LIST OF CONTRIBUTORS

Dr MD Bower PhD FRCP FRCPath
Consultant Medical Oncologist
Department of Oncology
Chelsea and Westminster Hospital
London

Dr KM Bowles MB BS PhD MRCP(UK) MRCPath
Consultant Haematologist
Norfolk and Norwich University Hospital NHS Trust
Norwich

Dr CS Brock FRCP
Consultant Medical Oncologist
Department of Oncology
Charing Cross Hospital
London

Dr GG Dark FRCP
Clinical Senior Lecturer
Northern Centre for Cancer Treatment
Newcastle General Hospital
Newcastle-upon-Tyne

Dr KM Fife MD FRCP FRCR
Consultant Clinical Oncologist
Oncology Centre
Addenbrooke's Hospital
Cambridge

Dr DW Galvani MD MEd FRCP FRCPath
Consultant Haematologist
Haematology Department
Arrowe Park Hospital
Wirral

Dr ABK Olujohungbe Dip. Haem (Lond) MD FRCP FRCPath
Consultant Haematologist
Department of Haematology
University Hospital Aintree NHS Trust
Liverpool

Dr BE Shaw MRCP(UK)
Haematology Consultant
Royal Marsden Hospital
London

Royal College
of Physicians
Setting higher medical standards

Published by:
Royal College of Physicians of London
11 St. Andrews Place
Regent's Park
London NW1 4LE
United Kingdom

Set and printed by Graphicraft Limited, Hong Kong

First edition published 2001
Reprinted 2004
Second edition published 2008

ISBN: 978-1-86016-269-5 (this book)
ISBN: 978-1-86016-260-2 (set)

Distribution Information:
Jerwood Medical Education Resource Centre
Royal College of Physicians of London
11 St. Andrews Place
Regent's Park
London NW1 4LE
United Kingdom
Tel: +44 (0)207 935 1174 ext 422/490
Fax: +44 (0)207 486 6653
Email: merc@rcplondon.ac.uk
Web: http://www.rcplondon.ac.uk/

MEDICAL MASTERCLASS

EDITOR-IN-CHIEF

JOHN D FIRTH DM FRCP

Consultant Physician and Nephrologist
Addenbrooke's Hospital
Cambridge

HAEMATOLOGY AND ONCOLOGY

EDITORS

DAVID W GALVANI MD MEd FRCP FRCPath

Consultant Haematologist
Arrowe Park Hospital
Wirral

MARK D BOWER PhD FRCP FRCPath

Consultant Medical Oncologist
Chelsea and Westminster Hospital
London

Second Edition

Royal College
of Physicians

Setting higher medical standards

Disclaimer

Although every effort has been made to ensure that drug doses and other information are presented accurately in this publication, the ultimate responsibility rests with the prescribing physician. Neither the publishers nor the authors can be held responsible for any consequences arising from the use of information contained herein. Any product mentioned in this publication should be used in accordance with the prescribing information prepared by the manufacturers.

The information presented in this publication reflects the opinions of its contributors and should not be taken to represent the policy and views of the Royal College of Physicians of London, unless this is specifically stated.

Every effort has been made by the contributors to contact holders of copyright to obtain permission to reproduce copyrighted material. However, if any have been inadvertently overlooked, the publisher will be pleased to make the necessary arrangements at the first opportunity.

CONTENTS

CONTENTS

FOREWORD

Since its initial publication in 2001, *Medical Masterclass* has been regarded as a key learning and teaching resource for physicians around the world. The resource was produced in part to meet the vision of the Royal College of Physicians: *'Doctors of the highest quality, serving patients well'*. This vision continues and, along with advances in clinical practice and changes in the format of the MRCP(UK) exam, has justified the publication of this second edition.

The MRCP(UK) is an international examination that seeks to advance the learning of and enhance the training process for physicians worldwide. On passing the exam physicians are recognised as having attained the required knowledge, skills and manner appropriate for training at a specialist level. However, passing the exam is a challenge. The pass rate at each sitting of the written papers is about 40%. Even the most prominent consultants have had to sit each part of the exam more than once in order to pass. With this challenge in mind, the College has produced *Medical Masterclass*, a comprehensive learning resource to help candidates with the preparation that is key to making the grade.

Medical Masterclass has been produced by the Education Department of the College. A work of this size represents a formidable amount of effort by the Editor-in-Chief – Dr John Firth – and his team of editors and authors. I would like to thank our colleagues for this wonderful educational product and wholeheartedly recommend it as an invaluable learning resource for all physicians preparing for their MRCP(UK) examination.

Professor Ian Gilmore MD PRCP
President of the Royal College of Physicians

PREFACE

The second edition of *Medical Masterclass* is produced and published by the Education Department of the Royal College of Physicians of London. It comprises 12 textbooks, a companion interactive website and two CD-ROMs. Its aim is to help doctors in their first few years of training to improve their medical knowledge and skills; and in particular to (a) learn how to deal with patients who are acutely ill, and (b) pass postgraduate examinations, such as the MRCP(UK) or European Diploma in Internal Medicine.

The 12 textbooks are divided as follows: two cover the scientific background to medicine, one is devoted to general clinical skills [including specific guidance on exam technique for PACES, the practical assessment of clinical examination skills that is the final part of the MRCP(UK) exam], one deals with acute medicine and the other eight cover the range of medical specialties.

The core material of each of the medical specialties is dealt with in seven sections:

- Case histories – you are presented with letters of referral commonly received in each specialty and led through the ways in which the patients' histories should be explored, and what should then follow in the way of investigation and/or treatment.

- Physical examination scenarios – these emphasise the logical analysis of physical signs and sensible clinical reasoning: 'having found this, what would you do?'

- Communication and ethical scenarios – what are the difficult issues that commonly arise in each specialty? What do you actually say to the 'frequently asked (but still very difficult) questions?'

- Acute presentations – what are the priorities if you are the doctor seeing the patient in the Emergency Department or the Medical Admissions Unit?

- Diseases and treatments – structured concise notes.

- Investigations and practical procedures – more short and to-the-point notes.

- Self assessment questions – in the form used in the MRCP(UK) Part 1 and Part 2 exams.

The companion website – which is continually updated – enables you to take mock MRCP(UK) Part 1 or Part 2 exams, or to be selective in the questions you tackle (if you want to do ten questions on cardiology, or any other specialty, you can do). For every question you complete you can see how your score compares with that of others who have logged onto the site and attempted it. The two CD-ROMs each contain 30 interactive cases requiring diagnosis and treatment.

I hope that you enjoy using *Medical Masterclass* to learn more about
medicine, which – whatever is happening politically to primary care,
hospitals and medical career structures – remains a wonderful occupation.
It is sometimes intellectually and/or emotionally very challenging, and also
sometimes extremely rewarding, particularly when reduced to the essential
of a doctor trying to provide best care for a patient.

John Firth DM FRCP
Editor-in-Chief

ACKNOWLEDGEMENTS

Medical Masterclass has been produced by a team. The names of those who have written or edited material are clearly indicated elsewhere, but without the support of many other people it would not exist. Naming names is risky, but those worthy of particular note include: Sir Richard Thompson (College Treasurer) and Mrs Winnie Wade (Director of Education), who steered the project through committees that are traditionally described as labyrinthine, and which certainly seem so to me; and also Arthur Wadsworth (Project Co-ordinator) and Don Liu in the College Education Department office. Don is a veteran of the first edition of *Medical Masterclass*, and it would be fair to say that without his great efforts a second edition might not have seen the light of day.

John Firth DM FRCP
Editor-in-Chief

We have created a range of icon boxes that sit among the text of the various *Medical Masterclass* modules. They are there to help you identify key information and to make learning easier and more enjoyable. Here is a brief explanation:

> Iron-deficiency anaemia with a change in bowel habit in a middle-aged or older patient means colonic malignancy until proved otherwise.

This icon is used to highlight points of particular importance.

> Dietary deficiency is very rarely, if ever, the sole cause of iron-deficiency anaemia.

This icon is used to indicate common or important drug interactions, pitfalls of practical procedures, or when to take symptoms or signs particularly seriously.

HAEMATOLOGY

Authors:

KM Bowles, DW Galvani, ABK Olujohungbe and BE Shaw

Editor:

DW Galvani

Editor-in-Chief:

JD Firth

1.1 History taking

1.1.1 Microcytic hypochromic anaemia

Letter of referral to the general haematology outpatient clinic

Dear Doctor,

Re: Mrs Khamini Shah, aged 37 years

This Asian woman, who is 12 weeks pregnant, complains of increasing tiredness and lethargy. Her diet seems reasonable. The result of her FBC is as follows: haemoglobin (Hb) 8.9 g/dL (normal range 11.5–16); mean corpuscular volume (MCV) 69 fL (normal range 80–100); mean corpuscular haemoglobin (MCH) 22.5 pg (normal range 27–32); white blood cells 8.2×10^9/L (normal range 4–11); and platelets 169×10^9/L (normal range 150–400). Please advise on the cause and management of her anaemia.

Yours sincerely,

Introduction

This woman has a microcytic hypochromic anaemia, the causes of which include:

- iron deficiency;

- thalassaemia trait and syndromes (α or β)

- anaemia of chronic disease (although this more usually causes a normochromic, normocytic anaemia);

- sideroblastic anaemia;

- lead poisoning.

The commonest of these is iron deficiency (see Section 2.1.5), the causes of which are listed in Table 1.

In clinical practice there may be more than one reason for the anaemia and more than one cause of iron deficiency.

History of the presenting problem

The first aim of the history should be to elicit possible causes of iron deficiency as outlined in Table 1. You should then move on to consider other possible causes of microcytic anaemia, while also assessing the functional impact of anaemia on the patient.

Diet

The referral letter states that this woman's diet seems reasonable, but it is important to establish how many times a week (if any) she eats red meat, poultry or fish, which are sources of relatively well-absorbed haem-iron. Does she drink a lot of tea and/or eat a lot of chapatis? Both contain substances (tannins and phosphates/phytates,

TABLE 1 CAUSES OF IRON DEFICIENCY	
Mechanism	**Example**
Reduced intake of iron	Poor diet[1]
Reduced absorption of iron	Coeliac disease Atrophic gastritis Post gastrectomy
Increased iron requirements	Pregnancy Growth spurts Chronic haemolysis[2]
Increased loss of iron	Menstruation Gastrointestinal (GI) system: oesophageal/gastric/duodenal inflammation or ulcer, malignancy (upper or lower GI tract), angiodysplasia (most typically colonic) or hookworm infestation (common in tropical countries) Haematuria[2]

1. Dietary deficiency of iron is very rarely the sole cause of iron-deficiency anaemia, although it may be an exacerbating factor.
2. Rare causes of iron-deficiency anaemia.

respectively) that inhibit intestinal iron absorption.

⚠️ Dietary deficiency is very rarely, if ever, the sole cause of iron-deficiency anaemia.

Bleeding

Ask specifically about symptoms of GI blood loss, which is a common cause of iron deficiency, particularly in men and postmenopausal women. Patients will normally volunteer obvious blood loss, but ask directly about piles; those who have had them for years may have become so accustomed to them bleeding that they fail to mention them to you. Pursue a history that might indicate upper GI inflammation or ulceration. Ask directly: 'Do you get indigestion or heartburn? Do you take anything for indigestion? Have you ever had a barium meal or endoscopy test?' Take a careful history of the patient's bowel habit: iron-deficiency anaemia with a change in bowel habit in a middle-aged or elderly patient means colonic malignancy until proved otherwise.

Even though this patient is pregnant, ask about her menstrual cycle, as menorrhagia before becoming pregnant may have led to iron deficiency. Were her periods regular, and were they heavy (how many days did she bleed for, and how many pads did she have to use)?

Malabsorption

This is clearly not the likely diagnosis in this case, but abdominal symptoms of discomfort, bloating, excess wind or altered bowel habit should lead to further consideration of the possibility of malabsorption. In whites (but not Asians) coeliac disease is common

(prevalence about 1 in 300 people in Europe and North America) and often presents with iron-deficiency anaemia in the absence of obvious intestinal symptoms.

Pregnancies

How many previous pregnancies has she had? Each of these will have been a drain on her body iron stores.

Functional significance of anaemia

The letter of referral states that the patient has been feeling tired and lethargic, but establish what is meant by this more precisely. What is the most exercise that she can do at the moment (and confirm what limits this activity)? Compare this with her capacity before her pregnancy and a year or so ago to get a feel for the pace at which the anaemia may have developed and to provide a baseline from which to judge her response to treatment.

Other relevant past history

Aside from general screening questions, look at the causes of microcytosis (see Section 2.1.5). The history should be directed at establishing whether any of these factors are the cause(s) for this woman's anaemia. As an Asian woman, the most obvious diagnosis to consider is that she may have a thalassaemia syndrome (see Section 2.1.1). The patient (or relatives in routine clinical practice) may be able to provide you with this information. Ask directly: 'Did you know that you were anaemic? Has anyone told you this before? Do you know if anyone else in your family has anaemia or thalassaemia?'

Ascertaining the presence of a thalassaemia syndrome in this patient is not only important in explaining the anaemia but has implications regarding the risk of her child being born with

thalassaemia major: the male partner should be strongly encouraged to undergo testing if the woman is a thalassaemia carrier.

Plan for investigation and management

Explain to the woman that a number of blood tests are required to find the cause of this anaemia and that there may be an inherited element.

Blood count and film

The results of the FBC should be confirmed by examination of the blood film. In iron deficiency the red cells will be hypochromic and microcytic (Fig. 1) with pencil cells and the occasional target cell. The reticulocyte count will be low for the level of anaemia, and the red cell count will be low.

In β-thalassaemia trait the degree of anaemia is often mild for the degree of microcytosis (eg Hb 10 g/dL and MCV 60 fL) and the blood film shows target cells and hypochromic microcytes. In β-thalassaemia major the anaemia is severe with poikilocytosis, basophilic stippling of the red cells, target cells and nucleated red cells.

Haemoglobin electrophoresis

In β-thalassaemia trait, HbA_2 is >3.5% (but not always in the presence of iron deficiency). In β-thalassaemia major there may be no HbA, only HbF. Hb electrophoresis is normal in patients with α-thalassaemia: DNA analysis is required to make the diagnosis.

If the patient proves to have thalassaemia, then remember to recommend strongly that her partner be tested.

Biochemistry

Serum iron, ferritin and total iron-binding capacity should be

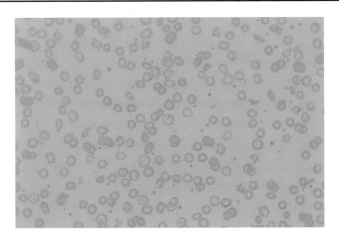

▲ **Fig.1** Iron-deficiency anaemia. Note the hypochromic and microcytic features, that the area of central pallor is enlarged and that there is an occasional target cell and pencil cell.

measured, as should B$_{12}$ and folate for completeness. A low ferritin is very suggestive of iron deficiency but beware: a normal or raised ferritin does not exclude iron deficiency, as it is an acute-phase protein that may be raised in the presence of inflammation.

Gastrointestinal studies

GI pathology seems unlikely to be the cause of anaemia in this case, but GI studies are essential investigations in middle-aged or older people where cancer is a major cause of anaemia.

> Iron-deficiency anaemia with a change in bowel habit in a middle-aged or older patient means colonic malignancy until proved otherwise.

Management

Although oral folic acid is recommended in pregnancy, obstetricians vary in their views on prophylactic iron because of side effects. In this case, commencing oral iron whilst laboratory tests are awaited is sensible. Plan to review the patient in a few weeks

when the results will be available, and in the mean time liaise with the obstetricians.

Further discussion

The recent UK antenatal screening programme has resulted in all pregnant women being screened for iron deficiency or haemoglobinopathy in order to reduce the risk of fetal haemoglobinopathy. If maternal MCH is below 27 pg, then iron studies and Hb electrophoresis are performed. If these tests are negative, then DNA analysis is performed to determine the presence of α-thalassaemia, following written consent from the patient. Testing the woman's partner will give information about whether the baby can inherit problems from both parents.

> If a pregnant woman has a thalassaemia trait, then the father should be strongly encouraged to undergo testing. Homozygous (or compound heterozygous) forms of thalassaemia can be devastating conditions for which counselling and prenatal testing should be offered.

1.1.2 Macrocytic anaemia

Letter of referral to the general haematology outpatient clinic

Dear Doctor,

Re: Mr Henry Fairchild, aged 62 years

This man has been feeling increasingly breathless, tired and depressed. He has been overweight for some years and is on a diabetic diet. He drinks 16 units per week and smokes 20 cigarettes per day. He is on atenolol for hypertension. He has worked in clerical jobs all his life. He has an anaemia of 9.9 g/dL (normal range 12–16.5) with a mean corpuscular volume of 107 fL (normal range 80–100), white blood cells 7.6 × 10^9/L (normal range 4–11) and platelets 78 × 10^9/L (normal range 150–400). Please advise on the cause and management of his anaemia.

Yours sincerely,

Introduction

This man has a macrocytic anaemia. The causes of macrocytosis are divided into those with a megaloblastic bone marrow and those with a normoblastic bone marrow (see Section 2.6). The commonest causes of megaloblastic anaemia are shown in Table 2. Common non-megaloblastic causes include liver disease and alcohol, hypothyroidism and the presence of a reticulocytosis (reticulocytes and young red cells being larger than older red cells).

TABLE 2 CAUSES OF MEGALOBLASTIC ANAEMIA

	B_{12} deficiency	Folate deficiency	Others
Reduced intake	Vegan diet	The elderly and alcoholics	
Increased requirements		Pregnancy Chronic haemolysis Dialysis Exfoliative dermatitis	
Reduced absorption	Pernicious anaemia Post gastrectomy Post ileal resection Crohn's disease Stagnant bowel loops Fish tapeworm	Coeliac disease Tropical sprue Crohn's disease Stagnant bowel loops	
Drugs		Reduced absorption: phenytoin, sodium valproate and combined oral contraceptive Antifolate drugs: methotrexate and co-trimoxazole Alcohol	Hydroxycarbamide (hydroxyurea), azathioprine, zidovudine and cytarabine

History of the presenting problem

This should seek to establish the likely cause of the anaemia and its functional significance for the patient.

Diet and alcohol consumption

Does the patient ever eat liver, fruit or fresh vegetables? These are the foods that contain the most folate. Dietary deficiency may be the sole cause of folate deficiency and is often a contributory factor.

Is the alcohol history correct in this case? It is common in routine clinical practice for a patient to give an underestimate of alcohol consumption on first enquiry (and in **PACES** it is common for the surrogate's briefing notes to say something along the lines of 'You drink more heavily than you have told your GP, but only

admit this if asked directly about your alcohol consumption'). A useful device to elicit this information is to explain to the patient why you want to know about his alcohol intake: 'Sometimes a high alcohol intake can cause anaemia . . . are you a heavy drinker now, or have you been in the past? How many drinks do you have on a typical day?'

Heavy alcohol consumption is often associated with a poor diet.

Malabsorption

Has the patient had any troubles with his bowels in the past? Enquire about abdominal symptoms of discomfort, bloating, excess wind or altered bowel habit that could indicate unrecognised malabsorption in this case. Folate deficiency is virtually universal in patients with untreated coeliac

disease, which is the commonest malabsorptive cause of folate deficiency (in the UK). Ask directly about previous abdominal surgery that might cause B_{12} deficiency (Table 2). Patients with long-standing type 1 diabetes can develop malabsorption for a variety of reasons, but this will clearly not be the explanation in an overweight 62-year-old whose diabetes is managed by diet alone.

> Always consider coeliac disease as a cause of unexplained iron- and/or folate-deficiency anaemia (in whites).

Drugs

Is the patient taking any of the drugs listed in Table 2 as causing folate deficiency?

Functional significance of anaemia

The letter of referral states that the patient has been feeling breathless and tired, but establish what is meant by this more precisely. What is the most exercise that he can do at the moment (and confirm what limits his activity)? Compare this with his capacity 6 months or so ago to get a feel for the pace at which his anaemia may have developed and to provide a baseline from which to judge his response to treatment.

Other relevant history

Aside from general screening questions, note that pernicious anaemia is an organ-specific autoimmune condition; therefore ask the patient whether he has other organ-specific autoimmune diseases or if such conditions run in the family. As stated above, he clearly will not have type 1 diabetes mellitus, but ask specifically about

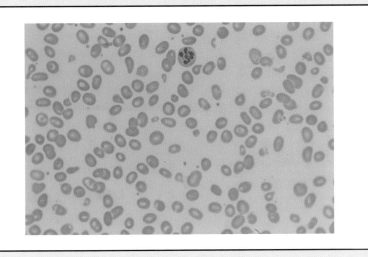

▲**Fig. 2** Pernicious anaemia. Note the poikilocytosis and oval macrocytes. The area of central pallor is less than normal indicating plenty of haemoglobin within the cells. Note the hypersegmented neutrophil.

thyroid problems or about any patches of discoloured skin (in routine clinical practice you would examine for vitiligo, but you cannot do so in the history station of PACES).

A very few patients with B$_{12}$ deficiency develop neurological symptoms. This is initially paraesthesia, but this sometimes progresses to permanent ataxia caused by subacute combined degeneration of the cord. Mental disturbance can also be a feature. Ask the patient whether he has any pins and needles or numbness in his feet, and if he has any difficulty walking, particularly in the dark.

A 'mixed picture' with both folate and iron deficiency is not uncommon, hence ask about bleeding as in Section 1.1.1.

Plan for investigation and management

FBC, blood film, reticulocyte count, clotting and direct antiglobulin test
The blood film will confirm the macrocytosis (Fig. 2). Changes in megaloblastic anaemia include:

- anisopoikilocytosis (there will be a wide variation in size and shape of the red cells);

- Howell–Jolly bodies;

- basophilic stippling;

- pancytopenia;

- hypersegmented neutrophils.

The reticulocyte count is low in megaloblastic anaemia. Reticulocytosis is common with bleeding, although not if the patient becomes iron deficient.

The direct antiglobulin test will be positive in autoimmune haemolysis. Check clotting as an assessment of synthetic liver function.

Biochemistry and haematinics
Check electrolytes, liver function (including γ-glutamyl transferase) and thyroid function. Measure serum B$_{12}$ and red-cell folate.

Immunology
Positive parietal cell antibodies occur in 90% of patients with pernicious anaemia, and intrinsic factor (IF) antibodies occur in 50% of cases. Look for the presence of anti-tissue transglutaminase antibodies in coeliac disease.

Bone marrow examination
This is rarely performed because modern serological methods are very reliable. Features of marrow megaloblastosis that will exclude malignancy are an expansion in the erythroid series, which typically have open sieve-like chromatin (Fig. 3), and the presence of giant metamyelocytes and band forms.

B$_{12}$ absorption studies
Unfortunately these are not widely available now due to

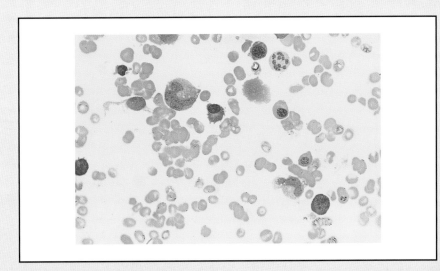

▲**Fig. 3** Megaloblastic marrow. Red-cell precursors show a chromatin appearance like a sieve. There is a hypersegmented neutrophil and a giant metamyelocyte away from the centre of the picture.

TABLE 3 INTERPRETATION OF SCHILLING'S TEST USING URINARY EXCRETION OF RADIOISOTOPES		
	Urinary excretion of B_{12} following:	
	Oral B_{12} alone	Oral B_{12}/IF
Vegan	Normal	Normal
Pernicious anaemia/gastrectomy	Low	Normal
Ileal resection	Low	Low
Stagnant loop syndromes	Low	Low[1]

1. Corrected by antibiotics.
Adapted with permission from Provan D and Henson A. *ABC of Clinical Haematology*. London: BMJ Publishing Group; 1998.

lack of isotope production, but the test remains an important one in terms of understanding the causes of B_{12} deficiency. In the Dicopac test, oral B_{12} labelled with cobalt-58 plus oral B_{12}/IF labelled with cobalt-57 are followed by intramuscular unlabelled B_{12}. The recovery of the two radioisotopes is then measured in the urine over 24 hours as a marker of absorption. The study needs to be carried out after correction of B12 (with or without folate) deficiency as megaloblastosis of the gut will cause malabsorption, masking the pattern of abnormality seen in pernicious anaemia. Table 3 shows how to interpret the results.

Upper gastrointestinal endoscopy

Atrophic gastritis is seen on gastric biopsy in cases of pernicious anaemia. This test will also pick up gastric carcinoma, which is more common in patients with this condition. Duodenal biopsy may show a cause of malabsorption in those with folate deficiency (classically subtotal villous atrophy in coeliac disease).

Management

Correct any haematinic deficiency and treat any underlying cause.

- B_{12} deficiency: administer hydroxocobalamin 1 mg im on alternate days for 10 days, then 250 μg weekly until the FBC is normal and then 1 mg im every 3 months.

- Folate deficiency: administer folic acid 5 mg orally once daily, but do not do this without excluding B_{12} deficiency, which it might exacerbate.

Do not give folate without excluding B_{12} deficiency.

Further discussion

Macrocytosis is a common cause of referral to clinic. Non-megaloblastic causes are common, as is the situation when no cause is found. It is important to exclude B_{12} and folate deficiency because they are so easily treated, and patients are extremely grateful within days of commencing replacement therapy.

When macrocytosis persists in the absence of an established cause, a marrow sample is usually necessary to exclude myelodysplasia and other haematological pathologies.

1.1.3 Lymphocytosis and anaemia

Letter of referral to the general haematology outpatient clinic

Dear Doctor,

Re: Mr John Leeds, aged 70 years

This retired bank manager reports a 7-month history of feeling 'tired all the time'. His haemoglobin (Hb) is 8.8 g/dL (normal range 11.5–16), mean corpuscular volume (MCV) 91 fL (normal range 80–100), platelets 196×10^9/L (normal range 150–400), white cell count (WCC) 83.6×10^9/L (normal range 4–11) with neutrophils 3.2×10^9/L (normal range 2–7) and lymphocytes 79.4×10^9/L (normal range 1–3). His blood film shows 'lymphocytosis and smear cells'. I am worried about these abnormalities, please investigate.

Yours sincerely,

Introduction

There are two main goals for this consultation. First is to establish the diagnosis/diagnoses for the anaemia and lymphocytosis, remembering that anaemia may be multifactorial in its aetiology, for example chronic lymphatic leukaemia (CLL) with marrow failure plus autoimmune haemolysis. Second is to assess the effect of the anaemia on the patient's quality of life, which will affect treatment decisions with respect to both the anaemia and its underlying cause. Asymptomatic patients with CLL who have mild anaemia, but otherwise preserved counts, no problems with adenopathy and no constitutional symptoms may initially be best served by a 'watch and wait' policy rather than chemotherapy.

Except in the most urgent cases, where the patient is clearly compromised by the degree of anaemia (eg heart failure or angina), time should be taken to find the cause of anaemia before arranging a blood transfusion. This is because transfusion is not necessarily required in some cases (eg haemolytic anaemia or haematinic deficiency) and may not help the situation. If transfusion is clinically indicated, ensure that appropriate tests are taken before the transfusion is started (eg vitamin B_{12}/folate) to obtain reliable results.

The possible causes of lymphocytosis are given in Table 4.

History of the presenting problem

Is the patient suffering from the anaemia? The letter of referral says that the patient is 'tired all the time', but establish his exercise capacity and ask the following questions in particular.

- Do you have chest pain? This would indicate myocardial ischaemia.

- Are you short of breath at rest, or waking up at night with breathlessness? This would suggest possible heart failure.

Try to determine the cause of the abnormal blood results. Ask the patient the following questions.

- Have you noticed any lumps? Suggests lymphadenopathy.

- Do you have abdominal pain? Indicates hepatosplenomegaly.

- Have you become yellow or jaundiced? This could mean a viral cause/haemolysis.

- Have you travelled recently and, if so, precisely where and when? Infections may have been contracted from these locations.

- Do you sweat at night or have fevers? Have you lost any weight? These are 'B' symptoms associated with haematological malignancy, or could possibly be due to an infection.

- Have you had any joint pains/swelling or rashes?

These are exceedingly unlikely in a 70-year-old man with a raised lymphocyte count, but – particularly in a young woman with haemolytic anaemia – always consider systemic lupus erythematosus.

- Are you more prone to infections than usual? Do you bruise or bleed easily? These are signs of bone-marrow failure.

- What medications are you taking? Check each drug the patient mentions in the *British National Formulary*/product data sheet to see if it can cause haemolytic anaemia, which is induced (via a variety of different mechanisms) by several drugs on rare occasions, eg methyldopa, penicillins/cephalosporins, quinine and sulphonylureas.

- What is your lifestyle? Make sure you exclude high-risk behaviour, even in a 70-year-old.

> In taking a systematic haematological history, ask about symptoms that might be due to problems with:
>
> - red cells (anaemia);
> - white cells (infection);
> - platelets (bleeding);
> - lymph nodes (swollen glands);
> - spleen (left upper quadrant pain/discomfort);
> - constitutional symptoms (weight loss and fever).

Other relevant history

A comprehensive past medical history is required as a patient's threshold for developing symptoms at a given level of Hb varies depending on their underlying general medical condition. Otherwise healthy patients will often tolerate their Hb falling

TABLE 4 CAUSES OF LYMPHOCYTOSIS	
Primary haematological	**Non-haematological**
ALL[1]	Viral infections: infectious mononucleosis (EBV), CMV, HIV, hepatitis A
CLL[1]	Bacterial infections (eg tuberculosis)
NHL[1]	Rickettsial infections Myocardial infarction (stress-related) Cigarette smoking Splenectomy Endocrine disorders (eg Addison's disease and thyrotoxicosis)

1. Significant anaemia is likely.
ALL, acute lymphoblastic leukaemia; CMV, cytomegalovirus; EBV, Epstein–Barr virus; NHL, Non-Hodgkin's lymphoma.

to 8 g/dL before becoming symptomatic. Patients with a history of ischaemic heart disease or other chronic illness will frequently develop symptoms as their Hb drops below 10 g/dL.

Plan for investigation and management

FBC, reticulocyte count and peripheral blood film

The patient's MCV (normal in this case) and reticulocyte count may be significantly raised due to haemolysis. Note the platelet count. The peripheral blood film may suggest the diagnosis immediately, eg blasts in ALL, mature lymphocytes in CLL (clearly the most likely diagnosis in this case) or atypical lymphocytes in viral infections (Fig. 4). Likewise, spherocytes and polychromasia will aid a diagnosis of haemolysis. In routine clinical practice, speak to your haematologist about these tests and arrange to go along and have a look.

Other blood tests

To establish the presence of haemolysis check liver function tests, including bilirubin (conjugated and unconjugated, since the latter will be elevated in haemolysis); lactate dehydrogenase (elevated in haemolysis); and serum haptoglobin (low in haemolysis).

To look for the cause of haemolysis check the direct antiglobulin test (also the Coombs' test; these will be positive in autoimmune haemolytic anaemia) and, as clinically appropriate, the Paul–Bunnell/ Monospot (will be positive in infectious mononucleosis), viral serology, and autoimmune rheumatic serology (for antinuclear antibodies and complement levels).

Also check vitamin B_{12} and folate (these may become deficient in chronic haemolysis), as well as ferritin and serum immunoglobulins (these may be suppressed in CLL and can be responsible for recurrent infections).

CXR and ECG

Look for hilar lymphadenopathy. Is there evidence of heart failure, ischaemia or strain?

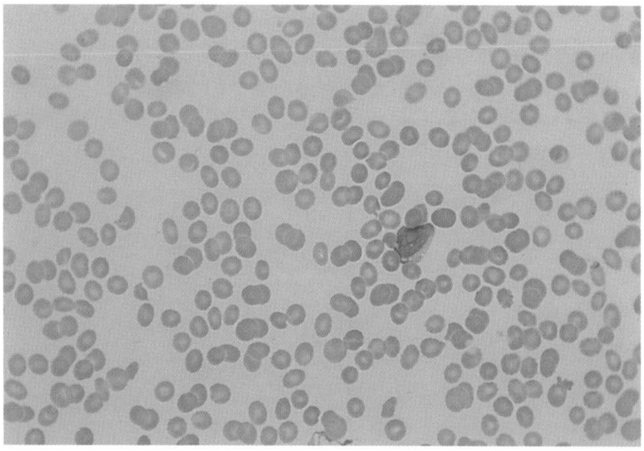

Management

This depends on the symptoms that the patient is suffering. Clearly if he is experiencing unstable angina as a result of the anaemia, then admission for transfusion will be appropriate. However, in routine practice most patients are not acutely unwell and their symptoms are chronic but not life-threatening. Outpatient follow-up in 4 weeks will give sufficient time for all the results to come back and a diagnosis be made. Patients should be told to contact their GP or the hospital should they become more unwell in the interim.

> **Patients should receive blood transfusions only if their anaemia is symptomatic, not because their Hb has fallen below a particular level.**

Further discussion

Anaemia is common and much can be resolved before a patient gets to a specialist haematology clinic. However, serious anxieties often arise before the outpatient appointment if a patient is told that a raised WCC may be 'leukaemia'. Such anxieties are often unnecessary and the 'L-word' is probably best avoided until a haematologist has made an assessment.

Specific treatment will depend on the underlying condition:

- ALL (see Section 2.2.2);
- CLL (see Section 2.2.3);
- NHL (see Section 2.2.5);
- HIV (see *Infectious Diseases*, Section 2.11).

▲**Fig. 4** Glandular fever cells are usually large and have an open chromatin pattern. They are typically indented by red cells. They may be difficult to distinguish from blasts.

1.1.4 Thromboembolism and fetal loss

Letter of referral to haematology outpatient clinic

Dear Doctor,

Re: Mrs Annie Burns, aged 36 years

Thank you for seeing this woman with a history of a low platelet count. The most recent result checked in our surgery was 95×10^9/L (normal range 150–400), but this has been low over 3 or 4 years. She has suffered one instance of deep vein thrombosis (DVT) at the age of 30, but there is no family history of thrombosis. In addition, she has a history of recurrent miscarriages and has also been referred to the obstetricians. I wonder if these pathologies are linked and would be grateful for your opinion and further investigation.

Yours sincerely,

Introduction

Each of the three individual aspects of this case is a relatively common problem: thrombocytopenia (see Section 2.3), venous thrombosis (see Section 1.4.6) and miscarriage. However, the combination of all three is most likely to be due to antiphospholipid antibody syndrome (APAS). Further questions should focus on confirming this diagnosis, but do not forget to consider other possibilities.

History of the presenting problem

The primary problem that the GP has asked you to investigate is the thrombocytopenia, but it is likely that the problem most distressing to the patient is the recurrent miscarriages. Establish if this is the case and discuss the miscarriages first if they are the patient's main concern, before proceeding to systematically enquire about the other aspects of her condition.

Recurrent miscarriages

How many pregnancies have failed, and at what stage in the pregnancies? In APAS, fetal loss tends to occur late, ie beyond the first trimester. Other questions related to fetal loss are likely to be better handled by the obstetricians and left to their clinic.

Thrombocytopenia

Is there a history of bleeding/bruising? In particular ask about any previous surgical or dental procedures.

In taking a history of a bleeding disorder, always ask directly about dental procedures, ie has there been prolonged bleeding after tooth extraction?

Venous thrombosis

Was the DVT confirmed (by Doppler/venogram) and, if so, for how long did she receive anticoagulation? Were there risk factors at the time of the thrombosis 6 years ago? Surgical procedures, immobility, smoking, oral contraceptives and pregnancy all predispose to thrombosis: are any of these risk factors still present? And was this the only episode of thrombosis? Ask directly whether there have been any other instances of unilateral leg pain or swelling, or of chest pains/breathlessness that might have been due to pulmonary emboli.

Other relevant history

- A family history of fetal loss or thrombosis should be elicited. APAS is not inherited, but many other causes of thrombophilia may be.

- Does she suffer from any systemic illness? APAS is associated with autoimmune rheumatic disorders, particularly systemic lupus erythematosus (SLE), and symptoms related to this syndrome should be elicited. Ask directly about joint pains/swelling and rashes.

- Ask about drugs or medications: phenytoin and phenothiazines may be associated with APAS.

Plan for investigation and management

Explain to the patient that a number of blood tests are required, some of the results of which may take a while to become available. Ascertain when she is seeing the obstetricians and explain, both in routine clinical practice and in PACES, that you will copy your letter to the GP to them, or even phone them, to keep them informed and prevent any inappropriate duplication of tests.

FBC and film

The thrombocytopenia should be confirmed and a blood film examined to exclude platelet clumps. The rest of the FBC and blood film is expected to be normal. If not, further investigations must be undertaken. The presence of anaemia (particularly haemolytic) may support a diagnosis of SLE and should trigger investigations as discussed in Section 1.1.3. Neutropenia would also be consistent with SLE.

Station 2: History Taking   **11**

Thrombophilia screen

In particular investigate for antiphospholipid antibodies and lupus anticoagulant.

Other tests

Dipstick the urine to look for proteinuria and/or haematuria, which could indicate lupus nephritis in this context. Perform blood tests to check renal function and liver function, and a screen for autoimmune rheumatic disorder, namely antinuclear antibodies (ANA), anti-double-stranded DNA antibodies (if ANA positive) and complement levels.

Management

Arrange to see the patient in the clinic with results in the next 3–4 weeks. She should obviously be advised to take adequate precautions against pregnancy while investigations are proceeding, but preferably not the oral contraceptive. It will be helpful if she has also seen the obstetricians before review. Ask her if she would like to bring her partner to the appointment. Some units will have a combined haematology/obstetric clinic where it may be most appropriate to review her.

Further discussion

The lupus anticoagulant is identified by a prolonged activated partial thromboplastin time (even though this is a prothrombotic syndrome). This is because antibodies bind to phospholipids on the platelet surface, interfering with clotting tests. The diagnosis of APAS is a serious one (see Section 2.4.2 for therapy), especially if related to underlying SLE. There are various support groups available for patients with recurrent fetal loss and she should be made aware of this.

For further discussion of SLE and autoantibody tests, see *Rheumatology and Clinical Immunology*, Sections 2.4.1 and 3.2

1.1.5 Weight loss and thrombocytosis

Letter of referral to general medical outpatient clinic

Dear Doctor,

Re: Mr Francis Green, aged 63 years

This man has lost 1 stone (about 6 kg) in weight, which is not due to dieting, and he has an abnormal FBC. He rarely troubles doctors, but has come to the surgery over the last year because of angina, for which I have given him bisoprolol and a glyceryl trinitrate spray to good effect. He has worked as a publican for 30 years, but keeps to 25 units of alcohol per week. His FBC shows haemoglobin (Hb) 12.2 g/dL (normal range 12–16.5), mean corpuscular volume (MCV) 91 fL (normal range 80–100), platelets 964×10^9/L (normal range 150–400), and a white cell count 10.6×10^9/L (normal range 4–11) with neutrophils 6.4×10^9/L (normal range 2–7). I am worried about these abnormalities, please investigate.

Yours sincerely,

Introduction

Thrombocytosis can be a feature of systemic disease, which needs to be excluded before a diagnosis of primary thrombocytosis can be established. Secondary thrombocytosis rarely causes thrombotic problems, even when the platelet count is over 1000×10^9/L, whereas primary thrombocytosis is associated with thrombotic episodes. Thrombocytosis can be divided into primary ('essential') thrombocytosis or myeloproliferative disease, and secondary ('reactive') thrombocytosis caused by:

- malignancy;
- infection;
- inflammation;
- haemorrhage;
- hyposplenism;
- iron deficiency.

History of the presenting problem

Most medical histories naturally begin with a discussion of the main symptom(s) identified by the patient. However, in this case there are few symptoms mentioned in the referral letter, only the very non-specific one of weight loss and angina, which is clearly not the reason for an opinion being sought although it must be briefly discussed. In conducting a careful functional enquiry you need to explore both potential causes of the high platelet count and possible complications arising from the thrombocytosis.

> ⚠ Primary ('essential') thrombocytosis is a diagnosis largely made on the basis of exclusion: do not make it too readily and miss an occult malignancy.

Causes of his thrombocytosis

Weight loss The loss of weight needs to be explored in detail. Has the patient actually weighed himself or is the estimate of one stone a guess?

But in the context of this case this symptom obviously suggests malignancy, so check carefully for clues.

- General: anorexia and night sweats.

- Respiratory: cough, haemoptysis and chest pain.

- Abdominal: nausea, dysphagia, vomiting, indigestion/abdominal pain and any change in bowel habit/rectal bleeding.

- Genitourinary: lower urinary tract symptoms and haematuria.

Alcohol intake and smoking Is the alcohol history correct in this case? As discussed in Section 1.1.2, it is common in routine clinical practice for patients to give an underestimate of their alcohol consumption on first enquiry and in PACES for the letter of referral to do so. Point out the issues connected with this to the patient and then ask directly about his drinking habits: 'Sometimes a high alcohol intake can cause this sort of problem with the blood . . . are you a heavy drinker now or have you been in the past? How many drinks do you have now on a typical day?' And (possibly) 'When you were drinking more heavily in the past, how many drinks would you have then?' Hepatoma may arise on a background of cirrhosis.

Smoking predisposes to many malignancies: if the patient is a smoker, then find out for how many pack-years; if not, then ask if he has been exposed to passive smoking (very likely given his occupation) and for how long this has occurred.

Complications of thrombocytosis
Evidence of thrombosis or ischaemia should be sought. The man's angina may be exacerbated by his thrombocytosis, although it is

unlikely to be the sole cause – but how bad is it now? Has he had any other thrombotic/ischaemic symptoms? Ask in particular about headaches, transient ischaemic attacks or strokes, paraesthesiae in hands or feet, and claudication or foot pains.

Thrombocytosis can also cause bleeding and bruising due to abnormal platelet function: has he been to the dentist recently? (See Section 1.1.4.)

> Thrombocytosis typically causes 'arterial' rather than 'venous' thrombotic events and is also associated with bleeding.

Other relevant history

- Consider the different causes of thrombocytosis as you proceed.

- Occult infection: consider tuberculosis. Has he been exposed to this? Has he done any foreign travel?

- Inflammation: does he have arthritis or any other chronic inflammatory process?

- Haemorrhage or iron deficiency: these seem unlikely here with a normal Hb and MCV.

- Hyposplenism: has he had his spleen removed? If this was done many years ago the patient may have forgotten about it, and in PACES the surrogate's briefing note may say 'do not mention this unless asked if you've had any operations'.

Plan for investigation and management

FBC and film
It is important to confirm the initial abnormalities with a repeat sample,

which will also identify any trend in the platelet count. In primary thrombocytosis the film will show a variety of platelet sizes and shapes, and megakaryocyte fragments may appear. In contrast, in reactive thrombocytosis platelets are plentiful but generally normal in size.

Inflammatory markers
Plasma viscosity and C-reactive protein may indicate inflammation.

Other blood tests
Biochemistry and liver function tests may indicate liver or kidney problems. Autoantibodies may indicate autoimmune rheumatic disorder. A low serum ferritin would indicate iron deficiency. A cancer marker screen is of variable utility: they are best used for monitoring established cancer rather than as a screening tool (but using them to obtain an estimation of alpha-fetoprotein could be justified).

CXR
Look for malignancy and infection.

The patient should be reviewed when the results are available, with further investigation dependent on the preliminary findings.

Further discussion
In the absence of secondary causes, a bone-marrow aspirate and trephine may indicate increased myeloid and/or megakaryocytic activity. Cytogenetic analysis will exclude chronic myeloid leukaemia as a cause of thrombocytosis if there is no Philadelphia chromosome.

If the patient asks whether cancer is a possibility, this should not be denied, but he must be assured that nothing is certain until the investigations are completed.

Station 2: History Taking **13**

Treating secondary causes often improves the platelet count, but where there is a thrombotic risk (eg angina) aspirin will offer some protection. In primary thrombocytosis, cytotoxic therapy needs to be considered in addition to aspirin (see Section 2.2.7).

1.2 Clinical examination

1.2.1 Normocytic anaemia

Instruction

This man has attended the Medical Outpatients Department for some years. He is more tired of late. Examine his hands and other relevant parts.

Locomotor examination

In PACES station 5 in particular it is important to do what you are told to do promptly, because you do not have much time. This is likely to be a case of arthritis, so perform a rheumatological examination, running through the differential diagnosis in your head as you do so (see *Rheumatology and Clinical Immunology*, Sections 1.2.1. and 1.2.3). Examiners sometimes struggle for things to ask in such cases because rheumatoid disease is so well rehearsed, hence the invitation in the instruction to think why this man might be tired. Anaemia is the most likely reason, but consider rheumatoid disease activity, and cardiac or pulmonary complications of rheumatoid arthritis. Concentrate on the possibility of anaemia in the next part of your examination, but also consider hypothyroidism, which is not related to rheumatoid arthritis

but is a common condition that causes tiredness.

Other examination

Aside from pallor in the hands, look for other evidence of anaemia and its causes.

- Conjunctival pallor.

- Jaundice (haemolysis).

- Say that you wish to palpate for splenomegaly (Felty's syndrome).

- Look for features of hypothyroidism: facial features, goitre, bradycardia and slow-relaxing tendon jerks.

Further discussion

How might rheumatoid arthritis cause anaemia?

Rheumatoid disease can cause anaemia in several ways.

- Medication: NSAIDs cause bleeding; gold causes myelosuppression; sulfasalazine causes haemolysis.

- Anaemia of chronic disease.

- Iron deficiency: consider upper gastrointestinal (GI) blood loss.

- Felty's syndrome: hypersplenism.

- Pernicious anaemia: an autoimmune association.

- Haemolytic anaemia: warm antibodies.

How would you investigate this anaemia?

FBC, blood film, direct antiglobulin test and bone-marrow aspirate Microcytosis would suggest iron deficiency, most probably due to GI bleeding; normocytosis would be consistent with anaemia of chronic disease; and macrocytosis could be due to haemolysis. Reviewing the blood film will distinguish between uniformly normocytic red cells and

combined microcytic and macrocytic populations; spherocytes and bite cells would indicate haemolysis. A positive direct antiglobulin test is associated with autoimmune haemolytic anaemia seen with autoimmune rheumatic diseases, ibuprofen and diclofenac. A marrow sample may be necessary to assess iron stores: in the anaemia of chronic disease the iron stain of the bone marrow will show stainable iron in the particles but not in the red-cell precursors (see Section 2.6). Primary haematological diseases and secondary metastatic cells may be seen in the marrow aspirate, but would not be expected in this case.

Biochemistry and haematinics
Look for evidence of renal and liver impairment. Measure C-reactive protein as an indicator of inflammation. Check B_{12}, folate, iron, total iron-binding capacity and ferritin. Check thyroid function, parietal cell antibodies, intrinsic factor antibodies (for pernicious anaemia), rheumatoid factor, immunoglobulins and calcium (for myeloma).

- A normal ferritin does not exclude iron deficiency.
- Ferritin is an acute-phase protein that may be raised in inflammatory states.

1.2.2 Thrombocytopenia and purpura

Instruction

This woman presented to the Emergency Department with a nose-bleed and 2-month history of menorrhagia. Her platelet count is $7 \times 10^9/L$ (normal range 150–400). Please examine her abdomen.

TABLE 5 CAUSES OF THROMBOCYTOPENIA

Type	Cause
Increased destruction (normal bone marrow)	
Non-immune	DIC (sepsis and malignancy)
	Chronic liver disease/hypersplenism
	Pregnancy (including haemolysis, elevated liver enzymes, low platelets)
	TTP/HUS
	Inherited thrombocytopenia (Wiskott–Aldrich syndrome and Bernard–Soulier syndrome)
Immune	Autoimmune diseases (SLE, rheumatoid disease, chronic lymphatic leukaemia and lymphoma)
	Drugs (heparin, gold, penicillins and digoxin)
	Infection (Epstein–Barr virus, hepatitis, HIV and malaria)
	Post-transfusion purpura
Reduced production (abnormal bone marrow)	Leukaemia
	Lymphoma
	Myelodysplasia
	Myelofibrosis
	Myeloma
	Metastatic malignancy
	Aplastic anaemia (primary or secondary, eg drugs)
	Megaloblastic haemopoiesis (B$_{12}$/folate deficiency)
	Congenital bone-marrow failure syndromes (rare: Fanconi anaemia and congenital megakaryocytic hypoplasia)

DIC, disseminated intravascular coagulation; HUS, haemolytic–uraemic syndrome; SLE, systemic lupus erythematosus; TTP, thrombotic thrombocytopenic purpura.

Introduction

Consider the causes of thrombocytopenia (Table 5) as you approach the patient and be alert to the possible signs.

General features

Look for signs of chronic blood loss: pallor (conjunctivae), and tachycardia but normotension.

Look for evidence of bleeding.

- Non-mucosal: look for bruising and purpura. Is the bruising extensive? Does bruising occur in areas not usually subject to trauma, eg the face, neck and body? If there is extensive bleeding in the limbs, then it is very important in routine clinical practice to look for evidence of a compartment syndrome, but this is very unlikely in PACES.

- Mucosal: look in the nose for blood and in the mouth for blood

blisters, making sure that you have a good look at the tongue and soft palate. If there is bleeding in the mouth or pharynx, then it is vital to check if the upper airway is compromised (this would indicate stridor/wheeze), but again this would be a remote possibility in PACES.

Abdominal examination

The key feature to look for in this case is clearly splenomegaly, which could be a feature of idiopathic thrombocytopenic purpura (ITP), leukaemia or liver disease in this context (see Section 1.2.5 for further discussion).

Further discussion

What factors are important in a bleeding history?

- When was the bleeding/bruising first noticed? If it occurred during

childhood, think of congenital causes; if during adult life, think of acquired causes.

- Where are the sites of blood loss? Is there a single site of blood loss or many? A single site suggests that there might be a structural cause that requires local treatment. Bleeding from multiple sites will often involve skin and mucosae (nose, mouth, gastrointestinal tract and menstrual).

- How much does the patient bleed and how often? How are their energy levels and how has the bleeding affected their life?

- Is the bleeding causing symptomatic anaemia? What is the most exercise the patient can take (and what stops them doing more)? Quality-of-life issues may affect any decisions to treat.

What is your differential diagnosis in a patient with a very low platelet count?

Review Table 5. Causes are broadly divided into those conditions associated with normal platelet production but reduced platelet survival and those presenting as a result of bone-marrow disease. Generally, reduced platelet survival is associated with isolated thrombocytopenia whilst reduced platelet production is frequently associated with other cytopenia.

Based on your differential diagnosis, which investigations would you arrange and what conditions might they detect?

- FBC: look for pancytopenia suggesting bone-marrow disease.

- Blood film: to confirm thrombocytopenia and look for evidence of haemic malignancy, eg circulating blasts in acute leukaemia, lymphocytosis and smear cells in chronic lymphocytic leukaemia, and also to look for red-cell fragmentation that is seen in TTP/HUS.

- Clotting studies: prothrombin time, activated partial thromboplastin time, fibrinogen and D-dimer to detect DIC.

- Renal and liver function tests, vitamin B_{12} and folate, and prostate-specific antigen (when appropriate): to detect renal failure (TTP/HUS), chronic liver disease, haematinic deficiency and prostate cancer.

- Blood cultures/viral studies/ Paul–Bunnell test: to look for sepsis and infection.

- Autoantibodies: SLE and rheumatoid disease.

- Bone-marrow aspirate: bone-marrow infiltration or failure.

- CT scan of the abdomen: to confirm any organomegaly and look (in particular) for lymphadenopathy.

This woman is diagnosed with ITP: what are the treatment options in the acute situation?

First-line treatment of ITP is generally oral prednisolone 1 mg/kg daily, to which most people respond within a week with a rising platelet count. Intravenous immunoglobulin (1 g/kg on two consecutive days) is also effective first- or second-line therapy. Tranexamic acid 1 g orally four times a day may improve clot stability and reduce bleeding.

In an acute scenario any bleeding needs to be controlled and the patient supported with fluids and red-cell transfusion as appropriate. Platelet transfusions are rarely helpful as platelet survival is so short, but they may be considered in extremis.

1.2.3 Jaundice and anaemia

Instruction

This 21-year-old (male) university student has presented with a fever and 'yellow' eyes. Please examine his abdomen.

Introduction

In PACES it is almost certain that patients will have a chronic condition, but acute conditions are possible and, even if the case is not an acute one, the examiner may decide to move discussion away from chronic diseases that you are likely to have rehearsed.

> Examiners often move discussion away from chronic conditions to acute presentations with similar physical signs, so be prepared for this.

General features

- Is the patient jaundiced? The history would suggest this – look at their skin colour and the sclerae.

- Are there any obvious rashes or petechiae? This may suggest an infective origin or associated low platelet count.

- Does the patient appear pale? (In this case he does.)

- Are there any abnormal masses visible? Cervical lymphadenopathy may be obvious from the end of the bed; if it is, then note whether this is symmetrical or not. Palpate the neck carefully and also feel for lymphadenopathy in the axillae.

- Are there any features of chronic liver disease? (See *Gastroenterology and Hepatology*, Section 1.2.2.)

Abdominal examination

- Examine the groins for lymphadenopathy.

- Look for the presence of hepatomegaly and splenomegaly, and pay particular attention to whether this is painful or not.

Further discussion

The clinical approach and differential diagnosis of the patient with jaundice is discussed in the *Gastroenterology and Hepatology* module, Sections 1.1.7 and 1.4.5, but given the instruction in this case the following would be likely issues for discussion.

What is the most likely cause of jaundice and pallor with tender hepatosplenomegaly and lymphadenopathy in a young patient?

An Epstein–Barr virus (EBV) infection (infectious mononucleosis). In such cases splenomegaly occurs in over 50% of patients, although hepatomegaly is less common. Symmetrical lymphadenopathy occurs in up to 75% of patients.

How would you confirm a diagnosis of infectious mononucleosis?

You would expect an FBC to show lymphocytosis, with reactive lymphocytes on the blood film and a positive Paul–Bunnell (monspot) test. A definitive diagnosis can be made by demonstrating a high EBV immunoglobulin M titre in the blood, although this is seldom necessary in routine clinical practice. The FBC may also show thrombocytopenia.

What is the likely cause of the anaemia and how would you investigate this?

Although anaemia and jaundice may coexist for a number of reasons, the most likely cause in this scenario is haemolysis secondary to infection. Appropriate tests would include bilirubin, reticulocyte count, haptoglobins, lactase dehydrogenase, Coombs' test (direct antiglobulin test) (see Section 3.4) and a blood film to demonstrate spherocytes.

Would you do any other tests?

Liver function tests may be deranged in an acute viral illness, and it would be appropriate to check the clotting tests. It may also be appropriate to test for other infections, in particular cytomegalovirus, and a wider differential diagnosis of infectious conditions would have to be considered if there was a travel

history or if the patient were immunocompromised.

⚠️ Acute lymphoblastic leukaemia may present in an identical manner to infectious mononucleosis.

See Section 1.2.5 for further discussion of the causes of hepatosplenomegaly.

1.2.4 Polycythaemia

Instruction

This man has a raised haemoglobin (Hb) of 20 g/dL (normal range 12–16.5). Please examine his abdomen.

Introduction

In the context of the abdominal PACES station these instructions clearly suggest that you will find splenomegaly, and a Hb concentration of 20 g/dL is most unlikely to be due to a secondary

cause. However, remember the common causes of secondary polycythaemia (Table 6) as you examine the patient and comment on them when asked to describe your findings. Mentioning relevant negatives will demonstrate that you are the sort of doctor who thinks about all aspects of a case, as you should do in routine clinical practice, and it will impress the examiners.

General features

Note the presence of plethora, which will be inevitable with this level of Hb. Consider the non-haematological causes of polycythaemia.

- Cyanosis: suggests a secondary cause.

- Clubbing: consider congenital heart disease and some forms of lung disease (cryptogenic fibrosing alveolitis or bronchiectasis), although these are most unlikely to feature in the abdominal station of PACES.

- Is the patient a smoker? Stained fingers, audible wheeze and a barrel-shaped chest are all suggestive of chronic obstructive pulmonary disease.

TABLE 6 CAUSES OF POLYCYTHAEMIA

Type of polycythaemia	Mechanism	Cause
True (primary)	Primary proliferative polycythaemia or PV	Clonal disorder
True (secondary)	Hypoxia (appropriate erythropoietin increase)	High altitude Cardiovascular disease Pulmonary disease Cigarette smoking Rare familial syndromes
	Inappropriate erythropoietin secretion	Renal disease Hepatic disease Uterine fibroids Cerebellar haemangioblastoma
Apparent/relative	Reduced plasma volume	Dehydration and diuretics Stress polycythaemia (middle-aged overweight smokers)

PV, polycythaemia vera.

Consider the haematological causes of polycythaemia.

- Is the patient scratching his skin? Polycythaemia vera (PV) may cause intractable itching.

- Other clues to suggest a diagnosis of PV include eyes (conjunctival suffusion and retinal engorgement) and limbs (any evidence of thrombosis).

Abdominal examination

- Are there excoriations from scratching?

- Abdominal mass: does this have the characteristics of an enlarged spleen? This clearly suggests a primary cause of polycythaemia.

- Are there other abdominal masses (eg renal or hepatic) suggesting a secondary cause?

- Examination of chest and heart would be needed to sort this case out, but the examiner is unlikely to let you proceed. Hypertension is common in polycythaemia.

Further discussion

Given the clinical scenario you will expect to find non-tender splenomegaly, suggesting a diagnosis of primary polycythaemia (see Section 2.2.7).

Do not forget, however, that there are other causes of splenomegaly that you may want to consider (see Section 1.2.5, Table 7).

If splenomegaly is not found, then secondary polycythaemia is more likely than primary. In routine clinical practice it is certainly commoner, hence be prepared to discuss the differential diagnosis shown in Table 6.

What questions would you ask to screen for causes of secondary polycythaemia?

History of chronic pulmonary or cardiac conditions (particularly congenital heart disease); smoking history; drug history (diuretics).

What investigations would you perform to diagnose the cause of secondary polycythaemia?

Pulse oximetry/arterial blood gases (to demonstrate hypoxia), proceeding (as appropriate) to lung function tests/chest imaging and to ECG/echocardiogram. If there is no evidence of significant respiratory or cardiac disease, then you will need to consider wider differentials and look for evidence of the rarer conditions in Table 6 and measure plasma volume.

1.2.5 Splenomegaly

Instruction

This 35-year-old woman has had upper abdominal discomfort for 3 weeks. Please examine her abdomen.

Introduction

The relatively non-specific instruction in this case gives no clue as to what you will find, but does suggest that whatever is there may be tender. Therefore, take particular care to feel gently to start off with and do not palpate an obviously tender organ at great length. To do so would not be kind, necessary or sensible in any circumstance, and examiners in PACES are instructed to fail any candidate who causes a patient an inappropriate amount of pain.

General features

Look for clues regarding the sort of condition that the patient has.

- Haematological: this can be associated with pallor or polycythaemia, petechiae/purpura, lymphadenopathy or an indwelling chemotherapy line.

- Hepatological: are there any stigmata of chronic liver disease? Look for hepatic fetor or flap, clubbing, leuconychia, Dupuytren's contracture, palmar erythema, spider naevi, bruising, jaundice and (in men) gynaecomastia and loss of secondary sexual characteristics.

- Renal: arteriovenous fistula (radial or brachial) or an indwelling dialysis line.

TABLE 7 CAUSES OF SPLENOMEGALY

Haematological	Non-haematological
Hodgkin's disease/non-Hodgkin's lymphoma[1]	Portal hypertension[1]
Chronic leukaemia (myeloid or lymphoid)[1,2]	Storage disease (eg Gaucher's or Niemann–Pick)
Myeloproliferative diseases[1,2]	Systemic disease (eg sarcoidosis, amyloidosis and systemic lupus erythematosus)
Thalassaemia major[2]	Acute infections (eg infectious mononucleosis[2], bacterial endocarditis and typhoid)
Haemolytic anaemia[2]	Chronic infections (eg tuberculosis, malaria and schistosomiasis)

1. Commonest causes in PACES.
2. FBC/film usually abnormal.

Abdominal examination

- Observation will show scars and swellings.

- Gentle then deeper palpation will elicit any tenderness and may reveal a viscus: formal examination for liver, spleen and kidneys should follow, taking care not to cause gross discomfort.

> ⚠️ If the spleen is obviously palpable and tender, do not keep pressing on it.

Further discussion

Causes of isolated splenomegaly are shown in Table 7. Try to assimilate the positive and negative signs related to the list of likely diagnoses, and commence with the most likely before moving onto the rarer causes. Making an inspired guess at a rarity looks foolish rather than clever.

How would you investigate a case of non-tender 12-cm splenomegaly?

To diagnose what is likely to be a haematological cause, perform an FBC and film, a bone-marrow examination, a CXR, and a CT scan of the chest, abdomen and pelvis (looking for lymphadenopathy). To screen for possible effects and complications of a haematological disorder or other medical problems, check electrolytes; renal, liver and bone function tests; glucose; a clotting screen; and immunoglobulins and protein electrophoresis.

1.3 Communication skills and ethics

1.3.1 Persuading a patient to accept HIV testing

Scenario

Role: you are a medical trainee working in a general medical outpatient clinic.

John Ward is a 21-year-old university student who has visited East Africa. Lately, he has complained of increasing lethargy and difficulty concentrating, has lost one stone (6.35 kg) in weight over the last 2 months and has developed swellings in the neck, armpit and groin area. At night-time his temperature has gone up to 39.7°C, when he would sweat profusely. The warden of his hall of residence noticed that he was unwell and sent him home, telling him that he should see his GP.

The family GP took a very detailed history covering all physical and social aspects of John's life. He examined him and confirmed generalised lymphadenopathy, also finding oropharyngeal candidiasis, and organised blood tests that showed elevated immunoglobulins and haemoglobin 9.6 g/dL (normal range 12–16.5), platelets 87×10^9/L (normal range 150–400), neutrophils 1.8×10^9/L (normal range 2–7) and lymphocytes 0.02×10^9/L (normal range 1–3).

John was referred to the medical clinic where you discussed the differential diagnosis of lymphoma and HIV. You recommended an HIV test after a thorough explanation of the possibility of HIV and the development of AIDS. John refused to discuss this, saying that 'he was worried about obtaining a mortgage in the future'. He asked if he could have his immediate symptoms treated. You gave him a prescription for high-dose fluconazole tablets and some paracetamol to bring his temperature down, and gave him an appointment at clinic in seven days time, to which he has now returned.

Your task: to convince the patient to allow you to test him for HIV.

Key issues to explore

- The differential diagnosis.

- The patient's understanding of and fears about HIV.

- Issues about insurance.

Key points to establish

- That best treatment cannot be provided without a definite diagnosis.

- Does he have recognised risk factors for HIV infection, or is there another explanation?

- Does he realise that there is effective treatment for HIV-positive people?

- That applications for life insurance require any significant illness to be disclosed.

Some answers to likely questions

Patient: can you not just treat me for my fevers and oral thrush?

Doctor: I could, but this would be just treating the symptoms and not the disease. If we do that, then whatever is causing the problem will simply get worse and it's very likely that you will develop other infections, more serious than thrush, and these could make you very ill indeed.

Patient: but if I've got HIV, you can't treat it, can you?

Doctor: no, that's not true nowadays. It is right that in the early days of HIV there was no effective treatment, but we now have combinations of drugs that can prevent or slow progression of the disease, so it's very worthwhile finding out whether or not it's the problem.

Patient: I used to have a boyfriend, but I have not seen him for a long time. We fell out over his new job, which he was determined to take. What should I do?

Doctor: I think we need to establish the diagnosis first, and then – if you are HIV positive – you need to think about informing him.

Patient: I have had some casual sexual contacts recently, what should I do about these?

Doctor: again this depends on whether or not you are HIV positive, but if you are, then there are a number of issues: your partners may already be infected, and my advice would be that they should see someone appropriate to discuss this. Also, you will need to adopt the appropriate sexual precautions to prevent infectivity because, as you may be aware, having unprotected sex knowing that you could be HIV positive is a legal issue.

Patient: I read on the Internet that Hodgkin's lymphoma causes these symptoms. Why could it not be lymphoma?

Doctor: you are right, it might be. But because, as you recognise, you are at risk of HIV, it makes sense to check this possibility rather than get a lymph node biopsy in the first place.

Patient: I also read that lymphoma occurs in HIV patients. Could it still be lymphoma?

Doctor: yes, that's possible. However, this sort of generalised gland swelling is more likely to be a feature of the HIV reaction at an early phase.

Patient: why are you so sure this is HIV?

Doctor: your lymphocyte count and blood picture is very suggestive of HIV infection in a homosexual person.

Patient: don't the drugs you give for HIV make these blood problems worse?

Doctor: occasionally drugs will suppress your bone marrow, but with all drugs it's a matter of balancing benefits and risks. At present the HIV – if that's what it is – is damaging your blood, so it is important to control the infection to minimise this damage.

Patient: if I have an HIV test, then I won't be able to get insurance, will I?

Doctor: you are right that this can cause difficulties, but I'm afraid that the fact of the matter is that you've almost certainly got a serious medical condition – HIV or lymphoma I think. Any substantial insurance that you take out will require you to declare if you have any serious medical problems, so I don't think that the issue can really be avoided by simply not having the test.

1.3.2 Talking to a distressed relative

Scenario

Role: you are the junior doctor on call at the weekend covering a general medical ward.

Mr Sutton is a 64-year-old man who has been admitted for investigation of anaemia, back pain and weight loss. He becomes confused and disruptive, is found to be hypercalcaemic (serum calcium 3.21 mmol/L, normal range 2.1–2.6) and the medical team have started appropriate treatment for this (intravenous saline and intravenous bisphosphonate).

Mrs Sutton has come to visit her husband, is distressed about his deterioration and feels that his medical team is missing something. Her mother had myeloma and a back pain similar to her husband. She tells the nurses that she wants to speak to a doctor, and they call you.

Before you see Mrs Sutton you review the notes and see that Mr Sutton has had a CXR and barium meal, which are normal; that his haematinics are normal; that a spinal X-ray showed a lytic lesion, but protein electrophoresis was normal. Although you cannot find any record of a test for Bence Jones protein being performed, you recall that 15% of myeloma cases are Bence Jones positive but without a serum monoclonal band.

Your task: to reassure Mrs Sutton that her husband is receiving appropriate treatment.

Key issues to establish

- That you are sympathetic to Mrs Sutton's worries.

- That investigations into Mr Sutton's condition are proceeding, but a diagnosis is still not clear.

- That hypercalcaemia is the probable cause of his confusion, and that treatment for this has been started.

- That a definitive management plan cannot be made until the diagnosis is established.

- That you will make sure that Mr Sutton's regular medical team knows about his wife's concerns.

Key points to explore

- What are Mrs Sutton's main concerns?

Appropriate responses to likely questions

Doctor: the nurses told me that you'd like to talk about your husband, Mr Sutton.

Patient's wife: *yes, that's right, thanks for coming. I'm very worried about him: he's confused, and he wasn't when I saw him yesterday.*

Doctor: yes, I agree that he's confused. That's almost certainly because he has high calcium in his blood. He's been put on treatment with the drip for that, but it often takes a while before things improve.

Patient's wife: *should he have a brain scan?*

Doctor: it is often difficult and unsafe to attempt to scan patients who are acutely confused, and I don't think that this is necessary at the moment. I think we know the cause of your husband's confusion – the high level of calcium in the blood – and I expect that things will improve as this comes down with the treatment. But if it doesn't, then we can review the situation.

Patient's wife: *why is his calcium high then?*

Doctor: we're not sure at the moment. There are a number of conditions that can do this. Have the regular doctors on the ward had a chance to talk to you about the possibilities?

Patient's wife: *yes, they've talked a bit. They've said it could be myeloma, or perhaps some sort of cancer. My mother had myeloma. Has my husband got myeloma or not doctor?*

Doctor: I don't know for certain, but it is possible.

Patient's wife: *but one of the doctors on the ward told me that the . . . what was it? Funny word . . . immunoglobulins were normal and that it wasn't myeloma.*

Doctor: I've looked in the notes and it's true that the immunoglobulins in his blood are normal, and they are usually abnormal when someone's got myeloma. But this isn't always the case and I think we need to see the result of a special urine test before we can say that we are certain.

Patient's wife: *why did the regular team not do this urine test?*

Doctor: I don't know, but I will discuss it with them.

Patient's wife: *I feel let down by his regular doctors. I am not happy!*

Doctor: I can understand your concerns and frustrations. You need to speak to the consultant in charge of your husband's case and take these concerns up with them. I will let the nurse in charge of the ward know that you want to do this and she should be able to tell you the best way of making contact.

Patient's wife: *have you seen more cases of myeloma than my husband's doctors?*

Doctor: I think that this is very unlikely, but discussions about difficult cases occur all the time between teams of doctors and this is how problems are solved.

Patient's wife: *will he end up in a wheelchair like my mother?*

Doctor: it's far too early to be able to say anything like this. We need to be sure of the diagnosis before we can say what might, or might not, happen in the future.

Patient's wife: *myeloma cannot be cured, can it?*

Doctor: I think that's right. It's certainly not a condition that we can guarantee to cure, but there are treatments that can help substantially. Some patients with myeloma can have many years of good-quality life, even if the disease does eventually come back.

See *Endocrinology*, Sections 1.1.1 and 1.4.2 for discussion of causes of hypercalcaemia.

1.3.3 Explaining a medical error

Scenario

Role: you are the medical junior doctor working over the weekend to cover a gastroenterology ward.

Mr Alistair Bates, a 66-year-old man with well-known alcohol-associated cirrhosis, portal hypertension and angina, is admitted with haematemesis. He is not severely shocked, and after receiving 500 mL of plasma expander and 500 mL of 0.9% saline intravenously his pulse and BP are satisfactory, but because his haemoglobin is 9.1 g/dL (normal range 12–16.5) a decision is made to give him a blood transfusion. Within half an hour of commencing the transfusion he develops chest pain and becomes profoundly hypotensive. There is concern that he might be bleeding and that this might be precipitating ischaemic cardiac pain, so his transfusion is speeded up and the haematology laboratory is phoned to ask for more blood. A urinary catheter is inserted and the urine passed is red. By this time Mr Bates is unresponsive to pain and arrangements are made for his urgent transfer to the intensive care unit (ICU).

The fact that Mr Bates had collapsed following transfusion and that he had haematuria clearly suggests a transfusion reaction. In discussion with the biomedical scientist in the haematology laboratory it rapidly becomes apparent that a Mr Alan Bateman had also been admitted through the Emergency Department at the same time as Mr Alistair Bates – your patient – and that blood had also been cross-matched for this patient.

A repeat sampling from Mr Bates is immediately organised: this reveals that he is group O Rhesus (D) positive with a strong Coombs' test, which is at variance with his first sample that was group A Rhesus (D) positive. The blood for transfusion had been issued on the basis of the first sample. The other patient with a similar name is also re-bled: Mr Bateman's first sample grouped O Rhesus (D) positive, but repeat testing reveals he is group A Rhesus (D) positive. Clearly there had been a transposition of samples during the admission of the two men in the Emergency Department leading to a haemolytic transfusion reaction for Mr Alistair Bates. Group O blood (correct) is now issued for him as he is transferred to the ICU for further management.

You discuss the case with the on-call gastroenterology SpR, who knows Mr Bates well. He tells you that Mr Bates has had several admissions over the last 6 months with gastrointestinal bleeding (always from varices) and/or ascites, and that his prognosis from the point of view of his liver is extremely poor. He does not think that attempts should be made to resuscitate him in the event of cardiac arrest.

Your task: you are asked by the senior nurse on the ward to talk to Mr Bates's wife, and explain what has happened and why he is to be transferred to the ITU.

Key issues to explore

- The wife's understanding of her husband's medical condition and prognosis.

- The blood transfusion error that has led to a serious transfusion reaction.

- The possibility of a fatal outcome.

- Does Mr Bates's wife know her husband's views about attempts to resuscitate him in the event of cardiac arrest? And what are her views?

Key points to establish

- Mr Bates has a very poor prognosis because of his liver disease.

- A transfusion reaction has occurred, with immediately life-threatening consequences.

- It is not clear who is to blame for the transfusion error at this point, but the issue will not be ignored.

- That an attempt to resuscitate Mr Bates in the event of him having a cardiac arrest is extremely unlikely to be successful.

Appropriate responses to likely questions

Patient's wife: why is my husband unconscious?

Doctor: he has had a serious bleed from his stomach, and I'm afraid that he has reacted to the blood transfusion. His blood pressure is very low, which is why his brain is not working properly at the moment.

Patient's wife: why has he reacted to the blood transfusion? I thought blood was life-saving! And he's had it before without any problems.

Doctor: I'm afraid that there seems to have been a mix-up with the blood samples and the blood he received has resulted in him becoming seriously ill with a transfusion reaction.

Patient's wife: what is a transfusion reaction?

Doctor: the sort of reaction that he's got happens when the body recognises that the transfused blood is the wrong sort. It destroys the transfused cells, which release substances that can damage the body.

Patient's wife: he was given the wrong sort of blood? Who is responsible for this mistake?

Doctor: I'm not hiding anything when I say that I'm not exactly sure how this mistake has happened, but there seems to have been a mix-up between two patients' blood samples. We are investigating this, and when we have found out what happened we will let you know. We will not sweep things under the carpet. The consultant in charge will speak to you but he is not here at the moment. However, I think the ICU staff may be able to help with your concerns until the consultant in charge can speak to you.

Patient's wife: can I speak to the doctor in charge please?

Doctor: I am sure that the consultant in charge will speak to you, but she is not here at the moment. The most important thing to do now is to get Mr Bates to the ICU, but before we finish I will take your contact details and pass them on to the consultant.

Patient's wife: will he die?

Doctor: I'm afraid that he might. His liver disease is very bad indeed and, as I've said, the transfusion reaction is a very serious thing in itself. Have any of the gastroenterologists, the doctors who look after him regularly, had a chance to talk to you about his liver?

Patient's wife: a bit. They've told me it's pretty bad.

Doctor: yes, that's right. As you know he's been in and out of hospital several times recently, sometimes with bleeding and sometimes with swelling due to fluid in the abdomen. All of which means that the liver is in very bad shape. So, if we put the transfusion problem to one side for the moment, even without this I'm sorry to say that his outlook isn't good at all. I spoke to one of the team of doctors that know him a few minutes ago, and he said he thought he was unlikely to live for more than a few months.

Patient's wife: what will happen if you can't get his blood pressure up?

Doctor: we are trying to get his blood pressure up, but if we are unsuccessful then I'm afraid that his heart could stop. Did your husband ever talk with you about what he would want done in this situation?

Patient's wife: no, he didn't. What do you think?

Doctor: that's a difficult question. If there's a problem that can be made better, then it's clearly right to try and do everything that you can to keep someone alive – to give them the 'kiss of life' and that sort of thing. But when there are problems that cannot be improved – like your husband's liver – then it's very unlikely indeed that things like that would work; and I think, and the doctor from the team that knows him also thinks, that we should make sure that he's comfortable.

1.3.4 Breaking bad news

Scenario

Role: you are a junior doctor working on a haematology ward.

A 24-year-old shop assistant presents with a 6-week history of increasing tiredness. She has also had several episodes of cystitis and more recently has noticed that she has started to bruise more easily. Her FBC is as follows: haemoglobin 7.8 g/dL (normal range 12–16.5), white blood cell count 5.1×10^9/L (normal range 4–11), neutrophils 0.2×10^9/L (normal range 2–7) and platelets 18×10^9/L (normal range 150–400). Bone-marrow aspirate confirms the diagnosis of acute myeloid leukaemia and cytogenetic analysis reveals a normal female karyotype in all metaphases examined.

The case is discussed at the multidisciplinary team meeting and it is agreed that with current combination chemotherapy (which should last about 6 months) the patient has an approximately 90% chance of going into remission, with a 5% risk of death during treatment, a 5% risk of refractory disease, a 50% chance of relapse in the next 5 years and a 40% survival at 5 years. In the case of refractory or relapsed disease, two out of three patients respond to alternative treatment and 5-year survival is about 30%. Failure to respond to treatment in instances of relapsed or refractory disease implies incurable leukaemia. Without treatment this woman would die in a matter of weeks.

Your task: you must explain the diagnosis, treatment options and prognosis to this woman and her husband.

Key issues to explore

- Find out what the patient believes is going on.

- Describe the outcome of the disease if it is not treated.

- Describe the treatment options (including the option of no treatment) and the prognosis for each of the treatment approaches – in this case her condition is potentially curable. Be honest about the side effects and risks of treatment, but emphasise that there is a whole system in place to provide her with 24-hour support both when in hospital and when at home.

Key points to establish

- The diagnosis is not in doubt: the patient has leukaemia, which is a cancer of the blood. You must use the word 'cancer': it is the only word that you are sure everyone understands in the same way. Do not use words like 'tumour', 'growth', 'neoplasm' and 'lesion' when talking about cancerous diseases because these can be ambiguous and confusing.

- That you and your colleagues will do everything possible to cure the leukaemia, although a cure cannot be guaranteed. Also that you will support the patient and her family throughout the process of treatment and recovery.

- That if there is no curative option, every effort will be made to control the disease for as long as possible and that any symptoms the illness might cause will be dealt with actively. Reinforce that there are extremely effective treatments for the control of all symptoms and that you are determined that at no point during the illness should your patient suffer.

- That you will always tell the patient the truth, whether it is good news or bad. Encourage the patient to ask questions and reaffirm your intention to be open and honest with your answers.

- It is uncommon today for relatives to ask for the patient to be kept ignorant of the facts of the illness. If the patient is to give informed consent to further treatment, then she has to be fully aware of the diagnosis. Chemotherapy is potentially lethal, and informed consent must be obtained. Gentle persuasion and logical reasoning help most relatives see that this is correct. Occasionally, where it is clear that the patient is going to die rapidly, it may be more appropriate to keep them comfortable and spare them the details. However, if the patient demands information you must be honest with them: relatives have no legal right to withhold information in the UK.

Appropriate responses to likely questions

Patient/husband: is it cancer doctor?

Doctor: yes, leukaemia is a form of cancer. It is cancer of the blood.

Patient/husband: are you sure that it's leukaemia? Could it be anything else?

Doctor: no, I'm afraid that it couldn't. I'd like to tell you something different, but I wouldn't be being honest if I did. You've got leukaemia.

Patient/husband: can it be cured?

Doctor: this form of leukaemia is curable in some people but not in others. We can make the leukaemia go away in nine out of ten people like you with our current treatments – we call that remission – and after treatment the disease never comes back in about half of these patients. However, in others it does, which we call relapse. In a few people the leukaemia doesn't respond well to treatment at all, but we will do everything we can to make your leukaemia go away and stay away.

Patient/husband: what does the treatment involve?

Doctor: it involves having injections of drugs and taking tablets, which we call chemotherapy.

Patient/husband: doesn't chemotherapy make you sick and ill?

Doctor: you're right that there can be side effects such as sickness. We will explain to you what these might be, and also tell you about the treatments that can prevent them or make them less severe. We won't give you any treatments without explaining to you what they're supposed to do, and what effects they might have on you.

Patient/husband: what if the treatment doesn't work?

Doctor: remember that most people like you do respond to treatment. However, if the first course of treatment doesn't work, we would have to change tack and use a different combination of drugs to try to make the leukaemia go away. Many people who do not respond to the first set of drugs do respond to this different combination. That said, if you didn't respond to the second course of treatment then I think we'd have to accept that no drugs available would be able to cure your leukaemia, and our emphasis would switch to dealing with the symptoms that it caused.

Patient/husband: if I go into remission with the treatment but the disease comes back, what then?

Doctor: unlike many other cancers, if people like you relapse with leukaemia there are still treatments available that can cure the disease. It is harder to cure the disease second time around, but it is still possible. We could talk more about treatment options at that stage if it were to happen.

Patient/husband: if I am cured, will I be able to have children? And would any children I have in the future be affected by the chemotherapy?

Doctor: many women treated with this type of chemotherapy do go on to have children. Fertility may be reduced after chemotherapy, and if you did have problems in getting pregnant in the future then there are a number of investigations we would want to do at that stage to see if we could identify and treat the cause. While you are on chemotherapy you must not get pregnant, as the chemotherapy would harm the developing child. Also, you must not assume the chemotherapy will stop you getting pregnant, so you must use contraception such as condoms. If you think you might be pregnant at any stage during treatment, then you should let us know immediately. Most doctors recommend waiting 2 years after finishing treatment before trying to get pregnant. But after you have recovered from chemotherapy and it has left your system, then we don't think there is an increased risk of cancer or of an abnormality in children whose

parents have previously received treatment for cancer.

Patient/husband: do we have to decide about this right now?

Doctor: no, we don't have to make a decision this minute. But we can't wait too long, because without treatment the disease will get worse and I'm sorry to say that it will probably kill you within a few weeks. I'd suggest that you think things over, and I'll come back later on today or tomorrow morning to discuss your decision. I'll also ask one of the specialist nurses to come and talk to you: they'll be able to give you more information about how the treatments are given and the support that is available for you and your family.

1.4 Acute scenarios

1.4.1 Chest syndrome in sickle cell disease

Scenario

A 19-year-old student with sickle cell disease presents to the Emergency Department. He reports a two-day history of cough, fever and increasing shortness of breath. Over the last few hours he has developed pleuritic chest pain and his breathing has rapidly deteriorated. The nurse tells you he is hypoxic with a tachycardia and is becoming distressed.

Introduction

The fundamental problem is that of sickling of red blood cells within the pulmonary circulation, which

leads to reduced perfusion and gas exchange in the lung, causing local hypoxia and acidosis. As the patient becomes more unwell, he becomes dehydrated and his blood viscosity increases. Pleuritic chest pain may cause segmental hypoventilation and exacerbate hypoxia, which together with increased viscosity and acidosis all promote further sickling of red cells. A vicious circle is set up (Fig. 5), leading to rapid clinical deterioration. The initial trigger may be infection within the lung or bony rib infarction. Repeated sickling within the lung eventually leads to pulmonary damage and an increased risk of embolism.

> ⚠️ Acute chest syndrome is one of the commonest causes of death in adults with sickle cell disease. This is a medical emergency and without prompt and appropriate treatment this young man will die.

History of the presenting problem

The clinical features of chest syndrome are shortness of breath, pleuritic chest pain and fever. These can make it difficult to distinguish from pneumonia or pulmonary embolism (PE). The patient may not be able to give a clear history of their condition, because there is often no obvious trigger. In this case a chest infection may have initiated the process by causing local hypoxia.

Ask the patient about features that would suggest pneumonia, eg travel (hotel rooms – this might make it worth considering *Legionella*), rigors and coloured sputum.

Ask about features that would suggest PE, such as previous episodes, risk factors, unilateral leg pain/swelling and haemoptysis.

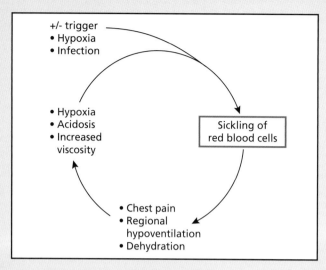

▲ **Fig. 5** The vicious circle. Sickling leads to hypoxia, acidosis and dehydration, an environment that promotes further sickling.

Other relevant history

- Has the patient had previous sickling episodes, and what were they like? In particular, has he had chest problems before?

- What is his vaccination status, presuming that he has a non-functioning spleen (this would mean there is a particular risk of pneumococcal infection)?

- The family history is relevant as patterns often follow through generations.

Examination: general features

Rapid assessment and resuscitation are required. Check the patient's airway, breathing (respiratory rate and pulse oximetry), circulation (peripheral perfusion, pulse and BP) and their position on the Glasgow Coma Scale. Is he in shock?

Examination: respiratory system

Look for decreased chest expansion, consolidation or a pleural rub. Rib tenderness may be a feature.

Investigation

FBC

Look for normochromic, normocytic anaemia with sickle cells (Fig. 6). Neutrophilia occurs with or without infection. Thrombocytopenia and reduced packed cell volume may occur as a result of sequestration within the pulmonary circulation. Thrombocytosis may occur in autosplenectomy.

Biochemistry and arterial blood gas analysis

Check electrolytes, renal and liver function and blood glucose. Measure arterial blood gases to confirm the degree of hypoxia and look for acidosis.

Microbiology

Culture his blood, urine and stool. Send his serology for respiratory pathogens.

Radiology

The CXR may show widespread patchy infiltrates that are difficult to distinguish from infection.

Management

Oxygen and intravenous fluids are essential.

- Sit the patient up and give high-flow oxygen through a rebreathing bag.

- Place intravenous access in both arms and rapidly infuse 1 L of 0.9% saline.

- Start intravenous antibiotics, eg ampicillin 500 mg iv 6-hourly.

- If the patient is in pain, administer analgesia: intravenous opiate (eg diamorphine 5 mg) is the most effective agent, but use with caution as it may cause respiratory depression. Consider patient-controlled analgesia once he is medically stabilised.

- Administer enoxaparin 20 mg sc once a day as prophylaxis against venous thromboembolic disease, or therapeutic anticoagulation if PE is strongly suspected.

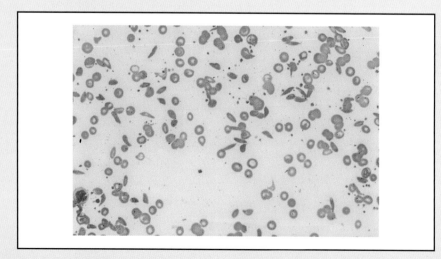

▲ **Fig. 6** Homozygous sickle cell anaemia. Note the elongated pointed red cells (the classical sickle shape is uncommon) and also fragmentation.

Severe crises, which require management in an intensive care unit, are indicated by:

- reduced level of consciousness;
- persistent hypoxia;
- unstable or deteriorating circulation/breathing.

Further comments

Few GPs in the UK are experienced in the management of the complications of sickle cell disease: all cases should be discussed with a haematologist who has the necessary expertise. Chest syndrome with hypoxia, neurological symptoms or priapism are all indications for exchange blood transfusion, the aim of which is to reduce haemoglobin (Hb) S to less than 30% (ie an HbA of >70%). Following complete recovery, the use of hydroxycarbamide (hydroxyurea) might be considered. This drug increases fetal Hb, increases mean corpuscular volume and reduces the white cell count. It significantly reduces the number of crises, without appearing to be leukaemogenic.

1.4.2 Neutropenia

Scenario

A 27-year-old man with epilepsy attends the Emergency Department with shortness of breath, dry cough and a fever of 39°C. On initial investigation he is found to be neutropenic and you are asked to see and advise him. His FBC is as follows: haemoglobin 13.8 g/dL (normal range 12–16.5), white blood cell count 2.9×10^9/L (normal range 4–11), neutrophils 0.4×10^9/L (normal range 2–7), lymphocytes 2.1×10^9/L (normal range 1–3) and platelets 201×10^9/L (normal range 150–400).

Introduction

Febrile neutropenia

Febrile neutropenia refers to all neutropenic patients (neutrophils $<2.0 \times 10^9$/L) who have a fever. Patients with a neutrophil count of less than 0.5×10^9/L are at greatest risk of life-threatening infection. Fever may be defined as two temperatures taken 1 hour apart that are both greater than 38.0°C or one temperature greater than 38.5°C.

Neutropenic sepsis

Neutropenic sepsis refers to neutropenic patients with a severe illness caused by overwhelming infection. Signs of sepsis include tachycardia, hypotension, postural hypotension, tachypnoea, confusion, a reduced consciousness level and fever, but not all patients have all these signs. Neutropenic sepsis is a medical emergency.

⚠ Severely neutropenic patients with infections may not appear at first glance to be very unwell, but this is misleading – they have a life-threatening illness and often deteriorate rapidly.

Consider neutropenia before the blood count is taken when the clinical context is appropriate, eg in patients on chemotherapy or following a bone-marrow transplant. Immediate action saves lives: when called by a GP, nurse, hospital doctor, patient or a relative about a (potentially) neutropenic patient with fever, remember that all neutropenic patients with fever (including this one) should be considered to have the life-threatening

condition 'neutropenic sepsis' until established otherwise.

What are the causes of neutropenia?

Neutropenia can be either an isolated finding, as in this patient, or part of a generalised pancytopenia. Problems with sepsis tend to be more significant when the neutropenia occurs as part of a generalised pancytopenia secondary to chemotherapy. There are two likely reasons for this. The first is that chemotherapy causes mucosal damage, particularly in the mouth and gut, which facilitates the passage of organisms into the bloodstream. The second is that monocyte function is preserved in isolated neutropenia: these phagocytose bacteria in a similar way to neutrophils and offer protection against infection. The causes of neutropenia are listed in Table 8.

History of the presenting problem

Respiratory/sepsis

The details given strongly suggest that the presenting illness is respiratory: is this pneumonia? Ask about rigors and pleuritic pain. Has he produced any sputum at all and, if so, what colour was it? (But remember that sputum production is often a late feature in pneumonia.) Check rapidly for other symptoms that might indicate a source of sepsis (dysuria/urinary frequency, abdominal/loin pain, diarrhoea, skin infection/abscess or a painful joint).

⚠ Patients with neutropenic sepsis may only have vague and non-specific symptoms such as malaise and lethargy.

TABLE 8 CAUSES OF NEUTROPENIA SEEN IN ISOLATION OR AS PART OF PANCYTOPENIA

Isolated neutropenia	Neutropenia as part of a pancytopenia
Drugs	Bone-marrow infiltration
Anticonvulsants, eg phenytoin and carbamazepine	Leukaemias
Antibiotics, eg co-trimoxazole and chloramphenicol	Lymphomas
Antidepressants, eg clozapine and mianserin	Metastatic malignancy
Phenothiazines, eg thioridazine and chlorpromazine	Myelodysplasia
Sulphonylureas, eg gliclazide	Myelofibrosis
Others, eg carbimazole, gold and penicillamine	Myeloma
Post infectious	
Viral, eg influenza and HIV	Bone-marrow failure
Bacterial, eg sepsis and tuberculosis	Aplastic anaemia
Autoimmune, eg isolated or systemic lupus erythematosus	Chemotherapy
Cyclical	Radiotherapy
Benign, eg chronic benign neutropenia and benign familial neutropenia	Splenomegaly

Other relevant history

Cause of neutropenia

The patient has an isolated neutropenia: note the conditions listed in Table 8 and take a careful drug history. Ask about symptoms that might suggest a recent infectious illness (could this be a post-viral problem?) and for symptoms that might suggest an autoimmune rheumatic disease. Ask about a family history of neutropenia or blood disorders.

Examination

The following aspects are particularly important.

- Check the patient's vital signs: temperature, pulse, BP including postural drop, respiratory rate and pulse oximetry. Are they in shock?

- Check the Glasgow Coma Scale (if appropriate).

- Examine them carefully for focal signs of infection: throat, chest and abdomen.

- Pay careful attention to the mouth and perianal area as sites of potential infection (as well as long lines if appropriate).

- Examine all lymph node groups.

⚠ Do not perform a digital rectal examination in a patient with neutropenia – this may cause infection.

Investigation

FBC and film

Ask the laboratory to confirm the findings of the FBC by reviewing the film in the unlikely event that they have not already done so. This review would principally look for evidence of dysplasia, in particular for nucleated red cells, primitive myeloid cells and blasts in the peripheral blood, all of which would suggest marrow infiltration. If there is a history of recent infectious illness, then check a Monospot test.

Other blood tests

Check electrolytes, renal and liver function, calcium, immunoglobulins and serum electrophoresis, and perform a clotting screen. Look for antinuclear antibodies, complement levels, rheumatoid factor and (if the patient is antinuclear antibody positive) double-stranded DNA antibody.

Microbiology

Culture blood, urine and stool. If there is a long line *in situ* (eg a Hickman line), take blood cultures from both the line and peripheral vein. Use a nasopharyngeal swab if there are symptoms of respiratory tract infection.

Radiology

Perform a CXR, looking in particular for pneumonic consolidation.

Bone-marrow examination

This should be carried out in all cases without a clear cause of neutropenia in order to exclude bone-marrow infiltration or failure. Occasionally, acute leukaemia will present in this way.

Other investigations

Depending on severity of illness and findings on pulse oximetry (is oxygen saturation 94% or more?), check arterial blood gases.

In this patient, who appears to have a neutropenic respiratory infection, high-resolution CT scanning of the chest and/or bronchoscopy with lavage and transbronchial biopsy may be required if initial cultures are not diagnostic and the patient does not improve with first-line management.

Management

Underlying condition

Treat any underlying condition appropriately. If a drug is believed to be responsible, then it should be stopped.

Neutropenic sepsis

Resuscitate if necessary.

- Administer high-flow oxygen, through a reservoir bag if needed, aiming for oxygen saturation >95%.

- Establish intravenous access and infuse colloid or 0.9% saline to support the patient's BP.

- Administer broad-spectrum intravenous antibiotics. Most hospitals have a policy with regard to antibiotic use in neutropenic sepsis, but a typical recommendation would be piperacillin 4 g iv qds and gentamicin 5–7 mg/kg iv daily (with gentamicin dose adjusted according to monitored levels, and recognition of the need for a reduced dose in cases of renal failure).

- Consider a urinary catheter and initiate an hourly input/output chart if the patient is shocked.

Get specialist advice.

- Discuss the case with a haematologist.

- Consider the use of granulocyte colony-stimulating factor.

- If not already *in situ*, consider insertion of central line to monitor circulation and aid treatment. Note that this may need platelet cover.

Further comments

If the patient remains hypoxic, hypotensive, unstable or continues to deteriorate, then arrange assessment by the intensive care unit (ICU) team. Outcome is better if patients are transferred to ICU before they suffer a cardiac arrest.

How long should you continue the antibiotics?

This frequently depends on the individual patient, but a reasonable guideline based on assessment at 72 hours is as follows.

- If cultures are all negative and the patient is well and afebrile, stop antibiotics and observe.

- If the cultures are positive and the patient is responding, continue with appropriate antibiotics and stop the antibiotics not useful in the treatment of the identified organism.

- If the patient is not responding or is deteriorating, re-culture and take microbiological advice. Consider alternative infective organisms and changing or adding antifungal (or antiviral or anti-*Pnuemocystis*) drugs to the regimen.

Can neutropenic patients with fever ever be treated as outpatients?

Yes, but only after discussion with a senior haematologist. Patients with neutrophil counts above 0.5×10^9/L, with no symptoms or signs of sepsis, who are clinically well and have good social support (eg do not live alone), and who can be brought quickly back to the hospital if they become unwell can be considered for outpatient oral antibiotic treatment with close clinical outpatient assessment. If they deteriorate then they need to be admitted urgently and managed as described above. All fevers and suspected infections in patients with a neutrophil count of less than 0.5×10^9/L and all septic patients, regardless of their neutrophil count, should be managed in hospital.

1.4.3 Leucocytosis

Scenario

A 34-year-old car dealer presents with a short history of impaired vision in his left eye. On examination his spleen is palpable 8 cm below the costal margin. His FBC revealed the following: haemoglobin 10.3 g/dL (normal range 12–16.5), white cell count (WCC) 348×10^9/L (normal range 4–11) and platelets 398×10^9/L (normal range 150–400).

Introduction

How can you relate this man's symptoms of visual loss to his blood count?

At this level, the high WCC can result in impaired blood flow through the capillary circulation, ie leucostasis. This is a medical emergency. Confirm and discuss the result with the haematologist immediately.

What is the differential diagnosis at this stage?

A genuine WCC of this magnitude means that the patient has a form of leukaemia/lymphoma until proven otherwise. Leucocytosis much more commonly occurs as a reaction to infection, infarction, inflammation, trauma or a drug (see Section 2.6), but in these cases it is extremely unusual for the WCC to be greater than 100×10^9/L.

History of presenting complaint

What specific questions would you ask patients in whom you had demonstrated extreme leucocytosis?

- Are there other symptoms, eg pain in the eye or headaches?

- Do you have chest pain or shortness of breath? (This would indicate cardiac and pulmonary leucostasis.)

- Do you have any weakness in the arms or legs? (This would suggest other neurovascular defects.)

- Are you tired all the time? Are you experiencing unexpected bleeding or bruising? (These are features of bone-marrow failure.)

- Are you in any pain? [Any left upper quadrant or chest pain is related to splenomegaly, and might be present in chronic myeloid leukaemia (CML).]

- Have you lost weight? Do you sweat excessively? Do you have fevers? (These are the constitutional symptoms of leukaemia.)

Other relevant history
Ask the patient if he has been exposed to radiation or received chemotherapy in the past. These may be implicated in cases of leukaemia.

Examination: general features
A general physical examination is required, particularly to look for signs of infection, bleeding or leukaemic infiltration. Hepatomegaly may occur as a result of sequestration of white cells in the liver. Confirm the size of the spleen, which is commonly large in CML. Look for skin or gum lesions as evidence of infiltration/granulocytic sarcomas in acute myeloid leukaemia (AML).

Examination: eyes/neurological
Assess visual acuity and fields. On fundoscopy, look for evidence of retinal haemorrhage or central retinal vein thrombosis (see *Ophthalmology*, Section 2.4). Assess cranial nerves and the rest

of the nervous system, including the patient's consciousness level and if there is any evidence of confusion (can be a result of cerebral leucostasis).

Investigation

Which quick investigation is required immediately?
A blood film will usually differentiate between acute and chronic leukaemia. In acute leukaemia the circulating cells are blasts, which characteristically have a high nucleocytoplasmic ratio and immature nuclear chromatin pattern. Chronic lymphocytic leukaemia (CLL) has the appearances of mature lymphoid cells with many disrupted 'smear cells' on the film. CML has increased numbers of myeloid cells in the peripheral blood (Fig. 7) and usually presents in the chronic phase, with more differentiated neutrophils and band forms predominating in the blood film and an associated basophilia and eosinophilia (and also sometimes a high platelet count). In chronic-phase CML, blast cells are rare but, less commonly, CML presents in either the accelerated or the blastic phase of the disease, when they are far more frequent.

Which subsequent tests would confirm the diagnosis?
Subsequent to the blood film, further information as to the nature of the cells can be gained by immunophenotyping of the peripheral blood (see Section 3.2). Monoclonal antibodies are used to detect the expression of cell markers in the population, and by the pattern of cell markers we are able to define the cell type (eg myeloid versus lymphoid, or immature versus differentiated) and therefore the disease.

Bone-marrow examination will also provide useful diagnostic information. Molecular techniques such as cytogenetic analysis and polymerase chain reaction (PCR) are used to identify specific genetic mutations that may have diagnostic importance. In CML the Philadelphia translocation, t(9;22), is seen, and *BCR–ABL* fusion transcript/gene by PCR/fluorescent *in situ* hybridisation can be confirmed. In acute promyelocytic leukaemia (FAB M3), the t(15;17) translocation is seen.

What other investigations would you request?
Check electrolytes, and renal and liver function. Also check baseline

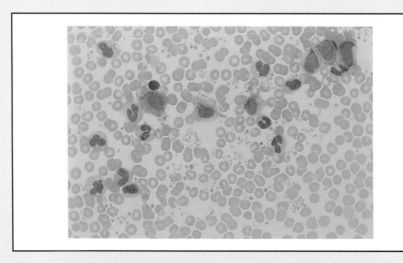

▲**Fig. 7** CML. There are plenty of neutrophils, but also some more primitive forms. A thrombocytosis is also present.

urate, calcium, phosphate and lactate dehydrogenase in view of possible tumour lysis syndrome.

Perform a CXR (to look primarily for pulmonary infiltrates), cultures (if there is clinical suspicion of infection) and an ECG (to check baseline).

Management

Request an urgent haematological opinion – the immediate aim must be to lower the WCC, which can be done by leucapheresis. This is a short-term holding measure, but may be enough to save this patient's sight pending specific treatment for the underlying condition. For sustained reduction of WCC this patient needs chemotherapy. Keep the patient well hydrated and commence allopurinol as prophylaxis against tumour lysis syndrome in preparation for chemotherapy.

Request an urgent ophthalmology opinion.

For management of CML, see Section 2.2.4; for AML, see Section 2.2.2; and for CLL and lymphoma see Section 2.2.5.

Further discussion

Remember that leukaemias are malignant diseases with far-reaching consequences. In initial discussion with this man and (if he wishes) his relatives, you will clearly need to say that there is very likely to be a serious underlying disease, but you must be absolutely certain that you know the diagnosis before telling the patient 'you've got leukaemia' (see Section 1.3.2). Ensure that if you are unable to answer the patient's questions you refer them to someone who is more experienced in this area. If the relatives have not been involved, you may want to suggest

that a relative is present during further discussions. Ideally a counsellor should be available, and relevant pamphlets and phone numbers (eg BACUP: http://www.cancerbackup.org.uk/ Home) should be obtained. The early/emergency management of patients with leukaemia often dictates how they approach their diagnosis and further treatment.

> ⚠️ In some patients anaemia is prominent, but be wary of transfusing blood into a patient with a very high WCC as this may further increase their total blood viscosity and precipitate leucostatic events.

1.4.4 Spontaneous bleeding and weight loss

Scenario

You are called to see a 27-year-old woman who has been brought to the Emergency Department by the ambulance crew with a major vaginal bleed. You notice that she is very pale, bruised and is bleeding from the cannula that has been inserted. Blood tests show a haemoglobin of 6.2 g/dL (normal range 11.5–16), platelets 3×10^9/L (normal range 150–400), white cell count 2.1×10^9/L (normal range 4–11), neutrophils 0.1×10^9/L (normal range 2–7), an activated partial thromboplastin time of 72 seconds (normal range 30–46) and a prothrombin time of 32 seconds (normal range 12–16).

Introduction

The pattern of bleeding, low platelets and abnormal clotting

suggest that this patient has disseminated intravascular coagulation (DIC). Although it is important to understand the cause of this, the immediate priority is to resuscitate her with platelets, clotting factors and blood. Although a few diseases may cause the pattern of deranged tests, pancytopenia associated with DIC in a young woman suggests acute promyelocytic leukaemia (AML M3) as the most likely diagnosis. This is a medical emergency.

History of the presenting problem

The history will generally be short (a period of days/weeks) in patients with acute myeloid leukaemia as this is an aggressive tumour. Ask in particular about:

- bruising/bleeding;
- infections;
- malaise;
- weight loss.

Other relevant history

Could the aetiology be obstetric or gynaecological?

- Is it possible that she is pregnant?
- Does she have a history of gynaecological/obstetric problems?

Are there other possible causes for the pancytopenia and DIC?

- Has she taken any drugs/medications?
- Has she done any recent travelling?
- Has she ever been diagnosed with a malignancy?
- Has she ever been diagnosed with a severe infection (eg tuberculosis) or had a recent (especially viral) infection?

Examination: general features

Check the patient's vital signs: temperature, pulse, BP including postural drop, respiratory rate and pulse oximetry. Is she in shock? Check the Glasgow Coma Scale (if appropriate). Is the abdomen tender? Is there any guarding?

Are there other areas of bleeding? Check the following.

- Look carefully at the skin and in the mouth for petechiae or purpura (Fig. 8); also look for any rashes or infiltration that might be leukaemic.

- Examine the ocular fundi for haemorrhages.

Look carefully for focal signs of infection on the throat, chest and abdomen (including the perianal area, but do *not* perform a rectal examination in this neutropenic patient).

Examine all lymph node groups.

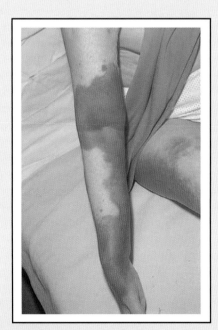

▲ **Fig. 8** Spontaneous bruising in an arm and leg as a consequence of DIC.

Investigation

What test will establish a definitive diagnosis?

The blood film will often show some evidence of leukaemia, but in some cases it may only show a 'leukoerythroblastic' picture (associated with many causes of bone-marrow failure). In practice a bone-marrow aspirate will be performed to make a definitive diagnosis and special tests (cytogenetics and immunophenotyping) will also be performed.

Other investigations

In this acutely ill woman it will clearly be appropriate to arrange an urgent cross-match and order blood (perhaps for 6 units to start with) and platelets (as recommended by a haematologist).

An FBC and DIC screen will need to be regularly repeated; you will also need to conduct checks of electrolytes, renal and liver function tests, and cultures (blood, urine and other sites as clinically indicated).

Check the patient's CXR and, given the presenting problem of vaginal bleeding, an ultrasound of pelvis/uterus (with/after review by a gynaecologist/obstetrician).

> ⚠ Do not check arterial blood gases in patients with thrombocytopenic bleeding unless absolutely necessary.

Management

It is likely that the haematologists will have been alerted directly by the laboratory in view of the grossly abnormal FBC, but if not seek haematology specialist advice urgently.

The immediate treatment is to resuscitate the patient with blood product support. Specific treatment for the leukaemia (all-*trans*-retinoic acid and chemotherapy; see Section 2.2.2) should be started as soon as possible by the haematology team, who will take over her management.

Request an urgent gynaecological/obstetric opinion.

Further comments

AML M3 is a type of leukaemia associated with a good prognosis (see Section 2.2.2). However, the highest risk of death is at the time of presentation, usually due to an inadequately managed coagulopathy or a catastrophic bleed (eg intracranial). Patients presenting to a unit with no on-site clinical haematology should be discussed and transferred as soon as it is safe to do so.

Be aware that the patient, although very unwell, will still be 'picking up' on what is going on around her. It is important not to lie to the patient. Explain to her that there is a problem with her blood counts and that a bone-marrow test and specialist input will be required to make a diagnosis.

1.4.5 Cervical lymphadenopathy and difficulty breathing

Scenario

A 30-year-old man presents to the Emergency Department on Christmas Day complaining of increased difficulty breathing over the last week. Today he could not swallow his dinner. He has noticed some lumps in his neck.

Introduction

Dyspnoea can be difficult to assess, but in previously fit individuals this symptom should always be taken seriously. Cervical lymphadenopathy is a common clinical problem: most cases are due to common viral infections, but nodes over 1 cm in size that persist for over 2 weeks should be considered for referral (in the UK), under the 2-week cancer rule, to either a haematology or ear, nose and throat (ENT) department.

> In cases of breathlessness in a patient with cervical lymphadenopathy, always consider upper airway obstruction, which is a medical emergency.

History of the presenting problem

Breathing

Aside from general enquiries to establish the degree of breathlessness ('Do you normally have any problems with your breathing? What makes you breathless? Is there a change in exercise tolerance or are you short of breath at rest?'), ask specifically about the problem of dysphagia and lumps in the neck ('Do you feel as if you are choking or have you inhaled anything?') because there is clearly the potential for upper airway problems.

In addition, ask about any problems with the throat, sinuses or ears (sites of local infection), any change in voice (suggests laryngeal problems) and haemoptysis (indicates lung cancer or tuberculosis).

Dysphagia

The history given suggests that this has been a problem today, but has he had previous difficulties?

Lymph nodes

Ask the patient the following questions.

- How long have you had the lumps in your neck (nodes)?

- Have they been present before?

- Are they changing in size? Decreasing size is usually reassuring, whereas increasing size alerts you to a progressive problem.

- Are they painful? Painless nodes are more ominous than pain associated with infection.

- Do you have any other lumps (glands)? This would suggest a generalised process.

General features

Has the patient undergone any weight loss? This could be a feature of infection, tuberculosis or malignancy. Also, has he had temperatures or night sweats? These are obviously a feature of infection, but intermittent persisting fever suggests lymphoma. Has he or any of his contacts had tuberculosis? This remains a cause of nodes and dyspnoea.

Other relevant history

Enquire about the following.

- Has the patient had any headaches? This is a feature of superior vena cava (SVC) obstruction.

- Has he been to the tropics? This broadens the infectious possibilities.

- Has he had any tumours or cancers in the past?

- Is he on any medication? Some drugs, eg phenytoin, can cause lymphadenopathy.

- Has he had arthritis or skin rash? Systemic lupus erythematosus can cause nodes and dyspnoea.

Examination: general features

Assess the patient for the following.

- Distress and anxiety.

- How is he breathing? Is there stridor?

- Can he talk and, if so, is his voice normal?

- Is he dribbling/drooling? This is a significant sign suggesting that he is unable to swallow secretions easily, and may have critical compromise of the airway.

- Check his vital signs: temperature, pulse, BP, respiratory rate and pulse oximetry.

- Pallor.

- Cyanosis.

- Pharyngeal swelling or infection: look carefully, but if a patient has stridor or is dribbling do not ask them to open their mouth as wide as possible as this may make a critical situation worse.

- Features of SVC obstruction: look for swelling of face and arms, jugular veins that will probably be prominent and non-pulsatile, and for superficial collateral vessels that may bypass the underlying venous obstruction.

Examination: respiratory and reticuloendothelial systems

Test for stridor by asking the patient to open his mouth and take a breath in and out as fast as he can (if necessary demonstrate, and get him to repeat). Localise the trachea. Is expansion equal?

Percuss and auscultate the chest for consolidation or fluid.

Examine the cervical nodes from behind the patient, including an assessment for thyroid swelling. Examine the axillae and groin systematically. Is there hepatosplenomegaly or nodal masses within the abdomen?

Investigation

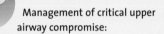

If a patient is extremely ill, then resuscitation must be started before investigation.

If the patient's breathing is severely compromised, then the immediate priority must be to secure the airway. If necessary, this must take precedence over investigation.

Management of critical upper airway compromise:

- sit the patient up;
- give them high-flow oxygen;
- call immediately for help from an anaesthetic or ENT specialist.

If the situation with the airway is not critical (or when the airway has been secured), then appropriate investigations would include the following.

To determine the cause of lymphadenopathy

FBC and film (may reveal features of lymphoma, Fig. 9), clotting screen (biopsy likely to be needed), electrolytes and a biochemical profile (hypercalcaemia is a feature of several conditions that can cause lymphadenopathy). Also check viral serology, tests for other infectious conditions and serological tests for

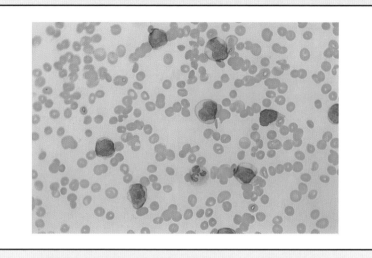

▲ **Fig. 9** Non-Hodgkin's lymphoma can spill over into the peripheral blood. These high-grade lymphoma cells can be difficult to distinguish from acute leukaemic cells (note that they are very big and have an irregular nuclear outline).

autoimmune rheumatic disorder if clinically appropriate.

Perform a CXR, looking in particular for hilar/nodal swelling (Fig. 10) or lung cancer. It is probably best followed by CT scan of the chest (and possibly abdomen and pelvis), and possibly by bronchoscopy (if indicated).

ENT referral for laryngoscopy will be appropriate if the

lymphadenopathy is confined to the patient's neck.

The single investigation most likely to establish the diagnosis is obviously lymph node biopsy: this will often be by fine-needle aspiration, but excision biopsy will be required for full lymphoma histology.

To assess respiratory compromise

Arterial blood gases, lung function tests and, in particular, flow–volume loops (see *Respiratory Medicine*, Section 3.6).

Management

As described above, if a patient with cervical lymphadenopathy has severely compromised upper airway, then securing the airway is the first priority and takes precedence over investigation.

Definitive management depends on the cause, but is the same as for SVC obstruction (see Section 1.4.3). If cervical lymphadenopathy is causing airway compromise, then steroids (dexamethasone 10 mg iv, followed by 4 mg po qds) can provide some relief, but it is best, if safely possible, to obtain diagnostic tissue before doing this.

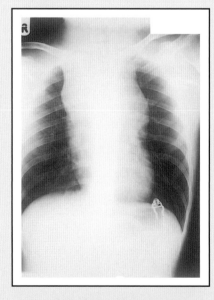

▲ **Fig. 10** Chest radiograph showing gross enlargement of the anterosuperior mediastinum of a man with Hodgkin's disease who presented with dyspnoea and dysphagia.

1.4.6 Swelling of the leg

Scenario

A 28-year-old woman had a left-sided deep venous thrombosis (DVT) in her first pregnancy 4 years ago. A thrombophilia screen at that time was normal. She was treated with heparin throughout the pregnancy, followed by warfarin in the postpartum period. She has avoided the oral contraceptive since and has not had a second pregnancy yet. She presents to the medical clinic with a swollen and painful left leg.

Introduction

The obvious clinical suspicion is that this woman has recurrent DVT. This is not an uncommon scenario, with recurrence of thromboembolism occurring in 10% of cases. Thrombophilia screens can lead to confusion in some cases, and having a normal or negative screen is no guarantee that a patient will not have a recurrent event.

History of the presenting problem

The expectation is that the woman has had another DVT, but it is necessary to confirm this by taking an appropriate history. Were there prolonged or recurrent leg problems following the initial DVT? How long has the recent swelling and pain been present, and how did it start? Were there any risk factors for thrombosis on this occasion (such as immobility or prolonged travel)? Initially, take a proper history and manage her as a DVT; note that if a comprehensive history is omitted, other less serious conditions may cause confusion, eg the symptoms may be due to a ruptured baker's cyst or because she had tripped over a step and twisted her ankle.

Check for features of pulmonary embolism (PE): pleurisy, cough, haemoptysis or breathlessness.

Other relevant history

A brief but thorough functional enquiry is needed, but questions of particular relevance include the following.

- Were there any problems associated with her heparin or warfarin therapy previously?
- Are there any contraindications to anticoagulation (such as recent surgery/significant bleeding)?
- Is she pregnant?
- Is there a family history of thromboembolism?

Examination: general features

Check the patient's vital signs: temperature, pulse, BP, respiratory rate and pulse oximetry. Also look for cyanosis.

Examination: leg and cardiovascular/respiratory systems

Are there signs in the leg consistent with a DVT? The most reliable are thigh swelling, asymmetric calf swelling (difference between the sides >2 cm), superficial venous dilatation and warmth of the affected leg (various studies have shown that Homan's sign, most often defined as discomfort behind the knee on forced dorsiflexion of the foot, is not reliable).

Are there features suggestive of PE? Look for elevated JVP, right ventricular heave, loud P2, gallop over the right ventricle and pleural rub.

Investigation

The key investigation is Doppler/ultrasound of the leg veins to confirm the presence of thrombosis.

Other routine investigations would include FBC, clotting screen, biochemical profile, ECG (looking for right heart strain), CXR (looking for any focal abnormality) and (if pulse oximetry shows oxygen saturation <94%) arterial blood gases. However, note that the following are *not* indicated.

- Thrombophilia screening: the 'acute phase' may elevate abnormally low levels.
- D-dimers: there is a high index of clinical suspicion that this woman has DVT, and whether the value is normal or elevated (as would be expected) will not influence the management of her condition. She needs imaging to look for thrombosis.

> ⚠ Do not measure D-dimers (or anything else) when the result will not inform the prognosis or management.

Management

Unless another diagnosis is made on clinical grounds, the patient should immediately be given a treatment dose of low-molecular-weight heparin.

> 🔑 If there is a high clinical likelihood of DVT or PE, start treatment directly unless diagnostic imaging is immediately available.

If a DVT is confirmed, then low-molecular-weight heparin should be continued and she should be started on warfarin, which will now be for life because this is the second episode.

The patient should be reminded about the side effects of anticoagulation, including issues related to pregnancy and the need for continued regular monitoring.

General advice about avoiding smoking, excess weight gain and dehydration is important, as is advice regarding long-distance travel (drink plenty of water, get up and move around, and wear compression stockings).

Further comments

Outpatient or inpatient?

Investigation and management of uncomplicated DVT can occur as an outpatient and the patient may not need to be admitted to hospital, although close liaison between the hospital and the community services is essential. The patient must know what to do and be able to do it in the event of deterioration.

Thrombophilia testing

Remember that thrombophilia testing needs to be performed outside the acute setting and with withdrawal of all anticoagulants, and should be performed by doctors who can give good advice based on the results. Do not hesitate to discuss the test findings with a haematologist. In a patient who has had a first thromboembolic episode a positive test does not in itself indicate a need for prolonged anticoagulation; indeed there is evidence to suggest that recurrence rates are no higher if the thrombophilia screen is positive.

Benefits and risks of long-term anticoagulation

The patient requires long-term warfarin. The balance of risks is a 10% annual recurrence rate versus a 1% annual incidence of bleeding on warfarin (only a 0.25% incidence of a fatal bleed);

hence most patients select warfarin in this situation. Monitoring can be performed with a finger-prick test at home using a hand-held device. Also, some patients can be taught to adjust dosage themselves, in which case warfarin therapy is not so onerous.

Pregnancy

Pregnancy and warfarin is a very important matter and needs emphasis with any woman of childbearing age, but take care with these discussions. Planning for pregnancy in the future will involve converting from warfarin to heparin during conception and continuing this throughout pregnancy, before re-instituting warfarin after delivery. Such conception planning needs sensitive handling and is probably best performed in a non-pressured outpatient setting, with involvement of obstetricians.

2.1 Causes of anaemia

Pathophysiology

There are several forms of haemoglobin (Hb), each characterised by the globin chains from which they are made. Two α chains are combined with either two β, two γ or two δ chains to give HbA, HbF and HbA_2, respectively. Four genes (two maternally inherited and two paternally inherited) code for the synthesis of the two α-globin chains. Two genes (one inherited from each parent) code for the synthesis of the two β-globin chains, and likewise for γ globin and δ globin. In fetal and neonatal life the principal Hb is HbF. Fetal HbF has a greater affinity for oxygen than the maternal HbA, thus facilitating transfer of oxygen from mother to child across the placenta. From 3 months after birth there is a switch from HbF production to HbA. In adults approximately 98% of Hb is in the HbA form.

Globin is a tetramer of two α and two β chains in HbA. Haem is a protoporphyrin ring that contains a single iron molecule. Each globin chain binds one haem group. In the lung, high oxygen tension promotes the uptake and binding of oxygen to Hb. In the tissues, a combination of lower oxygen tension and higher carbon dioxide tension facilitates oxygen release. Carbon dioxide may then bind to Hb forming carboxyhaemoglobin or is converted to carbonic acid by carbonic anhydrase. In the lung the Hb releases carbon dioxide and carbonic acid is converted back to carbon dioxide and water. The carbon dioxide then effluxes from the cells and oxygen is taken up.

> Anaemia is the result of a blood test, not a diagnosis. It should be thought of as the starting point of clinical investigation, not its end.

Anaemia occurs when red-cell loss exceeds red-cell production. Red cells are normally destroyed after about 120 days in circulation. Ineffective erythropoiesis as a result of haematinic deficiency, marrow failure or marrow infiltration may not be able to match the daily loss of senile red blood cells. Alternatively, bleeding or haemolysis may increase the daily loss to such a level that the marrow is no longer able to compensate by increased erythropoiesis. Anaemia is defined as a concentration of Hb in the peripheral blood below the lower limit of the normal range for age and sex (Table 9).

Anaemia can be subdivided clinically by the average size of the population of circulating red cells [mean corpuscular volume (MCV)] into microcytic, normocytic and macrocytic. It is important to note that the normal range for MCV is lower in children than in adults. Table 10, and the notes that follow, classify anaemia by aetiology.

> 'I have called this principle, by which each slight variation, if useful, is preserved, by the term natural selection.' Charles Darwin.

TABLE 9 CONCENTRATION OF HB IN BLOOD BY AGE

Age	Lower limit of Hb (g/dL)
Birth	13.5
1 week old	15
1 month old	12
1 year old	10.5
5 years old	11.5
10 years old	11.5
Adult male	13
Adult female	11.5
Pregnancy	10

TABLE 10 CLASSIFICATION OF ANAEMIA BY AETIOLOGY		
	Type of abnormality	**Example**
Congenital	Haemoglobinopathies	Sickle cell syndromes
		Thalassaemia syndromes
	Enzyme defects	Pyruvate kinase deficiency
		G6PD deficiency
	Membrane defects	Hereditary spherocytosis
		Hereditary elliptocytosis
Acquired	Deficiency states	Iron deficiency
		B_{12}/folate deficiency
	Acquired haemolysis	Immune
		Non-immune
	Marrow failure	Infiltration
		Aplasia

G6PD, glucose-6-phosphate dehydrogenase.

2.1.1 Thalassaemia syndromes

Pathophysiology

Thalassaemias occur because of an absence (or less commonly a defect) of one or more of the four α genes or one or both of the two β genes. This results in a quantitative abnormality and imbalance of globin chain synthesis. The clinical severity of the syndrome is proportional to the number of absent genes. The thalassaemias principally occur in populations of Mediterranean Europe, Central Africa, the Middle East, the Indian subcontinent and South-east Asia. It is believed that thalassaemia trait confers protection against falciparum malaria.

Aetiology

The α-thalassaemias

> The α-globin chains are present in both fetal and adult haemoglobin (Hb). Therefore genetic defects of α-globin may affect the fetus *in utero*. DNA studies are required to determine the diagnosis of α-thalassaemia.

Figure 11 illustrates the inheritance of the α-thalassaemias. The varying clinical syndromes are briefly discussed below.

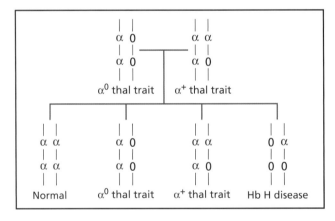

▲ **Fig. 11** Family tree illustrating inheritance of the α-thalassaemia syndromes. α, normal α gene; o, deleted α gene.

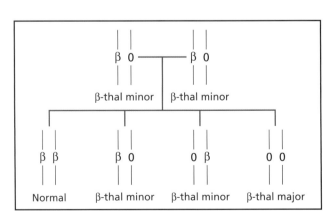

▲ **Fig. 12** Family tree illustrating the inheritance of the β-thalassaemia syndromes. β, normal β gene; o, deleted β gene.

The β-thalassaemias

> β-chain abnormalities do not become clinically significant until Hb synthesis switches from HbF to HbA in early infancy.

Figure 12 illustrates the inheritance of the β-thalassaemias. The two clinical syndromes are discussed below.

Clinical presentation

The α-thalassaemias
Genotype 00/00: hydrops fetalis
The absence of all four α genes leads to the formation of γ-globin tetramers known as Hb Barts within the fetal red cells. The fetus is anaemic and Hb Barts

has a high affinity for oxygen that results in poor tissue oxygenation. Clinically there is severe cardiac failure and death occurs in the third trimester or soon after delivery.

Genotype αo/oo: HbH disease
The absence of three α genes leads to the formation of tetramers of β-globin chains (HbH). Clinically there is a microcytic anaemia with Hb around 7 g/dL. Splenomegaly and haemolysis may occur. Normal survival is expected.

Genotype αα/oo and αo/αo: α-thalassaemia trait (α° trait and α⁺ homozygote trait) These two syndromes with two gene deletions are clinically identical. Affected individuals are well with a mild microcytic anaemia.

Genotype αα/αo: α-thalassaemia trait (α trait) Individuals with single gene deletions are clinically well. They have normal Hb with mild microcytosis.

The β-thalassaemias
Genotype β/o: β-thalassaemia minor These people are well. They have a mild anaemia with target cells and a microcytosis that may seem out of proportion to the degree of anaemia [eg Hb 10 g/dL and mean corpuscular volume (MCV) 60 fL]. On Hb electrophoresis HbA$_2$ is greater than 3.5%. Life expectancy is normal.

Genotype 0/0: β-thalassaemia major Patients with β-thalassaemia major present with profound microcytic anaemia and failure to thrive in infancy. Haemolysis leads to spheroctyes, anisopoikilocytosis, nucleated cells and fragmentation on the blood film (Fig. 13). The diagnosis is confirmed by the replacement of HbA by HbF on Hb electrophoresis. Marrow expansion occurs because of increased haematopoiesis, which leads to bony deformity. Extramedullary haematopoiesis occurs in an attempt to compensate for the severe anaemia, leading to hepatosplenomegaly. There is a reticulocytosis and the MCV and mean corpuscular Hb count are low. Multiple red-cell transfusions will eventually lead to secondary haemochromatosis so desferrioxamine therapy is required. Allogeneic bone-marrow transplant (BMT) from a sibling or matched unrelated donor is a potentially curative procedure. Ideally it should be performed before iron overload has caused significant organ damage. The significant initial risks of infection, graft failure, graft-vs-host disease and transplant-related mortality must be carefully weighed against the long-term benefits of transfusion independence and 'cure'. Without BMT, death usually occurs in the sufferer's early twenties secondary to cardiac failure.

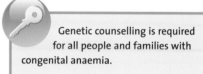

Genetic counselling is required for all people and families with congenital anaemia.

FURTHER READING
Olivieri NF. The beta-thalassaemias. *N. Engl. J. Med.* 1999; 341: 1407–20.

2.1.2 Sickle cell syndromes

Aetiology
In the sickle cell conditions there is a qualitative defect in the β-globin chain due to a single base-pair substitution resulting in valine replacing glutamic acid at position 6. Haemoglobin (Hb) C is formed after substitution of lysine for glutamic acid at the same position. The tendency to sickle is reduced by the presence and quantity of non-S haemoglobins, and high HbF levels are protective from acute complications. The heterozygote state confers protection against falciparum malaria, and the gene has been conserved in malaria-affected areas of sub-Saharan Africa. Geographically, HbC occurs in West Africa. In the UK, an estimated 15,000 individuals are affected by the sickling disorders. Figure 14 illustrates the inheritance of the sickle cell syndromes.

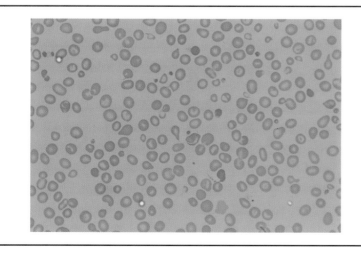

▲ **Fig. 13** β-Thalassaemia major. The severity of the changes on the film can vary considerably. The features are microcytosis, hypochromia and poikilocytosis. There are some target cells.

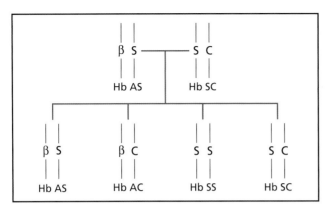

▲**Fig. 14** The inheritance of the sickle syndromes. β, normal β gene; S, sickle gene; C, HbC gene.

Clinical presentation

Genotype HbSS: sickle cell disease

Red cells are wider than the capillaries they have to pass through, and therefore the cells must fold to enable them to circulate. At low oxygen tensions the HbS crystallises and distorts the red cell shape, a phenomenon called sickling. The sickle cells are unable to fold and consequently block the capillaries; this prevents the further passage of red cells, lowering oxygen tension and resulting in local ischaemia.

The diagnosis is confirmed by a Sickledex test for Hb solubility and Hb electrophoresis (Fig. 15). Laboratories with a high throughput can utilise high-pressure liquid chromatography to separate the different haemoglobins.

The clinical course is one of chronic haemolytic anaemia punctuated by crises. Bone pain crises caused by marrow infarction are the most common hospital presentation. Crises may also occur within organs such as the spleen, lungs, liver and brain. Stroke, a devastating complication, is found in 8% of children. Repeated splenic infarction leads to functional hyposplenism by early childhood. Subsequently, patients are at increased risk of

infection, particularly by encapsulated organisms such as *streptococcus pneumoniae*. Aplastic crises may occur following infection with parvovirus B19, which usually requires transfusion support. The management of a sickle crisis, as well as the laboratory findings in sickle cell disease, is covered in Section 1.4.1. Hydroxycarbamide (hydroxyurea), which increases HbF, can reduce the incidence of painful crises, acute chest syndrome and the number of people and units transfused by 50%. However, even if those with sickle cell disease survive these potential problems, their life expectancy is reduced to about 50 years. Allogeneic bone-marrow transplants offers a potential long-term cure. All surgical procedures and pregnancies should be managed with the assistance of a haematologist.

Genotype HbAS: sickle cell trait

Patients with sickle cell trait are not anaemic and rarely suffer crises. However, in rare instances crises can be precipitated by severe hypoxia, being in an unpressurised aircraft or septicaemia. Once again, haematological advice should be taken for surgical procedures and pregnancies.

Genotype HbSC: haemoglobin SC disease

Patients with SC disease have a mild anaemia and suffer fewer crises than people with SS disease. Women are at increased risk of venous thromboembolic disease during pregnancy. Retinal ischaemia leads to proliferative retinopathy and may proceed to detachment. Yearly ophthalmological review is recommended in all adults with SC disease. As with the other sickle

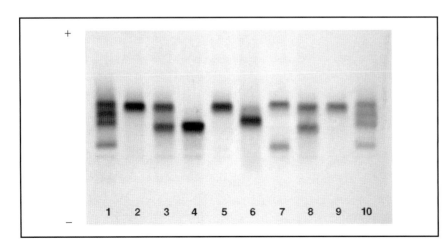

▲**Fig. 15** Hb electrophoresis (alkaline). The Hb is placed on the gel just above the row of numbers, and then an electric current is passed through the gel in the direction indicated. Lanes 1 and 10 are controls showing bands for HbC, HbS, HbF and HbA in ascending order. Lanes 2, 5 and 9 show HbA only. Lanes 3 and 8 show HbA and HbS. Lane 4 shows only HbS. Lane 6 shows mainly HbF from thalassaemia major (there is a small amount of HbA). Lane 7 shows HbA and HbC.

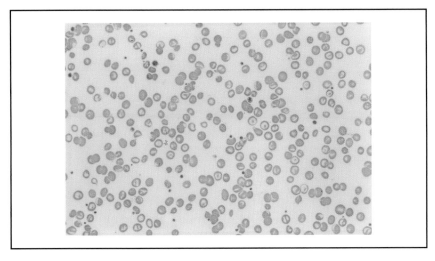

▲ **Fig. 16** Hb C. The presence of target cells is very striking, far more so than in liver disease.

syndromes, pregnancy and surgery should be discussed with a haematologist.

Genotype HbAC or HbCC

Both the heterozygous and homozygous forms cause minimal problems; homozygotes (HbCC) may have a mild microcytic anaemia and occasionally splenomegaly. The blood film shows many target cells (Fig. 16).

> Combinations of genetic defects in globin synthesis may occur in the same patient and present a wide variety of clinical problems. The further discussion of such syndromes is beyond the scope of this book.

FURTHER READING

Charache S, Terrin M and Moore R *et al*. Effect of hydroxyurea on the frequency of painful crises in sickle cell anemia. Investigators of the Multicenter Study of Hydroxyurea in Sickle Cell Anemia. *N. Engl. J. Med.* 1995; 332: 1317–22.

Walters MC. Bone marrow transplantation for sickle cell disease. *J. Pediatr. Hematol. Oncol.* 1999; 21: 467–74.

2.1.3 Enzyme defects

Glucose-6-phosphate dehydrogenase deficiency

Glucose-6-phosphate dehydrogenase (G6PD) is an enzyme that reduces glutathione in red cells. Deficiency of the enzyme is sex-linked: females are carriers and males are affected. Globally, 200 million people have reduced levels of G6PD. The female carriers are partly protected from falciparum malaria. The affected males are usually asymptomatic; however, dramatic intravascular haemolysis may be triggered by oxidative stress. Examples of such triggers include infection, drugs (eg dapsone, quinine and aspirin) and fava beans. The laboratory features are similar to those of the other haemolytic anaemias, with red-cell fragmentation, spherocytosis and reticulocytosis. The direct antiglobulin test is negative, unlike immune haemolysis. Denatured haemoglobin (Hb) clumps can be seen within the red cells and are known as Heinz bodies. Haemoglobinuria turns the urine red or a dark colour similar to that of a cola drink. Treat or remove the underlying cause, maintain the Hb with transfusion if necessary and support patients by keeping them well hydrated.

Pyruvate kinase deficiency

Pyruvate kinase deficiency causes a chronic haemolytic anaemia. The inheritance is autosomal recessive. Patients are often jaundiced from the haemolysis and many subsequently develop pigment gallstones. Marrow expansion occurs to compensate for the shortened red-cell survival. Splenectomy may prolong red-cell survival and reduce the level of anaemia, but because of the risks of surgery and the lifelong increased risk of infection this is reserved for the most severely affected.

2.1.4 Membrane defects

Hereditary spherocytosis occurs because of a structural defect in the cytoskeleton of the red blood cell (usually an abnormality of the protein spectrin). The red cells released into the peripheral blood appear morphologically normal, but as they circulate they lose their membranes, principally in the spleen. As more of the cell membrane is lost, the shape of the red cells changes from a biconcave disc to spherical. Red-cell survival is reduced, with the spherocytes eventually being destroyed in the spleen. There is wide variation in the clinical manifestations of this condition.

> The spleen destroys damaged spherocytic cells. Significant clinical illness can be treated by splenectomy, which enables spherocytes to live longer in the absence of the spleen.

In an adult, anaemia may lead to tiredness, lethargy and reduced exercise capacity. This may also be true in children, but height, weight and school performance can be more useful markers of the effects of disease.

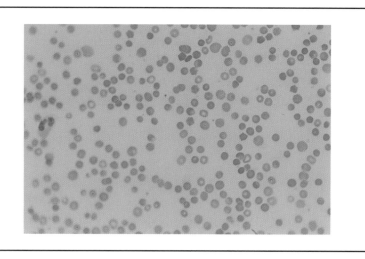

▲ **Fig. 17** Hereditary spherocytosis. Spherocytes are round and have no area of central pallor because of their spherical shape. They are rather smaller than the non-spherocytic normal cells. There is some polychromasia as well due to reticulocytosis.

Most cases of hereditary spherocytosis are inherited in an autosomal dominant fashion, with the severity often breeding true. Asking about the severity of the condition in older affected members within the family may give a guide to the extent of problems the individual is likely to experience. Particular attention to the following is warranted.

- Chronic haemolysis often leads to the formation of pigment gallstones, so document the frequency and severity of episodes of biliary colic and cholecystitis.

- Infection with a parvovirus may precipitate an aplastic crisis, the frequency and severity of which should also be recorded.

The degree of haemolysis in patients with hereditary spherocytosis is very variable and this is reflected by the level of haemoglobin (Hb), which may range from normal to severely anaemic (Fig. 17). The reticulocyte count is usually raised at between 5 and 20%. Because the spherocytes have a reduced cell volume and the reticulocytes an increased cell volume, the mean corpuscular value usually balances out within the normal range. The mean corpuscular Hb is often normal but the mean corpuscular Hb concentration will be raised because of the relative reduction in cell volume compared with cellular Hb. Aplastic crises may occur following viral infection, in particular by a parvovirus, which may lead to severe anaemia with no reticulocyte response. The direct antiglobulin test will be negative, whereas it will be positive in autoimmune haemolytic anaemia.

Hyperbilirubinaemia is common. In haemolysis the majority of bilirubin will be unconjugated and the liver enzymes should be within the normal range. In contrast, in common bile duct obstruction, bilirubin will be conjugated and liver enzymes will often be raised.

Spherocytes have reduced resistance to osmotic lysis (Fig. 18). An increasing degree of haemolysis of normal cells occurs in progressively hypotonic conditions, but spherocytes are more susceptible to lysis at any given concentration of saline. Reticulocytes are more resistant to lysis than normal red cells, and the reticulocytosis in hereditary spherocytosis is reflected in the tail of the curves. A positive test is not diagnostic of hereditary spherocytosis, but simply indicates the presence of spherocytes for any number of reasons.

Chronic haemolysis often leads to folate deficiency, and treatment of this may lead to symptomatic improvement. Many haematologists recommend folic acid 5 mg daily prophylactically.

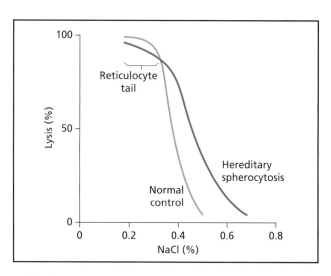

▲ **Fig. 18** Osmotic fragility curve. The normal control shows a steep curve over the range 0.3–0.4%. In hereditary spherocytosis the curve has a gentler slope with a marked reticulocyte tail.

Splenectomy will significantly reduce haemolysis, correct the anaemia and resolve the clinical problems, but these benefits will need to be weighed against the surgical risk of the procedure and the lifelong increased risk of infection in patients after splenectomy. If splenectomy is proposed, then the following should be considered.

- At least 2 weeks before the spleen is removed the patient should be given pneumococcal, meningococcal (AC) and *Haemophilus influenzae* B vaccinations, with a booster every 5–10 years.

- After splenectomy the patient should receive penicillin 250 mg orally twice a day for life, as prophylaxis against infection, and a yearly influenza vaccination.

- The patient should be educated and warned about the risk of infection and advised to seek medical help immediately should they become unwell. Individuals should also carry a supply of broad-spectrum antibiotics (eg co-amoxiclav) for immediate use should they develop symptoms or signs of infection.

- Splenectomy for those under the age of 5 years should be avoided if at all possible as the risks of overwhelming infection are greatest in this group.

2.1.5 Iron metabolism and iron-deficiency anaemia

Aetiology
There is approximately 4 g of iron in the human body of which two-thirds is present in haemoglobin (Hb); the rest is stored as ferritin and haemosiderin in the liver, spleen and bone marrow. A small amount of iron is used in enzyme systems. Iron is present in meat and vegetables, but is more effectively absorbed by the body if eaten in the haem form. Other factors that promote iron absorption include an acid environment, iron in the ferrous form, iron deficiency and pregnancy. Of the 15 mg of dietary iron that a person eats in a day, only 1–2 mg is absorbed, which may be increased to a maximum of 4 mg. Therefore, if iron loss consistently exceeds 4 mg/day, the iron stores will inevitably be used up and iron-deficiency anaemia will follow. In a healthy individual about 0.5 mg of iron is lost daily from the gut, while in women 1 mg/day is accounted for by menstruation. Pregnancy requires approximately 1.5 mg/day (although there is some compensation for this by the cessation of menstrual loss).

Pathophysiology
Iron is principally absorbed into the mucosal cells of the duodenum, where it is either taken up into the portal circulation or kept within the cell as ferritin and then lost when the mucosa is shed back into the gut. The majority of iron in the circulation is transported bound to transferrin, with a small quantity circulating as free iron within the plasma. Transferrin delivers the iron to developing erythroblasts in the bone marrow for Hb synthesis and to the reticuloendothelial system (liver, spleen and bone marrow) for storage. Tissue macrophages are the principal cells used for iron storage, most of which is bound to the protein apoferritin to form ferritin. Iron is reutilised following the breakdown of red cells.

> Ferritin rises in the acute phase, and a level within the normal range does not always truly reflect iron stores. A low ferritin always suggests iron deficiency, whereas a normal ferritin does not exclude iron deficiency.

The definitive test of iron status is a bone-marrow aspirate stained with Perl's stain. Iron deficiency is confirmed by the complete absence of stainable iron within the particles on the aspirate. Excess iron stores within the particles suggests iron overload.

> Approximately 1,500 million people worldwide (about one-third of the earth's population) suffer from iron-deficiency anaemia. In the developing countries this is most frequently due to hookworm and *Schistosoma*. In Europe the commonest cause is menstrual loss.

Clinical presentation
The diagnosis and causes of iron deficiency are considered further in Section 1.1. Consider the differential diagnosis of hypochromic microcytic anaemia in Table 11.

Treatment
Oral ferrous sulphate is well tolerated by most people at 200 mg tds. Constipation and gastrointestinal upset may cause intolerance, in which case intravenous iron can be considered. Newer preparations of intravenous iron are generally well tolerated, but they do not raise the Hb substantially faster than oral iron taken in full dose.

	Iron deficiency	Chronic disease	Thalassaemia trait (α or β)	Sideroblastic anaemia
TABLE 11	**CAUSES OF A HYPOCHROMIC MICROCYTIC ANAEMIA**			
Serum iron	Reduced	Reduced	Normal	Raised
Total iron-binding capacity	Raised	Reduced	Normal	Normal
Ferritin	Reduced	Normal/raised	Normal	Raised
Marrow particle iron	Absent	Present	Present	Present
Erythroblast iron	Absent	Absent	Present	Ring sideroblasts
Hb electrophoresis	Normal	Normal	$HbA_2 > 3.5\%$ (β)	Normal

2.1.6 Vitamin B_{12} and folate metabolism and deficiency

Pathophysiology

Vitamin B_{12} metabolism and deficiency

Vitamin B_{12} is an essential coenzyme for the synthesis of methionine and succinyl coenzyme A (CoA).

> Methionine is an essential amino acid and succinyl CoA is a metabolite within the citric acid cycle. Both are essential for nuclear maturation in all cells, and therefore megaloblastosis can affect all tissues, not just the red blood cells (namely demyelination of the spinal cord).

> B_{12} deficiency affecting the gut may cause malabsorption. The Schilling test should be carried out after correction of B_{12} deficiency, as any cause of megaloblastosis of the gut will cause malabsorption similar in pattern to that seen in pernicious anaemia.

B_{12} is found in fish, meat and dairy products. It is easily absorbed and body stores last for several years. Dietary deficiency is rare, but does occur in those people who keep to a strict vegan diet. B_{12} binds in the stomach to intrinsic factor (IF), a glycoprotein produced by gastric parietal cells. The B_{12}–IF complex binds to a receptor in the terminal ileum, where the B_{12} is absorbed but the IF is not. B_{12} is then transported in the blood bound to transcobalamin II to the tissues. IF is essential for the absorption of B_{12}. Antibodies to IF prevent formation of the B_{12}–IF complex and subsequent absorption of B_{12}. Antibodies to gastric parietal cells may reduce the production and release of IF as well as causing achlorhydria. Antibodies may be produced to the B_{12}–IF binding site in the terminal ileum, also causing malabsorption. The diagnosis, investigation and management of B_{12} deficiency is discussed further in Section 1.1.2.

Folate metabolism and deficiency

Folate is essential for the synthesis of amino acids and DNA. Folate is present in most foods, mainly leafy vegetables. It is absorbed in the proximal small bowel, and body stores last for approximately 4 months. Poor dietary intake is a common cause of folate deficiency, but any malabsorptive process affecting the small bowel may lead to folate deficiency (eg coeliac disease). There is an increased folate requirement in people who have chronic haemolytic anaemia and women who are pregnant (when folate deficiency is associated with an increased risk of neural tube defects in the fetus). Folate supplements are therefore recommended in pregnancy and chronic haemolysis. Unlike B_{12} deficiency, folic acid deficiency does not cause neurological damage. The haematological features in the blood and bone marrow are indistinguishable from those of B_{12} deficiency and the diagnosis is made on assay of red-cell folate. The diagnosis, causes and treatment are discussed further in Section 1.1.2.

2.1.7 Acquired haemolytic anaemia

Pathophysiology

Premature intravascular destruction of red cells is referred to as haemolysis. The mechanisms of acquired haemolytic anaemia are divided into immune-mediated destruction and mechanical destruction (Table 12).

All forms of intravascular haemolysis lead to the formation of spherocytes and a reticulocytosis. Following destruction of the red cells, haemoglobin (Hb) binds to haptoglobin. The serum haptoglobin transports the Hb to the liver where the iron is stored as ferritin, the globin chains are broken down to their constituent amino acids and the protoporphyrin ring is

TABLE 12 CAUSES OF ACQUIRED HAEMOLYTIC ANAEMIA

Immune	Mechanical
Autoimmune	Microangiopathic haemolytic anaemia
Warm (IgG) type	DIC, TTP, HUS, sepsis and burns
Cold (IgM) type	Physical trauma
Alloimmune	March haemoglobinuria and prosthetic heart
Haemolytic transfusion reaction	valves
Haemolytic disease of the newborn	Infection and toxins
Drug induced	Malaria (blackwater fever)
Oxidative (dapsone)	*Clostridium* sepsis
Hapten mechanism (penicillin)	Dengue fever
Autoantibody mediated (methyldopa)	Others
Innocent bystander mechanism	Paroxysmal nocturnal haemoglobinuria, burns,
(quinine)	renal failure and liver failure

DIC, disseminated intravascular coagulation; HUS, haemolytic–uraemic syndrome; TTP, thrombotic thrombocytopenic purpura.

metabolised to bilirubin. The serum haptoglobin level falls as it is used up and Hb then circulates unbound. The Hb may be excreted in the urine, turning the urine dark (blackwater fever of falciparum malaria). Hb may be taken up in the tubular cells of the kidney, where it forms haemosiderin which can be detected in urinary casts. Unconjugated bilirubin rises and patients may be clinically jaundiced. The non-immune haemolytic anaemias also cause red-cell fragmentation. Spherocytes, polychromasia and fragmentation can be seen on the blood film.

Autoimmune haemolytic anaemia

Autoimmune haemolysis occurs because the red cells become coated with autoantibody, complement (C3d) or both. The coating of the red cells leads to premature lysis within the circulation. The direct antiglobulin (DAG) test, also known as the Coombs' test, is positive (see Section 3.4). Autoimmune haemolytic anaemia is subdivided into warm and cold types depending on whether the antibody binds antigen most avidly at a warm temperature (37°C) or a cold temperature (4°C).

Warm haemolytic anaemia

Warm haemolytic anaemia may occur secondary to autoimmune disease or lymphoproliferative disorders or may be idiopathic. The DAG test is positive to IgG, C3d or both.

Prednisolone 1 mg/kg daily is the first-line treatment. Red-cell transfusion is indicated in severe symptomatic cases. If steroids fail, consider immunosuppression (eg azathioprine), intravenous IgG, ciclosporin, a monoclonal antibody (rituximab) directed against the B cells responsible for production of the warm antibody, and splenectomy.

Cold haemolytic anaemia

Cold haemolytic anaemia (cold haemagglutinin disease) is a condition principally of the elderly. The responsible antibody is IgM, which binds to the red cells as the blood cools in the peripheral circulation. As well as causing complement-dependent lysis, the pentameric IgM agglutinates red cells causing the hands and feet to turn blue in cold conditions (acrocyanosis). Haemolysis and agglutination can occur at different

temperatures and one may be more clinically problematic than the other. The condition is often idiopathic but may occur secondary to *Mycoplasma* infection, infectious mononucleosis or lymphoproliferative disorders.

Treatment is supportive. Keep the patient warm and transfuse using a blood warmer if necessary. Exclude an underlying treatable cause. Steroids are of no proven benefit. Resistant cases may respond to alkylator therapy such as low-dose cyclophosphamide.

Haemolytic transfusion reactions

Haemolytic transfusion reactions are discussed further in Sections 1.3.3 and 2.5.

The majority of blood group system (ABO) incompatibilities result from errors of identification at the bedside (when sampling or setting up a transfusion). Laboratory errors also occur.

Patients experience an immediate feeling of dread when they develop haemolysis. This is due to the development of shock and associated chest and back pain.

The transfusion should be discontinued immediately and the bag sent back to the laboratory. The laboratory and the consultant in charge need to know urgently about the matter. Blood for a Coombs' test and further antibody analysis is required, plus biochemistry and clotting profiles. Blood cultures are required in case there is an infective element.

Active resuscitation with fluids is necessary. Adrenaline (epinephrine) may be required intramuscularly. A brisk diuresis and close monitoring of central venous pressure is essential. There is a 10% mortality rate from haemolytic transfusion reactions.

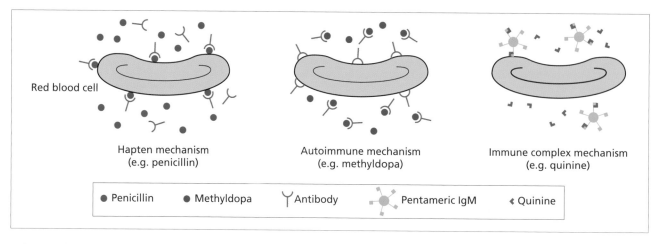

Red blood cell

Hapten mechanism
(e.g. penicillin)

Autoimmune mechanism
(e.g. methyldopa)

Immune complex mechanism
(e.g. quinine)

● Penicillin   ● Methyldopa   Y Antibody   Pentameric IgM   ◄ Quinine

▲ **Fig. 19** Antibody-mediated mechanisms for drug-induced haemolysis.

Drug-induced haemolysis

Many drugs can cause haemolysis by a variety of mechanisms (Fig. 19). Penicillin can attach to the red-cell membrane producing an antigen that stimulates antibody production and lysis (hapten mechanism). Methyldopa leads to antibody production. The antibodies cross-react with red-cell membrane antigens and stimulate haemolysis (autoimmune mechanism). Quinine forms an immune complex with an IgM antibody. The complex then binds to the red cell and complement-mediated lysis occurs (immune complex or innocent bystander mechanism). The appropriate treatment is to stop the drug, keep the patient well hydrated and support the Hb if necessary with red-cell transfusion. Steroids are of no proven value. The condition usually remits after stopping the drug.

Dapsone and sulfasalazine cause haemolysis by direct oxidative stress. Patients with glucose-6-phosphate dehydrogenase (G6PD) deficiency are particularly vulnerable, but all patients on these drugs should have regular counts checked. As with oxidative haemolysis in G6PD deficiency, Heinz bodies may be seen on the blood film and Hb may turn the urine dark.

Microangiopathic haemolytic anaemia

The haemolysis in microangiopathic haemolytic anaemias occurs because of the shredding of red cells as they flow through intravascular fibrin strands. This is often associated with a coagulopathy and organ damage due to microthrombi, and management is directed at resuscitation, supporting the cardiovascular system and the failing organ, and treating the underlying cause and correcting the coagulopathy. There is a significant mortality associated with these conditions. DIC, HUS and TTP are discussed in further detail in Sections 2.3.2 and 2.4.2.

2.1.8 Bone-marrow failure and infiltration

Marrow failure or damage will typically cause pancytopenia, of which anaemia is frequently a presenting feature. The leukaemias, lymphomas, myelodysplastic syndromes, myelofibrosis and myelomas can all result in marrow failure and are specifically discussed in Section 2.2.

2.2 Haematological malignancy

2.2.1 Multiple myeloma

Aetiology/pathophysiology

The cause of multiple myeloma (MM) is unknown. Radiation may be a factor in some cases (although there is no association with therapeutic radiation). Exposure to industrial/agricultural toxins or viruses (eg human herpesvirus 8) have all been considered, but proof is lacking. MM has been reported in familial clusters, suggesting a genetic element in some cases.

Myeloma is characterised by the accumulation of clonal, malignant plasma cells in the bone-marrow compartment, although the site of origin of the precursor cell is unknown. Recent advances in molecular biology suggest that the final oncogenic event occurs very late in B-cell differentiation. Chromosomal abnormalities have been identified, most commonly involving the immunoglobulin heavy chain switch region (on the long arm of chromosome 14).

However, it is likely that additional events are required to develop the malignant disorder. The tumour cells within the bone marrow are supported by a non-malignant population of stromal cells that produce cytokines (eg interleukin-6) that enhance myeloma cell growth and prevent apoptosis.

Epidemiology

MM accounts for about 10% of haematological malignancies. The annual incidence in the USA is 4 per 100,000 (it is slightly lower in the UK). Black people are affected twice as commonly as white people, and males more than females. The median age at diagnosis is 65 years, with fewer than 3% of patients presenting when they are younger than 40 years. It has been suggested that the incidence is increased in patients with HIV infection.

Clinical presentation

Common

- Bone pain and pathological fractures.

- Anaemia (bone-marrow failure).

- Recurrent infections (due to immunoparesis).

- Hypercalcaemia.

- Renal failure (multiple aetiologies: hypercalcaemia, direct effect of light chains, hyperuricaemia and non-steroidal drugs).

- Abnormal bleeding (due to platelet dysfunction).

Rare

- Hyperviscosity syndrome (ischaemia, heart failure and neurologial problems).

- Amyloid disease (eg carpal tunnel syndrome).

Investigations

There are a number of major and minor criteria required to make a diagnosis. In principle this rests on demonstrating two or more of the following.

- A monoclonal protein in the serum, urine or both. This is IgG in the majority of cases, but can be any class of immunoglobulin. Bence Jones protein (BJP) in the urine consists of free light chains, either κ or λ. Reduced levels of the normal immunoglobulins are supportive.

- Bone marrow showing increased plasma cells (>10%) (Fig. 20).

- Skeletal survey showing lytic lesions (Fig. 21).

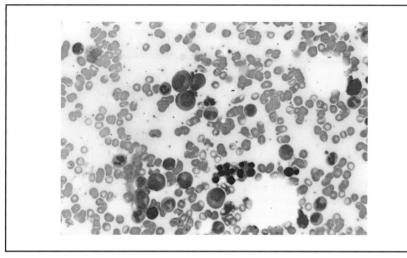

▲ **Fig. 20** Myeloma cells. This bone marrow shows a number of different types of cell. The larger cells with eccentric nuclei and basophilic cytoplasm are myeloma cells. Note the perinuclear transparency that represents the Golgi apparatus.

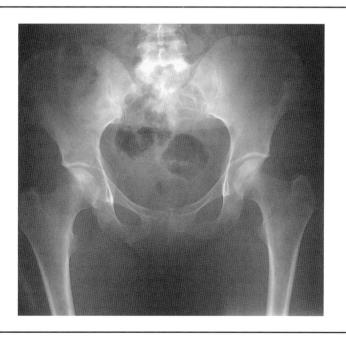

▲ **Fig. 21** Myeloma of bone. Note that the symphysis pubis has been eroded by myeloma. There are no apparent deposits in the upper femur or pelvis.

TABLE 13 STAGING OF MYELOMA (SALMON–DURIE)

	Stage I	Stage II	Stage III
Haemoglobin	<10 g/dL	Intermediate	<8.5 g/dL
Serum calcium	<12 mg/dL		>12 mg/dL
Radiography	Normal/single lesion		Multiple lesions
Paraprotein			
IgG	<50 g/L		>70 g/L
IgA	<30 g/L		>50 g/L
Urinary BJP	<4 g per 24 hours		>12 g per 24 hours

Other findings include:

- FBC and erythrocyte sedimentation rate (ESR) can reveal normochromic, normocytic anaemia. The ESR is raised because the positive charge of protein neutralises the negative charge of sialic acid on the erythrocyte membrane, and this reduces their natural tendency to repulse each other.

- Biochemistry can show raised calcium due to bony destruction, usually with a raised alkaline phosphatase. This may lead to dehydration and renal impairment.

Staging (Salmon–Durie)
Staging relates to disease bulk (Table 13).

Differential diagnosis of a serum paraprotein

Malignant

- Waldenström's macroglobulinaemia.
- Lymphoma.
- Chronic lymphocytic leukaemia.
- Primary amyloidosis.
- Plasma cell leukaemia.

Benign/stable

- Monoclonal gammopathy of uncertain significance.
- Cold haemagglutinin disease.
- AIDS.

Treatment
Myeloma may present as an acute emergency.

- Acute renal failure: prompt treatment of volume depletion is critical; involve the nephrologists early.

- Hypercalcaemia: fluids and bisphosphonates are critical.

- Spinal cord compression: a radiotherapy emergency.

- Hyperviscosity syndrome: consider plasmapheresis if there are hyperviscosity features.

Specific treatment depends on disease stage, as well as other factors such as age and the presence of poor prognostic factors (see below). There is no known cure for myeloma, but in recent years the treatments for it have improved dramatically. Many patients may now acheive a stable remission, lasting a number of years, through a combination of chemotherapy and autologous stem-cell transplantation.

Most haematologists will participate in trials, which ensures standard treatment for patients and access to drugs that may be financially unavailable otherwise.

Chemotherapy
Chemotherapy treatment, in combination with steroids, is the mainstay of treatment in newly

diagnosed patients. More recently, many trials will include treatment with thalidomide, which has been shown to have significant anti-myeloma effects.

These regimens can be given as pulsed therapy (ie repeated at regular time intervals), either orally or as intravenous infusions. The response rates are high: some patients enter complete remission, but most enter a 'plateau phase' with a lower but steady monoclone. All patients will eventually relapse. More intensive regimens are used in younger and fitter patients, and these can be used to debulk disease prior to transplantation.

Autologous stem-cell transplantation
The safety of these procedures (see Section 2.10) now means that they have become applicable to a larger number of patients. Many haematologists would consider patients up to the age of 60 as eligible for a transplant as part of their first-line treatment (ie debulk with chemotherapy first, but proceed directly to transplant therafter). This obviously depends on the overall condition of the patient and his or her response to chemotherapy. Second autologous transplants may also be performed, often with good results.

Allogeneic stem-cell transplantation
This is only an option for a minority of patients, particularly those who are young, fit and have a human leucocyte antigen-matched sibling (or well-matched unrelated) donor. Response rates are high, but unfortunately relapse is common.

Maintenance therapy
Interferon alfa has been used as maintenance therapy and this can prolong remission following

chemotherapy and transplantation, but it has not been shown to influence survival.

More recently, thalidomide is being used as maintenance therapy and early results are encouraging. Toxicities of this drug include thromboembolic events and peripheral neuropathy. Warfarin may be prescribed with thalidomide to reduce thromboembolism.

Plasmapheresis
Plasma viscosity may provide an indication for plasmapheresis but clinical features are far more important. Evidence of critical ischaemia, neurological syndrome or coma may improve following this intervention. There is also some evidence that this may be helpful in patients who present with severe acute renal failure.

Supportive care
Hypercalcaemia should be managed with fluids and bisphosphonates initially. Bisphosphonates should be continued on a monthly basis, even with a normal calcium level, as there is a suggestion that they may reduce bony disease and modulate the disorder.

Pain is common in myeloma and often requires opiate analgesia plus NSAIDs. Radiotherapy may be helpful in controlling pain due to localised bony lesions.

Recurrent blood transfusions and antibiotics may be required as a result of both the disease and the treatment. Weekly erythropoietin injections may prevent anaemia. In patients who have recurrent infections prophylactic infusions of intravenous immunoglobulins should be considered.

Psychological support
The patient will almost certainly need some help in coming to terms with the diagnosis. Try to involve family or friends, particularly when first explaining the situation. Societies exist for support and information, and the patient should be given access to these.

Prognosis
Median survival with chemotherapy is about 3–5 years. Poor prognostic factors at diagnosis include:

- higher stage;
- high β_2-microglobulin;
- raised C-reactive protein;
- renal failure (urea >14 mmol/L);
- certain chromosomal abnormalities;
- low albumin;
- older age.

Recent studies suggest that a combination of β_2-microglobulin and albumin are the most important factors.

> ### FURTHER READING
> Bataille R and Haroussseau JL. Multiple myeloma. *N. Engl. J. Med.* 1997; 336: 1657–72.
>
> - - - - - - - - - - - - - - - -
>
> Shipman C. Bisphosphonates induce apoptosis in human myeloma cell lines: a novel antitumour activity. *Br. J. Haematol.* 1997; 98: 665–72.

2.2.2 Acute leukaemia: acute lymphoblastic leukaemia and acute myeloid leukaemia

Aetiology
Only in some cases are aetiological factors identified. These include environmental agents as well as host susceptibility.

- Ionising radiation: this was discovered following the increased incidence of leukaemia after nuclear disasters, particularly acute myeloid leukaemia (AML). The suggestion that the incidence of acute lymphoblastic leukaemia (ALL) is increased in children living near nuclear power installations remains suspected but unproven. There is no definite evidence for increase in those exposed to modern diagnostic X-rays (except infants exposed to radiation *in utero*).

- Chemicals: benzene and alkylating agents (used to cure a prior malignancy).

- Viruses: human T-cell leukaemia/lymphoma virus is directly implicated in adult T-cell leukaemia/lymphoma.

- Genetic factors: Down's syndrome, Bloom's syndrome, Fanconi's anaemia and being the child of a nuclear power-plant worker.

- Acquired haematological abnormalities: this includes conditions that may transform into acute leukaemia, eg myeloproliferative disorders, aplastic anaemia and myelodysplasia.

Epidemiology
ALL is largely a disease of the young (peak incidence is in those aged 4–5 years). It is well recognised in adults and in infants, although less common. In contrast, AML is predominantly a disease of adulthood and the elderly. There is no geographical variation, except where the aetiological factors mentioned above play a role.

Clinical presentation
The history tends to be short. Symptoms and signs can be grouped as shown in Table 14.

Investigations

Blood film
The diagnosis will frequently be suggested by examining the blood

TABLE 14 SYMPTOMS AND SIGNS OF ACUTE LEUKAEMIA

Type of leukaemia	Symptoms and signs
Bone-marrow failure	Pallor Malaise (anaemia) Bleeding Bruising (thrombocytopenia) Infections (leucopenia; see Fig. 22)
Tissue infiltration	Bone pain Lymphadenopathy Hepatosplenomegaly Gum hypertrophy in AML M5 Skin infiltration in AML M5 (see Fig. 23) Headaches, vomiting and eye symptoms (meningeal involvement in ALL or AML M4/5) Mediastinal enlargement (T-cell ALL) Testicular swelling (ALL)
Other	Bleeding and thrombosis (DIC in AML M3) and joint pain resembling rheumatoid arthritis (ALL)

DIC, disseminated intravascular coagulation.

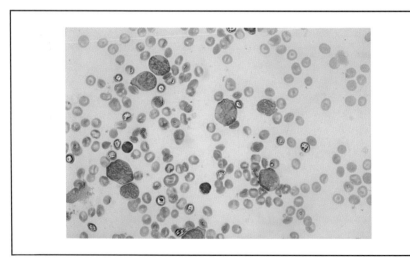
▲ **Fig. 23** Skin infiltration with AML.

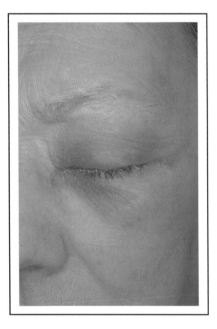

▲ **Fig. 22** *Pseudomonas* infection of the eye in a patient with AML. The infection responded to broad-spectrum antibiotics and vision was not impaired.

film thoroughly. The white cell count may be high, normal or low, but in many cases blasts will be apparent. The distinction between lymphoid and myeloid malignancy may not be obvious at this stage, unless particular morphological features are found, eg Auer rods in AML (Fig. 24).

Bone-marrow aspirate and trephine
The marrow is hypercellular with numerous blasts (usually well in excess of 50%). Morphological distinction can be made between ALL (Fig. 25) and AML, and the subtypes within each category.

Cytogenetics
Certain entities of the disease are strongly associated with recurrent chromosomal abnormalities. As well as aiding in diagnosis,

these may also confer prognostic value: the t(15;17) translocation of promyelocytic leukaemia confers good prognosis, but the t(9;22) translocation of ALL confers a poor prognosis.

Immunophenotyping (cell markers)
These techniques are helpful in identifying particular cell types and their clonality. AML is then subclassified into eight subtypes (M0 to M7).

▲ **Fig. 24** AML. Note that all the blood cells apart from two lymphocytes in this film are abnormal and are myeloblasts. One of them contains an Auer rod.

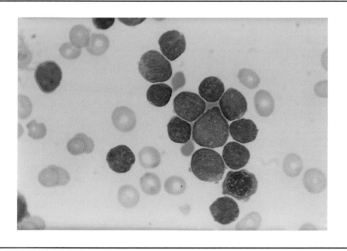

▲ **Fig. 25** ALL. The lymphoblasts are large with nucleoli. There is very little cytoplasm and no granularity. (Reproduced with permission from Bain B. *Slide Atlas of Blood Cells in Haematological Malignancy*. Oxford: Blackwell Science, 1996.)

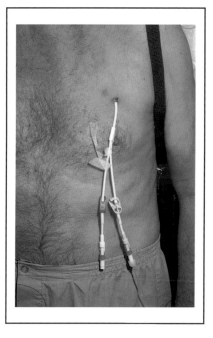

▲ **Fig. 26** This patient has had a Hickman line placed in the left subclavian vein and tunnelled under the skin to exit on the chest wall. This is a two-lumen device.

Cytochemistry

These stains are useful in identifying the lineage of the leukaemia.

Treatment

If you are unsure about a diagnosis of acute leukaemia and the treatment options, ask for help before discussing the diagnosis with the patient. Your local haematologist is likely to take over care of the patient and should be involved early.

When explaining the diagnosis, especially for the first time, try to ensure that the patient has some support available. Remember that in some cases you will be explaining matters to the parents of the patient. Individuals will respond to this news in their own way; try to be supportive. Most haematology departments will have booklets and numbers to call for further counselling or information.

The treatment in almost all cases will involve periods of prolonged hospital admission, as well as periods at home with frequent hospital attendances. Not only will the patient's life be disrupted, but also family life as well. Do not neglect the schooling, working, social and financial aspects of the care of these patients.

In all but the very elderly or unfit, intensive chemotherapy is the treatment of choice, at least in the first instance. In all patients the insertion of a long-term indwelling central venous catheter is indicated (Fig. 26). This facilitates the administration of chemotherapy and the sampling of blood. However, it is associated with risk of infection and thrombosis, and its care should be scrupulous.

In an adolescent or adult of childbearing age the likelihood of infertility following chemotherapy should be discussed and semen or ovarian cryopreservation offered.

Adequate precautions should be taken to prevent infections both during and after chemotherapy. Prophylactic oral antimicrobials should be given to sterilise the gut. A diet free of yogurt and soft cheese is necessary.

Thrombocytopenia will cause a fatal haemorrhage, so platelets should be given prophylactically when counts drop below 10×10^9/L. A platelet count of $>20 \times 10^9$/L associated with minor bruising is not generally treated and a watch-and-wait policy is observed; however, a platelet count of $<20 \times 10^9$/L with mucosal or severe bleeding is generally actively treated in order to raise the platelet count to $>50 \times 10^9$/L. Intracerebral and intraocular bleeding/surgery should be treated to achieve and maintain a platelet count above 100×10^9/L.

The principles of management differ according to the diagnosis.

Acute lymphoblastic leukaemia

Combination chemotherapy is used. This induces remission and then consolidates with stronger chemotherapy. Certain aspects of treatment should be noted.

- Central nervous system (CNS) therapy: in all patients with ALL, prophylactic treatment should be given. Prior to this being routine there was a high incidence of CNS relapse, probably due to the inadequate eradication of disease. (The CNS is a 'sanctuary site' and many drugs cannot cross the blood–brain barrier.)

- Maintenance therapy: continuous treatment for up to 2 years has been shown to increase disease-free survival.

Acute myeloid leukaemia
Treatment usually consists of four to five courses of intensive chemotherapy, each lasting 5–10 days. Maintenance therapy has not been shown to be of benefit. Special situations include the following.

- AML M3: due to the high incidence of DIC found in this subtype of leukaemia, these patients should be managed aggressively with platelet and clotting factor support. The chromosomal translocation that is characteristically found makes the disease responsive to treatment with all-*trans*-retinoic acid, which is started prior to the administration of chemotherapy.

- AML M5: due to the higher incidence of CNS disease in this subtype, prophylactic intrathecal chemotherapy may be indicated.

- In both ALL and AML the indications for autologous and allogeneic stem-cell transplantation are well established (see Section 2.10).

Complications
These occur in the long-term survivors of therapy (mainly children):

- secondary malignancy;
- neuropsychological effects;
- endocrine dysfunction (children especially);
- infertility;
- cardiac/respiratory sequelae.

Prognosis

Acute lymphoblastic leukaemia
In childhood, good-risk disease has a long-term disease-free survival with chemotherapy alone of 60–80%. This is only 20–30% in poor-risk disease. The risk factors are shown in Table 15. In adult ALL, survival mimics adult AML.

Acute myeloid leukaemia
Disease-free survival with chemotherapy alone is about 40% in good-risk disease (favourable cytogenetic abnormalities, younger age and no evidence of pre-existing myelodysplasia). Allogeneic bone-marrow transplant can be curative in younger patients (<50 years). However, the majority of patients over 65 years of age have a median survival period of 2 years.

FURTHER READING

Hoffbrand AV, Lewis SM and Tuddenham EGD, eds. *Postgraduate Haematology*. Oxford: Butterworth–Heinemann, 1999.

2.2.3 Chronic lymphocytic leukaemia

Aetiology/pathophysiology
The cause of chronic lymphocytic leukaemia (CLL) is unknown. There is evidence of a familial tendency, which shows the phenomenon of anticipation (ie CLL occurs at an ever earlier age in succeeding generations).

CLL is a disease of deregulated programmed cell death (apoptosis). CLL cells accumulate because they survive for an abnormally long time, not because they divide at an accelerated rate.

Epidemiology
CLL accounts for about 25% of all leukaemias. It is most common in the elderly, with an incidence close to 50 per 100,000 individuals after the age of 70. It is extremely rare under the age of 30. It is twice as common in males. In the Far East (and in Japanese immigrants to America) the disease is less common than in whites and Africans.

Clinical presentation

Currently, the vast majority of patients with CLL will be diagnosed while being investigated for another reason. A large proportion of these will never require treatment. It is important to remember, however, that 'leukaemia' is a frightening diagnosis: ensure that someone with experience in this disease can discuss it with the patient.

TABLE 15 RISK FACTORS OF ALL IN CHILDHOOD

	Good	Bad
Age (years)	1–10	<1, >50
Sex	Female	Male
White blood cells	<50 × 10⁹/L	>50 × 10⁹/L
CNS disease	No	Yes
Cytogenetics	eg hyperdiploidy	eg t(9;22)
Response to therapy	Complete	No complete response

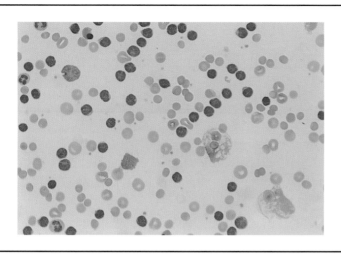

▲**Fig. 27** CLL. There is a predominance of mature lymphocytes. These have very little cytoplasm and no nucleoli. There are a few smear cells. There is a degree of polychromasia due to a reticulocytosis in the presence of autoimmune haemolysis.

Up to 80% of patients will be diagnosed following the finding of a lymphocytosis in the course of investigations for another reason (eg preoperative assessment). The features of disease are discussed below.

Common

- Symmetrical lymphadenopathy.

- Splenomegaly (50% of cases).

- Recurrent/severe infections (due to hypogammaglobulinaemia).

- Anaemia.

Less common

- Hepatomegaly.

- Constitutional symptoms (sweating, fevers and weight loss).

- Bone-marrow failure (thrombocytopenia and anaemia).

Investigations

- Lymphocytic infiltration of the peripheral blood. The cells are mature and uniform in appearance. Smear cells are seen (Fig. 27).

- Lymphocytic infiltration of the bone marrow. A trephine may be

helpful to indicate the pattern of involvement.

- Immunophenotyping of the cells will confirm the diagnosis (cells are characteristically positive for CD5 and CD23, negative for FMC7, with weak expression of CD22 and surface immunoglobulin).

- Anaemia and thrombocytopenia may be present (due to either bone-marrow failure or autoimmune causes).

- Direct antiglobulin test is positive in autoimmune haemolytic anaemia (10% of CLL is detected this way).

- Hypogammaglobulinaemia tends to be common in advanced cases of the disease.

- Chromosomal abnormalities are found in at least 50% of patients.

Staging
See Table 16.

Treatment
The indications for active treatment depend on the stage and activity of the disease (bulky or rapidly progressive disease, or disabling systemic symptoms). There is no evidence that earlier treatment of asymptomatic or early-stage disease is beneficial. The treatment options in stage B or C disease include the following.

- Corticosteroids: these are particularly helpful in the early treatment of patients and in those who have autoimmune phenomena.

- Chlorambucil: this can be given continuously or as monthly courses. Other types of chemotherapy have been tried alone and in combination. Fludarabine has given promising results, especially in combination with cyclophosphamide.

- Monoclonal antibodies are increasingly used, particularly rituximab (anti-CD20) and alemtuzumab (anti-CD52).

- Splenectomy: this can be of use to debulk disease as well as to treat refractory immune cytopenias.

TABLE 16 STAGING OF CLL			
Stage	Organ enlargement[1]	Haemoglobin[2] Hb in g/dL	Platelets[2] p/ts $\times 10^9$
A	0–2 areas		
B	3–5 areas	>10	>100
C	Not considered	<10	<100

1. Lymph node group or liver or spleen.
2. Other causes must be excluded (eg autoimmune or deficiency).
Produced by the International Workshop on CLL.

Remember that in this situation vaccination may not be effective, as antibody formation is greatly reduced. It is therefore important to maintain these patients on prophylactic penicillin (or erythromycin if allergic).

- Transplantation (autologous and allogeneic) is useful in selected younger cases.

- Prompt antibiotic therapy for infections.

- Consideration of prophylactic infusions of intravenous immunoglobulin in patients who have recurrent troublesome infections.

- Avoiding/treating the side effects of steroids with antifungals and histamine H_2 blockers.

Complications

In a small proportion of patients with CLL the disease may transform to a more aggressive type. This may manifest as refractoriness to treatment, systemic symptoms, increase in disease bulk and a change in the morphological features.

Prognosis

The stage is important in determining prognosis in CLL. Other adverse factors include:

- atypical lymphocyte morphology;

- lymphocyte doubling time <12 months;

- bone-marrow trephine showing diffuse involvement;

- certain chromosomal abnormalities;

- stage B/C;

- males;

- high expression of CD38;

- unmutated immunoglobulin *VH* gene status.

The median survival in all patients with CLL is 10 years. Patients who have early-stage disease have at least a 30% chance of dying due to an unrelated cause. Death due to CLL is usually as a result of infection or bone-marrow failure.

FURTHER READING

Child JA, Jack AS and Moya GJ. *The Lymphoproliferative Disorders.* London: Chapman & Hall, 1998.

Oscier D, Fegan C and Hillmen P. Guidelines on the diagnosis and management of chronic lymphocytic leukaemia. *Br. J. Haematol.* 2004; 125: 294–317.

2.2.4 Chronic myeloid leukaemia

Aetiology/pathophysiology

The occurrence of chronic myeloid leukaemia (CML) is regarded as 'sporadic'. No significant risk factor has been uncovered for its development, except previous high-dose ionising radiation.

CML is the best-studied molecular model of leukaemia as it was the first neoplastic process to be associated with a consistent acquired genetic abnormality. The crucial genetic event in CML is the generation of a reciprocal chromosomal translocation between chromosomes 9 and 22, the so-called Philadelphia (Ph) chromosome, in a haematopoietic stem cell. This translocation creates new genes, one of which is *BCR–ABL* on the Ph chromosome. The end-product of this genetic rearrangement is an oncoprotein responsible for most of the phenotypic abnormalities of chronic-phase CML. The fusion proteins are activated tyrosine kinases.

Epidemiology

The incidence of CML (stable worldwide) is 1–1.5 per 100,000 population. The median age of onset is 40–50 years, but CML can occur at all ages, with a variant form occurring in childhood. Males are slightly more commonly affected than females.

Clinical presentation

Common

- Bone-marrow failure (anaemia and thrombocytopenia).

- Hypermetabolism (weight loss, anorexia and sweats).

- Splenomegaly (abdominal pain and bloating) in 60–80%.

Rare

- Leucostasis (visual impairment and priapism).

- Hyperuricaemia (gout and renal failure).

Investigations/staging

- A leucocytosis of $50–400 \times 10^9$/L is found, with a full spectrum of myeloid cells represented in the peripheral blood.

- Increased numbers of eosinophils and basophils.

- Reduced neutrophil alkaline phosphatase.

- Normochromic, normocytic anaemia.

- High platelet count (but this may be normal or reduced).

- Serum uric acid is raised.

- Serum vitamin B_{12} and vitamin B_{12}-binding capacity are increased.

- Bone marrow is hypercellular with granulocytic predominance.

- The Ph chromosome (and BCR–ABL fusion protein) can be isolated from blood or bone marrow.

The disease course of CML usually starts with a chronic phase which lasts for 2–5 years. An accelerated phase follows when blood counts become difficult to control. Blast transformation follows soon after: as the leukaemic problem is in an early stem cell, transformation can be to acute myeloid leukaemia (AML) or acute lymphoblastic leukaemia (ALL). Patients may present in any phase.

Treatment

> Emergency treatment is not often needed, but may be required if there are symptoms of leucostasis when leucopheresis should be arranged urgently.

Tyrosine kinase inhibitor (imatinib)

The management of CML has changed dramatically since this agent was introduced into clinical practice in 1998. Owing to the ability of this drug to keep the BCR–ABL molecule in an inactive configuration, it is able to reverse the blood and marrow abnormalities rapidly, and can 'clear' the cytogenetic abnormality (Ph chromosome) from the bone marrow in up to 80% of patients. However, this drug is not thought to offer a cure in most patients, as withdrawing the drug results in return of the abnormalities. It is therefore necessary to continue the drug long term in those who acheive a good response with minimal side effects.

Side effects are generally mild and include nausea, fluid retention

and, in a few cases, neutropenia or thrombocytopenia. Occasionally these are severe enough to require reduction in the dose or complete withdrawal of the drug. The side effects are reversible.

Transplantation

The only treatment with a prospect of cure for most patients is allogeneic stem-cell transplantation. Currently, most patients will commence treatment with imatinib and progress to transplantation only if they do not respond. However, there remains a good argument for offering an allograft early in the disease for fit patients with a human leucocyte antigen-matched sibling/donor. Prior to cytotoxic therapy and, in particular, stem-cell transplantation, all patients should be offered the opportunity to cryopreserve sperm or oocytes.

Other therapies

Newer kinase inhibitors are in clinical trials. Alternative treatments include combinations of chemotherapeutic agents, interferon alfa and autologous stem-cell transplantation. These are used with far less frequency since the introduction of imatinib, except for hydroxycarbamide (hydroxyurea) which is still often used as a cytoreductive agent when the patient first presents.

Accelerated phase/blast transformation

Transformation to AML or ALL will eventually occur in all patients who have not had curative treatment. Treatment is with chemotherapy. In a few patients a second chronic phase is restored, but in the majority the treatment can only be hoped to prolong life slightly. Transplantation typically has a poor outcome in this setting.

Prognosis

In the chronic phase of chronic lymphatic leukaemia the median survival time is 2–5 years, although patients often survive longer. Once the transformation to AML or ALL has occurred, the survival period is typically 3–6 months.

> **FURTHER READING**
> Goldman J. ABC of clinical haematology: CML. *BMJ* 1997; 314: 657–60.

2.2.5 Malignant lymphomas: non-Hodgkin's lymphoma and Hodgkin's lymphoma

Classification

The malignant lymphomas are a broad group of diseases with a variety of clinical presentations and outcomes. Classification systems for the lymphomas are often confusing and have changed substantially over the years. The basis of classification systems is to take into account a number of properties of the tumour. These include morphology, immunophenotype, genotype, normal cell counterpart and clinical features (site of origin, aggressiveness and prognosis). The current World Health Organisation (WHO) classification is shown in Table 17.

Lymphomas can also broadly be described as high grade or low grade, which can be a guide to treatment. Hodgkin's lymphoma (HL) represents a group of diseases with distinct histological features (including a pathognomonic cell, the Reed–Sternberg cell), although many of the clinical features overlap with other lymphomas.

TABLE 17 WHO CLASSIFICATION OF LYMPHOMA (MAJOR CATEGORIES ONLY REPRESENTED)	
Classification	Frequency (%)
B-lineage	
Diffuse large B-cell lymphoma	30.6
Follicular lymphoma	22.0
Marginal zone B-cell lymphoma and mucosa-associated lymphoid tissue	7.6
Chronic lymphocytic leukaemia/small lymphocytic lymphoma	6.7
Mantle cell lymphoma (MCL)	6.0
Primary mediastinal large B-cell lymphoma	2.4
Burkitt's/Burkitt-like lymphoma	2.5
T-lineage	
Peripheral T-cell lymphoma	7.0
Anaplastic large-cell lymphoma	2.4
Lymphoblastic lymphoma	1.7
Hodgkin's lymphoma (30% of lymphomas)	
Nodular lymphocyte-predominant HL	5
Classical HL (nodular sclerosis classical HL, lymphocyte-rich classical HL, mixed cellularity classical HL and lymphocyte-depleted classical HL)	95

Aetiology/pathophysiology

Non-Hodgkin's lymphoma

In the large majority of cases the cause is not identified, although a number of factors are known to play a role in their development.

- Inherited disorders affecting DNA damage/repair (eg Fanconi's syndrome and ataxia telangiectasia).

- Infective agents: bacterial (eg *Helicobacter pylori* and gastric lymphoma) and viral [eg Epstein–Barr virus (EBV) and human T-cell leukaemia/lymphoma virus 1].

- Immunodeficiency/dysregulation (eg inherited syndromes, immunosuppressive therapy, HIV infection and autoimmune disorders).

- Ionising radiation.

- Carcinogenic chemicals.

Hodgkin's lymphoma

Certain factors may play a role.

- Genetic and occupational factors (eg familial aggregations, human leucocyte associations, benzene and nitrous oxide).

- EBV.

Epidemiology

Non-Hodgkin's lymphoma

In the UK the annual incidence is 11 per 100,000. It is slightly more common in males and increases with age. It has become much more common since the 1970s. Geographical variation in certain subtypes is marked.

Hodgkin's lymphoma

The annual incidence in the UK is 3 per 100,000 males and 1.8 per 100,000 females. There is a peak incidence in the third decade. In those aged 15–34 years old, this is the second most common tumour in men and the fourth most common in women.

Clinical presentation

Lymphomas present in a number of different ways.

- Lymphadenopathy: in early-stage HL this is most likely to be localised above the diaphragm. Non-Hodgkin's lymphoma (NHL) is more likely to present with generalised lymphadenopathy. The lymph nodes are classically painless, non-tender, asymmetrical and rubbery.

- Hepatosplenomegaly: more common in NHL.

- Mediastinal involvement: may occur in both (see Section 1.4.5).

- Constitutional 'B' symptoms: fever (may be cyclical in HL and 'Pel–Ebstein' fever), night sweats and weight loss (>10% of body weight in 6 months). HL may also present with pruritis or alcohol-induced pain.

- Bone-marrow failure: features of anaemia, thrombocytopenia and neutropenia.

- Oropharyngeal involvement: in NHL this may cause noisy breathing or a sore throat.

- Skin manifestations include non-specific rashes, infiltration and mycosis fungoides (Fig. 28).

- Other organs: much more frequent in NHL. Affected areas include gastrointestinal tract, brain, testis and thyroid.

Investigations

- Histopathological examination of the affected nodes/tissues will help to define the subtype of disease.

- Normochromic, normocytic anaemia (haemolytic anaemia may complicate NHL).

- Leucocytosis: abnormal lymphocytes on the blood film in NHL (Fig. 29); eosinophilia and neutrophilia in HL.

- Bone-marrow aspirate and trephine: in HL the aspirate is often 'reactive', although not involved by disease.

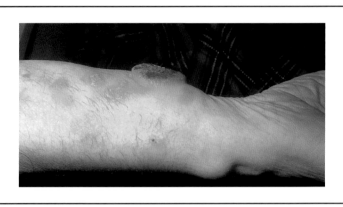

▲ **Fig. 28** Mycosis fungoides. There is a large plaque of lymphoma raised above the ventral aspect of this man's lower forearm. The rash on the rest of his forearm is also lymphomatous infiltration. This disappeared completely with intravenous cytotoxics.

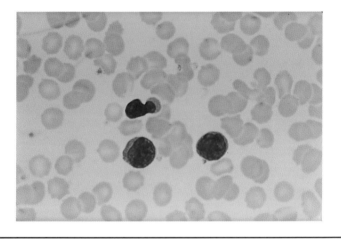

▲ **Fig. 29** Sézary cells. The lymphocytes are cleaved and have an overlapping nuclear conformation. (Reproduced with permission from Bain B. *Slide Atlas of Blood Cells in Haematological Malignancy*. Oxford: Blackwell Science, 1996.)

- Immunophenotyping of blood or bone-marrow samples can show the clonality and characteristics of the malignant cells.

- Lymphopenia: in HL (consider coexisting HIV infection).

- Raised erythrocyte sedimentation rate and lactate dehydrogenase.

- Paraprotein (NHL).

- Imaging: CT, MRI or PET (see below) scans of the pelvis, abdomen and chest.

- Cytogenetics: a number of subtypes are defined by specific chromosomal translocations, eg t(11;14) in MCL. This is now considered a routine investigation.

- Tests such as gene microarrays are becoming increasingly important in this group of diseases, but are not yet available or validated for routine use.

> 🔑 PET scan using fluorodeoxyglucose (performed with or without a CT scan) is used in patients with lymphoma for staging, response assessment and prediction of relapse. It is currently a very expensive technique and not readily available in all areas.

Staging

The updated Ann Arbor classification is shown in Table 18.

Treatment

Non-Hodgkin's lymphoma

In general, the management of this diverse group of diseases is performed with chemotherapy, and depends on whether it is predominantly of an aggressive or indolent nature. The use of both autologous and allogeneic transplantation (usually as part of the management for relapsed disease) has increased in recent years due to the increased safety of these procedures and the good outcomes seen.

TABLE 18 STAGING OF HL (ANN ARBOR)

Stage	Disease extent
I	Disease in one lymph node area only
II	Disease in two or more lymph node areas on the same side of the diaphragm
III	Disease in lymph node areas on both sides of the diaphragm (the spleen is considered to be nodal)
IV	Extensive disease in liver, bone marrow or other extranodal sites

Additional information is provided by the following suffixes: A, no constitutional symptoms; B, presence of constitutional symptoms; E, localised extranodal disease.

- Low-grade disease, which may be asymptomatic and have no significant effect on quality of life in some cases, often requires no treatment or only intermittent treatment with oral chemotherapy. This disease is not curable by chemotherapy (or an autograft) alone.

- In aggressive (high-grade) disease, combination chemotherapy is usually indicated. The gold standard treatment in most of these patients will be R-CHOP chemotherapy. This is a cyclical regimen of chemotherapeutic drugs (cyclophosphamide, vincristine, daunorubicin and prednisolone) with the addition of the anti-CD20 monoclonal antibody rituximab (see Section 2.9). Up to 50% of patients can be cured. Stem-cell transplantation is often recommended at relapse.

- Those patients with a large disease bulk are at risk of developing tumour lysis syndrome and appropriate preventative measures should be taken (see Section 2.9).

- Newer treatment strategies are constantly being evaluated. These include newer monoclonal antibodies, anti-angiogenesis agents (eg thalidomide) and vaccines.

Hodgkin's lymphoma
Radiotherapy is usually used in conjunction with shortened combination chemotherapy in stage I and IIA disease. The use of combination chemotherapy in instances of more advanced disease has been very successful, with a number of regimens reported to induce complete remission in 60–90% of patients. Again, stem-cell transplantation is usually reserved for relapse.

> Because many patients with malignant lymphomas are young, it is essential to discuss the potential loss of fertility that may result as a side effect of intensive chemotherapy. The patient should be offered the opportunity to cryopreserve semen or ovarian tissue prior to commencing treatment.

Complications (particularly of Hodgkin's lymphoma)
In view of the success of the above-mentioned treatment strategies, there are increasing numbers of long-term survivors who may experience a range of delayed side effects:

- second malignancies;
- infections;
- endocrine abnormalities;
- cardiac and pulmonary toxicity;
- psychosocial problems.

FURTHER READING

Child JA, Jack AS and Moya GJ. *The Lymphoproliferative Disorders.* London: Chapman & Hall, 1998.

Hoffbrand AV, Lewis SM and Tuddenham EGD, eds. *Postgraduate Haematology.* Oxford: Butterworth–Heinemann, 1999: 479–504.

Maloney DG. Advances in immunotherapy of haematological malignancies. *Curr. Opin. Haematol.* 1998; 5: 237–50.

2.2.6 Myelodysplastic syndromes

Aetiology
The aetiology of most cases of myelodysplastic syndrome (MDS) is unknown; however, in a proportion of cases there is an obvious associated factor.

- Exposure to benzene, ionising radiation and organic chemicals.

- Previous cytotoxic chemotherapy (eg alkylating agents and procarbazine). The median time to development of MDS in these cases is 4–5 years.

- Certain genetic disorders may predispose to MDS (eg Down's syndrome, Fanconi's anaemia and neurofibromatosis type 1).

Epidemiology
This is largely a disease of the elderly (median patient age, 69 years). In those of the population over 70 years of age, the incidence is >30 per 100,000. The incidence is very low in those under the age of 50 (with no recognised predisposing factors). Males are more commonly affected than females.

Clinical presentation
About one-quarter of patients will be diagnosed following an incidental finding on the blood count. Most patients present because of features of bone-marrow failure: 80% due to anaemia, 20% due to the consequences of neutropenia and thrombocytopenia.

Investigations
The diagnosis is usually first suspected from the blood count and film.

- FBC may show pancytopenia, anaemia or isolated cytopenias of other lineages. Macrocytosis (mild) may be present.

- The blood film shows dysplastic neutrophils (Fig. 30) and odd-looking platelets. Blasts may also be seen (Fig. 31).

- Bone-marrow aspirate and trephine are crucial for the diagnosis of MDS in any patient in whom treatment would be contemplated. In an elderly

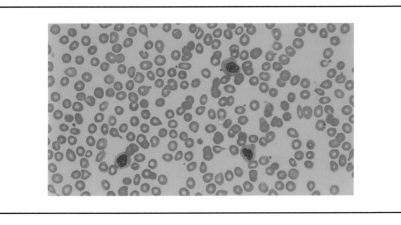

▲ **Fig. 30** Myelodysplastic neutrophils. Note the hypogranular nature of the cytoplasm. The nuclear conformation is also very abnormal for mature neutrophils.

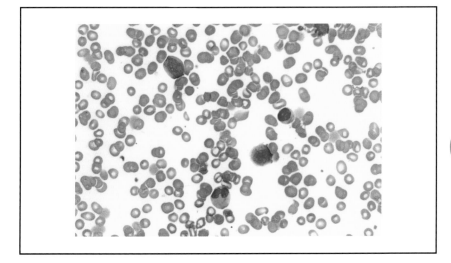

▲ **Fig. 31** This blood film shows the presence of myeloblasts in addition to a myelodysplastic neutrophil.

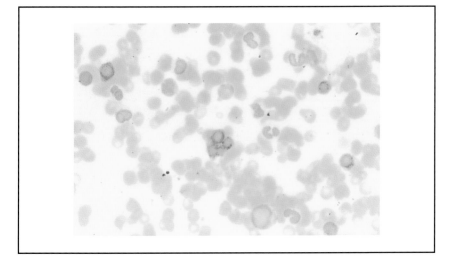

▲ **Fig. 32** Ring sideroblast. This bone marrow has been stained with Perl's stain. Note the blue perinuclear ring representing mitochondrial staining.

patient, where management would not be altered, this need not be done. The marrow is hypercellular in most cases. All three lineages may show abnormalities. Ring sideroblasts (due to abnormal iron accumulation in the mitochondria) may be seen on Perl's stain (Fig. 32).

- Chromosomal abnormalities are common, particularly in the group with MDS related to previous cytotoxic chemotherapy.

- Autoantibodies are found in up to half of the patients.

Classification
The current World Health Organization (WHO) classification is shown in Table 19.

Treatment

> MDS is a classic example of a disease where active treatment may be the wrong choice. The vast majority of these patients are elderly and many have other medical problems. Taking the quality of life into account is essential, and treatment should be tailored to best suit this objective. More aggressive approaches will be indicated in younger, fit patients.

Supportive care
This is the approach taken in the majority of patients. Red-cell transfusions should be given according to symptoms. (Remember that iron chelation with desferrioxamine may be indicated in patients who are recurrently transfused, but this is only really indicated in a patient in whom very long-term transfusion therapy will be indicated.) Platelet transfusions should be reserved for bleeding complications or prophylactically for procedures. Antibiotics are given as needed.

TABLE 19 WHO CLASSIFICATION OF MDS

Classification	Presenation
Refractory anaemia	Erythroid dysplasia only (<5% blasts)
Refractory anaemia with ringed sideroblasts	As above with >15% ringed sideroblasts
Refractory cytopenia with multilineage dysplasia	Dysplasia in ≥10% of cells in two or more myeloid cell lines (<5% blasts)
Refractory cytopenia with multilineage dysplasia and ringed sideroblasts	As above with ≥15% ringed sideroblasts
Refractory anaemia with excess blasts, type 1	Unilineage or multilineage dysplasia, 5–9% blasts
Refractory anaemia with excess blasts, type 2	Unilineage or multilineage dysplasia, 10–19% blasts
MDS, unclassified	Unilineage dysplasia in granulocytes or megakaryocytes
MDS associated with isolated del(5q)	Normal to increased megakaryocytes with hypolobated nuclei (<5% blasts). Isolated del(5q)

FURTHER READING

Bowen D, Culligan D, Jowitt S, *et al*. Guidelines for the diagnosis and therapy of adult myelodysplastic syndromes. *Br. J. Haematol.* 2003; 120: 187–200.

Heany P and Golde D. The myelodysplastic states. *N. Engl. J. Med.* 1999; 340: 1649–60.

Growth factors

These can be used in the short or long term and include erythropoietin and granulocyte colony-stimulating factors. The latter can be helpful in increasing the number of neutrophils and improving their function in patients with infections in the short term, and may therefore reduce the duration of their hospital stay and antibiotic treatment. Growth factors used in combination can cause an improvement in blood counts in certain patients, thus reducing the transfusion requirements, but survival benefit is not yet proven. The cost of such regimens remains high.

Immunosuppression

There are data to support the use of immunosuppressive regimens (anti-lymphocyte globulin and ciclosporin) in certain patients, particularly those with a hypocellular bone marrow. Clearly the patient's general health and the side-effect profile need to be considered.

Cytotoxic chemotherapy

Cytotoxic chemotherapy ranges from palliative treatment with outpatient regimens to aggressive combination chemotherapy with acute myeloid leukaemia (AML)-type regimens.

Transplantation

Allogeneic transplantation can be recommended in a proportion of well-selected fitter patients and this can offer a long-term event-free survival rate of up to 50%.

Prognosis

All patients with MDS have a reduced life expectancy. The International Prognostic Scoring System stratifies patients according to the number of blasts in the bone marrow, chromosomal abnormalities and the number of cytopenias. Patients will fall into low-, intermediate- or high-risk categories. On the basis of this, median survival is more than 10 years in low-risk patients but less than 6 months in high-risk patients. The risk of transforming to AML is 20% at 10 years in low-risk patients but 50% at 3 months in high-risk patients. Patients who do not transform to AML will usually die as a result of the effects of bone-marrow failure.

2.2.7 Non-leukaemic myeloproliferative disorders (including polycythaemia vera, essential thrombocythaemia and myelofibrosis)

Aetiology/pathophysiology

This diagnosis encompasses a group of conditions in which there is clonal proliferation of one or more haemopoietic components in the bone marrow. The trigger for the initiation of disease is unknown. These conditions are closely linked, transitional forms exist and evolution from one entity to another is not uncommon. In 2005 a single point mutation in JAK2 (a cytoplasmic tyrosine kinase with a key role in signal transduction) was identified in over half of the patients with myeloproliferative disorders (MPD). This is found in over 80% of those with polycythaemia vera (PV) and about half of those with essential thrombocythaemia (ET) or myelofibrosis (MF). This finding has provided insight into the pathogenesis of MPD, as well as a simple test that is very helpful if positive.

Epidemiology

Polycythaemia vera (or primary proliferative polycythaemia)

The median age at presentation is 55–60 years, but PV may occur at any age.

Essential thrombocythaemia

The majority of patients are aged over 50 years. There appears to be an increasing incidence in younger people, especially women.

Myelofibrosis

This is predominantly a disease of the elderly.

Clinical presentation

Some features are common to all three disorders.

- Splenomegaly: rare in ET as the diagnosis is frequently made early; often massive in MF.

- Haemorrhage and thrombosis: less common in MF.

- Headaches, dizziness, migraine and blurred vision.

- Gout/hyperuricaemia: uncommon in ET.

More specific features are described below.

Polycythaemia vera

- Pruritis.

- Plethoric appearance.

- Hypertension.

- Peptic ulceration.

Myelofibrosis

- Metabolic disturbance: weight loss, night sweats and fever.

- Bone-marrow failure.

- Bone pain.

- Painful splenomegaly.

Investigations

Polycythaemia vera

- Haemoglobin and packed cell volume (PCV) are raised.

- Raised red-cell mass (with low/low-normal plasma volume).

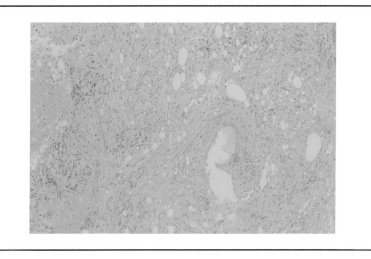

▲ **Fig. 33** Myelofibrosis. There is reduced fat space. There is a lot of fibrotic and hypercellular tissue consistent with MF. Reticulin staining would be strongly positive.

- Half the patients have raised leucocyte and platelet counts.

- Raised neutrophil alkaline phosphatase.

- Raised serum vitamin B_{12} and B_{12}-binding capacity.

- Raised urate.

- Hypercellular bone marrow; a small proportion of patients have a detectable chromosomal abnormality at presentation.

- Low erythropoietin levels.

Essential thrombocythaemia

- Raised platelet count ($>600 \times 10^9$/L).

- Hypercellular bone marrow, with abnormal megakaryocyte clumping, particularly on trephine biopsy.

- No consistent chromosomal abnormality is found.

- White cell count may be raised.

Myelofibrosis

- White cell and platelet counts are often high, and pancytopenia occurs late.

- Leucoerythroblastic blood film, with characteristic red-cell changes.

- Usually, the bone marrow cannot be aspirated and trephine biopsy shows evidence of fibrosis (Fig. 33).

- High serum urate and lactate dehydrogenase.

Differential diagnosis

It is essential to exclude chronic myeloid leukaemia, usually on the basis of cytogenetics.

To some extent both PV and ET are diagnoses of exclusion, and hence it is crucial to have actively sought and excluded all the causes of secondary/reactive polycythaemia and thrombocythaemia (see Sections 1.1.5 and 1.2.4). The recent identification of a JAK2 mutation in over half of the patients with MPD means the criteria for diagnosis are changing and, in many cases, may be more straightforward.

Treatment

Polycythaemia vera

The aim is to maintain PCV under 45%. No treatment is curative. Prior to commencing treatment the risks and benefits of each strategy need to be carefully considered in discussion with the patient.

1. Venesection: this is an efficient method of lowering the red-cell count rapidly and can be used as maintenance therapy, particularly in young patients to avoid other therapy with greater side effects. The patient must have reasonable venous access and should realise the time commitment involved.

2. Aspirin.

3. Cytoreductive therapy: this may be required in those who do not tolerate venesection or who progress despite this.

   (a) For young patients this should be with interferon; second-line therapy with hydroxycarbamide (hydroxyurea) or anegrelide.

   (b) In older patients hydroxycarbamide is the first choice; second-line therapy includes interferon, anegrelide, busulfan or radioactive phosphorus.

   (c) Radioactive phosphorus is effective, but in view of long-term effects should only be used for patients over 75 years old.

4. Other interventions: allopurinol for gout/hyperuricaemia. Pruritis is difficult to control but may respond to histamine H_1 or H_2 antagonists, cholestyramine or interferon.

Essential thrombocythaemia
Treatment is based on risk stratification.

Low risk Age <40 years and has:

- no history of thrombosis;
- platelet count <1500 × 10⁹/L;
- no cardiovascular risk factors (smoking, obesity, hypertension or diabetes);

Treat with aspirin alone or observe.

High risk Age >60 years or has:

- previous history of thrombosis;
- hypertension and diabetes;
- platelet count >1500 × 10⁹/L.

These patients should all be treated with hydroxycarbamide (hydroxyurea) and aspirin.

> ⚠ Some of these patients may be of childbearing age and should be counselled about the use of contraception.

Intermediate risk (ie fits neither category) Treatment options include aspirin alone or aspirin and hydroxycarbamide.

Myelofibrosis

This is incurable and treatment is supportive. Cytotoxic agents, splenic irradiation and even splenectomy can be employed to reduce transfusion requirements and for symptom control.

Complications
All types of myeloproliferation may progress to MF or acute leukaemia.

Prognosis

Polycythaemia vera
Median survival is 8–15 years.

Essential thrombocythaemia
Median survival is 10–14 years.

Myelofibrosis
In general the survival period is <2 years.

FURTHER READING

Harrison CN. Essential thrombocythaemia: challenges and evidence-based management. *Br. J. Haematol.* 2005; 130: 153–65.

McMullin MF, Bareford D, Campbell P, *et al*. Guidelines for the diagnosis, investigation and management of polycythaemia/erythrocytosis. *Br. J. Haematol.* 2005; 130: 174–95.

2.2.8 Amyloidosis

Pathophysiology
A variety of very different processes lead to the extracellular deposition of fibrillar protein aggregates that interfere with tissue structure and function. All amyloid proteins share a similar core structure of β sheets with strands perpendicular to the long axis. The precursor proteins may derive from serum amyloid A (reactive systemic amyloidosis, AA), monoclonal light chains (systemic amyloidosis associated with lymphoid dyscrasias, AL) or inherited abnormalities of amyloidogenic proteins (transthyretin, apolipoprotein A1 and the fibrinogen α chain). Glycosaminoglycans are deposited on top of these proteins. The process is very dynamic and cumulative, but it can be affected by reducing the relevant building blocks.

The process may involve the deposition of amyloid systemically throughout the body (systemic AL and systemic AA amyloidosis) or focal deposition (cerebral deposition in Alzheimer's disease).

Epidemiology
Systemic AL amyloidosis occurs in up to 10% of patients with myeloma. The majority of people with AL amyloidosis will have no apparent lymphoproliferative disorder at diagnosis.

Between 5 and 10% of patients with rheumatoid arthritis develop systemic AA amyloidosis. Hereditary forms of systemic amyloidosis are autosomal dominant, eg familial amyloid polyneuropathy due to abnormal transthyretin. Amyloidosis occurs in 2% of patients on the European dialysis programme.

Clinical presentation

Systemic AA amyloidosis

A high level of serum A (a high-density lipoprotein derived from hepatocytes) is required for sustained periods to produce this disease. This may be associated with chronic inflammatory disorders, chronic microbial infections or malignancy. The commonest presentation is with proteinuria, with or without nephrosis and uraemia. Visceromegaly is common (liver, spleen and kidneys). Cardiac and gut involvement are less common. Patients in 50% of cases die due to renal failure (if not supported by dialysis).

Systemic AL amyloidosis

This is caused by deposition of fragments of the variable region of light chains present in monoclonal proteins associated with myeloma, lymphoma, etc. The most common clinical features at diagnosis include nephrotic syndrome (in about one-third of patients), congestive cardiomyopathy (restrictive in nature), peripheral neuropathy (usually sensory and symmetrical), autonomic neuropathy and hepatomegaly. Any organ may be affected except the brain. Occasionally, AL amyloidosis may also be localised.

Hereditary amyloidosis

There are a variety of different types of inherited protein abnormality that produce

amyloidogenic proteins. These are exceptionally rare.

Dialysis-related amyloid

This is associated with the excess deposition of β_2-microglobulin, leading to amyloid formation.

Investigations

Histology

The red/green birefringence under polarised light following staining with Congo red remains the standard for diagnosis. This can be performed on fine-needle aspiration samples from fat or on rectal biopsies (these give a positive yield in up to 80% of cases), which should then be followed by immunohistochemical staining for the specific amyloid type. This can also be performed on the bone-marrow trephine biopsy that is usually performed to exclude an underlying lymphoproliferative disorder.

Serum amyloid P

This is a normal plasma protein. Radiolabelled serum amyloid P (SAP) scans can now be performed to assess the extent of the disease and this is 100% sensitive in cases of systemic AA amyloidosis (Fig. 34). It forms a baseline against which treatment can be measured.

Echocardiogram

Echocardiography and ECG to assess cardiac function.

Biochemistry

Check renal and liver function.

Immunoglobulins

Monoclonal immunoglobulins or Bence Jones proteins are found in AL amyloid. Some patients with systemic AL amyloidosis

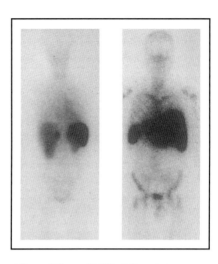

▲**Fig. 34** SAP scan: ^{123}I-SAP scintigraphy in two young adults with systemic amyloidosis. On the left is an anterior whole-body scan of a 26-year-old man showing uptake of tracer into the liver, spleen and marrow, the diagnostic distribution of systemic AL amyloidosis. On the right is a posterior whole-body scan showing AA amyloid deposits in the spleen, adrenals and kidneys of a 34-year-old woman with rheumatoid arthritis. The presence and type of amyloid were corroborated histologically in both cases. (Reproduced with permission from Gilmour JD, Hawkins BN and Pepys MB. Amyloidosis. *Br. J. Haematol.* 1997; 99: 245–56.)

will have no apparent monoclonal band in serum or urine and no excess of plasma cells in the marrow. However, monoclonality can be confirmed by looking at immunoglobulin gene rearrangements at the DNA level. Factor IX and factor X can sometimes be low in association with amyloidosis.

Management

This can be divided into supportive measures and those which reduce the supply of amyloid protein. Supportive measues include those associated with the renal, cardiac or gastrointestinal involvement. Patients with amyloidosis frequently experience bleeding problems due to multiple pathologies, the most common of which is a vasculopathy due to the deposition of amyloid in blood vessels. This should be remembered, as patients may bleed extensively following biopsies or surgical procedures.

Systemic AA amyloidosis

Suppression of inflammation or chronic infection is paramount. Oral chlorambucil may improve survival possibilities and SAP scans. The serum A protein can also be measured as a response parameter.

Systemic AL amyloidosis

Melphalan and prednisolone will improve amyloid deposition and SAP scans in up to 50% of patients. The responses can take over 12 months. High-dose therapy with vincristine and Adriamycin (doxorubicin hydrochloride) plus dexamethasone can produce higher responses, even after two cycles. However, the myelotoxicity and potential cardiotoxicity of such regimens have to be very carefully followed in these patients. Autologous bone-marrow transplantation is an option for fitter, younger individuals. Cardiac transplantation is also an option. Thalidomide has been shown to have some efficacy, but side effects are common.

Familial amyloid polyneuropathy

Hepatic transplantation can remove the source of the transthyretin protein.

FURTHER READING

Bird J, Cavenagh J, Hawkins P, *et al.* Guidelines on the diagnosis and management of AL amyloidosis. *Br. J. Haematol.* 2004; 125: 681–700.

- - - - - - - - - - - - - - - - - -

Gilmore JD, Hawkins PN and Pepys MB. Amyloidosis: a review of recent diagnostic and therapeutic developments. *Br. J. Haematol.* 1997; 99: 245–56.

- - - - - - - - - - - - - - - - - -

Hall R and Hawkins PN. Cardiac transplantation for amyloidosis. *BMJ* 1994; 309: 1135–7.

2.3 Bleeding disorders

2.3.1 Inherited bleeding disorders

Pathophysiology

Bleeding involves more than just clotting factors.

Vasoconstriction occurs following vessel injury. Platelets adhere to damaged vessels because von Willebrand factor (vWF) acts as an anchor. Further platelet aggregation occurs to reduce blood loss (primary haemostasis) and the activated platelet surface acts as a nidus for the activation of clotting factors (secondary haemostasis). Platelets and vWF are as important in bleeding as clotting factors (Fig. 35).

Most clotting factors are produced in the liver, but vWF derives from endothelium. The division into an intrinsic system (activated by contact) and an extrinsic system (activated by tissue factor and factor VIIa) always seemed somewhat artificial; trauma produces both triggers. The division was useful in explaining the differences between the laboratory prothrombin time (extrinsic system) and activated partial thromboplastin time (APTT, intrinsic system). The whole importance of the intrinsic system *in vivo* was in question because factor XII does not produce severe clinical bleeding when deficient. Factor VII deficiency, however, causes severe bleeding despite a normal intrinsic system.

In recent years the clotting pathway has been reviewed in an attempt to provide a better explanation for *in vivo* activity. Tissue damage produces tissue factor, which binds and activates factor VII. Activated factor VII goes on to activate factor X and factor IX. The cascade is amplified through the intrinsic system, and thrombin and fibrin are produced within the clot.

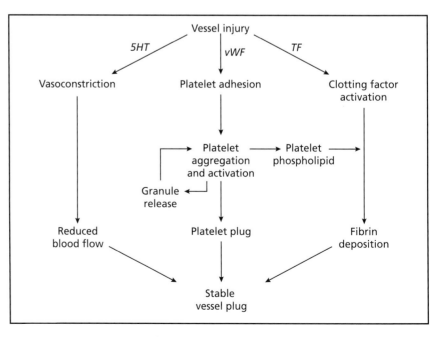

▲ **Fig. 35** Consequences of vessel injury. 5HT, 5-hydroxytryptamine; vWF, von Willebrand factor; TF, tissue factor. The arrows indicate the main pathways of activation.

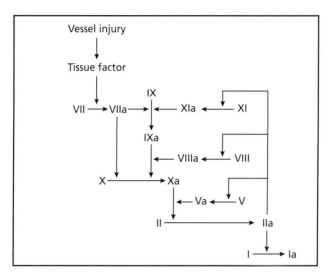

▲**Fig. 36** Clotting cascade. Roman numerals denote clotting factors (the suffix 'a' denotes activation). Arrows denote the principal activating pathways.

The production of thrombin (IIa) itself activates factors V, VIII and XI to amplify the cascade (Fig. 36). Thrombin generation is central to the clotting cascade model. This revised hypothesis puts greater emphasis on those factors which through their absence produce profound bleeding. The cascade is regulated in a number of ways. A tissue factor pathway inhibitor acts to inhibit excess factor IX and X formation. In addition, plasminogen, protein C, protein S and antithrombin III are activated to limit excess clot formation (Fig. 36).

Epidemiology

Each inherited clotting factor abnormality has a variety of possible genetic abnormalities underlying it. It is not surprising that there are a variety of clinical phenotypes.

- Von Willebrand's disease (vWD) occurs in 1% of the population and is usually very mild (autosomal dominant and affecting chromosome 12).

- Factor VIII deficiency is X-linked and occurs in 100 per 1,000,000 population. Haemophilia A is

caused by a variety of different types of mutation within the factor VIII gene and about 30% of these are spontaneous mutations rather than inherited.

- Factor IX deficiency is also X-linked (haemophilia B) and occurs in 20 per 1,000,000 population. It is usually associated with deletion within the factor IX gene.

Clinical presentation

A thorough bleeding history is essential when considering whether a patient has a congenital bleeding diathesis. Carefully document all episodes of potential haemostatic stress (eg surgery, dental extractions, periods and childbirth) in the patient's life. A patient who describes excessive blood loss after every haemostatic stress is much more likely to have a congenital bleeding disorder than an individual who reports bleeding problems only in recent years, or excessive blood loss on some occasions but has demonstrated good clotting on others. Also ask about family members as many bleeding disorders are inherited.

Von Willebrand's disease

The majority of vWD is mild. Many patients are unaware that they have mild vWD and are labelled as easy bruisers or bleeders without explanation. Many women with mild vWD have abnormally heavy periods that they do not seem to regard as atypical, perhaps because their mothers or sisters (who also have vWD) have similarly heavy periods so female members of the family believe it to be normal. Equally, many doctors are unfamiliar with the diagnosis of vWD and how common it is, and patients are not infrequently seen in a haematology clinic later rather than sooner. Unfortunately, it is not unusual to diagnose women with mild vWD in the haematology clinic only after they have had a hysterectomy for menorrhagia. Other than heavy periods, mild vWD sufferers commonly present with bleeding following tooth extraction, nosebleeds or easy bruising. Moderate deficiencies will be associated with more substantial blood loss related to trauma or surgery, but rarely haemarthrosis. Only 1% of patients with vWD have symptoms severe enough to mimic those of haemophilia A or B.

Haemophilia

Two-thirds of boys with severe haemophilia A and B (where <1% of the normal level of factor VIII or IX is present) are diagnosed at birth when the boy is born to a known or suspected carrier. The remaining cases occur as a result of a new mutation and present in childhood when the baby begins to crawl and falls, or with the eruption of dentition. Traumatic and spontaneous joint and muscle bleeds are the most frequent manifestation in children and young adults with severe haemophilia. Historically, joint

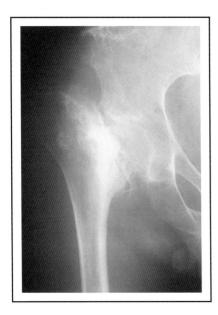

▲**Fig. 37** Left hip joint showing destruction of the femoral head due to recurrent haemarthrosis in a 45-year-old man with haemophilia A.

damage has often progressed to a deforming arthropathy (Fig. 37). The aim of modern treatment is to prevent deforming arthropathy by the use of regular prophylactic recombinant clotting factor treatment, physiotherapy and education about how to avoid bleeds and the need for early treatment.

Some patients have a milder clinical phenotype relating to higher factor levels (1–5% of normal levels produces moderate haemophilia, while 6–49% of normal levels produces mild haemophilia). These boys present following trauma or surgery (eg tonsillectomy) with excessve blood loss. Generally, individuals with mild and moderate haemophilia require treatment on demand, ie in response to bleeding or in preparation for surgery.

Cerebral haemorrhage was the major killer of haemophiliacs before the advent of AIDS. Extensive use of blood products has led to a high incidence of hepatitis B and C in addition to HIV amongst the haemophiliac population. Furthermore, many patients alive today have been exposed to the prion responsible for variant Creutzfeldt–Jakob disease, although the clinical impact of this is presently unknown. The availability of a recombinant factor now free of all human-derived components should hopefully ensure that blood product-transmitted infections for children born with haemophilia will no longer be a major concern.

Platelet disorders

Bernard–Soulier and Glanzmann's disease result in defective platelet function and quantity. They are rare, but can cause severe bleeding in children. The problem principally concerns primary haemostasis, and patients suffer with mucosal-type bleeding (eg nose-bleeds, mouth bleeds and menorrhagia).

Investigations

Clotting tests

A clotting screen may reveal a slightly prolonged APTT in vWD, haemophilia A or haemophilia B. Specific factor assays are required for diagnosis. Deficiency of factor VIII is found in haemophilia A and vWD. Deficiency of factor IX is found in haemophilia B. In vWD, vWF antigen is low (but normal in haemophilia A) and its function as measured by the ristocetin cofactor assay is reduced (but is normal in haemophilia A).

Blood count

FBC and blood film will give information about platelet count and morphological abnormalities. Platelet function tests using a number of different stimuli can reveal patterns of defective function.

Treatment

Only treat vWD and haemophilia after discussion with a senior haematologist and/or a haemophilia centre. The principles of treatment are discussed below.

Von Willebrand's disease

1-Deamino-8-D-arginine vasopressin (DDAVP) can stimulate vWF release from endothelium when given by either intravenous or intranasal routes. For more significant bleeds or prior to major surgery, DDAVP should be infused over half an hour at a concentration of 0.4 µg/kg. This can be repeated two or three times to cover surgery. It should increase factor levels approximately three-fold over the baseline. Tranexamic acid is an antifibrinolytic drug and can be used to increase clot stability. Occasionally, in more severely affected patients or for prolonged/major haemorrhage in less severely affected patients, factor VIII concentrates containing vWF may be required. This product is derived from plasma and carries potential risks of transfusion-transmitted disease.

Haemophilia

Generally, severe haemophiliacs require prophylactic treatment with recombinant clotting factor to prevent bleeding. About one-third of boys with severe haemophilia A develop an inhibitor to factor VIII after factor VIII treatment. This compounds the bleeding further and complicates therapy. Treatment of haemophilia and patients with inhibitors should be directed from a specialist centre. Patients with mild or moderate deficiencies of factor VIII or IX will need infusions of these concentrates for bleeding episodes. Recombinant factors are now used routinely for all patients. In the milder forms of haemophilia A, DDAVP infusions may stimulate factor levels as with vWD.

Prognosis

The life expectancy for patients with haemophilia A and B should now be well into middle age in the era of blood product-free concentrates.

FURTHER READING

Darby SC, Ewart DW, Giangrande PLF, *et al.* Mortality before and after HIV infection in the complete UK population of haemophiliacs. *Nature* 1995; 377: 79–82.

- - - - - - - - - - - - - - - -

Hoffbrand AV, Lewis SM and Tuddenham EGD, eds. *Postgraduate Haematology*. Oxford: Butterworth–Heinemann, 1999: 479–504.

- - - - - - - - - - - - - - - -

Rapaport SI and Rao LV. The tissue factor pathway. *Thromb. Haemost.* 1995; 74: 7–17.

2.3.2 Aquired bleeding disorders

Pathophysiology

> Liver disease causes clotting factor production to become defective and thrombocytopenia is common. The quality of the fibrinogen is often defective.

In liver disease there may be vitamin K deficiency, which is associated with jaundice. Factor VII levels can act as an indicator of liver damage in a number of clinical situations (eg paracetamol overdose).

Vitamin K deficiency related to biliary obstruction, malabsorption or warfarin overdosage is usually apparent from the history. It will result in a prolongation of the prothrombin time (PT) rather than the activated partial thromboplastin time (APTT), which is less dependent on vitamin K-related factors.

Disseminated intravascular coagulation (DIC) results from excess thrombin formation in the presence of suppressed fibrinolysis and physiological anticoagulants (protein C, protein S and antithrombin III). Interleukin-6 has been strongly connected with DIC. Major tissue damage or malignancy will cause tissue factor and factor VII to trigger fibrin formation. Protein C/S and antithrombin III levels fall due to ongoing coagulation and impaired synthesis. Plasminogen activator inhibitor type I is increased and inhibits fibrinolysis. As DIC progresses, factor levels fall and platelets are consumed within the clot. Fibrinolysis results in rising fibrin degradation products (FDPs) and the consumption of fibrinogen. DIC can be acute and fulminant as seen in major trauma cases, or chronic and subtle as in malignancy and liver disease.

> The bleeding tendency associated with renal disease is due to poor platelet function rather than an acquired clotting defect. Dialysis will improve platelet function and reduce bleeding.

Autoantibodies to clotting factors such as factor VIII and von Willebrand factor (vWF) occur in autoimmune disorders, inflammatory arthritis, malignancy and with certain medications. This produces a severe acquired haemophilia that is often fatal.

Finally, any cause of severe thrombocytopenia will produce an acquired bleeding disorder (see Section 2.3.3). Bleeding does not usually occur spontaneously until platelet levels fall below 20×10^9/L. However, bleeding may occur in the presence of a normal platelet count if the platelets have become qualitatively abnormal, eg in renal disease, malignancy and myeloma.

Clinical presentation

Acquired bleeding disorders usually present as extensive superficial bruising; purpura is typically a feature of thrombocytopenia. Mucosal bleeding from gums and throughout the gastrointestinal tract can be torrential. Haematuria is usually due to local causes but can be a feature of acquired bleeding disorders. Joint bleeds are uncommon. DIC may be associated with both bleeding and active thrombosis/infarction (due to platelet deposition), resulting in the failure of all organ systems. Causes of DIC include:

- sepsis;

- trauma (burns, surgery, road traffic accident and fat embolism);

- cancer;

- obstetric (amniotic embolism and abruption);

- transfusion reaction;

- vascular abnormalitites (Kasabach–Merritt syndrome);

- toxins (venom and drugs);

- transplant rejection;

- liver disease.

Investigations

Patients with liver disease are usually easily spotted clinically, and liver function tests confirm the suspicion. However, the coagulation disturbance of liver disease can merge with, and be difficult to distinguish from, DIC; it is usually a matter of degree. Prolongation of the PT and APTT along with a falling fibrinogen level is highly suggestive

	PT	APTT	Fibrinogen	VIII	vWF	RICOF
TABLE 20 DIFFERENTIAL DIAGNOSIS OF BLEEDING DISORDERS						
Liver disease	↑	N/↑	↓	N/↓	N	N
DIC	↑	↑	↓↓	↓	↓	N
Haemophilia A	N	↑	N	↓	N	N
vWD	N	↑	N	↓	↓	↓

VIII, factor VIII; vWD, von Willebrand's disease; RICOF, ristocetin cofactor.

of DIC. FDPs, in particular D-dimers, indicate that fibrin is being actively broken down and they are raised in DIC. However, perhaps the most sensitive marker for DIC is a rapidly falling platelet count. Protein C/S and antithrombin III levels fall. Table 20 will help to distinguish the causes of bleeding.

Acquired clotting factor inhibitors produce a very specific and profound fall in an individual clotting factor. This usually prolongs the PT or APTT. Specialised clotting tests will then show that incubation for 2 hours with normal plasma does not correct the abnormality.

FBC and blood film may reveal microangiopathic features in DIC. The film may be informative about causes of thrombocytopenia (see Section 1.2.2).

Management

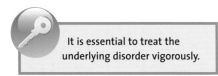

It is essential to treat the underlying disorder vigorously.

In liver disease, intravenous vitamin K should be given over a number of days. Infusion of fresh frozen plasma (FFP; 15 mL/kg) or factor concentrates should be considered if there is bleeding. Further bleeding despite infusion of FFP may be due to defective fibrinogen and require cryoprecipitate.

In DIC it is important to replace clotting factors with FFP (aim to restore PT and APTT to within 1.5 times normal), cryoprecipitate (aim to restore fibrinogen to >1.5 g/L) and platelets (aim to restore count to >20 × 10^9/L if not bleeding, to >50 × 10^9/L if bleeding and to >100 × 10^9/L if bleeding in head or eye). Clotting tests should be repeated a few hours after infusion to check if any correction has been produced and further infusions given if necessary. It will not always be possible to correct laboratory results, but clinical bleeding may improve. Watch out for fluid overload. If antithrombin III levels are very low, then antithrombin III concentrates should be considered.

There is no set formula for giving blood products in the presence of massive blood transfusion; clotting results and clinical bleeding are the best guides. Always seek advice from a haematologist.

Acquired clotting factor inhibitors need to be managed in specialist centres. Infusion of porcine factor VIII or factor concentrates to bypass factor VIII deficiency (eg factor VIII inhibitor bypassing agent or recombinant factor VIIa) may be used.

Defects in platelet quality and quantity can be treated with platelet infusions. 'One dose' of platelets is equivalent to platelets from four individuals. An infusion of one dose should produce an increment of about 40 × 10^9/L in the platelet count 1 hour after infusion in previously untransfused patients, and should be considered for anybody bleeding with a low platelet count. Patients with platelet levels of <20 × 10^9/L (due to marrow failure) without bleeding should be given a prophylactic platelet infusion.

Always repeat abnormal clotting results and FBCs. Do not overreact to a single abnormal result; it may be false, eg a blood clot in the sample tube may produce profound thrombocytopenia.

FURTHER READING

Levi M and Cate HT. Disseminated intravascular coagulation. *N. Engl. J. Med.* 1999; 341: 586–92.

2.3.3 Idiopathic throbocytopenic purpura

Aetiology

Idiopathic thrombocytopenic purpura (ITP) is immune mediated: a circulating antibody binds to an antigen on the surface of the platelet and leads to destruction in the reticuloendothelial system, particularly the spleen. These may be directed against the glycoprotein Ib and IIb/IIIa complexes.

Epidemiology

Similar incidence in boys and girls; commoner in women than men.

Clinical presentation

Common

Ranges from few purpuric spots to extensive purpura and bleeding from mucous membranes. A history of viral prodrome is common in children, but not in adults. Many adult patients have no symptoms and the diagnosis is made incidentally when a 'routine' FBC is performed.

Uncommon

- Retinal haemorrhage is usually only seen if there is anaemia in addition to thrombocytopenia.

- Intracranial haemorrhage, which may be preceded by complaints of headache and neck stiffness.

Physical signs

Apart from haemorrhage there are usually no abnormal physical signs. Splenomegaly is not a feature: if the spleen is palpable, this suggests that the diagnosis is not ITP.

Investigation

The platelet count is usually $<50 \times 10^9/L$ and often $<10 \times 10^9/L$, when there is substantial risk of serious bleeding. FBC and clotting tests are otherwise normal. Bone-marrow examination may be performed in older patients to exclude myelodysplasia and typically shows increased numbers of megakaryocytes. Platelet autoantibodies (IgG in particular) can be found, but these are not measured routinely.

Differential diagnosis

Usually the diagnosis is straightforward, but is one of exclusion: ITP is defined as isolated thrombocytopenia with no clinically apparent associated disorders. Other causes of thrombocytopenia need to be considered (see Section 1.2.2), in particular drug-induced thrombocytopenia, systemic lupus erythematosus and HIV infection.

Treatment

The aim of treatment is the prevention of bleeding not cure of the ITP. In children the disease is usually self-limiting and treatment is not indicated. Corticosteroids are the mainstay of treatment in adults, prednisolone 0.5–1.0 mg/kg daily producing a response in 60–70% of cases within 3 weeks. As the differential diagnosis includes acute lymphoblastic leukaemia (ALL), the commonest malignancy of childhood, never start steroids without first confirming a normal bone marrow by aspirate. Both ALL and ITP may respond initially to steroids but clearly patients with ALL will subsequently deteriorate rapidly.

High-dose intravenous immunoglobulin (0.4 g/kg daily for 3–5 days) is sometimes used in refractory cases. Splenectomy may be performed for chronic refractory ITP, but is associated with a subsequent increased risk of life-threatening infection and should be avoided if possible in children under the age of 5 years old. Patients will need vaccinations before splenectomy and lifelong prophylactic antibiotics after splenectomy (see Section 2.1.4). A variety of immunosuppressants has been used in refractory cases with occasional success.

Platelet transfusion is used in life-threatening situations but is of limited value because transfused platelets are rapidly destroyed.

Complications

The main risk is of intracerbral haemorrhage.

Prognosis

In children ITP is an acute self-limiting illness, which resolves over 1–2 weeks. In adults a similar pattern can be seen, but the disease more often follows a relapsing/remitting course (chronic ITP). Death due to haemorrhage is rare in ITP.

FURTHER READING

George JN. Platelets. *Lancet* 2000; 355: 1531–9.

2.4 Thrombotic disorders

Despite all the recent scientific advances in the identification of genetic risk factors for venous thromboembolism, it is the acquired and clinically assessable risk factors of deep vein thrombosis (DVT)/ pulmonary embolism (PE) that still have the greatest impact on risk and decision-making for the great majority of individuals. These include patient age, surgery, malignancy, combined oral contraceptive pill, pregnancy, patient weight, smoking, inactivity, hospital admission, past history of DVT/PE and family history of DVT/PE, irrespective of identifiable genetic thrombophilic abnormalities.

2.4.1 Inherited thrombotic disease

Pathophysiology

The clotting cascade activates, and is modulated by, a number of naturally occurring 'anticoagulants'. When protein C is activated it inhibits factors V and VIII with the help of protein S. Antithrombin III binds to most activated clotting factors to control their activity and is the mediator of heparin activity. Plasminogen is converted to plasmin when clotting is activated, and plasmin begins to limit the extent of fibrin deposition. Deficiencies of these natural anticoagulants will lead to a prothrombotic or thrombophilic state in the same way as deficiencies of clotting factors lead to haemophilic states.

> The most frequently identified genetic thrombophilic state is resistance to activated protein C, which leads to a functional protein C abnormality. This results from a mutation of the factor V gene (the Leiden mutation) that renders factor V resistant to the modulating effects of protein C.

Many genetic mutations are now recognised in the genes for protein C, protein S and antithrombin III and these cause both quantitative and qualitative abnormalities in these proteins. A prothrombin gene mutation (G20210A) results in overactivity of prothrombin.

Hyperhomocysteinaemia has become generally accepted as an independent risk factor for arterial thrombosis (evidence for venous is weaker). It causes abnormalities within vessel endothelium leading to plaque formation.

Note that these inherited prothrombotic states manifest in the heterozygous form (ie they are partially dominant). Homozygous protein C deficiency is fatal in the neonate. In contrast, homozygosity for factor V Leiden is not fatal but further increases the risk of thromboembolism.

Although deficiencies in the fibrinolytic pathway have been intensively investigated, they seem to be clinically irrelevant.

Epidemiology
Amongst white patients presenting with their first DVT, 12–20% will be heterozygous for factor V

Leiden and 6% heterozygous for prothrombin G20210A (this compares with 6% and 2%, respectively, in the asymptomatic white population). Approximately 9% of patients presenting with their first DVT will be heterozygous for a defect in protein C, protein S or antithrombin III. About 12% of the population are homozygous for methylenetetrahydrofolate reductase abnormalities that lead to increased homocysteine levels.

It is clear, therefore, that the factor V Leiden and prothrombin mutations are the major players in inherited thrombophilia. It is important to recognise, however, that the majority of people with their first thromboembolism have no demonstrable underlying genetic predisposition and that the majority of people with the factor V Leiden and prothrombin mutations never have a venous thromboembolic event. For the whole population the major risk factors for venous thromboembolism are not genetic but the acquired risk factors of surgery, malignancy, combined oral contraceptive pill, pregnancy, patient weight, smoking, inactivity, and past history of DVT/PE.

Clinical presentation
Inherited thrombophilia usually presents as typical venous thromboembolism, but it is not a major risk factor for arterial disease. However, given that 6% of the population is heterozygous for factor V Leiden, only a minority of these actually develop thromboembolism. Trigger factors are usually required to precipitate the event, eg immobility and pregnancy. Unusual sites of venous thromboembolism (eg sagittal sinus and mesenteric vein) should result in a search for a thrombophilic tendency.

Following a single venous thromboembolic event, patients with inherited thrombophilia should be routinely anticoagulated for the usual time period. There are data that suggest that long-term anticoagulation in this situation reduces the risk of further venous embolism, but this is not normal practice at present unless the initiating event was life-threatening or occurred in the presence of antithrombin III deficiency. Indefinite anticoagulation is indicated for recurrent episodes of venous embolism whether thrombophilia tests are positive or negative: the target INR should be 2.5.

Asymptomatic individuals who have positive thrombophilia tests but no personal history of venous embolism do not require routine anticoagulation, but vigorous attention to prophylaxis is required during periods of high risk.

Pregnancy itself produces a predisposition to venous embolism due to venous pooling, hormonal changes and a natural fall in protein S. This remains the chief cause of maternal mortality (see Section 2.7).

The factor V Leiden mutation occurs in one-third of women who have venous thromboembolism on the pill. Screening for thrombophilia prior to commencing the pill is not performed because the detection of factor V Leiden might deprive a large number of women of the potential benefits of these agents. Given that 6% of women are positive for factor V Leiden, a tiny fraction actually develop venous thromboembolism on the pill; the vast majority have no problems. Any personal history of venous thromboembolism is a contraindication to the pill.

The use of hormone-replacement therapy (HRT) has produced benefits for many women. A personal history of any venous thromboembolism is now considered a relatively strong contraindication to HRT. Positive thrombophilia tests with no personal history of venous thromboembolism are not a contraindication as such, but a strong family history of venous thromboembolism makes HRT hazardous.

In what circumstances should someone be tested for thrombophilia?

- If they have recurrent thromboembolism.
- If they have a venous thromboembolism before 40 years of age.
- If they suffer from arterial thrombosis before 30 years of age.
- If they have thrombosis in an unusual site.
- If they have relatives who are positive cases.

Investigations

Thrombophilia testing should not be performed in the acute phase of venous thromboembolism because this can confuse results. Similarly, testing should not be performed during anticoagulation, except for factor V Leiden and prothrombin gene mutations that are performed on DNA.

Most laboratories will perform a 'thrombophilia screen', which consists of protein C, protein S, antithrombin III, activated protein C resistance, diluted Russell's viper test and antiphospholipid antibodies. Genetic testing for factor V Leiden and prothrombin gene mutations may need to be sent to a reference laboratory. Testing for homocysteine levels is becoming more frequent.

Treatment

For practical details of how to initiate anticoagulation or to reverse over-anticoagulation, see Section 3.6.

Heparin

Low-molecular-weight (LMW) heparin has nearly replaced unfractionated heparin for the immediate treatment of DVT and PE. This has been a triumph for a more expensive option that confers quality improvement through the abolition of laboratory testing and multiple subcutaneous or intravenous infusions. LMW heparin enables some patients to be treated in the community.

The USA led the way on this because the improvement in quality of anticoagulation which LMW heparin confers over unfractionated heparin has meant a reduction in the number legal cases based on the premise that further venous thromboembolism was a result of poor control with unfractionated heparin.

LMW heparin has superseded the use of unfractionated heparin in pregnancy.

Routine monitoring of LMW heparin levels is not required as the majority of patients only receive the drug for short periods of time. However, LMW heparin can accumulate in renal failure. Patients in renal failure treated with LMW heparin should have an anti-Xa assay performed after 3–5 days of treatment to monitor for evidence of toxicity. If levels are high, then the dose can be adjusted accordingly. Monitoring of anti-Xa levels is also recommended for patients on long-term LMW heparin, such as those taking the drug daily throughout pregnancy.

Bleeding is an unusual toxicity of LMW heparin and should be managed by stopping the heparin and giving protamine. Get advice! (See Section 3.6.)

Warfarin

Warfarin is familiar to most doctors who realise that serious bleeding complications are the main risk of inadequate control; however, if you read the package insert you will see that there is a multiplicity of idiosyncratic associations. A loading dose-type regimen such as Fennerty remains common, but increasingly with elderly patients in chronic atrial fibrillation a gentler approach, commencing with 2–3 mg/day, is being explored. More emphasis is put on treating arterial problems with aspirin rather than warfarin.

The main drugs that interfere with warfarin are antibiotics, NSAIDs and amiodarone (see the interaction table in the *British National Formulary*).

FURTHER READING

Baglin TP, Keeling DM and Watson HG. British Committee for Standards in Haematology. Guidelines on oral anticoagulation (warfarin): third edition, 2005 update. *Br. J. Haematol.* 2006; 132: 277–85.

Boushey W, Beresford SA, Omenn GS, *et al.* A quantitative assessment of plasma homocysteine as a risk factor for vascular disease. *JAMA* 1995; 274: 1049–57.

British Committee for Standards in Haematology. Guidelines on oral anticoagulation. *Br. J. Haematol.* 1998; 101: 374–87.

Cumming AM and Shiach CR. The investigation and management of inherited thrombophilia. *Clin. Lab. Haematol.* 1999; 21: 77–92.

2.4.2 Acquired thrombotic disease

🔑 **Pathophysiology**
Virchow's triad states that three things should be considered in thrombosis: the vessel, the blood constituents and flow characteristics.

The majority of arterial thromboses relate to abnormal vessels, eg atheroma. Cellular blood components can increase total blood viscosity when present in excess, eg polycythaemia, thrombocythaemia and hyperleucocytosis. Similarly, increases in plasma viscosity (myeloma or Waldenström's macroglobulinaemia) can produce cerebral, spinal and cardiac ischaemia. It is difficult to predict what level of plasma viscosity will cause problems because each individual will have a different threshold for symptoms/problems.

Antiphospholipid antibody syndrome

Aetiology

The antiphospholipid antibody syndrome (APAS) produces the paradox of prolonged clotting times but also an arterial and venous thrombotic tendency. This is because the antibody binds the phospholipid on the platelet surface and inhibits the clotting cascade from proceeding efficiently, prolonging the activated partial thromboplastin time (APTT, the 'lupus anticoagulant'). At the same time the antibody binds to thrombomodulin on endothelium and slows protein C activation,

producing a prothrombotic tendency locally. It is now clear that the specificity of the antibody is for β_2-glycoprotein 1, which in turn binds phospholipid, thereby acting as a natural anticoagulant.

Epidemiology

Antiphospholipid antibodies are associated with:

- inflammatory arthritis, eg refactory anaemia and systemic lupus erythematosus (SLE);

- acute infection, eg malaria and HIV;

- thromboembolic vascular disease;

- medication, eg phenothiazine and phenytoin.

The majority of antibodies arise without any obvious predisposition. Note that antiphospholipid antibodies only occur in about 10% of patients with SLE. In unselected patients with these antibodies, 2.5% per year will develop thromboembolism.

Clinical presentation

🔑 The definition of APAS is the association of one or more clinical features with either the lupus anticoagulant or antiphospholipid antibodies tested on more than one occasion.

- Thromboembolism: venous > arterial.

- Recurrent fetal loss in the second or third trimester. The presence of IgG antiphospholipid antibodies confers a relative risk of 3.5. The placenta becomes infarcted and necrotic.

- Thrombocytopenia: platelet aggregation.

- Non-thrombotic central nervous system problems: chorea, epilepsy and Guillain–Barré syndrome.

- Skin lesions: ulcers and livedo reticularis.

- Endocardial disease.

- Haemolytic anaemia.

Investigations

Full blood count Check FBC for thrombocytopenia and a biochemical screen for renal impairment.

Clotting studies Antiphospholipid antibodies are detected by an enzyme-linked immunosorbent assay. It is likely that this will be superseded by β_2-glycoprotein 1 assays in the future.

A prolonged APTT may be a feature of, but is not specific for, APAS. Typically the APTT is not normalised by mixing with normal plasma. The dilute Russell's viper venom test (DRVVT) is prolonged in APAS due to activation of the antibody-blocking factor X by the venom. The DRVVT is expressed as a ratio of a patient's test to control, and the further step of adding excess platelets to swamp the effect of the antiphospholipid antibody and normalise the DRVVT confers even better specificity. Testing during anticoagulation is unreliable.

Other tests CXR and ECG to assess previous thrombotic episodes.

🔑 When considering APAS, both clotting and antibody tests should be repeated after an interval of 6 weeks for confirmation.

Treatment

Patients identified as having APAS should be referred to a specialist haematology clinic. Other risk factors for thromboembolism such as obesity, smoking and the oral contraceptive should be reviewed and considered. Patients with deep vein thrombosis (DVT)/pulmonary embolism (PE) should be given heparin in the acute phase; the use of low-molecular-weight (LMW) heparin has removed the complexity of adjusting the heparin dose in the presence of an already abnormal APTT. A first event of DVT/PE should be treated with warfarin at a target INR of 2.5 and the duration of the therapy requires specialist assessment. A previous history of thromboembolism is an indication for long-term warfarin therapy, with a target INR of 2.5 if the recurrent DVT/PE occurred while the patient was off warfarin therapy, or a target INR of 3.5 for patients who develop a recurrence of DVT/PE while on warfarin at a lower target INR.

For arterial thrombotic events aspirin is insufficient therapy and a target INR of 3.5 is recommended as long as the bleeding risk at the higher intensity of anticoagulation is taken into consideration.

Recurrent fetal loss is treated with LMW heparin and aspirin, preferably before conception. This is superior to steroid therapy.

A positive antiphospholipid antibody or DRVVT with no clinical history is not an indication for anticoagulation. The patient should be kept under review.

FURTHER READING

Baglin TP, Keeling DM and Watson HG. British Committee for Standards in Haematology. Guidelines on oral anticoagulation (warfarin): third edition, 2005 update. *Br. J. Haematol.* 2006; 132: 277–85.

Kandiah DA, Sali A, Sheng YH, *et al*. Current insights into the antiphospholipid syndrome: clinical, immunological and molecular aspects. *Adv. Immunol.* 1998; 70: 507–20.

Khamashta MA, Cuadrado MJ, Mujic F, *et al*. The management of thrombosis in APAS. *N. Engl. J. Med.* 1995; 332: 993–7.

Rai R, Cohen H, Dare M, *et al*. Randomised controlled trial of aspirin plus heparin in pregnant women with recurrent miscarriage associated with APA. *BMJ* 1997; 317: 253–7.

Thrombotic thrombocytopenic purpura

Aetiology

Aetiology is unknown in most cases. It can occasionally be associated with haemorrhagic colitis, administration of cytotoxic drugs (mitomycin), SLE/connective tissue disorders, pregnancy and the oral contraceptive. There are rare familial forms.

Pathophysiology

Physiologically, ultra-large von Willebrand factor (vWF) multimers are released from vascular endothelium and broken down into smaller vWF multimers by a metalloproteinase enzyme present in the plasma now known as ADAMTS-13. Patients with thrombotic thrombocytopenic purpura (TTP) have a deficiency of ADAMTS-13 (either as an acquired inhibitor or more rarely a congenital deficiency), which results in a build-up of ultra-large vWF multimers that themselves are highly active at causing spontaneous platelet aggregation and microvascular thrombosis, particularly in high shear stress circulations (eg kidney and brain).

Platelets are consumed in this process and patients become thrombocytopenic.

Incidence

The annual incidence is about 1 per 1,000,000, with a slight female preponderance. TTP affects all ages, with incidences peaking at 30–40 years.

Clinical presentation

There is fever, purpura (although it may not be dramatic), non-immune intravascular haemolytic anaemia associated with fragmented red cells, consumptive thrombocytopenia, neurological features and renal failure.

Neurological features may be 'general' (eg irritability, fits, drowsiness and coma) or focal (eg stroke syndromes).

Diagnosis

Diagnosis is suggested by FBC and blood film showing thrombocytopenia and fragmented red cells in the appropriate clinical context. A clotting screen will be normal or show only minor abnormalities.

Differential diagnosis

- From other causes of thrombocytopenia in a patient with an acute systemic illness. The commonest of these are infections: viral (HIV, cytomegalovirus, Epstein–Barr virus and hantavirus), bacterial (septicaemia) and others (eg malaria). In these situations a low platelet count is usually associated with disseminated intravascular coagulation, whereas in TTP it is not.

- From haemolytic–uraemic syndrome (HUS). 'Typical' cases of HUS and TTP probably represent the extreme ends of a continuum.

In TTP renal failure is not usually severe: if it is, and neurological features are not prominent, then the term HUS will be applied (see *Nephrology*, Section 2.7.3).

- From other causes of thrombotic microangiopathy: malignant hypertension, acute scleroderma, APAS and renal allograft rejection.

Treatment
The management of suspected or confirmed TTP needs expert haematological supervision. Management is based on supportive care (eg dialysis) and plasma exchange (or infusion of fresh frozen plasma when plasma exchange is not immediately available). Plasma exchange removes the ADAMTS-13 inhibitors with the ultra-large vWF multimers and replenishes normal ADAMTS-13. Continue daily plasma exchange until the patient's platelet count is normal for two consecutive days, then slowly increase the interval between plasma exchanges. Given the risk of thromboses with this condition, consider the use of aspirin or LMW heparin when the platelet count begins to rise.

This is a rare disease with a high mortality rate. Many different immunosuppressive regimens have also been tried, particularly in patients refractory to plasma exchange. However, each drug has been given only to small numbers of patients and without controls, so it is difficult to know how effective they are.

Complications
The greatest fear is intracerebral haemorrhage.

Prognosis
Mortality was 90% before the introduction of plasma exchange in the 1970s; now it is around 20%.

However, mortality can still occur after a relapsing and remitting course in 10% of cases.

FURTHER READING

George JN. Platelets. *Lancet* 2000; 355: 1531–9.

2.5 Clinical use of blood products

Principle
Blood products should be used in the following circumstances:

- replacement of something that the patient does not have (eg factor VIII for treatment in haemophilia A);

- replacement of something that is lost/decreased (eg correction of anaemia or platelets for thrombocytopenia post chemotherapy);

- to decrease the problems associated with exposure to a previously unseen antigen (eg anti-D in Rh D-negative pregnant women or specific immunoglobulin after exposure to infection).

Indications
Wherever possible, national and local guidelines should be followed. Each NHS Trust should supply you with these (often in the form of the junior doctor's handbook). Special requirements exist for the transfusion of products in some patients [eg cytomegalovirus (CMV) negative and irradiated blood]. All blood products are now leucocyte depleted at source in view of the theoretical risk of transmission of variant Creutzfeldt–Jakob disease. Irradiated blood products such as

platelets are used in patients with Hodgkin's disease, those receiving stem-cell transplant therapy, patients receiving purine analogues like fludarabine or profoundly immunocompromised patients. Blood transfusion has received a lot of political interest recently.

Packed (red) cells
It is impossible to provide a trigger haemoglobin (Hb) for transfusion that would be appropriate in all cases, in view of the numerous confounding factors that may coexist (eg age and systemic disease). Anaemia due to haematinic deficiency should not be transfused but the relevant haematinic replaced. There is no doubt that the appropriate transfusion can be life-saving, but it is also clear that a large number of patients are exposed to blood transfusions unnecessarily. Recent studies have suggested that patients whose Hb is allowed to fall to around 8 g/dL may have a more favourable outcome than those transfused with higher Hb values. The number of units to be transfused depends on the clinical situation and the Hb. Blood conservation mechanisms should be explored and recombinant human erythropoietin may reduce or prevent transfusion requirements in carefully selected patients who have anaemia due to cancer or other systemic chronic illness. Timely preoperative assessment clinics (at least 4 weeks before elective surgery) with judicious use of iron (orally or parenterally) may lead to less usage of packed red cells in surgery.

Platelets
Once again, strict criteria cannot be applied to all clinical situations. Platelets should be given if the patient is bleeding and the platelet count is 50–100 × 10⁹/L, for example

patients who have received massive transfusions and in the setting of disseminated intravascular coagulation (DIC). The maximum increment that can be expected following one dose of platelets is 40×10^9/L (pooled from four donor units). Usually only one dose of platelets is given at a time. Prophylactic platelets are given to patients with counts below 10×10^9/L to reduce the risk of spontaneous haemorrhage.

Fresh frozen plasma
Definite indications are acute DIC, thrombotic thrombocytopenic purpura and the replacement of a single coagulation factor deficiency if the specific concentrate is not available. Conditional uses arise in liver disease or a massive transfusion associated with bleeding and abnormal coagulation tests. The dose of fresh frozen plasma (FFP) is 12–15 mL/kg (this is usually 3–4 units). Substantial bleeding in patients on warfarin should now be treated with a prothrombin complex concentrate rather than FFP.

Cryoprecipitate
The chief indication is for the replacement of fibrinogen, eg DIC, hypofibrinogenaemia or dysfibrinogenaemia. The dose of cryoprecipitate is 10 units given intravenously. The fibrinogen level should be greater than 1 g/L in these situations.

Immunoglobulins (intravenous or intramuscular)
These are used for patients who have inherited or acquired deficiencies of gamma-globulins such as chronic lymphatic leukaemia or severe combined immunodeficiency, in people exposed to infections (eg hepatitis A or B) and in certain diseases thought to have an immune component (eg immune

thrombocytopenic purpura and Kawasaki disease).

Albumin
Treatment with albumin is controversial and operator dependent. Some anaesthetists insist on albumin as a plasma expander.

Anti-D immunoglobulin
This is given to Rh D-negative women when there is a risk that Rh D-positive fetal cells may enter the maternal circulation, thus causing the mother to become immunised with a possibility of haemolytic disease of the newborn in subsequent pregnancies. It is given prophylactically in the third trimester, as well as within 72 hours of any sensitising event (eg delivery, abortion or amniocentesis).

Contraindications
Blood products should not be used outside the recommended indications unless discussed with the haematologist. Blood products should never be used simply for volume expansion except in the context of haemorrhage or significant anaemia.

Practical details

> The most important aspect of blood transfusion relates to complications due to administration errors.

Before treatment
The blood sample for cross-matching must be taken from a patient with an armband, who is identified by you as the correct person. The blood sample must then be labelled by you at the patient's bedside. Prelabelling of

tubes is completely unacceptable due to the high error rate. There should be at least three independent identifiers on the bottle and the form, such as name and surname, date of birth and hospital number.

Laboratory work
The patient's blood is grouped (ABO and rhesus) and serum screened for antibodies. A cross-match is not routinely carried out for patients who have not received any transfusions or for those who have no antibodies. The blood grouping is established and an antibody screen is carried out. If the screen is negative, blood can be issued electronically, ie without physically mixing the patient's serum with prospective donor cells. Patients with a positive direct antiglobulin test will have a cross-match carried out. In a routine cross-match, the patient's serum is mixed with red cells from the prospective donor units, looking for cell aggregation due to antibodies (incompatibility). Compatible units are then labelled with the patient's details and set aside in the refrigerator for use.

The treatment
A qualified person, who has a written request form containing the patient's details, must fetch the cross-matched products from the blood fridge. Two qualified members of staff on the ward must check the blood products at the patient's bedside with the patient's details. There are moves towards an electronic patient identification system that uses a bar code attached to the patient's wrist and matches it with the number on the unit of blood component to be transfused. The information on the armband must exactly match that on the blood bags, the drug chart and

the information provided by the transfusion laboratory before transfusion can take place. Ensure that the correct armband is on the correct patient!

Complications

The most frequent complication reported to the SHOT (Serious Hazards of Transfusion) committee is where a patient has received blood components intended for someone else. About two-thirds of these involved one or more error, due to deviation from the guidelines mentioned above. An incompatible blood transfusion may result in few adverse effects or may cause an acute fatal reaction (see Section 1.3.3).

Other complications include:

- allergic reactions due to platelets or white cells;

- febrile reactions to human leucocyte antibodies or plasma proteins;

- circulatory overload;

- transfusion-transmitted infections (eg hepatitis C, HIV, malaria and CMV);

- graft-vs-host disease;

- transfusion-related acute lung injury due to FFP;

- immune sensitisation (eg to Rh D antigen);

- reactions due to bacterial infection of products;

- clotting abnormalities (in massive transfusions).

FURTHER READING

British Committee for Standards in Haematology, Blood Transfusion Task Force. Royal College of Nursing and the Royal College of Surgeons of England. The administration of blood and blood components and the management of transfused patients. *Transfus. Med.* 1999; 9: 227–38.

National Blood Authority. *Summary of SHOT Annual Report.* 2006.

Provan D. Better blood transfusion. *BMJ* 1999; 318: 1435–6.

Thurer RL. Evaluating transfusion triggers. *JAMA* 1998; 279: 238–9.

2.6 Haematological features of systemic disease

Anaemia of chronic disease

The picture is usually of a normocytic normochromic anaemia (see Table 21 for differential diagnosis). Ordinarily there is a low serum iron and total iron-binding capacity. In more severe cases, a microcytic hypochromic picture may develop: iron stores in the marrow are normal but incorporation into erythroblasts is defective. The underlying reason for this is probably due to loss of erythropoietin sensitivity, which may relate to release of cytokines such as tumour necrosis factor α. Erythropoietin in pharmacological doses may be of some benefit, whereas the effect is dramatic in the anaemia of uraemia (due to reduced renal production of erythropoietin). Better disease control with immunomodulatory drugs may improve the haemoglobin. Note that ferritin, globulins and erythrocyte sedimentation rate may all be raised as a feature of the chronic disease process. Any condition associated with prolonged inflammation, infection or malignancy can produce this type of anaemia. Key examples are rheumatoid arthritis and Crohn's disease.

Liver disease

Chronic liver disease is often associated with a raised mean corpuscular volume (MCV), target cells, mild anaemia and thrombocytopenia. Acanthocytes (spur cells) and echinocytes (burr cells, which are smaller and with more spikes) are also features of advancing liver disease. Zieve's syndrome occurs following acute alcohol poisoning, producing haemolysis and red-cell damage due to hyperlipidaemia and changes within the red-cell membrane.

Alcohol excess frequently suppresses platelet production, which recovers during abstinence. This thrombocytopenia is not steroid sensitive and can cause problems for liver biopsy. Hypersplenism suppresses all

TABLE 21 CAUSES OF A NORMOCHROMIC NORMOCYTIC ANAEMIA	
Mechanism	**Example**
Anaemia of chronic disease	Rheumatoid disease and polymyalgia rheumatica
Combined deficiencies	Iron and folate deficiency in coeliac disease
Haemic malignancy	Acute and chronic leukaemias, and myelodysplasia
Organ failure	Kidney, liver, thyroid and pituitary
Acute blood loss	Haemorrhage

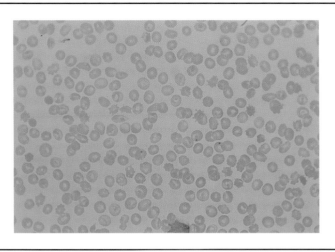

▲ **Fig. 38** Blood film where three Howell–Jolly bodies are present. There are also some target cells and acanthocytes, typically seen in hyposplenism.

blood elements due to dilution/pooling of the circulating volume by the enlarged spleen. However, do not miss a haematinic deficiency as a cause of pancytopenia in these patients. The diagnosis of hypersplenism requires a marrow of normal cellularity with an enlarged spleen.

Clotting disorders in liver disease are dealt with under acquired bleeding disorders (see Section 2.3.2).

Hyposplenism

The extremes of age are associated with relative hyposplenism. This causes a relative immunodeficiency and reduction in the response of antibodies to infection.

Splenectomy may be performed during laparotomy for tumour or trauma. The spleen may be infiltrated by amyloid, lymphoma or sarcoid. The spleen frequently atrophies in coeliac disease, inflammatory bowel disease and systemic lupus erythematosus (SLE). Infarction of the spleen occurs in sickle cell anaemia and massive splenomegaly may be due to haemic malignancy, including chronic myeloid leukaemia and myelofibrosis.

These causes result in reduced splenic function, which may be seen on the FBC as leucocytosis and thrombocythaemia. Target cells, acanthocytes and Howell–Jolly bodies (Fig. 38) appear on the film as a result of the spleen not functioning properly. Myelocytes and normoblasts may also be seen.

Patients with a non-functioning spleen or who have had a splenectomy should receive phenoxymethylpenicillin (penicillin V) or, if they are allergic, a suitable alternative for life, and should carry a card in the event of an accident. Vaccination with Pneumovax (polysaccharide) and meningococcal and *Haemophilus influenzae* B vaccines will improve immunity. Where possible, this should be performed 4 weeks prior to splenectomy to maximise the antibody response. Revaccination should occur every 5–10 years; pneumococcal antibody levels will prove helpful in this decision.

⚠ Do not underestimate the seriousness of infections following splenectomy. Even fit young adults can die with an overwhelming postsplenectomy infection.

Drugs

Many drugs can produce an oxidative stress to the red cell and produce haemolysis in patients with glucose-6-phosphate dehydrogenase deficiency. However, people with normal enzyme levels can also suffer from oxidative damage to red cells during periods of extreme ill-health. Drugs can also be associated with antibody formation and a positive Coombs' haemolysis (see Section 2.1.7).

The commonest problem caused by drugs is mild cytopenia(s). Nearly every drug has been described as producing a blood dyscrasia, even if only in a single idiosyncratic case report. A decision has to be made about whether to stop the drug and see if the blood count improves (usually within 1–2 weeks) or tolerate a mild cytopenia(s) because the overall benefit of the drug outweighs the mild toxicity (eg anticonvulsants). Sometimes, a brief course of granulocyte colony-stimulating factor may help during periods of neutropenic sepsis.

⚠ Some drugs, such as carbimazole, phenytoin and methotrexate, are well recognised as causing marrow damage. Always be vigilant with patients who are taking such medication long term.

Drugs associated with aplastic anaemia/cytopenias include:

- antithyroids (carbimazole and propylthiouracil);

- antipsychotics (chlorpromazine);

- anticonvulsants (phenytoin);

- antibiotics (chloramphenicol and sulphonamides);

- anti-inflammatories (phenylbutazone, gold and indomethacin).

Macrocytosis

Several conditions cause a raised MCV without a megaloblastic marrow. Always consider the following:

- alcohol and liver disease;

- pregnancy;

- hypothyroidism;

- chronic obstructive airways disease;

- reticulocytosis (haemorrhage or haemolysis);

- scurvy.

Alterations in the white cell count

Variations in elements of the white cell count occur frequently. Tables 22–26 highlight the common situations.

FURTHER READING

Party of the British Committee for Standards in Haematology Clinical Haematology Task Force. Guidelines for the prevention and treatment of infection in patients with absent or dysfunctional spleen. *BMJ* 1996; 312: 430–4.

Weiss G and Goodnough LT. Anaemia of chronic disease. *N. Engl. J. Med.* 2005; 352: 1011–23.

TABLE 22 CAUSES OF NEUTROPHILIA AND NEUTROPENIA

Neutrophilia	Neutropenia
Acute infection	Drugs
Chronic inflammation	Postinfectious
Steroids	Autoimmune neutropenia
Stress, eg surgery and postictal	Bone-marrow infiltration: usually associated with other cytopenias
Chronic myeloid leukaemia	Severe sepsis

TABLE 23 CAUSES OF A RAISED AND REDUCED EOSINOPHIL COUNT

Eosinophilia	Eosinopenia
Drugs: gold, sulphonamides and penicillin	Drugs: corticosteroids and aminophylline
Parasitic infection (eg *Strongyloides*, schistosomiasis, filariasis and *Echinococcus*)	Acute severe illness (eg myocardial infarction, trauma, surgery and burns)
Allergy/hypersensitivity (eg asthma, eczema and allergic bronchopulmonary aspergillosis)	Cushing's syndrome
Malignancy: lymphoma and eosinophilic leukaemia	
Sarcoid	

TABLE 24 CAUSES OF AN INCREASED AND REDUCED BASOPHIL COUNT

Basophilia	Basopenia
Myeloproliferative disorders	Sepsis
Chronic inflammatory diseases, eg rheumatoid	Haemorrhage
IgE-mediated hypersensitivity	Cushing's syndrome
Hyperlipidaemia	Thyrotoxicosis

TABLE 25 CAUSES OF MONOCYTOSIS AND MONOCYTOPENIA

Monocytosis	Monocytopenia
Infection: malaria, tuberculosis and subacute bacterial endocarditis	Autoimmune disease, eg rheumatoid and SLE
Myelodysplasia	Steroids
Lymphoma	Cytotoxic drugs
Granulocyte–macrophage colony-stimulating factor therapy	Hairy cell leukaemia

TABLE 26 CAUSES OF LYMPHOCYTOSIS AND LYMPHOPENIA

Lymphocytosis	Lymphopenia
Viral infections	Acute stress, eg trauma and surgery
Bacterial infections, eg pertussis, tuberculosis and typhus	Cancer and renal failure
Exercise	AIDS
Splenectomy	Medication
Lymphoid leukaemias	

2.7 Haematology of pregnancy

There are several haematological changes that occur during normal pregnancy and in the peripartum period.

> It is important to be aware that all primary haematological diseases may present during pregnancy and therefore think carefully before making the diagnosis 'normal for pregnancy'.

Full blood count

Maternal erythropoiesis increases from the first trimester. However, rather than resulting in a rise in the haemoglobin (Hb) concentration, the normal range for Hb during pregnancy is lower than in the non-pregnant state, with anaemia defined as a Hb of less than 10 g/dL. This is because even though the red-cell mass increases by 25%, the plasma volume expands by approximately 40%. There is therefore a dilutional effect. A mild neutrophilia is also common in pregnancy.

> A mean corpuscular volume of up to 103 fL is considered to be within normal limits in pregnancy. Anything greater than this should be investigated.

Anaemia

Anaemia does occur with increased incidence in pregnancy. The increase in erythropoietic activity, the fetal demand for iron, and antepartum and postpartum haemorrhage all lead to an increased incidence of iron deficiency around pregnancy. The increased metabolic activity is also a drain on the limited folate stores.

Folate deficiency can cause a megaloblastic anaemia in pregnancy. It has also been shown that maternal folate deficiency in the first trimester is associated with an increased incidence of neural tube defects in the fetus. Folic acid prophylaxis is therefore recommended, starting prior to conception. Serum B_{12} falls in pregnancy, but rarely sufficient to cause problems.

Thrombocytopenia

Thrombocytopenia occurs in approximately 5% of all pregnancies. The majority of these cases comprise benign gestational thrombocytopenia, which is mild (platelet count $<80 \times 10^9$/L), isolated (all other parameters of the FBC are normal) and not associated with any physical symptoms or signs, and which resolves spontaneously postpartum. The mother and the obstetricians should be reassured that this presents minimal risk of significant bleeding to the mother or the child. Mild cases of idiopathic thrombocytopenic purpura (ITP) can occur.

A bone-marrow assessment should only be performed if there is suspicion of leukaemia and the platelet count is <20×10^9/L. Similarly, features suggestive of intercurrent disease, eg systemic lupus erythematosus, should be investigated. If the bone marrow is morphologically within normal limits, this suggests that the thrombocytopenia is a result of increased peripheral destruction and shortened platelet survival, the causes of which include:

- ITP;

- drugs (eg heparin, methyldopa and penicillins);

- eclampsia;

- haemolysis, elevated liver enzymes and low platelets (HELLP) syndrome;

- disseminated intravascular coagulation (DIC);

- haemolytic–uraemic syndrome/thrombotic thrombocytopenic purpura;

- antiphospholipid antibody syndrome (APAS).

If the platelet count falls below 20×10^9/L at any time during the pregnancy or if the thrombocytopenia is leading to clinically significant bleeding, the mother should be started on prednisolone (1 mg/kg orally). This usually brings about a rise in the platelet count within 14 days. If this fails, then intravenous immunoglobulin 1 g/kg should be given on two successive days; this usually works within 5 days. Vaginal delivery is acceptable with a platelet count >50×10^9/L. Epidural anaesthesia should not be used in women with a platelet count of less than 80×10^9/L.

Eclampsia is a syndrome of proteinuria, oedema, hypertension, epigastric pain, brisk reflexes,

renal impairment and fitting in pregnancy. Thrombocytopenia and DIC may occur. Urgent senior obstetric review is needed to consider immediate elective delivery of the child. Supportive management is aimed at controlling the fits and BP.

HELLP syndrome is an uncommon but serious complication of eclampsia. Treatment is as for eclampsia. There is significant maternal and fetal mortality.

Even severe ITP rarely causes a significant bleeding problem in the child.

Clotting abnormalities

There is about a 10-fold increase in the risk of venous thromboembolic disease during pregnancy, which lasts well into the puerperium. This is because the gravid uterus places direct pressure on the pelvic veins (particularly the left) and leads to venous stasis in the legs; protein C levels fall in pregnancy, resulting in a relative prothrombotic state; and APAS can develop during pregnancy.

Thromboembolism remains the chief cause of maternal mortality. More than half of pregnant women with venous thromboembolism will have factor V Leiden mutation. Anticoagulation should be with low-molecular-weight heparin to term, then warfarin for 12 weeks' postpartum (warfarin does not enter breast milk). Further pregnancies require anticoagulation to prevent a recurrence in all patients, whether thrombophilia tests are positive or negative (see Section 2.4.1). The presence of inherited thrombophilia increases the risk of abruption, stillbirth and eclampsia.

Management of DIC in pregnancy is aimed at treating the obstetric

cause, together with haematological management (as discussed in Section 2.3.2).

The causes of pregnancy-induced DIC include:

- pre-eclampsia and eclampsia;

- HELLP syndrome;

- placental abruption;

- septic abortion;

- retained products of conception;

- amniotic fluid embolus.

FURTHER READING

British Committee for Standards in Haematology. Guidelines for the investigation and management of ITP in adults, children and pregnancy, 2003. Available at http://www.bcshguidelines.com/

2.8 Iron overload

Pathophysiology

Iron overload may be iatrogenic (excess oral iron or blood transfusion) or pathophysiological (haemochromatosis). There is no secretion pathway for iron in the body, and about 1 mg is lost per day due to gut mucosal cell loss. Absorption of luminal iron is controlled by the enterocyte, which is sensitive to iron stores in the body. The enterocyte is influenced by its own transferrin receptor that regulates transferrin uptake from the plasma. The behaviour of the transferrin receptor is modulated by the HFE protein, which lies adjacent to it on the cell surface. In haemochromatosis the enterocyte absorbs excess iron because an abnormal HFE protein has dysregulated the transferrin receptor; this results in expansion of the total body pool of cellular iron. The exact mechanism by which the HFE protein controls the transferrin receptor is not known, but the defect in the HFE protein in haemochromatosis results in a structural change that alters its relationship to that receptor.

Epidemiology

In white populations, 10% are heterozygous and 0.5% homozygous for the HFE gene mutation.

Approximately 85% of homozygotes have a mutation involving a change from cysteine to tyrosine at amino acid 282 within the HFE protein. A small percentage are due to mutations at amino acid 63, and a few more are yet to be determined. The mutation occurred over 2,000 years ago, and the heterozygous state is thought to confer a survival advantage for blood loss.

Clinical presentation

In individuals with haemochromatosis iron absorption is increased from birth, resulting in raised percentage transferrin saturation, even in childhood. Iron is progressively deposited in tissue, with increased hepatic iron in men by the end of the second decade. Menstruation slows iron accumulation in women. The serum ferritin continues to rise as hepatic iron stores increase, and liver fibrosis occurs by the mid-thirties in men. Deposition of iron within tissues leads to superoxide radical formation and tissue damage. Clinical manifestations are usually seen within the fifth decade in men, and later in women. However, the clinical phenotype is very variable,

with some families having more severe disease than others. Not all present with 'bronzed diabetes', and features can include:

- skin (pigmentation and hair loss);

- endocrine (end-organ damage in pancreas, pituitary, thyroid and gonads);

- cardiac (restrictive cardiomyopathy and dysrhythmias);

- liver (fibrosis and cirrhosis);

- joints (pyrophosphate disease).

Investigations

Serum iron levels are generally unreliable.

Making the diagnosis

Homozygotes will have a transferrin saturation greater than 55% (males) or 50% (females). Percentage transferrin saturation is a more sensitive screening test and indicator than the serum ferritin, which may be raised as an acute-phase protein in many conditions and also in liver disease. Confirmation may be obtained by genetic analysis for the HFE gene mutation. Once detected, families of an affected individual should be offered the opportunity of testing.

Looking for complications

Homozygotes need FBC, liver function, alpha-fetoprotein, blood sugar, thyroid-stimulating hormone, follicle-stimulating hormone, luteinising hormone, testosterone and cortisone levels to be checked. An ECG and echocardiogram are required. Radiographs of knees and wrists may show pyrophosphate disease.

Management

Regular venesection will reduce body iron levels in the majority of cases of haemochromatosis. This can be monitored using ferritin levels as a rough guide to response. Once the ferritin is <50 mg/L, venesections are discontinued until levels begin to rise above normal. Normalising the ferritin does not reverse tissue damage but may slow progress of the disease. Desferrioxamine is not normally used in haemochromatosis and oral iron chelators can be difficult to tolerate.

Heterozygotes usually have normal ferritin levels. If the ferritin is raised, consider intercurrent pathology such as liver disease. It is unclear what the long-term outcome is in patients who are heterozygous for the HFE gene mutation.

Iron overload due to transfusion begins to become a problem after 20 units have been given or if serum ferritin has risen above 1000 mg/L. Subcutaneous or intravenous desferrioxamine is required on a regular basis to leach iron out of the body. Such desferrioxamine regimens are troublesome for patients and staff, and should only be considered if there is likely to be overall benefit for the patient, for example an 80-year-old woman with acute myeloid leukaemia is unlikely to benefit.

Complications

Recognised complications include:

- hepatoma;

- liver failure;

- cardiac failure;

- diabetes mellitus.

Screening

Population screening may reveal asymptomatic homozygotes and early venesection may prevent morbidity and mortality. There are a number of screening studies taking place in the USA. Such screening programmes usually use the percentage transferrin saturation as an initial test, followed by genetic confirmation.

FURTHER READING

British Committee for Standards in Haematology. Guidelines on the diagnosis and therapy of genetic haemochromatosis, September 2003. Available at www.bcshguidelines.com/

Edwards W. Haemochromatosis. In: Lee GR *et al.*, eds. *Wintrobe's Clinical Haematology*, Vol. 1. Baltimore: Williams & Wilkins, 1999.

Olynyk JK, Cullen DJ, Aquilia S, *et al.* A population-based study of the clinical expression of the HFE gene. *N. Engl. J. Med.* 1999; 341: 718–26.

Salter-Cid L, Brunmark A, Li Y, *et al.* Transferrin receptor is negatively modulated by the HFE protein: implication for cellular iron haemostasis. *Proc. Natl Acad. Sci. USA* 1999; 96: 5434–46.

2.9 Chemotherapy and related therapies

Chemotherapy

Chemotherapy should kill a tumour but enable damaged normal tissues to recover between treatments. The cumulative effect should be to maximise tumour damage but minimise normal tissue damage.

Principle

Chemotherapy can be designed to:

- make a disease disappear, eg acute myeloid leukaemia (AML) or acute lymphoblastic leukaemia;

- suppress the disease, eg the plateau phase in myeloma;

- normalise the blood count, eg essential thrombocythaemia;

- merely improve the blood count with no intention of cure, eg palliation in certain cases of AML.

A complete remission is defined as the disappearance of the disease from blood and marrow (although molecular techniques may still reveal traces). Partial remission is defined as an improvement in blood and marrow with significant residual disease.

Chemotherapeutic agents usually damage cells during cell division (see *Cell Biology*, Cell Cycle and Apoptosis). Combining agents that act on different parts of cell division will maximise cell damage. However, within a tumour some cells will not be dividing and can therefore be relatively resistant to the effects of chemotherapy. Thus, if a tumour has a high proportion of dividing cells, such as high-grade non-Hodgkin's lymphoma (NHL), it is more susceptible to chemotherapy. More indolent tumours, such as low-grade NHL, are less susceptible to chemotherapy. (Note that low-grade NHL has a better survival than high-grade NHL because it is less aggressive even though it is less chemosensitive.)

Chemotherapeutic agents and their properties

Alkylating agents These include cyclophosphamide, chlorambucil, busulphan and melphalan. They transfer alkyl groups to DNA, resulting in double-strand linking that prevents cell division. High-dose intravenous cyclophosphamide can

cause haemorrhagic cystitis, so mesna is infused to limit bladder damage. Myelosuppression, alopecia and emesis are all common with cyclophosphamide. Oral chlorambucil and melphalan are well tolerated; they produce some myelosuppression but rarely cause significant emesis or alopecia.

Anthracyclines These include Adriamycin (doxorubicin) and mitoxantrone. They were originally designed as antibiotics and inhibit topoisomerase 2, a DNA repair enzyme, and also intercalate DNA base pairs to disrupt DNA templates. They are usually given intravenously and cause major myelosuppression, emesis, alopecia and mucosal damage. Cardiotoxicity is significant, and transient ECG changes occur in one-third of patients. Patients should not receive more than 450 mg/m^2 of doxorubicin during their lifespan as cardiomyopathy and heart failure are dose dependent.

Vincristine Vincristine and its relatives crystallise cytoplasmic tubulin, preventing spindle formation and cell division. These drugs do not cause significant myelosuppression, alopecia or emesis. However, nerve damage may produce paraesthesiae, foot drop, ileus and constipation. Vinblastine should replace vincristine if neurological toxicities are problematic.

Antimetabolites The antimetabolite group of cytotoxics comprises a number of very different drugs, including methotrexate, cytarabine and fludarabine.

- Methotrexate inhibits dihydrofolate reductase, which paralyses the folic acid and B$_{12}$ metabolism central to purine/pyrimidine formation. Methotrexate is often used in low doses by rheumatologists; always be vigilant for sudden and potentially fatal myelosuppression. Intrathecal methotrexate is given in some high-grade lymphoid malignancies that may be present in the cerebrospinal fluid. High-dose intravenous methotrexate typically causes myelosuppression, damages the gut mucosa (causing mucositis and diarrhoea) and produces renal impairment. Folinic acid rescue is given intravenously to minimise the damage to normal tissues; folinic acid bypasses the methotrexate-sensitive step. Alopecia and emesis are not common.

- Cytarabine (cytosine arabinoside) is a pyrimidine analogue. It becomes incorporated into DNA and terminates DNA synthesis by inhibiting DNA polymerase. It is a major player in the treatment of acute leukaemia. It is myelosuppressive, emetogenic and produces mucositis. Occasional cerebellar damage and conjunctivitis are seen.

- Fludarabine is a purine analogue that is converted to fludarabine triphosphate within the cells. This inhibits ribonucleotide reductase and curtails DNA synthesis. Fludarabine is given orally with very little toxicity apart from myelosuppression. It forms the second line of treatment in chronic lymphatic leukaemia (CLL).

Hydroxycarbamide (hydroxyurea)
Oral hydroxycarbamide is widely used in myeloproliferative disorders. It may cause drowsiness but is otherwise very well tolerated. Careful dose adjustment limits marrow suppression. Hydroxycarbamide inhibits ribonucleotide reductase.

Asparaginase This is an unusual drug: it hydrolyses asparagine and inhibits protein synthesis. It may cause hypersensitivity, pancreatitis and somnolence. Myelosuppression and emesis are not major problems.

Others Steroids have a cytotoxic effect in certain lymphoid malignancies. Their exact mode of action is unclear, but they probably destabilise the nuclear membrane. Etoposide (VP16) is a semi-synthetic derivative of podophyllotoxin. It is a topoisomerase 2 inhibitor that produces myelosuppression and emesis.

> - A dedicated chemotherapy pharmacist can make life simpler and safer for everybody.
> - Over the last 30 years different combinations of chemotherapeutic agents have been used in haemic malignancy under the guidance of the Medical Research Council. Gradually, improvements in survival and toxicity have been produced by this coordinated approach. Such national/international initiatives enable statistically significant patient numbers to be obtained and are thought to be best practice in cancer units.

Dose scheduling
Finding the correct dose and schedule for drug combinations is very dependent on the limiting toxicities. Dose is calculated according to body surface area. Myelosuppression is the commonest toxicity that limits therapy; marrow function should recover sufficiently between courses before further treatment. Marrow transplantation is a technique that uses supralethal chemotherapy, plus or minus radiotherapy, to kill residual tumours, after which the patient is 'rescued' by an infusion of bone marrow/stem cells (see Section 2.10).

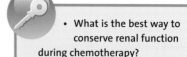

> - What is the best way to conserve renal function during chemotherapy?
> - What advice should be given about fertility?

Cytokine therapy

Erythropoietin
Erythropoietin is very effective in the treatment of the anaemia of renal failure. In haematology it can significantly improve the anaemia of myeloma, especially if renal impairment is present. However, it does not consistently improve the anaemia of myelodysplasia or chemotherapy and is only used in selected cases or trials.

Colony-stimulating factors
Colony-stimulating factors were discovered in the laboratory to stimulate granulocyte growth, monocyte growth or combinations of both. Given subcutaneously to patients, they boost the recovery of such cells following chemotherapy, transplantation or severe infection. There are many clinical studies using such agents, and the broad picture is that although infections can be reduced, overall survival is not improved.

Interleukin-2
Interleukin (IL)-2 stimulates the division of cytotoxic T cells and improves immune function. In the 1980s, IL-2 was used in high doses in cancer patients, with major toxicities. Smaller subcutaneous/intravenous doses are now being examined to see if the agent can stimulate the natural host response to suppress any residual disease following chemotherapy.

Interferon alfa

This has been used clinically for over 30 years. It has not been a panacea for cancer. In modest subcutaneous doses it can improve and control hairy-cell leukaemia, chronic myeloid leukaemia and hepatitis B/C. In younger people the influenza-like symptoms it causes are well tolerated and disappear after a few weeks. The elderly do not tolerate interferon alfa very well. High doses have been used in renal cancer and melanoma with improvements in about 30% of cases, but there are major toxicities at such doses.

Monoclonal antibodies

In recent years the use of monoclonal antibodies (antibodies directed at antigens on tumour cells that bind to the antigen and damage the cells, either by antibody cytotoxicity or by direct killing) has increased dramatically in haematology practice. Although these are not, strictly speaking, chemotherapy agents, some newer monoclonal antibodies may be conjugated to a drug or may be radiolabelled for better efficiency. Side effects may occur at the time of infusion and are generally mild and manageable (fever, rigors and urticaria), but may occasionally be severe (hypoxia and hypotension). Infusions are usually started slowly for this reason. Late side effects mostly relate to immunity and infections.

Currently the most commonly used include the following.

- Rituximab (anti-CD20). CD20 is widely expressed on most normal B cells and B-cell malignancies. This agent is now recommended as part of first-line therapy (with chemotherapy) in patients with diffuse large B-cell lymphoma, and is approved by the National Institute for Health and Clinical Excellence (NICE) for use in this setting. The evidence for its efficacy in numerous other lymphoproliferative diseases is accruing fast and the applications for this agent are broad.

- Alemtuzumab (anti-CD52). This agent is used extensively in stem-cell transplantation as a T-cell-depleting agent (although it also depletes B cells, natural killer cells and dendritic cells, which all express CD52). It has also been used with some success in CLL.

- Gemtuzumab ozogamicin (anti-CD33 with antitumour antibiotic). This agent is being investigated in AML and is being used in a number of Medical Research Council trials.

Other agents

Note that opioids and antiemetics are discussed in *Pain Relief and Palliative Care*, Sections 2.1 and 2.3.

- Chemotherapy will decrease fertility, so think about freezing sperm or eggs. Fertility may return after chemotherapy, so contraception is required.
- Chemotherapy should be accompanied by plenty of intravenous fluid and allopurinol to protect against urate nephropathy.

Complications

If you are worried about extravasation of chemotherapy, seek expert advice.

Major myelosuppression can result in rapidly fatal infections. Early use of broad-spectrum antibiotics is important in this situation. Sterilising the gut also reduces the risk of gut flora causing septicaemia.

There is no effective way to minimise alopecia.

Modern emesis control with 5-hydroxytryptamine (5HT$_3$) antagonists means that chemotherapy is much better tolerated, and patients rarely have to be deeply sedated.

Infertility

Fertility is permanently lost following some treatments such as allogeneic stem-cell transplantation. In such cases this must be discussed with an honest but sensitive approach before treatment.

All men (even those who have no plans for starting a family – their views may change) should be offered the chance of sperm storage before starting chemotherapy. This process is usually carried out over 3 days, and the delay is usually acceptable in terms of starting treatment.

For women requiring chemotherapy, storage of eggs or embryos (created by *in vitro* fertilisation) is possible, but these processes require ovarian stimulation and usually take weeks. In acute leukaemia this length of delay before starting chemotherapy is not possible. Storage of ovarian tissue is at an experimental stage at present, although there is the concern that reimplantation of ovarian tissue taken before chemotherapy could be associated with the reimplantation of leukaemia. Ovarian tissue storage may also be impractical because of the need to start chemotherapy immediately. Many women who do regain fertility after chemotherapy go on to have an early menopause.

Tumour lysis syndrome

This is a medical emergency with a high morbidity and mortality. It should be anticipated and prevented, but if it occurs treatment should be prompt and multidisciplinary (eg involve the renal physicians and/or intensivists). Tumour lysis syndrome occurs because of the rapid breakdown of the tumour, which results in metabolic derangement (hyperphosphataemia, hypocalcaemia, hyperkalaemia and hyperuricaemia) and clinical features (oliguria, cramps, seizures, cardiac failure and arrhythmias).

All patients at risk should be adequately hydrated prior to and during chemotherapy. Those at high risk should receive rasburicase (a urate oxidase enzyme that results in rapid degradation of uric acid), others should receive allopurinol. Blood tests should be done after chemotherapy to detect abnormalities.

FURTHER READING

Galvani DW and Cawley JC. *Cytokine Therapy*. Cambridge: Cambridge University Press, 1992.

Polliack AA. *Handbook of Essential Drugs in Haematology*. Reading: Harwood Academic Publications, 1991.

2.10 Principles of bone-marrow and peripheral blood stem-cell transplantation

Principle

Malignant cells can be destroyed by chemotherapy or radiotherapy if the doses are high enough. However, the doses required to eradicate disease can be so toxic that irreversible vital organ damage would occur, thus killing both the tumour and the patient.

The principal dose-limiting side effect of conventional chemotherapy and radiotherapy is bone-marrow toxicity. In many malignant diseases the higher the dose of treatment given, the greater the chance of cure. Infusing stem cells that will reconstitute the bone marrow enables doses of chemotherapy and radiotherapy to be given that would otherwise cause fatal irreversible bone-marrow failure.

Autologous transplantation refers to material reinfused into the same individual it was taken from. Allogeneic transplantation refers to material infused from a different individual. Over time it has been noted that patients transplanted from allogeneic donors have less disease relapse than those receiving autologous transplants. This and other evidence has led to the demonstation of a graft (donor) versus leukaemia/malignancy (patient) – or GVL – effect as one of the main mechanisms for preventing disease relapse after transplantation.

Knowledge of this mechanism has enabled transplanters to develop a different approach to transplantation, known as non-myeloablative or reduced-intensity conditioned transplants. This uses less toxic treatment prior to the transplant, relying on the immunity of the donor to suppress any residual malignant cells. As this is less toxic, these transplants can be performed in much older patients (up to 70 years old in some circumstances) and in those who have organ dysfunction before transplantation.

Practical details

Before treatment

Haematopoietic stem cells must be collected before the transplant. If this is from the patient (autologous),

the stem cells are usually stored frozen until they are needed. Stem cells from an allogeneic donor are usually (but not always) used fresh. Allogeneic donors may be human leucocyte antigen (HLA)-matched siblings, HLA-matched unrelated individuals or family members (haplo-identical). HLA-matched cord blood may also be used. In bone-marrow transplant (BMT) the source of the stem cells is the marrow, whereas in peripheral blood stem-cell transplant (PBSCT) the source is blood. Currently nearly all autologous, and about 50% of allogeneic, collections use peripheral blood stem cells. Stem cells in the peripheral blood can be collected following stimulation with growth factors (granulocyte colony-stimulating factor) or chemotherapy (in patients). The cells are then harvested on a leucapheresis machine. Marrow donations are performed under general anaesthesia, during which approximately 1 L of marrow is removed from the posterior pelvis.

The patient receives 'conditioning' chemotherapy and/or radiotherapy and/or immunotherapy to reduce any residual disease, and prepare the bone-marrow environment to receive the transplanted cells.

The transplant itself

The marrow or leucapheresis collection is infused into the patient through a Hickman line just like a blood transfusion. The transplanted stem cells travel to the bone-marrow space where they engraft and proliferate to produce a full complement of mature blood cells over the next few weeks.

The immunosuppression and myelosuppression requires the patient to be isolated in a transplant room and looked after by trained transplant staff. Immunosuppression to prevent reactions between the graft and host, and prophylactic antibiotics are used routinely. Once neutrophils and platelets begin to appear in the circulation, isolation restrictions are relaxed and the patient is allowed home after a matter of weeks.

Indications

Leukaemia
Allogeneic transplantation can cure acute and chronic leukaemia in up to 60% of suitable patients. The indications for transplantation in this setting are usually very straighforward and agreed upon by societies such as European Blood and Marrow Transplantation (EBMT). Many of the current clinical leukaemia trials include criteria for transplantation, or randomisation to receive a transplant.

Autologous BMT in acute leukaemia may prolong survival compared with chemotherapy alone, but there is substantial extra hospitalisation and morbidity.

Lymphoma and other malignancies
A lymphoma that relapses after conventional chemotherapy is still potentially curable with high-dose chemotherapy and autologous transplantation. Lymphomas are more common in older patients and the advent of reduced-intensity conditioning has now increased the application of allogeneic transplants in these patients, with very satisfactory outcomes.

High-dose chemotherapy and autologous transplantation is also used to prolong survival in myeloma, but it is not curative. Many protocols currently include

an autologous transplant as part of the first-line management in these patients.

Trials of high-dose chemotherapy and autologous transplantation are underway in the treatment of other solid tumours such as teratoma and breast cancer.

Non-malignant disease
Allogeneic transplant has also been used in the management of β-thalassaemia major and sickle cell disease.

Complications
Complications following transplants can generally be divided into toxicity, infection and immunological. All complications become more common after allogeneic transplant, especially when using an unrelated donor, ie as the genetic disparity increases. Toxicity more commonly occurs early (related to the conditioning), but infections can occur at any time due to the patient's altered immunity.

Acute graft-vs-host disease (GVHD) occurs in the first 100 days after allogeneic BMT (after 100 days it is termed chronic GVHD). GVHD and GVL both occur because the donor's immune system recognises the patient's cells as being 'not self'. Immunosuppression is used in the prophylaxis and treatment of GVHD. Any organ system may be affected, but the most common are the liver, skin and gut.

Outcome
Transplantation offers the possibility of cure to a significant proportion of patients who would otherwise succumb to their disease. However, the risks of the transplant

may be correspondingly high. The risk–benefit of the procedure must be assessed on an individual basis, taking into account the patient's age and general health as well as the disease prognosis with and without transplant.

There is a 10–50% transplant-related mortality with allogeneic BMT. Death usually occurs secondary to infection or GVHD. Autologous BMT is associated with <5% mortality.

The procedure must be explained in detail to the patient (and relatives) and careful notes of the discussion should be kept. The patient must give fully informed consent if transplantation is to proceed.

BMT and PBSCT have become much safer over the years (due partly to better supportive care), but are still associated with risk. It is vital that the patient is central to the decision-making process if these treatments are being considered. It is the haematologist's responsibility to educate and inform patients honestly as to the risks, benefits and potential outcomes of all the therapeutic options, guiding them in deciding between transplant, standard chemotherapy or even no treatment at all.

FURTHER READING
Barrett J and Treleaven JG, eds. *The Clinical Practice of Stem Cell Transplantation*. Oxford: Isis Medical Media, 1998.

Hoffbrand AV, Lewis SM and Tuddenham EGD, eds. *Postgraduate Haematology*. Oxford: Butterworth–Heinemann, 1999.

3.1 The full blood count and film

Principle

A busy haematology laboratory often processes as many as 1,000 blood samples a day. A written or computer-generated request is received with each blood that arrives and the sample is analysed by automated cell counters. These cell analysers pass a single cell suspension in front of a light/laser source and record number, refractile characteristics and size of cells on a photoelectric/photomultiplier tube. Abnormalities flagged by the machine may prompt further investigation such as a blood film, reticulocyte count or Coombs' test. The results are verified and a formal report is then issued. Quality assurance is an essential part of good laboratory practice.

The blood film remains the means by which an accurate morphological diagnosis is made, and this still involves humans looking down a microscope! See Further reading for good sources of information and photographic material.

Red blood cells

The mean corpuscular volume (MCV) is very useful as it helps to categorise anaemia. When multiplied by the red-cell count the haematocrit is computed by the analyser. It is important to be aware that the MCV is an average of many cells; a value in the normal range may therefore represent a single population of similarly normal-sized cells or two populations, one of microcytic and one of macrocytic cells (Fig. 39). The red-cell distribution width (RDW) is an estimate of the diversity of size of the red cells in the measured population. A raised RDW may suggest the measured population is dimorphic, and this should prompt examination of the blood film to assess the variation in size of the cells (for anisocytosis) and variation in shape (for poikilocytosis).

The mean corpuscular haemoglobin (MCH) can also be assessed and tends to rise and fall in line with the mean cell volume. The concentration of haemoglobin (Hb) within the cell is reported as the MCH concentration (MCHC). This rises if the reduction in cell volume is not matched by a reduction in cellular Hb, a phenomenon most commonly seen with spherocytosis. Acanthocytes are red cells with small membrane processes, seen in some cases of liver disease, hypo-β-lipoproteinaemia and hyposplenism (Fig. 40).

On entering the circulation, young red cells are larger and more basophilic due to their RNA content. On supravital staining these immature forms can be identified clearly and quantified accurately by their reticular appearance, leading them to be referred to as reticulocytes. In health, reticulocytes account for approximately 1% of circulating red cells, but this rises in response to acute blood loss, haemolysis or severe hypoxia. The variation in staining of red cells is referred to as polychromasia (Fig. 41).

Inclusions within the red cell are uncommon. Howell–Jolly bodies are remnants of DNA that have

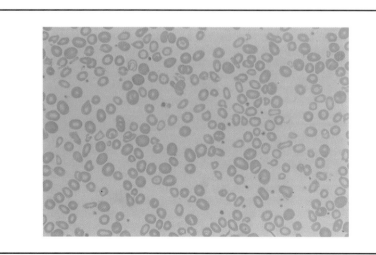

▲ **Fig. 39** Dimorphic blood film. This person with iron-deficiency anaemia has recently started iron replacement therapy. The larger normochromic reticulocytes are in marked contrast to the iron-deficient cells.

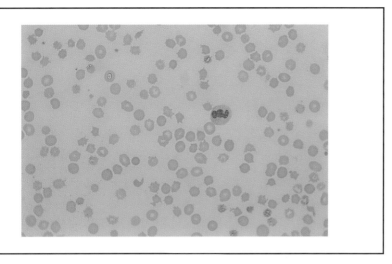

▲ **Fig. 40** Acanthocytes. This person with liver disease has marked acanthocytosis. There are also some fragments.

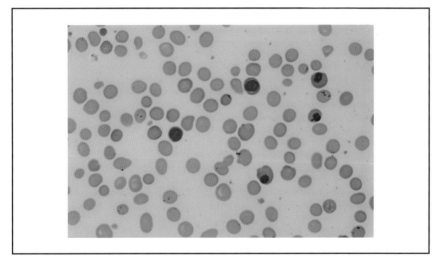

▲ **Fig. 41** Polychromasia. Variation in red/blue staining of erythrocytes due to reticulocytosis.

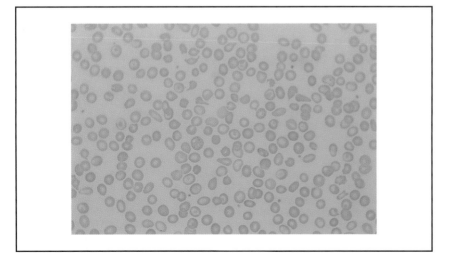

▲ **Fig. 42** Punctate basophilia. There are two cells showing basophilic stippling.

not been removed by the spleen. Basophilic stippling (Fig. 42) is due to ribosomal RNA aggregates within the cell; they do not stain with Perl's stain. Pappenheimer bodies are small collections of ferritin precipitating in mitochondria within the cell. They are smaller than Howell–Jolly bodies but bigger than basophilic stippling.

White blood cells

Granulocytes

Neutrophils Neutrophils have a dense nucleus that is divided into two to five lobes and cytoplasm that contains lysozyme granules. In the presence of infection, increased numbers of immature neutrophils enter the circulation. These cells often have fewer lobes in the nucleus and the picture is referred to as 'left-shifted'. In infection the neutrophil granules become more prominent, which is termed 'toxic granulation'.

At any one time approximately 50% of the neutrophils in the peripheral blood are attached to the vascular endothelium by cell adhesion molecules. This marginated pool of cells is not measured in a peripheral blood count. Steroids cause demargination and therefore a rise in the measured neutrophil count. Following their release into the circulation, granulocytes circulate for approximately 10 hours before entering the tissues, where they survive for a further 2–5 days before being destroyed.

Eosinophils Eosinophils are usually bilobed and contain larger, more densely staining granules than neutrophils.

Basophils Basophils contain histamine granules that often cover and obscure the nucleus. The surface is coated with IgE.

On entering the tissues they are referred to as mast cells.

Monocytes

Monocytes are larger than granulocytes. They have folded and convoluted nuclei with abundant vacuolated cytoplasm. Monocytes circulate for approximately 36 hours before entering the tissues to become macrophages, where they can survive for months.

Granulocytes and monocytes migrate to areas of inflammation where they phagocytose microorganisms, disrupted cells, and cells coated with immunoglobulin and complement. Granulocytes also release cytokines, recruiting and activating more cells to the inflammatory response.

Lymphocytes

Lymphocytes are subdivided into B and T cells. T cells originate in the bone marrow but spend some of their development in the thymus, while B cells originate and develop purely in the bone marrow. Lymphocyte survival in the peripheral blood ranges from a couple of weeks to many years. Lymphocytes are found in both the peripheral blood and the bone marrow; however, plasma cells (in health) are confined to the bone marrow. Both B and T lymphocytes look identical on the blood film, but staining with monoclonal antibodies easily distinguishes them on the basis of their antigens. (See *Scientific Background to Medicine 1*, Immunology and Immunosuppression.)

Platelets

Platelets are fragments of megakaryocyte cytoplasm that survive in the circulation for about 7 days without a nucleus. About one-quarter of the platelets

are sequestered in the spleen. Platelets have a central role in haemostasis. Platelet granules contain several substances, such as adenosine diphosphate, adenosine triphosphate, serotonin and factor VIII, that promote aggregation following injury.

> ### FURTHER READING
>
> *Scientific Background to Medicine 1*, Immunology and Immunosuppression.
>
> ----------------
>
> Bain B. *Blood Cells. A Practical Guide*, 3rd edn. Oxford: Blackwell Science, 2002.
>
> ----------------
>
> Bain B. *A Beginner's Guide to Blood Cells*, 2nd edn. Oxford: Blackwell Science, 2004.

3.2 Bone-marrow examination

Principle

To perform a marrow aspirate the needle is passed through the bone cortex close to the posterior iliac spine. The needle introducer is then removed and 1 mL of bone marrow is aspirated through the hollow needle. It is rare to perform sternal aspirates now.

For a trephine biopsy a larger hollow needle is pushed through the bone (pelvis only). On removal a core of bone comes out within the hollow needle.

Indications

Investigation of suspected bone-marrow pathology.

Practical details

Before the procedure

Explain carefully what you are about to do and why you feel it is necessary. Ask if the patient is

allergic to iodine. Written consent should be obtained.

Explain that despite local anaesthetic some patients feel discomfort for a short period of time as the needle passes into the bone. A nurse should provide practical help for you and moral support for the patient. Lie the patient on his or her left side as for a lumbar puncture.

Equipment

Dressing pack, sterile gloves, iodine, bone-marrow aspirate needle, trephine needle, one green needle, one orange needle, one 20-mL syringe, two 5-mL syringes, 5–10 mL 1% lidocaine, one size 15 blade, swabs, Elastoplast, one 5-mL ethylenediamine tetra-acetic acid (EDTA) bottle, one tissue-culture medium tube and one formalin pot.

Procedure

Performed with aseptic technique under local anaesthetic. Open up the dressing pack and put the syringes, blade, needles, sterile swabs, gloves and iodine on the towel. Give the EDTA bottle, tissue-culture medium and lidocaine to the nurse.

Feel for the patient's right posterior iliac crest, just above the sacroiliac joint. Assess how much soft tissue you will have to traverse to get to the bone.

Wash your hands, put on the gloves and clean the patient's back with iodine. Infiltrate the skin with the local anaesthetic, initially using an orange needle. Infiltrate deeper to the periostium with the green needle. Make a small cut in the skin with the blade.

Pass the aspirate needle through the soft tissues to the periosteum. Warn the patient that the following may cause some discomfort. Push through the bony cortex approximately 1 cm. Withdraw the central introducer and with a 20-mL syringe (it provides better suction) aspirate 4 mL. Put 2 mL in the EDTA tube and 2 mL in the tissue-culture medium. Ask the nurse to agitate the bottles gently and confirm the samples have not clotted. Withdraw the aspirate needle.

Take the trephine needle and push through the soft tissue to the periosteum. Once on the surface of the bone withdraw the central introducer and then push the hollow needle through the bone. When you are approximately 2–3 cm into the bone, confirm the size of the core by gently replacing the central introducer and seeing how far it sticks out of the end of the needle at the point resistance is felt. Remove the introducer, rotate the needle and then withdraw. Push the core into the formalin pot.

After procedure
Apply direct pressure until bleeding stops and apply the dressing. Help the patient into the supine position and allow to rest. Twenty minutes' rest and a cup of tea is usually enough for most patients to recover. If after 20 minutes there has been no further bleeding and the patient feels well enough, he or she can go home. Simple analgesia is recommended for any pain.

Label bottles and cards correctly.

Complications
Occasionally patients may bleed. Sometimes a suture is required.

Interpreting the bone-marrow aspirate

Staining techniques
The various stages of differentiation and maturation of haematopoiesis can be identified and counted by staining the marrow slides with

May–Grünwald–Giemsa stain and examining them under the light microscope. Morphological examination of bone marrow is at the very centre of the diagnosis of haematological disease and the monitoring of response to therapy. Assessment is made by counting the numbers of cells in the various stages of maturation (for which normal ranges have been established) and their morphological form, ie whether they look normal or abnormal.

A reduction in the numbers of a given cell type in the peripheral blood may be due to either reduced production in the bone marrow or reduced survival within the peripheral circulation. For example, normal numbers of megakaryocytes in the bone marrow of a patient with thrombocytopenia strongly suggests that there is reduced survival of platelets in the peripheral circulation. Conversely, the absence of megakaryocytes in the bone marrow of a patient with thrombocytopenia suggests the low platelet count has occurred because of reduced platelet production.

Immunohistochemical staining techniques can further clarify the lineage and degree of maturity of the cells in the marrow, eg myeloperoxidase and Sudan black stain myeloid cells, and periodic acid–Schiff stains lymphoid cells.

Cytometry
Cells of different lineages and stages of maturation can also be identified by the different cluster of differentiation (CD) molecules they express on their surface. This requires the use of a flow cytometer using a technique known as immunophenotyping. Antibodies to specific CD molecules are added to the cell population being examined. The antibodies are labelled with fluorescent markers that can be detected by the flow cytometer, thus enabling the number of cells with a given CD marker to be counted (Fig. 43).

Combinations of certain CD markers identify a given type of cell. For example the combination of CD13, CD33 and CD34 on a cell identify it to be a myeloid blast. If 90% of the cells in the bone marrow

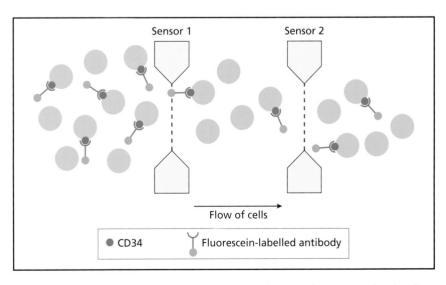

▲ **Fig. 43** Immunophenotyping. As all the cells pass through the first sensor they are counted. As the cells pass through the second sensor, only those bound to fluorescein-labelled antibodies are counted. The machine then gives a percentage of the population that expressed the CD marker.

label this way, then the diagnosis is acute myeloid leukaemia.

Cytogenetics

Following incubation and culture of marrow, chromosomes within the cells can be examined under the microscope. Large chromosomal deletions, breaks and translocations occur in many haematological malignancies. An example of this would be the translocation of genetic material between the long arms of chromosomes 9 and 22, the Philadelphia chromosome t(9;22). Cytogenetic results are important in leukaemia prognosis.

Interpreting the marrow trephine

The bone-marrow trephine is decalcified in acid over several days before sections can be made. These are then stained with haematoxylin and eosin plus other stains, eg immunohistochemical stains to mark certain cells in the trephine. The architecture of the bone and marrow are viewed at low power; also the amount of fat and haemic tissue present. Higher power reveals the types and pattern of cells present. The individual cell detail is not as clear as on an aspirate, but the trephine is vital in some conditions, eg myeloma, where an aspirate may miss a patch of the disease.

3.3 Clotting screen

Principle

A citrated blood sample cannot clot because the calcium required for the process is chelated by the citrate. Laboratory clotting tests take the patient's plasma and add calcium and stimuli to initiate clotting.

Indications

The clotting screen is performed in anybody with active bleeding of an unknown cause. Patients on warfarin will routinely have an INR check and do not need the other tests involved. Patients on unfractionated heparin will have an activated partial thromboplastin time (APTT) test without the other investigations.

Practical details

Prothrombin time

In this test, thromboplastin is used to stimulate clot formation. The thromboplastin is usually made from rabbit brain and is of a standardised activity. Although it is classically taught that the prothrombin time (PT) measures the extrinsic clotting system, factors II and V are also assessed (they form part of the final common pathway of the clotting cascade). The INR is a way of expressing the prothrombin ratio by adjusting for any local variations in the thromboplastin used in the test; this has made discrepancies in PT and warfarin control a lot less problematic.

Activated partial thromboplastin time

This test is also known as the kaolin cephalin clotting time. The test measures clotting time following the activation of contact factors, but without added tissue thromboplastin. The plasma is incubated with kaolin to activate the contact factors within the intrinsic systems. Standardised phospholipid is then added to generate clot. The APTT measures more heparin-sensitive clotting factors than the PT and is therefore more sensitive for monitoring heparin. In deficiencies of factors VIII and IX the APTT is prolonged, but when the patient's plasma is mixed with normal plasma this prolongation is corrected. Further analysis is required to assay the specific clotting deficiency.

Fibrinogen

Dilutions of the patient's plasma and normal plasma are made. Standardised thrombin solution is then used to cause these dilutions to clot. The patient's result is compared with the control plasma.

D-dimers

These are fibrin degradation products with a dimeric structure resulting from the way the fibrin has been cut by plasmin. They are non-specifically raised in a variety of situations such as disseminated intravascular coagulation, liver disease and malignancy. However, although the absence of D-dimers is a strong indication that there is no active thromboembolic activity, the presence of them is not an indication of thromboembolic disease as such. The test is based on agglutination of antibody-coated latex beads. The test can be automated or performed on a glass slide.

3.4 Coombs' test (direct antiglobulin test)

Principle

The Coombs' reagent consists of monoclonal antibodies that detect human antibody on the surface of red cells.

Indications

- Haemolytic anaemia (evidenced by polychromasia and reticulocytosis).

- Blood transfusion reaction.

Practical details

The patient's red cells are washed free of plasma. The red cells are then resuspended in the Coombs' reagent. Incubation enables the reagent to cross-link the antibodies on the red-cell surface. Free Coombs' reagent is then washed off. If the red cells are agglutinated due to cross-linking of the red cells, then a positive Coombs' test is recorded.

3.5 Erythrocyte sedimentation rate versus plasma viscosity

Principle
The acute-phase response results in acute-phase proteins rising and increasing the viscosity of blood. This is best seen by direct viscosity measurement. An indirect measurement of viscosity is observing the sedimentation of erythrocytes over 1 hour.

Indications

- Features of hyperviscosity syndrome.

- Any inflammatory or infective process.

- Temporal arteritis.

- Any cause for raised immunoglobulins, eg myeloma.

Practical details

Plasma viscosity
Plasma viscosity is measured by comparing the flow rate of plasma and distilled water under equal pressure and constant temperature through capillary tubes of equal diameter. The result is expressed as millipascals per second (mPa/s). The test can be performed on an ordinary blood count sample in ethylenediamine tetra-acetic acid. This is a highly reproducible measurement without the confounding problems of cellular constituents being present.

Erythrocyte sedimentation rate
The problem with the erythrocyte sedimentation rate (ESR) is that anaemia and polycythaemia can interfere with the test. A mixed blood sample is drawn up a capillary tube >100 mm in length, which is then stood vertically. At the end of 1 hour the fall of the red-cell level compared with the original plasma meniscus at the top of the tube records the ESR. This is very high in cases of myeloma and malignancy, where proteins surround red cells and reduce the repelling negative charges present on them. Conversely, in polycythaemia where there is an excess of erythrocytes, cellular repulsion is at a maximum and the sedimentation rate is very low (ie 1 mm/hour).

Performing an ESR or plasma viscosity test is no substitute for taking a history and examining patients for evidence of disease. Blindly performing an ESR or plasma viscosity test on the off-chance of detecting something (a screening test) is wasteful. On the other hand, the ESR or plasma viscosity are useful in monitoring an established disease process.

3.6 Therapeutic anticoagulation

Initiation of anticoagulation
Two types of anticoagulation are commonly used: low-molecular-weight (LMW) heparin and warfarin. Standard (unfractionated) heparin is only used in certain circumstances, eg perioperative management of patients with artificial heart valves. You should consult your local protocol or haematology team for advice on instances such as this.

LMW heparins are much easier to prescribe and administer than standard heparin, and have been shown to be equal to or better than standard heparin in a variety of conditions. Be clear whether you are prescribing for prophylactic or therapeutic anticoagulation levels. Check to see if the patient has ever had complications with heparin before.

Warfarin is usually commenced at the same time as heparin. Warfarin decreases factors II, VII, IX and X and protein C. There should be an overlap of 4–5 days so that heparin can protect against falling protein C causing thrombosis. Initiation of warfarin is a hazardous phase of therapy and a Fennerty-type regimen is preferred (Fig. 44). Be aware that older people may require lower doses. Transferring care to the haematology team or GP when discharging the patient needs careful attention to prevent disasters.

Warfarin (gradual introduction)
Occasionally, patients in chronic atrial fibrillation can be warfarinised more gradually, dispensing with the need for loading doses. This practice is quite common in DME and cardiology. Follow the procedure below.

1. Do not give heparin (of any sort).

2. Check INR.

3. Administer warfarin 2 mg po once daily.

4. Check INR in 1 week.

5. Increase warfarin to 3 or 4 mg once daily.

6. Check INR in 1 week.

7. Continue until INR reaches therapeutic target.

Warfarin dose - LOADING ONLY

Day	Date	INR Ordered	INR Result	Warfarin Dose (mg)	Doctor Prescribed	Nurse Signed	Nurse Signed
1st							
2nd							
3rd							
4th							

The Warfarin schedule is only valid for the first 4 days, then continue at Dr's discretion

After 4 days, loading is complete: please record warfarin dosing after 4th day on regular drug chart

Once a patient is established on warfarin, a daily INR is not needed.

▲ **Fig. 44** Warfarin loading regimen used at Addenbrooke's Hospital, Cambridge, UK. (Courtesy of Dr Trevor Baglin.)

Reversal of anticoagulation

Low-molecular-weight heparin
Old-fashioned unfractionated intravenous heparin has a half-life of 30 minutes, and discontinuation of the infusion was often sufficient if bleeding occurred. Difficulties arise when serious bleeding occurs on subcutaneous LMW heparin because the half-life is longer. Proceed as follows.

- Stop the heparin prescription.

- Administer protamine 50 mg by slow intravenous injection. Note that too much protamine is also an anticoagulant.

- Blood products will only be needed if there is torrential haemorrhage.

Warfarin
High INR and bleeding If a patient is bleeding and a clinical decision is made that the effect of warfarin should be reversed, proceed as follows immediately.

- Stop the warfarin prescription.

- Administer vitamin K 5–10 mg iv.

- Specific blood products will reverse the warfarin more quickly. Prothrombin complex concentrates are virally inactivated, provide good responses and are increasingly used in the UK. Fresh frozen plasma is not virally inactivated, requires larger volumes (up to 2 L) and is less used now.

High INR but not bleeding If the patient is not bleeding but INR is above the therapeutic range, then proceed as follows.

- INR up to 8: stop warfarin. Recheck the INR after 3 days. Do not recheck earlier unless clinically indicated because the value would not be expected to alter substantially in the first 24–48 hours.

- INR above 8: many would proceed as above. However, if there is a bleeding risk, give vitamin K 0.5 mg po or iv. Recheck in 24 hours.

- When the patient's INR is back in the therapeutic range, continue with warfarin at lower dose.

> Whenever a patient has ended up with a high INR, try to find out why anticoagulation 'went wrong'.
>
> - Did the patient get into a muddle with the pills?
> - Is there an interaction or change in health, eg liver failure?
> - How strong is the indication?

FURTHER READING

Scientific Background to Medicine 2, Clinical Pharmacology.

- - - - - - - - - - - - - - - -

British Committee for Standards in Haematology. Guidelines on oral anticoagulation. *Br. J. Haematol.* 1998; 101: 374–87.

4.1 Self-assesement questions

Question 1

Clinical scenario

A 56-year-old woman has a family history of haemochromatosis and is homozygous for the C282Y mutation. Her ferritin is 927 mg/L (normal range 15–150), haemoglobin 12.5 g/dL (normal range 11.5–16) and aspartate aminotransferase 87 U/L (normal range <40).

Question

Which is the best course of action?

Answers

A Weekly venesection until she is anaemic
B Intravenous desferrioxamine
C Venesect to drop her ferritin into the low-normal range
D Monitor the ferritin levels
E Test all first-degree relatives

Question 2

Clinical scenario

A 73-year-old woman has been anaemic for some months. Her daughter says she has 'gone off her feet' and is more confused. A bone-marrow examination is performed (see Fig. 45).

Question

What is the diagnosis?

Answers

A Acute myeloid leukaemia
B Chronic lymphatic leukaemia
C Disseminated cancer of the bone
D Myeloma
E Myelofibrosis

Question 3

Clinical scenario

A 25-year-old woman is at 30 weeks in her second pregnancy. She has been tired for 1 week and has had vague abdominal pain and dyspepsia for 2 days. Her haemoglobin is 9.2 g/dL (normal range 11.5–16), platelets 22×10^9/L (normal range 150–400), white cell count 14×10^9/L (normal range 4–11) with neutrophils 10.1×10^9/L (normal range 2–7), INR 1.8 (normal range <1.2), kaolin-cephalin clotting time 42 seconds (normal range 30–46) and fibrinogen 1.0 g/L (normal range 2–4).

Question

The two most likely causes of these results are:

Answers

A Thrombocytopenia of pregnancy
B Fatty liver of pregnancy
C Disseminated intravascular coagulation
D Acute myeloid leukaemia
E Idiopathic thrombocytopenia
F Thrombotic thrombocytopenic purpura
G Haemolysis, elevated liver enzymes and low platelets (HELLP) syndrome
H Placental abruption
I Amniotic embolus
J Haemolytic anaemia

Question 4

Clinical scenario

This 79-year-old man has swollen cervical glands and is receiving

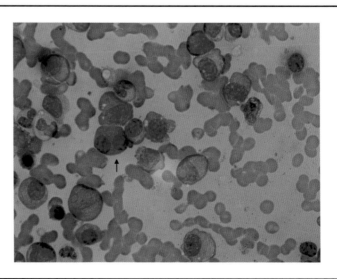

▲ **Fig. 45** Question 2.

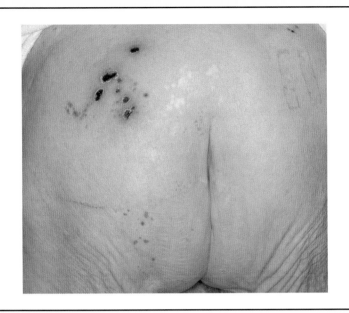

▲**Fig. 46** Question 4.

fludarabine for chronic lymphocytic leukaemia. His blood count shows haemoglobin of 11.5 g/dL (normal range 12–16.5), platelets 12 × 10⁹/L (normal range 150–400) and white cell count 23 × 10⁹/L (normal range 4–11). He has developed a rash on his bottom (see Fig. 46).

Question

What is the most likely cause of this rash?

Answers

A Purpura
B Leukaemic infiltrate
C Pressure sore
D Shingles
E Henloch–Schönlein purpura

Question 5

Clinical scenario

A 45-year-old man has had a sore throat for 2 weeks. He has been previously well. His FBC reveals haemoglobin 11.2 g/dL (normal range 11.5–16), white cell count 33 × 10⁹/L (normal range 4–11) and platelets 89 × 10⁹/L (normal range 150–400). Fig. 47 shows his blood film.

Question

What are the two most likely diagnoses?

Answers

A Infectious mononucleosis
B Myeloma
C Acute lymphoblastic leukaemia
D Acute myeloid leukaemia
E Chronic lymphatic leukaemia
F Chronic myeloid leukaemia
G Influenza
H Myelofibrosis

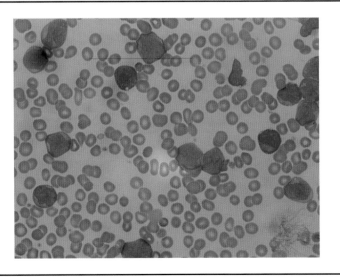

▲**Fig. 47** Question 5.

I Infective 'leukaemoid' reaction
J Idiopathic thrombocytopenic purpura

Question 6

Clinical scenario

A 77-year-old woman was admitted to the medicine for the elderly ward having become confused and fatigued. She had numbness in her feet. Her FBC showed haemoglobin 6.7 g/L (normal range 11.5–16), white cell count 4.3 × 10⁹/L (normal range 4–11) and platelets 76 × 10⁹/L (normal range 150–400). Her blood film is shown in Fig. 48.

Question

The most likely diagnosis is:

Answers

A Myelodysplasia
B Acute myeloid leukaemia
C Pernicious anaemia
D Iron deficiency
E Myeloma

Question 7

Clinical scenario

A 63-year-old man was admitted with fever and dyspnoea. He had been previously well. Investigation

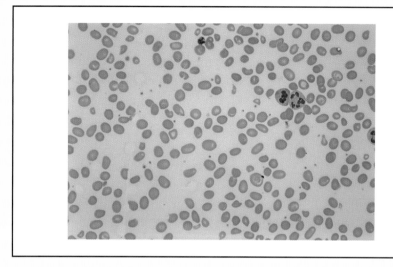

▲ **Fig. 48** Question 6.

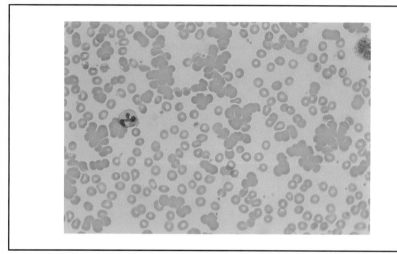

▲ **Fig. 49** Question 7.

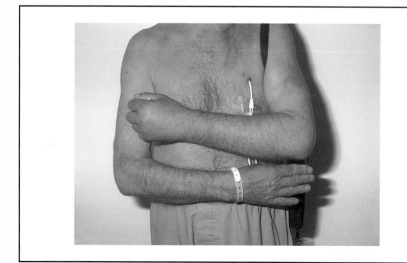

▲ **Fig. 50** Question 8.

revealed haemoglobin was 9.2 g/dL (normal range 12–16.5), mean corpuscular volume 113 fL (normal range 80–100), white cell count 14×10^9/L (normal range 4–11) and platelets 23×10^9/L (normal range 150–400). His blood film is shown in Fig. 49.

Question
What is the most likely diagnosis?

Answers
A Acute myeloid leukaemia
B Chronic myeloid leukaemia
C Myeloma
D Chronic lymphatic leukaemia
E *Mycoplasma* pneumonia

Question 8

Clinical scenario
A 65-year-old man has received chemotherapy for acute myeloblastic leukaemia through his Hickman line. His arm has become swollen (see Fig. 50).

Question
What investigation would you perform next to establish the diagnosis?

Answers
A D-dimer
B Chest radiograph
C Spiral CT scan of chest
D Venography of arm
E Blood cultures

Question 9

Clinical scenario
A 39-year-old factory worker was seen in clinic with a 4-week history of increasing fatigue and a swelling in his neck (Fig. 51). Investigation showed haemoglobin 8.7 g/dL (normal range 12–16.5), platelets 97×10^9/L (normal range 150–400), white cell count 12.2×10^9/L (normal range 4–11) with neutrophils 3.0×10^9/L (normal range 2–7), plasma

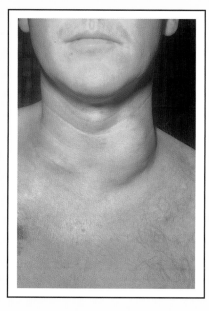

▲**Fig. 51** Question 9.

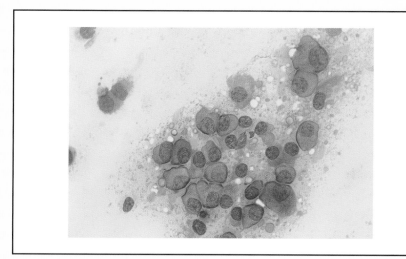

▲**Fig. 52** Question 9.

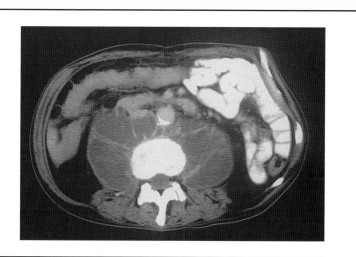

▲**Fig. 53** Question 10.

viscosity 2.9 mPa/s (normal range 1.50–1.72) and creatinine 256 μmol/L (normal range 70–110). A fine-needle aspiration was performed on the neck swelling and the stained material appears in Fig. 52.

Question
The most likely diagnosis is:

Answers
A Acute leukaemia
B Myeloma
C Lymphoma
D Epstein–Barr virus infection
E Tuberculosis

Question 10

Clinical scenario
A 73-year-old man had been treated for myeloma for 6 months, with treatment consisting of continuous intravenous chemotherapy (infused through a Hickman line) over a 4-day period every month. During this time he had several episodes of pyrexia, which were settled with broad-spectrum antibiotics. He was admitted with lower abdominal pain and difficulty walking. There were no hard neurological signs in his legs, but he had difficulty moving them due to pain. His haemoglobin was 9.1 g/dL (normal range 12–16.5), white cell count 15.9 × 10⁹/L (normal range 4–11) with neutrophils 7 × 10⁹/L (normal range 2–7) and platelets 110 × 10⁹/L (normal range 150–400). A CT scan of his abdomen was performed and a mid-lumbar section is illustrated in Fig. 53.

Question
The diagnosis is:

Answers
A Osteomyelitis of the spine
B Psoas abscess
C Aortic rupture
D Plasmacytoma surrounding the spine
E Hydronephrosis

Question 11

Clinical scenario
A 26-year-old woman was found to have mild anaemia in her first pregnancy, with a mean corpuscular volume of 71 fL (normal range 80–100). Her blood film appears in Fig. 54 and shows a clear abnormality.

Question
Which condition does this abnormality *not* usually appear in?

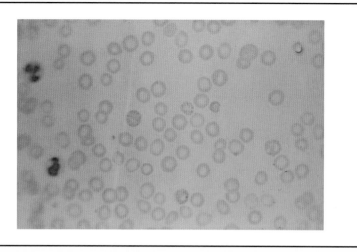

▲ **Fig. 54** Question 11.

Answers
A Thalassaemia
B B$_{12}$ deficiency
C Myelodysplasia
D Iron deficiency
E Lead poisoning

Question 12

Clinical scenario

A 40-year-old journalist has returned from Africa. Her FBC reveals haemoglobin 7.3 g/dL (normal range 11.5–16), platelets 50 × 10^9/L (normal range 150–400) and white cell count 9 × 10^9/L (normal range 4–11). The blood film is shown in Fig. 55.

Question

What is the diagnosis?

Answers

A Vivax malaria
B Falciparum malaria
C Trypanosomiasis
D Loa loa
E Schistosomiasis

Question 13

Clinical scenario

A 24-year-old woman presents with purpura (Fig. 56). Investigation reveals haemoglobin 12.1 g/dL (normal range 11.5–16), mean corpuscular volume 81 fL

(normal range 80–100), platelets 147 × 10^9/L (normal range 150–400), white cell count 10 × 10^9/L (normal range 4–11), prothrombin time 14 seconds (normal range 12–16), activated partial thromboplastin time 32 seconds (normal range 30–46) and fibrinogen 4.1 g/L (normal range 2–4). She had similar appearances of purpura on her other leg and on the flexor aspects of her forearms.

Question

What is the most likely diagnosis?

Answers

A Henoch–Schönlein purpura
B Acute leukaemia
C Factitious purpura
D Idiopathic thrombocytopenia
E Thrombotic thrombocytopenia

Question 14

Clinical scenario

A 70-year-old man was admitted for a prostatectomy. His haemoglobin was 12.9 g/dL (normal range 12–16.5), mean corpuscular volume 85 fL (normal range 80–100),

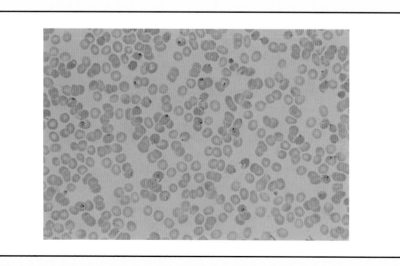

▲ **Fig. 55** Question 12.

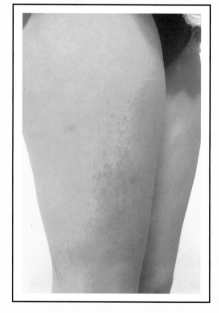

▲ **Fig. 56** Question 13.

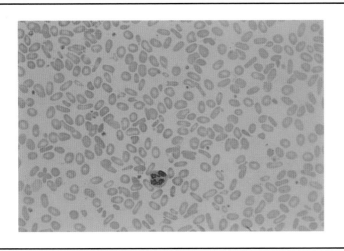

▲**Fig. 57** Question 14.

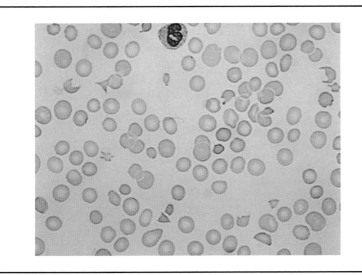

▲**Fig. 58** Question 15.

platelets 367×10^9/L (normal range 150–400) and white cell count 9×10^9/L (normal range 4–11). The blood film is shown in Fig. 57.

Question
What is the diagnosis from the blood film?

Answers
A Hereditary spherocytosis
B Hereditary elliptocytosis
C Folate deficiency
D Iron deficiency
E Coombs' positive haemolysis

Question 15

Clinical scenario
A 31-year-old woman was admitted to the Emergency Department having been found unconscious at home. Her relatives said that she had recently had 'flu-like symptoms and been confused. She had a fever of 38.7°C. Laboratory investigations revealed haemoglobin 9.7 g/dL (normal range 11.5–16), platelets 16×10^9/L (normal range 150–400), white cell count 15×10^9/L (normal range 4–11) with neutrophils 11×10^9/L (normal range 2–7),

prothrombin time 14 seconds (normal range 12–16), activated partial thromboplastin time 37 seconds (normal range 30–46) and fibrinogen 4.1 g/L (normal range 2–4). The blood film is shown in Fig. 58.

Question
What is the diagnosis?

Answers
A Idiopathic thrombocytopenia
B Acute myeloid leukaemia
C Thrombotic thrombocytopenic purpura
D Viral marrow suppression
E Disseminated intravascular coagulation

Question 16

Clinical scenario
A 72-year-old man is admitted for hernia repair. Investigation reveals haemoglobin 14.2 g/dL (normal range 12–16.5), white cell count 25×10^9/L (normal range 4–11) and platelets 374×10^9/L (normal range 150–400). His blood film is shown in Fig. 59.

Question
What is the diagnosis?

Answers
A Acute myeloid leukaemia
B Chronic myeloid leukaemia
C Chronic lymphatic leukaemia
D Myeloma
E Non-Hodgkin's lymphoma

Question 17

Clinical scenario
A 64-year-old woman has non-Hodgkin's lymphoma, for which she has received chemotherapy, and has also had multiple blood transfusions for anaemia. She is also receiving tamoxifen for breast cancer. She has become sensitive to sunlight and developed a rash on her hands (Fig. 60).

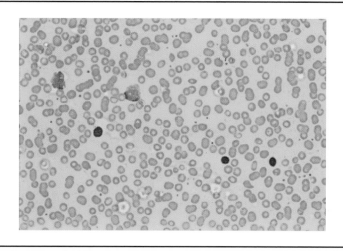

▲**Fig. 59** Question 16.

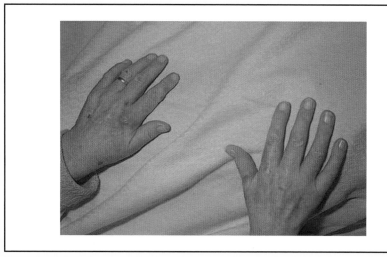

▲**Fig. 60** Question 17.

Question

What is the diagnosis?

Answers

A Mycosis fungoides
B Drug reaction
C Metastatic cancer
D Porphyria cutanea tarda
E Psoriasis

Question 18

Clinical scenario

A 50-year-old man has isolated lymphocytosis on his FBC (25 × 10^9/L; normal range 1–3 × 10^9/L). Immunophenotyping is performed and confirms a diagnosis of chronic lymphatic leukaemia (CLL). He is well and his examination is normal.

Question

Which are the two most accurate statements?

Answers

A It is important to perform a bone-marrow aspirate and trephine
B This is stage A disease
C Due to the high white cell count, this is stage B disease
D Treatment should be initiated as soon as he is investigated fully
E His blood count should be monitored weekly
F CLL cannot be confirmed on immunophenotyping
G There is no indication to treat at this stage
H He should have a CT of his chest and abdomen
I The median survival in such patients is 3 years
J Women have a worse prognosis than men

Question 19

Clinical scenario

A 60-year-old man with a high-grade lymphoma has commenced on chemotherapy. Blood tests are taken 2 hours after commencing and you are asked to review these to exclude tumour lysis syndrome.

Question

Which result would *not* suggest the development of tumour lysis syndrome?

Answers

A Hyperuricaemia
B Hypocalcaemia
C Hyperkalaemia
D Hypophosphataemia
E Hyperphosphataemia

Question 20

Clinical scenario

A 72-year-old man, who is known to have myeloma, is brought to the Emergency Department because he is generally 'unwell'.

Question

Which of the following is *not* a usual feature of hypercalcaemia?

Answers

A Impaired renal function
B Constipation
C Confusion
D Dehydration
E Diarrhoea

Question 21

Clinical scenario

A 57-year-old man is found to have polycythaemia vera, with a haemoglobin of 20 g/dL (normal range 12–16.5) and a haematocrit of 0.48 (normal range 0.38–0.50). He is asymptomatic.

Question

Which is the single best treatment option?

Answers

A Observation alone
B Hydroxycarbamide oral therapy
C Venesection
D Aspirin
E Subcutaneous interferon injections

Question 22

Clinical scenario

A 38-year-old man has had two deep venous thromboses in the absence of any recognised precipitating events. You ask the haematology laboratory to screen for causes of a thrombophilic state.

Question

Which one of the following conditions will they *not* look for?

Answers

A Protein C deficiency
B Protein S deficiency
C Antithrombin III deficiency
D Factor VIII deficiency
E Lupus anticoagulant

Question 23

Clinical scenario

A 55-year-old woman presents with tiredness. She had been given a diagnosis of rheumatoid arthritis at the age of 35 years, but has been fit and well for many years, without any joint

problems. Her FBC is as follows: haemoglobin 9.3 g/dL (normal range 11.5–16), mean corpuscular volume 85 fL (normal range 80–100), mean corpuscular haemoglobin 28 pg (normal range 27–32), white blood cell count normal and platelet count normal.

Question

Which one of the following statements is correct?

Answers

A Sideroblastic anaemia is a likely diagnosis
B Felty's syndrome is a likely diagnosis
C Acute blood loss is likely
D Anaemia of chronic disorders is the most likely diagnosis
E A normal ferritin excludes iron deficiency as a cause of her anaemia

Question 24

Clinical scenario

A tall, thin 18-year-old man with sickle cell disease presents to the Emergency Department with a 36-hour history of cough, fever, breathlessness and pleuritic chest pain.

Question

The most likely diagnosis is:

Answers

A Pulmonary embolism
B Myocardial infarction
C Pneumococcal pneumonia
D Pneumothorax
E Acute chest syndrome

Question 25

Clinical scenario

A 49-year-old man presents with malaena of 1 week's duration. On investigation his platelet count is found to be elevated.

Question

Which of the following is the most likely cause of the thrombocytosis?

Answers

A Blood loss
B Chronic myeloid leukaemia
C Infection
D Essential thrombocytopenia
E Inflammatory bowel disease

Question 26

Clinical scenario

A previously well 34-year-old woman (gravida II, para II) who is 24 weeks' pregnant presents with a low platelet count of 84×10^9/L (normal range 150–400). She is asymptomatic and experienced similar problems in her last pregnancy, following which she gave birth to a normal healthy boy. She denies any previous medical history or family history of a blood disorder.

Question

Which one of the following statements is true?

Answers

A A bone-marrow aspirate will confirm chronic idiopathic thrombocytopenic purpura
B A Caesarean section should be the preferred delivery method
C The baby has a 10% risk of intracranial bleed
D No investigations are required and platelets should normalise post partum
E Platelet-associated immunoglobulins will be high

Question 27

Clinical scenario

A 24-year-old woman presents to the Emergency Department with a history of a painless swelling in her neck. She is otherwise well.

Question

What is the most likely diagnosis?

Answers

A Acute leukaemia

B Infectious mononucleosis

C Non-Hodgkin's lymphoma

D HIV seroconversion illness

E Hodgkin's disease

Question 28

Clinical scenario

A 16-year-old boy has been diagnosed with acute lymphoblastic leukaemia. His white cell count is 10×10^9/L (normal range 4–11), platelet count 100×10^9/L (normal range 150–400) and haemoglobin 14 g/dL (normal range 12–16.5) at diagnosis.

Question

Which one of these factors is associated with a better outcome?

Answers

A His age

B His gender

C His haemoglobin

D His white cell count

E His platelet count

Question 29

Clinical scenario

A 68-year-old woman has had chronic lymphatic leukaemia for 4 years without marrow failure or any need for medication. At follow-up, her haemoglobin has dropped to 7.8 g/dL (normal range 11.5–16), with other tests showing mean corpuscular volume 122 fL (normal range 80–100), platelets 211×10^9/L (normal range 150–400), lymphocytes 43×10^9/L (normal range 1–3) and reticulocyte count 12% (normal range 0.5–2).

Question

Which test is most likely to give you the correct diagnosis?

Answers

A Serum B_{12} level

B Coombs' test

C Marrow aspirate

D Red-cell folate level

E Serum ferritin level

Question 30

Clinical scenario

A 71-year-old man was treated with fludarabine for Waldenström's macroglobulinaemia. His IgM band fell from 36 g/L to a plateau of 5 g/L and he was stable for 5 years before suddenly presenting with haemoglobin (Hb) 6.7 g/dL (normal range 12–16.5), platelets 79×10^9/L (normal range 150–400), creatinine 130 µmol/L (normal range 70–110) and plasma viscosity 2.5 mPa/s (normal range 1.5–1.75). During blood transfusion he developed a tachycardia and chest pain, and was transferred to the Coronary Care Unit. The next day results showed Hb 7 g/dL, a positive Coombs' test and creatinine 377 µmol/L.

Question

What is the most likely diagnosis?

Answers

A Renal failure due to hyperviscosity

B Pulmonary embolism with circulatory failure

C Fludarabine-induced haemolysis

D Relapse of Waldenström's disease with haemolytic transfusion reaction

E Transformation to acute leukaemia

Question 31

Clinical scenario

A 78-year-old woman presents with a 3-month history of worsening back pain. Her FBC reveals haemoglobin 10.2 g/dL (normal range 11.5–16) and

there are rouleaux on her blood film. She has moderately impaired renal function. You suspect myeloma, but dipstick testing of her urine is negative for protein and serum electrophoresis fails to demonstrate a monoclonal band.

Question

Which one of the following statements is true?

Answers

A She does not have myeloma

B Polymyalgia rheumatica is the most likely diagnosis

C She may have myeloma that produces only free light chains

D Bone pain is an unusual presentation of myeloma

E Negative protein on dipstick testing of urine excludes the presence of Bence Jones protein

Question 32

Clinical scenario

A 26-year-old woman attends the anticoagulation clinic for monitoring of her warfarin, which she is taking because of recurrent pulmonary embolism. She is quite well with no evidence of bleeding or increased bruising. She is on no other medication. Unexpectedly her INR is 7.5.

Question

What is the correct course of action?

Answers

A Administer 10 mg of vitamin K intravenously

B Administer 10 mg of vitamin K orally

C Admit her for fresh frozen plasma infusion

D Stop warfarin and recheck her INR in 3 days

E Admit her overnight for observation

4.2 Self-assessment answers

Answer to Question 1

C

Venesection, which may need to be performed every 2–4 weeks, should be used to drop the ferritin level into the low-normal range. Do not be too vigorous and make the patient anaemic. First-degree relatives are usually tested to complete the family investigations.

Answer to Question 2

D

This aspirate shows plasma cells with eccentrically placed nuclei. One cell indicated by the arrow on Fig. 45 is binucleate. Note also the clumping of red cells on the film, which is typical of myeloma.

Answer to Question 3

C and G

The thrombocytopenia of pregnancy is normally around 80×10^9/L. This thrombocytopenia is much lower, with prolonged clotting tests indicating disseminated intravascular coagulation or HELLP syndrome.

Answer to Question 4

D

Shingles is a common problem in patients with lymphoid malignancy and/or receiving chemotherapy.

Answer to Question 5

C and D

These leucocytes are large and have nucleoli suggesting acute leukaemia. It is difficult to tell which type from this photograph.

Answer to Question 6

C

Note the macrocytosis and poikilocytosis typical of pernicious anaemia, and also that one of the neutrophils is hyperlobulated. A slightly low platelet count is not uncommon in pernicious anaemia.

Answer to Question 7

E

Note the clumping of red cells on the film caused by cold agglutinins, which are a feature of *Mycoplasma* pneumonia.

Answer to Question 8

D

Indwelling lines are a nidus for both thrombosis and infection. In this case thrombosis is the obvious diagnosis and a venogram is required to confirm this. The line should be removed and he may require anticoagulation.

Answer to Question 9

B

This poor man had myeloma with a soft tissue plasmacytoma in the neck.

Answer to Question 10

B

This man had suffered several episodes of methicillin-resistant *Staphylococcus aureus* sepsis related to his Hickman line, and this organism produced the florid psoas abscesses shown. These were successfully drained and antibiotics were administered.

Answer to Question 11

D

Punctate basophilia (seen as small blue dots in some red cells) occurs in all these conditions except iron deficiency.

Answer to Question 12

B

The intracellular parasites are too small for vivax and there are no gametocytes, hence this is falciparum malaria.

Answer to Question 13

C

The distribution on the forearms and thighs and the results of the normal investigations are typical of factitious purpura, an uncommon condition of uncertain (presumed psychological) aetiology.

Answer to Question 14

B

The erythrocytes are predominantly elliptical rather than spherical. Hereditary elliptocytosis is often asymptomatic and may be discovered in the elderly.

Answer to Question 15

C

Note the fragmented erythrocytes. The clinical picture with normal clotting and thrombocytopenia make this thrombotic thrombocytopenic purpura.

Answer to Question 16

C

There is an increase in lymphocytes. Occasional smear cells are not specific for chronic lymphatic leukaemia.

Answer to Question 17

D

Porphyria cutanea tarda has developed due to iron overload

following transfusion and tamoxifen. Venesection improved the rash. Chloroquine is an alternative treatment.

Answer to Question 18

B and G
Early-stage chronic lymphatic leukaemia shows no marrow failure and requires observation only. CT scanning is not essential, but some haematologists think that a bone marrow may help with staging.

Answer to Question 19

D
Tumour lysis causes hyperphosphataemia due to cell death. Patients with bulky chemosensitive tumours are particularly liable to tumour lysis syndrome, which can be prevented in most cases by establishing a saline diuresis and giving allopurinol and/or rasburicase.

Answer to Question 20

E
Hypercalcaemia causes constipation rather than diarrhoea. Management is by inducing a saline diuresis and giving intravenous bisphosphonate, with careful monitoring of renal function.

Answer to Question 21

C
Venesection should aim to get the haematocrit below 0.45 in primary polycythaemia.

Answer to Question 22

D
Haemostasis and thrombosis are finely regulated processes that depend on the level and configuration of prothrombotic proteins and natural anticoagulants. In up to 50% of cases of venous thrombosis it is possible to demonstrate an inherited abnormality of coagulation. The inherited thrombophilias are:

• activated protein C resistance due to an abnormal factor V, ie factor V Leiden;

• protein C deficiency;

• protein S deficiency;

• antithrombin III deficiency.

Inherited hyperhomocysteinaemia is also associated with arterial and venous thrombosis.

The lupus anticoagulant is an acquired anticoagulant that prolongs phospholipid-dependent tests *in vitro* but predisposes to thrombosis in patients.

Factor VIII deficiency is an X-linked predisposition to bleeding called haemophilia A.

Answer to Question 23

D
Ferritin is an acute-phase reactant, so a normal value does not exclude iron-deficiency anaemia. A low ferritin would be a useful result, strongly supporting the diagnosis of iron deficiency.

Anaemia of chronic disorders is a feature of rheumatoid arthritis, most marked in the acute phase of the illness. Felty's syndrome is very uncommon.

The differential diagnosis of her anaemia is wide. Appropriate tests would include B_{12}, folate, iron, total iron-binding capacity and ferritin, inflammatory markers (C-reactive protein), thyroid function, rheumatoid factor, immunoglobulins (could this be myeloma?), liver, renal and bone function tests, and a CXR.

Answer to Question 24

E
This is a typical presentation of acute chest syndrome, one of the commonest causes of death in adults with sickle cell disease. Pulmonary embolism and pneumonia cannot be excluded, but are less likely diagnoses.

Key aspects of management include the following.

• Give high-flow oxygen via a reservoir bag.

• Rapid intravenous infusion of 1 L of 0.9% saline.

• Start intravenous antibiotics, eg ampicillin 500 mg qds.

• Intravenous opioid for pain, eg diamorphine 5 mg, with antiemetic.

• Prophylaxis against venous thromboembolism, eg enoxaparin 20 mg sc od.

• Call for specialist advice if the patient deteriorates or does not improve rapidly.

• Exchange transfusion may be indicated if the patient becomes hypoxic.

Answer to Question 25

A
Thrombocytosis is much more commonly a secondary phenomenon than part of a primary malignant process. Blood loss results in increased marrow activity and hence a raised platelet count. Treatment of the underlying cause will serve to bring the platelet count down gradually.

Answer to Question 26

D
The diagnosis is gestational thrombocytopenia, which is

seen in 1–4% of pregnancies and suggested in this case by the history of a similar picture in a previous pregnancy. Idiopathic thrombocytopenic purpura and HELLP syndrome are unlikely in someone who is asymptomatic, particularly in the absence of petechiae/purpura. HIV infection can cause thrombocytopenia, but the absence of risk factors makes it unlikely here. The baby should have its platelet count checked at birth and 1 week later.

Answer to Question 27

E

Hodgkin's disease and non-Hodgkin's lymphoma can both present with isolated cervical lymphadenopathy, but this is more commonly seen in Hodgkin's disease in this age group. The node(s) are classically painless and non-tender. The patient is often otherwise well, but may have 'B' symptoms (weight loss, fevers and night sweats).

Answer to Question 28

D

The good prognostic features in childhood acute lymphoblastic leukaemia include age between 1 and 10 years, female gender, low white cell count ($<50 \times 10^9$/L), no evidence of central nervous system disease or particular chromosomal abnormalities, and complete response to early chemotherapy. Haemoglobin concentration and platelet count do not significantly influence prognosis.

Answer to Question 29

B

The clue is the raised reticulocyte count, which causes the raised mean corpuscular volume. This is due to Coombs'-positive haemolysis, seen in 10% of cases of chronic lymphatic leukaemia (CLL). Although B_{12}, folate and iron deficiency can occur in CLL, they do not raise the reticulocyte count. A marrow aspirate would not give the answer here.

Answer to Question 30

D

Most patients with Waldenström's macroglobulinaemia or myeloma relapse, with a rise in their paraprotein. When measured, this man's IgM had risen to 29 g/L and his anaemia was due to active disease. He developed chest pain due to an acute haemolytic transfusion reaction that caused the Coombs' test to become positive. This was due to a Jka red cell antibody that had not previously been detected.

The plasma viscosity is only slightly raised and is unlikely to produce renal failure at this level. Fludarabine can cause Coombs'-positive haemolysis, but not usually 5 years after treatment. There is no evidence for acute myeloid leukaemia.

Answer to Question 31

C

Bone pain is a common presenting feature of multiple myeloma. In 80% of patients with myeloma there is a paraprotein in the serum, usually of the IgG or IgA class. However, in 20% of patients only free light chains are produced (Bence Jones-only myeloma). Stick tests of the urine do not detect Bence Jones proteins.

Answer to Question 32

D

The British Committee for Standards in Haematology has published guidelines for the reversal of warfarin effect. A patient who is not bleeding, who has no additional risk factors for bleeding (eg older age, peptic ulceration) and has an INR of less than 8 may stop their warfarin and wait for the level to come down without intervention.

ONCOLOGY

Authors:

MD Bower, CS Brock, GG Dark and KM Fife

Editor:

MD Bower

Editor-in-Chief:

JD Firth

ONCOLOGY: SECTION 1
PACES STATIONS AND ACUTE SCENARIOS

1.1 History taking

1.1.1 A dark spot

> **Letter of referral to diabetic outpatient clinic**
>
> Dear Doctor,
>
> **Mrs Sarah Patterson, aged 35 years**
>
> This woman with well-controlled insulin-dependent diabetes mellitus is well known to your clinic. She has noticed a dark spot on her forearm that she thinks may have appeared over the last few months, as she cannot recall it being there previously. I would be grateful for your advice: is it a complication of her diabetes? Does anything need to be done about it?
>
> Yours sincerely,

Introduction

Black spots on the skin are not a complication of diabetes, and in this scenario the important issue is to establish the nature of the lesion and if it could be a malignant melanoma.

History of the presenting problem

What are the features of the lesion?

In routine clinical practice you would clearly examine the spot whilst talking to the patient, but this is not possible in the history-taking station of a PACES examination. However, some of the most important diagnostic information comes from the patient's history. Important features that should alert suspicion include the following.

- How long has it been there? A recent lesion is more likely to be significant than one that has been there for a long time.

- Has it bled? Bleeding is a sinister feature.

- *Asymmetry* (irregular shape).

- *Border* (not smooth edge).

- *Colour* (uneven, variegated or changing). Has its colour changed?

- *Diameter* (larger than 6 mm in diameter or growing). Is it getting bigger?

If there was a pre-existing mole, then aside from checking the above, ask if it is itching or painful? These changes may indicate malignant change.

Other relevant history

The following features increase the risk of melanoma.

- Light complexion; blond or red hair; and multiple pigmented skin lesions, including freckles and moles.

- Intermittent sun exposure and severe sunburns. This is particularly the case if it occurs during childhood or because of poor tanning and the use of sun beds.

TABLE 1 SKIN TYPES, WITH TYPE 1 BEING THE MOST AND TYPE 6 THE LEAST SUSCEPTIBLE TO SKIN MALIGNANCY

Skin type	Description
1	White skin, never tans and always burns
2	White skin, burns initially and tans with difficulty
3	White skin, tans easily and burns rarely
4	White skin, never burns and always tans (Mediterranean type)
5	Brown skin, eg natives of the Indian subcontinent
6	Black Afro-Caribbean skin

- A family history of melanoma: this is present in up to 10% of cases.

- A past medical history of melanoma: this increases the risk of a second primary melanoma 10-fold.

The risk of skin malignancy is related to skin type (see Table 1).

Directly explore the patient's concerns about the lesion. Ask if there is any particular reason why she is worried about it or if she knows what it might be due to. Many patients will not volunteer such information unless prompted to do so (both in routine clinical practice and in PACES examinations), and eliciting this information is vital to understanding and managing the patient.

General issues

It will also be appropriate to ask about the patient's general health and in particular the control of her diabetes: 'How have things been going with the diabetes?' Blood sugar can sometimes be difficult to control when there are problems or anxieties of any sort. Intercurrent illness is obviously a well-known precipitant of poor diabetic control, but anxiety and stress, such as might be caused in this case by the appearance of a potentially malignant spot, can do the same. Patients will often neglect the routine monitoring and treatment

of their diabetes if their attention is directed elsewhere, and may not volunteer this information unless questioned in a sympathetic manner about the matter.

Plan for investigation and management

Any suspicious skin lesion requires urgent referral to skin cancer services (in the UK this is in accordance with the National Cancer Plan 2-week wait guidelines). Excision biopsy under local anaesthetic is required to confirm the diagnosis and is usually followed by radiological investigations to establish the stage of the melanoma. (For further advice on management, see Section 2.7; *Dermatology*, Sections 2.20, 2.21 and 2,22. See also http://www.dh.gov.uk/PolicyAndGuidance/HealthAndSocialCareTopics/Cancer.)

Routine monitoring of the patient's diabetes will be required, in particular a review of her blood glucose recordings and HbA_{1c} level. If she were finding it difficult to maintain good control of these, then referral to the specialist diabetic nurse for advice and help would be sensible. It is important that other aspects of her diabetic management are not neglected because all attention is directed to her skin lesion, eg the checking of her eyes and feet, and awareness and treatment of other cardiovascular risk factors should continue as usual.

1.2 Clinical examination

1.2.1 A lump in the neck

Instruction

This 55-year-old woman has had a painless lump in her neck for 3 months. Please examine her neck.

General features

Neck lumps are most likely to be due to lymphadenopathy or related to the thyroid gland. If lymphadenopathy has been present for 3 months, then this suggests a malignant rather than infective cause. In such a case look for signs of weight loss and/or cachexia, as well as for pallor and jaundice.

Is there nicotine staining of the patient's hands (smoking is associated with a range of malignancies) and are the fingers clubbed?

Look in particular for signs of hyperthyroidism or hypothyroidism, and also for eye signs of Graves' disease (see *Endocrinology*, Sections 1.2.5 and 2.3.2).

Note whether the patient is breathless at rest (if so, consider smoking-related lung disease) and ask them: 'Open your mouth and take a deep breath in and out as fast as you can.' This will elicit stridor if any mass in the neck is causing tracheal compression.

Look for other scars, in particular from previous breast or lung surgery.

Neck examination

Observe the position of the lump and any other lumps and scars. Ask the patient to swallow, giving her a sip of water from the cup that is likely to be available at the side of

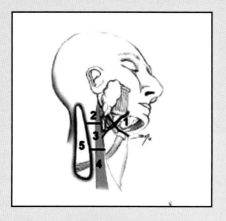

▲ **Fig. 1** Lymph node groups of the neck. Level 1, submental/submandibular nodes; levels 2–4, upper, mid and lower deep cervical nodes; level 5, posterior cervical nodes.

TABLE 2 COMMON MALIGNANT CAUSES OF AN ENLARGED LYMPH NODE IN THE NECK	
Orign of tumour	**Pathological diagnosis**
Primary tumour	Head and neck squamous cancer Thyroid tumour Parathyroid tumour Salivary gland tumour
Lymphoid malignancy	Hodgkin's disease Non-Hodgkin's lymphoma
Metastatic cancer	Lung cancer Oesophageal cancer Breast cancer Melanoma

the chair/bed. Does this make the lump move? Inspect the patient's oral cavity.

Examine the patient from behind and feel the lymph node areas systematically, starting with the occipital and preauricular. Then proceed to the upper, mid and lower deep cervical nodes and the submandibular, submental and supraclavicular regions (levels 1–5, Fig. 1). Examine any enlarged node for fixity, consistency and size (this must be measured accurately).

For discussion of the approach to a lump in the thyroid gland, see *Endocrinology*, Section 1.2.7.

Further discussion
In the instructions for the case, you have been told that the lump has been present for 3 months. This makes an infective cause of lymphadenopathy extremely unlikely, except for tuberculosis in some parts of the world, and discussion will focus on the various malignant causes (Table 2).

Supraclavicular fossa or lower cervical nodes may be the result of a thoracic malignancy (lung or oesophagus) or breast cancer. Squamous carcinoma in neck nodes may be secondary to a primary site

in the head and neck, which can include the oral cavity, pharynx, larynx, sinuses and salivary glands. Thyroid carcinoma is a possibility that is histologically distinctive (papillary, follicular, medullary or anaplastic).

Left supraclavicular fossa nodes (part of level 5) can arise from infradiaphragmatic carcinomas such as stomach, bowel, pancreas, endometrium or cervix via drainage into the thoracic duct.

After a full clinical examination, particularly the lungs and the breasts, the first investigations required to establish the diagnosis will be an FBC (examine any features that suggest lymphoma), a CXR (to check for lung cancer and bone secondaries) and obtaining tissue from the lymph node, either by a needle biopsy performed radiologically under ultrasound guidance or an open surgical biopsy.

Further investigations will depend on the findings of these tests. If histology reveals a squamous carcinoma, then unless there is a suspicious lesion on the CXR the patient should have endoscopy of the upper aerodigestive tract, with blind biopsies of the nasopharynx if no primary is seen. In the case

of an adenocarcinoma, upper gastrointestinal endoscopy and mammography may be required.

Remember that some cancers are treatable with chemotherapy, even if the primary cannot be found:

- breast cancer;
- ovarian cancer;
- lymphoma;
- testicular tumours;
- neuroendocrine cancers;
- squamous cell carcinoma of the head and neck.

1.3 Communication skills and ethics

1.3.1 Am I at risk of cancer?

Scenario

Role: you are the medical junior doctor on duty on the oncology ward

Mr Ian Booth, the son of a 56-year-old woman with advanced colon cancer who is an inpatient under your care, asks whether he and his children are at risk of colon cancer. You have checked his mother carefully, including taking a full family history. Her brother died of colorectal cancer aged 45 years and her older sister has endometrial cancer. Their father also died of colon cancer aged 52 years.

At the multidisciplinary team meeting, it has been noted that the occurrence of cancers in different members of this family raises the possibility of hereditary non-polyposis colon cancer (HNPCC), and there was a presentation on the topic. The mode of inheritance for HNPCC is autosomal dominant. A set of criteria, referred to as the 'Amsterdam Criteria', has been established to assist in the clinical diagnosis of HNPCC:

1. three or more members of a family have histologically confirmed colorectal cancer, one of whom is the first-degree relative of the other two;

2. colorectal cancer extends over two or more generations;

3. colon cancer in one member of the family has been diagnosed before the age of 50 years;

4. exclusion of familial adenomatous polyposis.

The risk of colorectal cancer in HNPCC patients is about 70% by the age of 70 years compared with 2% in the general population.

Your task: the son asks you about the risk of him and his children developing cancer and what to do about it.

Key issues to explore

This scenario raises a number of issues, including:

- a member of the public asking for advice without appropriate referral;

- consent to release information about one member of the family to another;

- implications of genetic testing not confined to an index case;

- dealing with an anxious relative.

Key points to establish

You are not allowed to release medical details about one person to another without consent. You are not responsible for his or his children's medical care, and if any medical testing is necessary he should be advised to seek this via his GP. Nonetheless, it would be appropriate and caring to answer his enquiries to help guide him, and it may be appropriate to obtain blood from his mother (your patient) for genetic testing with her consent.

Appropriate responses to likely questions

Son: am I at risk of colon cancer?

Doctor: several cases of cancer within a family can occur by chance since one in three people in the UK will develop cancer. However, the young age of your uncle (45 years) and the pattern of cancers in your family are both suspicious, indicating that some cancers might run in your family.

Son: how high is the risk?

Doctor: I cannot be sure at the moment, but I am concerned that your family may be affected by a condition called – I'm afraid it's a bit of mouthful – hereditary non-polyposis colorectal cancer, that's HNPCC for short. I'll write it down for you. This increases the risk

of colon and some other forms of cancer. If your mother has this form of cancer – and I don't know for certain if she does, but she might – then she has a one in two chance of passing this risk on to you.

Son: how can I know if our family is affected by HNPCC?

Doctor: there are a number of criteria that are used to define families with HNPCC and your family's history does suggest that you may have a higher risk of cancer. Genetic testing of blood samples from as many members of your family as possible may help to work out whether you and your children have inherited this increased risk. This service can be provided, with consent and explanation, by a cancer genetics clinical service. Your GP can refer you to the doctors who run this service and will know how to do this.

Son: if my mother needs a blood test, how can we ask her now?

Doctor: you first need to see a cancer geneticist to find out if they recommend that a blood sample from your mother would be useful in establishing the risk for you and your children. If so, we can discuss with your mother the reasons for asking for a blood sample to help find out if other family members are at risk, explaining that it will not be of help in treating her. She will need to give permission for the drawing of the blood sample and its use for genetic testing.

Son: what can I do if I am affected by HNPCC?

Doctor: if you (and your children) have inherited this risk, then there are screening programmes that aim to detect a cancer early at a curable stage. This involves regular inspection of the bowel with a special telescope, called a colonoscope, every 2 years to look for early cancers that are not yet producing any symptoms. In addition you should look out for any symptoms that might be suspicious, such as a change in the way your bowels are working – diarrhoea or constipation, and blood in your motions – or in your general health, for instance if you lose weight. These should be reported immediately to your GP, who would then refer you to the appropriate hospital specialist.

1.3.2 Consent for chemotherapy (1)

Scenario

Role: you are the medical junior doctor working on the oncology day unit

Mr Chris Thomson, a 28-year-old single man with newly diagnosed stage 4B Hodgkin's lymphoma, is about to start six cycles of intravenous chemotherapy of Adriamycin (doxorubicin hydrochloride), bleomycin, vinblastine and dacarbazine (ABVD), given as an outpatient on day 1 and 14 of each 28-day cycle.

The patient has already been given written information concerning the treatment, including the CancerBACUP booklet about Hodgkin's disease and summary information about ABVD chemotherapy covering the drugs that are used, how the treatment is given, how often treatment is given, and the possible side effects.

The information provided states that with no treatment the patient is likely to die in weeks or months; that with the treatment proposed the chance

of surviving 5 years is 70–80% (with the possibility of high-dose chemotherapy and peripheral stem-cell transplant in the event of relapse); and that the most significant side effect of chemotherapy is vulnerability to infection.

Your task: you are asked by the chemotherapy clinical nurse specialist to obtain written consent.

Key issues to explore

Before you examine, treat or care for competent adult patients you must obtain their consent. The main issues here are to establish competence to consent, and to explain the benefits and risks of the treatment proposed or of other courses of action.

Adults are assumed to be competent unless demonstrated otherwise. If you have doubts, the question to consider is: can this patient understand and weigh up the information needed to make this decision? Unexpected decisions do not prove the patient is incompetent, but may indicate a need for further information or explanation. Patients need sufficient information before they can decide whether to give their consent (in this case, the benefits and risks of chemotherapy).

> Is the patient competent? Can he or she understand and weigh up the information needed to make the decision?

> ⚠ An unexpected decision does not mean that the patient is not competent.

Key points to establish

Does Mr Thomson understand the key issues, ie prognosis without treatment, prognosis with treatment, side effects of treatment, and possibility (or lack) of alternative treatments?

Appropriate responses to likely questions

Patient: what are the aims of giving me chemotherapy?

Doctor: the aim of this treatment is to cure you of the disease. With this chemotherapy, your chances of surviving for 5 years are probably around 70–80%. Furthermore, even if the disease were to come back, it is often still possible to cure Hodgkin's disease using high-dose chemotherapy and peripheral stem-cell transplantation – that is a sort of bone-marrow transplant using your own cells.

Patient: what will happen if I don't have any of this treatment?

Doctor: if you have no treatment for your Hodgkin's disease, then I'm afraid that there's no doubt that it will continue to grow and spread, and will lead to your death. This is likely to occur within weeks or months.

Patient: what does having chemotherapy actually involve?

Doctor: the ABVD chemotherapy regimen is given by injection through a flexible plastic tube into the vein, with you being treated as an outpatient every 2 weeks for 24 weeks. Before each cycle a blood test is performed to ensure that it is safe to give the chemotherapy.

Patient: how can you tell if the chemotherapy is working?

Doctor: it may be possible to tell simply by examining you, for instance if the swollen glands that we can feel get smaller, or we may repeat the CT scan after 2–3 months of chemotherapy, which will tell us more about the swollen glands inside your chest and abdomen.

Patient: what are the side effects?

Doctor: chemotherapy often causes unwanted side effects and it is difficult to predict who will develop these. Some people are lucky and get very few side effects whilst others have a rougher ride. Many possible side effects can happen and some are more common than others. I will tell you about the more common ones and will give you a written patient information leaflet that describes them in greater detail. If you have any questions, either before you start the treatment or during the course of therapy, then please ask me or one of the nurses.

Patient: the information sheet says that the chemotherapy can affect my fertility.

Doctor: yes, that is one of the possible side effects: your ability to father a child may be affected by the chemotherapy. You should already have had the chance to store a sperm sample so that if your fertility is affected then it can be used for you to have a child in the future, but if you have not done so then we can make arrangements. However, despite this, you must not assume that because you are on chemotherapy you are not fertile. It is important that you do not father a child whilst on the chemotherapy because the drugs could affect the growing baby. It is important that you use effective contraception whilst on the chemotherapy and for at least a few months afterwards.

Patient: the information sheet is very long, what is the most important part?

Doctor: the most important thing to be aware of is that chemotherapy lowers your resistance to infection. If at any time after starting the chemotherapy you get a high temperature (over 38°C or 100.5°F), feel hot and sweaty or shivery, or you suddenly fell unwell then you must contact the hospital oncology team right away. This is the most important thing because it may happen to you when you are at home and it is something that you have to deal with. I have written down all the ways to contact us any time, day or night. If you cannot get in touch with us, come straight to the Accident and Emergency Department and explain that you are a patient on chemotherapy.

Patient: what will happen if I do get an infection?

Doctor: if you do get an infection you will be admitted to hospital, have blood tests and other tests taken to find out the cause of the infection, and be given injections of antibiotics into your veins. This normally settles things down within a few days or a week.

Patient: but can't infections sometimes kill you?

Doctor: yes, I am afraid that they can, but this isn't likely. They usually settle with antibiotics and other treatments, but it's true that sometimes they can get very bad.

Further comments

Excellent patient information is available for cancer patients from resources such as CancerBACUP (www.cancerbacup.org.uk) and these should be provided for all patients as part of the informed consent process. In addition all cancer patients should have a 'key worker' who helps to coordinate their care pathway and is usually their first point of contact. All patients starting chemotherapy must be provided with instructions on how to access the oncology team in the event of an emergency at any time of the day or night.

1.3.3 Consent for chemotherapy (2)

Scenario
Role: you are the medical junior doctor working in the oncology clinic

Mr Frank Lewis, a previously healthy 51-year-old man, is found to have a 3-cm right upper lobe mass on his CXR during a medical insurance check-up. He has a 30 pack-year smoking history, but no history of hypertension, diabetes or heart disease. A CT scan confirms the right upper lobe mass. No hilar or mediastinal nodal enlargement is seen, and there is no evidence of chest wall, liver or adrenal involvement. A transbronchial biopsy of the mass reveals squamous cell cancer (SCC). A PET scan is positive in the primary tumour and in the right hilum, but is otherwise negative. The patient undergoes a right upper lobectomy and full hilar/mediastinal node dissection. He tolerates the procedure well and has a rapid, uneventful postoperative recovery.

Pathology confirms a 4-cm SCC. Two hilar lymph nodes are involved with the tumour, but the mediastinal nodes are clear. The pathologic stage is T2N1M0 (IIB). At the multidisciplinary team meeting following surgery, adjuvant cisplatin-based chemotherapy is recommended.

Your task: explain to the patient the rationale and benefits of the adjuvant chemotherapy that was described in the multidisciplinary team meeting as follows: data from a large (1,867 patients), randomised, controlled trial suggest a modest survival advantage (44% vs 40% at 5 years) for patients who receive postoperative adjuvant platinum-based chemotherapy. Patients with good performance status should be offered the option of adjuvant chemotherapy provided they understand that the expected benefit will be very modest. The side effects reported in the trial included 0.8% of the patients dying from chemotherapy toxicity, whilst 23% of them had at least one episode of grade 4 toxicity: severe neutropenia (17%), severe thrombocytopenia (3%) and severe vomiting (3%).

Key issues to explore

As in the previous scenario, the issue again is one of consent, which in this case involves the discussion and understanding of a finely balanced risk–benefit analysis.

> There are many times in medicine when the benefits and risks of treatment are finely balanced and there is no 'right' and 'wrong' answer.

Key points to establish

Discuss the risk of recurrence and the estimation of the benefit of adjuvant chemotherapy compared with its side-effect profile.

Appropriate responses to likely questions

Patient: my surgeon told me he had removed the entire tumour. Why do I need anything else done?

Doctor: even after the operation there is a chance that the lung cancer can come back, probably because some cancer cells had already spread but were too small to be seen on any of the scans that you had before the operation. Giving people anticancer drug treatments into the blood can help to kill any cancer cells that could be present and this will reduce the chance of the disease returning. Unfortunately it does not completely eliminate the risk of the cancer returning and does potentially have many unpleasant side effects.

Patient: how do I know if the chemotherapy is working?

Doctor: there is no way of telling for an individual person if the chemotherapy is helping because at the time it is given there are no cancer cells visible on scans. All we do know is that giving chemotherapy after curative surgery for your type and stage of lung cancer reduces the chance of the disease coming back and improves your chances of being cured. The chemotherapy improves your chances of being alive in 5 years' time by about 4%, from 40% to 44%. Or putting it another way, if we give 25 people this treatment, then one of them will be cured that would not have been if they did not have it.

Patient: what is the downside of chemotherapy?

Doctor: of course the chemotherapy does have many side effects and I will discuss these further with you before you decide, but the chance of dying because of the chemotherapy is under 1%. I will give you some written information that has been produced for patients in your position who have to make this difficult decision.

Patient: will you still look after me in the clinic if I don't have chemotherapy?

Doctor: yes, of course. Whether you decide to have the chemotherapy or not we will still look after you in this clinic.

Patient: what would you do?

Doctor: that's a very hard question to answer! There are some people who will put up with any treatment, however unpleasant, to increase their chance of being cured of lung cancer. There are others who feel that the small increase in survival is not worth the possible side effects and interference in quality of life. Without being flippant, it really is like the half-drunk pint of beer: to some it is half full and to others half empty. There isn't a right or a wrong answer.

Patient: do I need to decide right now?

Doctor: no, I would suggest that you read the information that I've given you and think about it, and about the things we've just talked over. Once you have done that then we need to talk things over again, perhaps along with someone from your family or a friend if you'd prefer. But we do need to decide within the next couple of weeks.

Further comments

Caring for people with cancer requires careful deliberation and consultation with the patient. To enable patients to participate in this decision-making process they have to be fully informed, and thus clear delivery of information is essential. A number of resources are available to supplement the information given by clinicians to their patients. These include web-based resources as well as patient information leaflets published by charities including CancerBACUP and individual tumour-type patient groups.

1.3.4 Don't tell him the diagnosis

Scenario

Role: you are the medical junior doctor working on the oncology clinic

The daughter of a 72-year-old man approaches you immediately before you are due to call her father in for his first visit to your outpatient clinic. The father has been referred by the urologists, who have made a diagnosis of metastatic prostate cancer. His histology and radiology have been reviewed in the multidisciplinary team meeting. The patient has T4N1M1 poorly differentiated (Gleason 4+5) adenocarcinoma of the prostate. There are widespread bone metastases on the bone scan and bilateral obstructive hydronephrosis causing chronic renal failure. The daughter states emphatically that 'Doctor, you must not tell him what's the matter. I know it will kill him. He will fall apart like Mum did.'

Your task: to discuss the situation with the daughter.

Key issues to explore

Collusion is generally an act of love that aims to protect the patient. Colluders often argue that they know the patient better than the doctor and are better able to judge what the patient should be told. It is important to first acknowledge the colluder's unique relationship with the patient. The next step is to explain that it is your responsibility and duty to give her father the information that he wants about his illness.

> 🔑 Collusion is generally an act of love, which should be acknowledged.

> ⚠️ Information should never be forced on a patient who clearly does not want to receive it.

Key points to establish

You must explain that her father is unlikely to request information that he is not ready to hear, and reassure her that you will check this out with him with each piece of news. Any information will be given gently and sensitively, with opportunities to reflect and ask questions.

Appropriate responses to likely questions

Daughter: he's my dad and I know he'll go to pieces.

Doctor: I understand why you say that: you want to protect your father and that is because you care so much about him. Of course you have known him all your life and I have yet to meet him. I will only be asking him what information he wants to know – it's my responsibility and

duty to tell him what he wants to know about his illness, and answer any questions or anxieties that he has. However, I won't force any information onto him that he doesn't want to hear.

Daughter: whatever you do, don't tell him he's got cancer.

Doctor: he is not likely to ask questions about his illness if he is not ready to hear the answers. I will answer honestly any questions that he asks me, but I will make sure that he wants to hear the answers before giving them. I won't ram the cancer diagnosis down his throat if he doesn't want to discuss it, but equally I will not lie to him if he asks me directly if his illness is cancer. Very often I find that the patient already knows it's cancer, but is trying to hide the truth from loved ones to protect them too. When that happens it becomes a lot easier if both of you know the diagnosis and then you can talk to each other about it.

Daughter: I still don't want him to be alone when you tell him.

Doctor: I agree, and I will ask him if he wants anyone to be present when we discuss the test results. If he says yes, then we can all talk together. If he says no – which I think is very unlikely – then I will talk with him first, and then ask if he's happy for us all to talk. Answering his questions about the diagnosis with you present will help you both to talk openly about the cancer. It will allow him to discuss his feelings with you. In my experience, being able to talk within the family about the diagnosis can dramatically improve the quality of life of someone with cancer and often helps everyone in the family.

1.4 Acute scenarios

1.4.1 Acute deterioration after starting chemotherapy

Scenario

As on-call medical junior doctor you are asked to see a 27-year-old man who started his first cycle of cyclophosphamide, cytarabine, vincristine, doxorubicin and methotrexate combination chemotherapy for stage 4B Burkitt's lymphoma that is affecting his bone marrow and cerebrospinal fluid. On the second day of his chemotherapy he feels faint and a 12-lead ECG is performed that show runs of broad complex tachycardia of up to four beats.

Introduction

The acute destruction of large numbers of cancer cells is associated with metabolic sequelae caused by the release of intracellular contents into the systemic circulation, and is termed 'tumour lysis syndrome' (TLS). The most immediate and dramatic of its consequences are caused by release of the electrolyte potassium, which can cause fatal hyperkalaemia. Nucleic acid breakdown leads to hyperuricaemia and this, unless treated appropriately, can be complicated by renal failure, partly due to the precipitation of uric acid crystals within the renal tubules. The release of calcium and phosphate into the bloodstream can cause transient hypercalcaemia (hypocalcaemia is a later and more typical feature) and hyperphosphataemia, although these rarely cause any significant consequences, except that calcium and phosphate may co-precipitate and contribute towards the impairment of renal function.

The onset of cardiac arrhythmias during the first cycle of chemotherapy for high-grade lymphoma or leukaemia is highly suggestive of TLS.

History of the presenting problem

The information given states that the patient felt faint, which led to the recording of his ECG. Aside from general questions about how he is feeling, it will clearly be relevant to find out when he first felt faint, whether he has noticed any palpitations ('Have you been aware of your heart beat doing anything out of the ordinary?') and whether he has had any other cardiorespiratory symptoms, eg breathlessness or chest pain (and what type of chest pain if any).

Other relevant history

A brief cardiac history to exclude any known pre-existing cardiac abnormality would be appropriate, although unlikely to reveal anything in a 27-year-old man.

It will also be necessary to check for other features of metabolic upset such as muscular weakness, which is sometimes a symptom of hyperkalaemia. However, with many other potential causes for a condition such as this, several other factors have to be considered: urinary symptoms such as oliguria (has the patient's urine output been monitored?); flank pain and haematuria may indicate acute renal failure; and cramps, seizures, spasms and tetany may rarely be caused by hypocalcaemia.

Examination: general features

The first priority in assessment will be to decide how unwell the patient is. Is he talking sensibly or is he confused? What are his vital signs?

Given the documentation of arrhythmia, a specific examination will clearly focus on the cardiovascular system, but a general examination may identify the presence of bulky tumour, which increases the risk of TLS. In any patient with haematological malignancy who is unwell, it will also be sensible to look in particular for evidence of infection or of bruising/bleeding that may indicate thrombocytopenia, although these are unlikely to be problematic so soon after the initiation of chemotherapy.

Carpopedal spasm and tetany are rare consequences of hypocalcaemia in this context.

Examination: cardiovascular system

A full cardiovascular examination is clearly required, the key elements of which are as follows.

- Check peripheral perfusion: are the patient's hands cold?

- Pulse rate and rhythm: is there an arrhythmia now?

- BP, including postural measurement lying and sitting: hypotension (systemic blood pressure <100 mmHg) or postural hypotension (fall in systemic blood pressure of over 10 mmHg on sitting) would be worrying signs indicating that the patient was very ill. A fall in BP on sitting indicates significant intravascular volume depletion in this context.

- JVP: a low JVP (not visible in the root of the neck) would indicate intravascular volume depletion, whereas a normal or high JVP shows that the patient has adequate (or excessive) intravascular volume. This would mean that the patient should not be given further intravenous fluid without very careful monitoring to prevent iatrogenic fluid overload.

- Lung bases: there are many causes of crackles in the lungs, but bibasal crackles would point to the possibility of pulmonary oedema and be a warning of the dangers of giving intravenous fluid.

Investigation

The first priority is to inspect the 12-lead ECG, not just to extract as much information as possible about the broad complex tachycardia, but for changes suggestive of hyperkalaemia.

All doctors should be familiar with the ECG changes of hyperkalaemia. The following changes occur progressively as the serum potassium rises:

- tenting (peaking) of T wave;
- PR interval lengthens and QRS complex widens;
- P wave becomes indistinct and disappears;
- broad QRS complex slurs into tented T wave;
- sinusoidal morphology.

Emergency biochemistry is mandatory, including electrolytes (particularly serum potassium), creatinine, calcium, phosphate, urate and lactate dehydrogenase, which will be elevated and is probably the best test to evaluate treatment response in TLS.

Analysis of arterial blood gases, looking particularly for acidosis (a common feature of renal failure associated with tumour lysis) as well as to confirm oxygenation and ventilation, is essential.

Management

The metabolic chaos of tumour lysis results in rapid changes in electrolytes and carries a significant mortality in an otherwise curable tumour type.

This patient requires urgent transfer to a high-dependency monitored bed. Pending this, it will be important to arrange for him to be placed on a cardiac monitor and pulse oximeter, and to provide him with high-flow oxygen if his saturation is less than 92% (with no harm done if it is above this level).

Management of hyperkalaemia

If the ECG shows any evidence of hyperkalaemia that is more severe than simply tenting of the T waves, then emergency treatment for hyperkalaemia should be given immediately, even before laboratory confirmation of the diagnosis.

All doctors must know the emergency treatment for severe hyperkalaemia:

- Intravenous injection of 10 mL 10% calcium gluconate: acts instantly to stabilise the cardiac membranes.
- Intravenous injection of 50 mL 50% dextrose with 10 units short-acting insulin (eg Actrapid) over 15–30 minutes, with frequent monitoring of fingerprick blood glucose. This drives potassium into the patient's cells.

For further details of the management of hyperkalaemia, see *Acute Medicine*, Section 1.2.19; *Nephrology*, Section 1.4.1.

Recognition and treatment of renal failure

What is the patient's urine output? Look at the fluid balance charts

(if available). Arrange for insertion of a urinary catheter: in this context the benefit of accurate monitoring of urine output outweighs the disadvantage that a catheter may introduce infection.

If there is intravascular volume depletion (hypotension/postural hypotension and low JVP), give intravenous 0.9% saline rapidly to restore volume, stopping when postural change in BP is abolished and the JVP is restored to normal.

Assuming that the patient is not oliguric (defined as a urine output of less than 30 mL/hour), commence 'hyperhydration' with infusion of 0.9% saline (1 L every 4 hours) with diuresis assisted by furosemide (40–80 mg iv) or mannitol (25 g iv) if the patient's urine output is less than expected (this regimen would be expected to induce an output of over 100 mL/hour). Remember, however, that this patient is at risk of acute renal failure, and pulmonary oedema will be induced if this fluid regimen is given in the face of oliguria, so frequent clinical checks are required by you and whoever is on the next shift. This is a patient whose details for examination need to be handed over: what is the urine output, where is the JVP and what do the lung bases sound like?

Fluid management in the very ill:

- Resuscitate quickly: 0.9% saline until there is no postural fall in BP and the JVP is easily seen.
- Then pause: is the patient passing urine?
- Do not be responsible for iatrogenic drowning.

If the patient remains oliguric despite adequate fluid resuscitation, then give no more fluid and call local renal services: urgent dialysis may be necessary.

Management of hyperuricaemia

Hyperhydration with intravenous fluids to induce a diuresis will lower the patient's serum urate and the risk of renal failure. Urate is more soluble at high pH; hence its excretion can also be increased by urinary alkalinisation. This can be achieved by adding intravenous sodium bicarbonate to the fluid regimen in order to achieve a urine pH of 7–7.5 (measured by dipstick). This is most easily and safely done by giving 250 mL of 1.26% sodium bicarbonate in place of 0.9% sodium chloride for 1 hour. The infusion of high-concentration solutions of bicarbonate (eg 8.4%) is to be avoided, except *in extremis*.

The prophylactic use of allopurinol (a xanthine oxidase inhibitor) should have been started prior to chemotherapy, but if it has not then it should be started (standard dose 300 mg daily). A relatively new drug, recombinant urate oxidase (rasburicase), converts insoluble uric acid into the soluble allantoin. Clinical trials have shown that urate oxidase controls hyperuricaemia faster and more reliably than allopurinol: its use is indicated for children and haematological malignancy, such as in this case.

If the patient remains oliguric, then haemodialysis will be required: this removes urate from the body very effectively.

Further comments

How would this have been prevented? TLS results from spontaneous or treatment-related apoptosis and usually occurs within 5 days of commencing chemotherapy. It is associated with a number of factors:

- bulky chemosensitive disease;

- elevated pretreatment serum uric acid;

- elevated serum lactate dehydrogenase;

- impaired renal function.

It is important to identify those at risk and institute prophylactic measures prior to commencement of chemotherapy. These measures include allopurinol, intravenous fluids, urinary alkalinisation and rasburicase.

1.4.2 Back pain and weak legs

Scenario

You are an junior doctor in the Emergency Department and are asked to see a 70-year-old ex-serviceman with known metastatic prostate cancer. He had been diagnosed 8 months previously with T4NXM1 adenocarcinoma of the prostate. At diagnosis a transrectal ultrasound-guided biopsy demonstrated a Gleason grade 4+3 tumour and his serum prostate-specific antigen (PSA) level was grossly elevated at 492 ng/mL (nominal level 4 ng/mL). A radionuclide bone scan was positive and he was started on antiandrogen therapy consisting of flutamide and goserelin.

There had been a good initial decline in his serum PSA, but over the past couple of weeks he has been complaining of mid-thoracic back pain that radiates around his chest when he coughs. This morning he got out of bed and his legs gave way.

Introduction

Spinal cord compression affects up to 5% of patients with metastatic cancer and is an important source of morbidity, despite treatment being effective in 90% of patients if an early diagnosis is made. The most common underlying cancers causing spinal cord compression are breast, lung and prostate cancer, lymphoma, myeloma, renal cancer and sarcomas.

The initial symptoms can be vague, with the patient only seeking medical attention when their problems worsen. Any cancer patient complaining of back pain and bladder or bowel dysfunction, and who has bilateral upper motor neuron signs in the legs or a sensory level should be considered to have spinal cord compression until proven otherwise and requires urgent investigation. Autonomic dysfunction occurs late and carries a poor prognosis.

Any cancer patient with back pain and bladder or bowel dysfunction plus bilateral upper motor neuron signs in the legs or sensory level has spinal cord compression.

History of the presenting problem

The patient's presentation with new-onset back pain and weak legs clearly points towards cord compression due to metastatic disease. It is clearly important to take a detailed history of his bladder and bowel function.

- Are they working properly?

- Does he get the feeling that he wants to pass urine and open his bowels normally?

- Has he had difficulty holding his bladder or bowels and perhaps been incontinent?

• Does it feel normal when he wipes himself after opening his bowels?

It would also be appropriate to enquire whether he has had any previous back problems. These are common, but everything in this case points away from a diagnosis of an exacerbation of non-malignant back pain.

Examination: general features

It will be important to assess the patient's pain and his general condition.

• Is he wasted and cachectic?

• Is he dehydrated?

• Is he anaemic, or does he have petechiae/purpura (bone-marrow involvement)?

In his abdomen, is the liver enlarged and craggy? And of more relevance to the presenting problem, is the bladder palpable to indicate urinary retention? Rectal examination will be essential.

• Ask if he can feel your finger.

• Is there a 'frozen pelvis' of locally invasive cancer?

• Is there faecal overload/impaction?

Examination: neurological system

Are the patient's legs weak and, if so, is the neurological deficit typical of spinal cord compression? Look for bilateral weakness and increased tone with extensor plantar responses. Look for a sensory level consistent with the description of girdle-type pain. Remember to check perianal sensation at the same time as you perform rectal examination.

Look at the back for obvious spinal deformity. The patient may also have pain on palpation consistent with vertebral collapse secondary to metastatic tumour.

Investigation

The priority is obviously to obtain imaging of the spine: plain radiographs may reveal obvious vertebral collapse or associated vertebral disease (Fig. 2). However, the definitive test, required urgently, is an MRI scan of the spinal axis to define the presence and level(s) of spinal cord compression (Fig. 3a). Gadolinium contrast enhancement helps to delineate between leptomeningeal disease and intramedullary metastases.

It will also be appropriate to check FBC, creatinine, electrolytes, bone and liver function tests and a CXR.

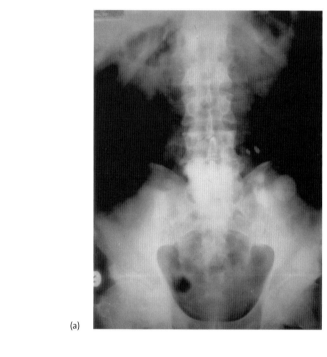
(a)

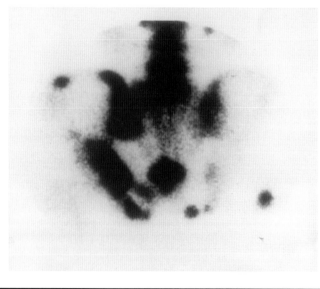
(b)

▲**Fig. 2** **(a)** Plain pelvic radiograph and **(b)** technetium-99 pyrophosphate bone scan of the corresponding area from a patient with sclerotic bone metastases of prostate cancer.

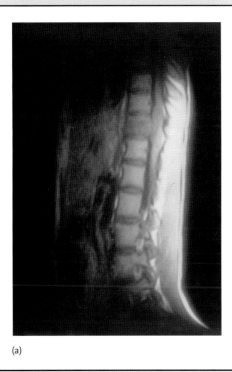
(a)

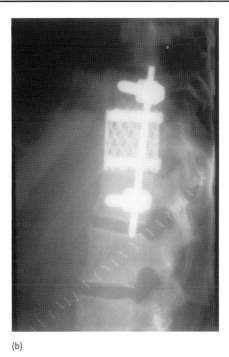
(b)

▲ **Fig. 3** (a) MRI demonstrating cord compression at T11 due to vertebral metastasis with soft-tissue extension and (b) plain radiograph following surgical decompression and stabilisation.

Management

> 🔑 Spinal cord compression is a medical emergency: treatment should be started immediately on clinical suspicion.

High-dose intravenous corticosteroids should be initiated on clinical suspicion alone to prevent further evolution of any neurological deficit: give dexamethasone 10 mg iv stat, then 4 mg po qds.

If the overall condition of the patient makes it appropriate, a neurosurgical opinion should be obtained about the potential for surgical decompression, especially if there is vertebral instability (Fig. 3) or if the level of the compression has been previously irradiated. Otherwise, the definitive treatment is urgent local radiotherapy.

Other aspects that require attention include pain relief (see *Pain Relief and Palliative Care*, Section 2.1), bladder catheterisation (if the patient is suffering from urinary retention) and nursing care to avoid pressure area damage (if he has severe paresis and/or sensory loss).

Further comments

> 🔑 Preservation of gait and continence requires prompt diagnosis and treatment.

If the patient can walk at presentation with malignant cord compression, there is an 80% chance that his ability to walk can be preserved with appropriate treatment. A multidisciplinary team approach with active rehabilitation following treatment is required to optimise neurological recovery.

1.4.3 Breathless, hoarse, dizzy and swollen

Scenario

You are asked to see and assess a 65-year-old woman who has been sent for assessment as a medical emergency. She had been booked an appointment for the chest clinic in 2 week's time, but has deteriorated over the last 2 days with worsening shortness of breath and dizziness.

She is a heavy smoker (50 pack-years) and has been complaining of a persistent but worsening productive cough with occasional streaks of blood in the sputum for some months. In the last few days she has noted that she is becoming more short of breath when she walks to the shops for her cigarettes; also she feels dizzy when bending forward.

She says that her friends have noticed that her voice has deepened and become hoarser over the past few weeks. She also feels she has been putting on weight, as her fingers are swollen and she can no longer wear her rings. She sleeps poorly at night and often wakes in the morning with 'puffy bags' under her eyes.

Introduction

The diagnosis of superior vena cava obstruction (SVCO) depends on recognising the clinical features that arise from obstruction of the venous drainage of the upper body: headaches, oedema of the arms and face, distended neck and arm veins, and a dusky skin coloration over the chest, arms and face. Collateral venous circulation may develop over a period of weeks, with the direction of blood flow – towards the drainage territory of the inferior vena cava – helping to confirm the diagnosis.

The most frequent malignant causes of SVCO are:

- small-cell lung cancer (SCLC);

- non-small-cell lung cancer;

- lymphoma;

- germ-cell tumours;

- breast cancer.

The severity of symptoms relates to the rate of onset, degree of obstruction and development of compensatory collateral venous return. The symptoms may worsen on lying flat or bending as this further stresses the obstructed venous return, hence this woman's dizziness.

History of the presenting problem

The history suggesting SVCO due to a lung malignancy is clear-cut in this case; indeed it is very unlikely that any other diagnosis could account for it.

It would be important to explore the patient's exercise capacity before the recent deterioration in her health since this will indicate her underlying cardiopulmonary function. Ask her: 'How far could you walk 3 months ago, before these problems started?'

Examination: general features and respiratory system

> Airway compromise is an emergency.

The first priority must be to assess the patient's airway because airway compromise is an emergency. She has a hoarse voice, but is she short of breath at rest, does she speak in broken sentences and is she cyanosed? In particular, does she have inspiratory and/or expiratory stridor? Elicit this (if it is not obvious when she breathes normally) by asking her to open her mouth and take a deep breath in and out as fast as she can.

> Elicit stridor by asking the patient to open his or her mouth and take a deep breath in and out as fast as possible.

General examination will obviously include noting if there is evidence of weight loss or even cachexia. Also check the following:

- pulse rate (for tachycardia);

- BP (for pulsus paradoxus – a fall in systolic pressure on inspiration

– suggesting severe compromise to venous return in this context);

- respiratory rate (for tachypnoea), but do not be deceived by the patient who is exhausted and has a normal respiratory rate – they may die soon.

> ⚠ Beware the patient with a respiratory problem who has a normal respiratory rate but looks exhausted – they may be about to die.

Given the clinical suspicion in this case, look carefully for oedema and discoloration of the face and arms, and also for collateral veins. Check for lymphadenopathy in the neck. The most important clinical sign in making the diagnosis of SVCO is loss of pulsation in the veins of the neck.

In the chest itself, look for the likely signs of chronic obstructive pulmonary disease, as well as for evidence of a pleural effusion. Palpate the breasts carefully and note if the liver is palpable in the abdomen and, if so, whether it is likely to contain secondaries.

Investigation

The combination of symptoms and signs of SVCO are unmistakable. The priority is to obtain imaging to confirm this and indicate the likely cause. A plain CXR will demonstrate superior mediastinal widening, perhaps with the presence of a pleural effusion. A CT scan of the thorax will provide more detailed information regarding the superior vena cava and the bronchi.

Sputum cytology may establish the diagnosis of SCLC in up to 50% of cases, because most patients with SVCO (65%) have lung cancer and SCLC is the main histological type that presents in this way.

Bronchoscopy can yield malignant cells for cytological analysis, but in some cases biopsy of the mediastinal mass may be necessary. This can be achieved either transbronchially, by mediastinoscopy, or under CT guidance.

If a lymph node is palpable, then lymph node biopsy may prove to be the best way of diagnosing the tumour. It is less invasive and has a lower likelihood of complication than other techniques that can be used to obtain tissue.

It will also be appropriate to check FBC, creatinine, electrolytes, bone and liver function tests and (probably) arterial blood gases.

Management

Treatment of SVCO depends on the aetiology and severity of the obstruction, and on the patient's overall prognosis. It is important to relieve symptoms as well as treating the underlying cause. Immediate treatment is required in the presence of airway compromise and should be started before biopsy results are available.

Sit the patient upright and give her high-flow oxygen. Monitor her oxygen saturation with a pulse oximeter and check arterial blood gases at least once to look for carbon dioxide retention. If the airway is compromised then give her high-dose steroid treatment (dexamethasone 10 mg iv stat, then 4 mg po qds).

When possible, a histological diagnosis should be obtained urgently as some tumours are better treated with chemotherapy than radiotherapy. Radiologically placed stents in the superior vena cava may relieve symptoms while a histological diagnosis is awaited. However, mediastinal radiotherapy is the optimal treatment for most tumours and relieves symptoms in up to 90% of patients within 2 weeks. Patients with chemosensitive tumours such as lymphoma, SCLC and germ-cell tumours gain symptomatic relief within days from appropriate systemic chemotherapy.

Further comments

> Patients with SVCO can have a good prognosis, although many do not.

The outcome of treatment depends on the aetiology of the SVCO and the response of the patient to therapy. Patients with lymphoma, SCLC and germ-cell tumours can have a good long-term outcome even in the presence of SVCO.

For patients with recurrent SVCO or those whose underlying disease cannot be treated effectively, insertion of expandable wire stents under radiological guidance can give instantaneous symptomatic relief and should be considered as a palliative manoeuvre.

2.1 Breast cancer

Aetiology/pathophysiology

Both genetic and hormonal factors play a role in the aetiology. Hereditary predisposition is implicated in around 10% of breast cancer cases, including those women with the *BRCA1* and *BRCA2* mutations and those with Li–Fraumeni syndrome (see Section 2.13). Prolonged exposure to oestrogen is also thought to be a factor, and both early menarche and late menopause are established risk factors, as are late first pregnancy (over 35 years old) and nulliparity.

The role of the combined contraceptive pill is controversial, although a meta-analysis in 1996 suggested a 1.24 relative risk for current users, falling to 1.07 5 years after they stopped taking the pill. Many of these studies were based on use of older versions of the pill when the oestrogen dosage was up to five times higher than in the current pill. Hormone-replacement therapy has been shown by the Million Women Study to increase the incidence of breast cancer in current long-term users (relative risk 1.66) and is no longer recommended for first-line treatment of osteoporosis.

Pathology

Invasive ductal carcinoma with or without ductal carcinoma *in situ* (DCIS) is the commonest histology, accounting for 70% of cases, whilst invasive lobular carcinoma accounts for most of the remainder. DCIS constitutes 20% of screen-detected breast cancers. It is multifocal in one-third of women and has a high risk of becoming invasive (10% at 5 years following excision only). Pure DCIS does not cause lymph node metastases, although these are found in 2% of cases where nodes are examined owing to undetected invasive cancer. Lobular carcinoma *in situ* (LCIS) is a predisposing risk factor for developing cancer in either breast (7% at 10 years).

Epidemiology

Breast cancer is the most frequent cancer in women after non-melanotic skin tumours; it is the commonest cause of death in women aged 35–54 years in England, and follows an unpredictable course with metastases presenting up to 20 years after initial diagnosis. For these reasons it is one of the most feared diagnoses in the developed world. In 2002 there were 41,700 breast cancer diagnoses in the UK and 12,600 breast cancer deaths. England has one of the highest age-standardised rates of incidence and mortality from breast cancer in the world. The lifetime risk of breast cancer is 1 in 9. In England and Wales the 5-year age-standardised survival rate in 1990 was 62%, in contrast to over 70% in France, Italy and Switzerland. However, this has improved recently with earlier detection by screening and improved treatment: the 5-year survival was 80% for women diagnosed in 1998–2001 in England.

Clinical presentation

Breast cancer usually presents as a mass that persists throughout the menstrual cycle. A nipple discharge occurs in 10% of cases, and pain in only 7%. Less common presentations include inflammatory carcinoma with diffuse induration of the skin of the breast, which confers an adverse prognosis. Increasingly, women present as a consequence of mammographic screening.

Around 40% of breast cancer sufferers will have axillary nodal disease, the likelihood rising with the size of the primary tumour. The involvement of axillary nodes by tumour is the strongest prognostic predictor. Distant metastases are infrequently present at presentation. The commonest sites of spread are bone (70%), lung (60%), liver (55%), pleura (40%), adrenals (35%), skin (30%) and brain (10–20%).

Paget's disease of the nipple accounts for 1% of all cases and presents with a relatively long history of eczematous change in the nipple with itching, burning, oozing or bleeding. There may be a palpable underlying lump as the nipple will contain malignant cells singularly or in nests. The prognosis is related to the underlying tumour.

Treatment

Early breast cancer

Standard treatment is wide local excision and axillary node surgery (dissection, sampling or sentinel lymph node biopsy) followed by

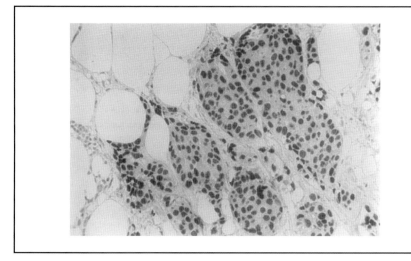

▲**Fig. 4** Invasive ductal breast cancer showing immunocytochemical staining for ER.

adjuvant breast radiotherapy. This achieves similar local control and survival rates to mastectomy with less mutilating surgery.

Women without axillary node involvement may be divided into two groups.

1. High-risk patients who have a tumour smaller than 1 cm or that does not express the oestrogen receptor (ER) (Fig. 4). The 5-year disease-free survival for these women is less than 80% and they should receive adjuvant treatment.

2. Those with smaller ER-positive tumours do not require adjuvant treatment.

Women with histological spread to the axillary nodes are candidates for adjuvant chemotherapy, which delays recurrence and improves survival. The adjuvant therapy for premenopausal women will be:

• chemotherapy for ER-negative tumours;

• chemotherapy and a luteinising hormone-releasing hormone analogue or tamoxifen for ER-positive tumours.

The adjuvant therapy for postmenopausal women is:

• chemotherapy with tamoxifen for ER-negative tumours;

• tamoxifen for ER-positive tumours.

The role of adjuvant treatment has been unravelled by a number of meta-analyses performed by the Early Breast Cancer Trialists' Collaborative Group based in Oxford. Recent data support the use of adjuvant Herceptin (trastuzumab), a humanised monoclonal antibody to human epidermal growth factor receptor 2 (HER2), in addition to chemotherapy for women with early breast cancers that express HER2.

Advanced breast cancer
The management of metastatic disease includes symptomatic radiotherapy to palliate painful bone metastases, and standard second-line endocrine therapy with aromatase inhibitors that inhibit peripheral oestrogen production in adrenal and adipose tissues. Advanced ER-negative disease may be treated with combination chemotherapy. A recent advance in the management of advanced breast cancer is the use of trastuzumab. Bisphosphonates reduce skeletal morbidity in women with bony metastases.

In situ breast cancer
The management of carcinoma *in situ* is less clearly defined. The traditional surgery for DCIS was simple mastectomy. However, although breast-conserving surgery and radiotherapy has a higher relapse rate, conducting a salvage mastectomy for these relapses produces similar survival rates to initial management by mastectomy. The suggested treatment options for LCIS range from observation with annual screening to bilateral prophylactic mastectomy in highly selected patients. There appears to be no place for chemotherapy in either DCIS or LCIS, and the role of endocrine therapy for both is under evaluation.

Complications
Tamoxifen is a selective ER modulator that has important side effects, including menopausal symptoms of vasomotor instability and fluid retention, depression and ophthalmological side effects such as cataracts and retinopathy. In addition, tamoxifen is associated with an increased risk (approximately seven-fold) of endometrial polyps and cancer, so any abnormal vaginal bleeding requires prompt investigation.

Tamoxifen also has beneficial side effects, including reduced postmenopausal osteoporosis and a reduced incidence of second primary breast cancer in the contralateral breast. This suggests that it could have a role in prevention of breast cancer in high-risk women, which is under investigation at present.

Prognosis
See Table 3 for 5-year survival by stage for breast cancer.

TABLE 3 THE 5-YEAR SURVIVAL OF BREAST CANCER BY STAGE

Tumour stage (AJCC)	Simplified stage definition	5-year survival (%)
Stage I	Tumour smaller than 2 cm, no nodes	96
Stage II	Tumour 2–5 cm and/or moveable axillary nodes	81
Stage III	Chest wall or skin fixation and/or fixed axillary nodes	52
Stage IV	Metastases	18

AJCC, American Joint Committee on Cancer.

Prevention

Chemoprevention with tamoxifen has been shown to reduce the incidence of breast cancer in a randomised controlled American trial of 13,000 healthy women at high risk of developing breast cancer. However, these results have not been reproduced in two similar European trials.

Breast cancer screening is covered in Section 3.4.

FURTHER READING

Burstein HJ, Polyak K, Wong JS, Lester SC and Kaelin CM. Medical progress: ductal carcinoma *in situ* of the breast. *N. Engl. J. Med.* 2004; 350: 1430–41. Million Women Study Collaborators. Breast cancer and hormone replacement therapy in the Million Women Study. *Lancet* 2003; 362: 419–27.

– – – – – – – – – – – – – – – –

NHS Centre for Reviews and Dissemination. Management of primary breast cancer. *Effective Health Care* 1996; 2: 1–16.

– – – – – – – – – – – – – – – –

National Institute for Health and Clinical Excellence. *Breast Cancer Clinical Service Guidelines*, 2002. Available at www.nice.org.uk

– – – – – – – – – – – – – – – –

National Institute for Health and Clinical Excellence. *Familial Breast Cancer: The Classification and Care of Women at Risk of Familial Breast*

Cancer in Primary, Secondary and Tertiary Care, 2004. Available at www.nice.org.uk

– – – – – – – – – – – – – – – –

Rodger A, Stebbing J and Thompson A. Breast cancer (non-metastatic). *Clinical Effectiveness*, 2005. Available at www.clinicalevidence.com/ceweb/conditions/onc/onc.jsp

– – – – – – – – – – – – – – – –

Sainsbury JRC, Anderson TJ and Morgan BAL. ABC of breast diseases: breast cancer. *BMJ* 2000; 321: 745–50.

– – – – – – – – – – – – – – – –

Stebbing J, Crane J and Gaya A. Breast cancer (metastatic). *Clinical Effectiveness*, 2005. Available at www.clinicalevidence.com/ceweb/conditions/onc/onc.jsp

2.2 Central nervous system cancers

Aetiology

The cause of most adult brain tumours is not known. Several inherited phakomatoses are associated with brain tumours including:

- tuberous sclerosis (gliomas, ependymomas);
- von Reckinghausen's disease–neurofibromatosis (cranial and root schwannomas, meningiomas, ependymomas and optic gliomas);

- von Hippel–Lindau disease (cerebellar and retinal haemangioblastoma);
- Gorlin's basal naevus syndrome (medulloblastoma);
- Turcot's syndrome (gliomas);
- Li–Fraumeni syndrome (glioma) (see Section 2.13).

Pathology

Primary brain tumours may be:

- glial tumours;
- non-glial tumours;
- primary cerebral non-Hodgkin's lymphoma.

Gliomas account for 50% of brain tumours and are divided into four grades:

- grade I (non-infiltrating pilocytic astrocytoma);
- grade II (well to moderately differentiated astrocytoma);
- grade III (anaplastic astrocytoma);
- grade IV (glioblastoma multiforme).

The prognosis deteriorates with increasing grade of tumour.

Other glial tumours include:

- ependymomas that arise from ependymal cells that usually line the fourth ventricle;
- oligodendrogliomas that arise from oligodendroglia;
- medulloblastomas are tumours of childhood that usually arise in the cerebellum and may be related to primitive neuroectodermal tumours elsewhere in the central nervous system (CNS).

Non-glial brain tumours include:

- pineal parenchymal tumours;
- extragonadal germ-cell tumours (see Section 2.4);

- craniopharyngiomas;

- meningiomas;

- choroid plexus tumours.

Meningioma is the commonest non-glial tumour and constitutes 15% of brain tumours.

The majority of spinal axis tumours in adults are extradural:

- metastatic carcinoma;

- lymphoma;

- sarcoma.

Primary spinal cord tumours include:

- extradural meningiomas (26%);

- schwannomas (29%);

- intramedullary ependymomas (13%);

- astrocytomas (13%).

Epidemiology
Metastases to the brain are commoner than primary brain tumours. The most common primary sites of brain metastases are lung, breast, melanoma and renal. In addition, nasopharyngeal cancers may directly extend through the skull foramina. Meningeal metastases occur with leukaemia and lymphoma, breast and small-cell lung cancer, and from medulloblastoma and ependymal glioma as a route of spread. Brain tumours account for 2–5% of all cancers and 2% of cancer deaths. Fewer than 20% of CNS tumours occur in the spinal cord.

Clinical presentation

Glial tumours
General symptoms from the mass effect include increased intracranial pressure, oedema, midline shift and herniation syndromes, as well as progressively altered mental state and personality, headaches, seizures

TABLE 4 CLINICAL FEATURES OF MENINGIOMA BY SITE	
Site	**Clinical features**
Parasagittal falx	Progressive spastic weakness and/or numbness of legs
Olfactory groove	Anosmia, visual loss, papilloedema (Foster–Kennedy syndrome) and frontal lobe syndrome
Sella turcica	Visual field loss
Sphenoid wing	Cavernous sinus syndrome (medial), exophthalmos and visual loss (middle), and temporal bone swelling and skull deformity (lateral)
Posterior fossa	Hydrocephalus (tentorium); gait ataxia and cranial neuropathies V, VII, VIII, IX and X (cerebellopontine angle); suboccipital pain and ipsilateral arm and leg weakness (foramen magnum)

and papilloedema. Focal symptoms depend on the location of the tumour. Fewer than 10% of first fits are due to tumours and only 20% of supratentorial tumours present with fits.

Meningioma
These tumours, which are more common in women, present as slowly growing masses that produce headaches, seizures, motor and sensory symptoms, and cranial neuropathies depending on their site (Table 4). Meningiomas are one of the few tumours that produce characteristic changes on plain skull radiographs: they lead to bone erosion, calcification and hyperostosis (Fig. 5).

Spinal axis tumours
The frequency of tumour sites is 50% thoracic, 30% lumbosacral and 20% cervical or foramen magnum. These tumours present with:

- radicular symptoms due to root infiltration;

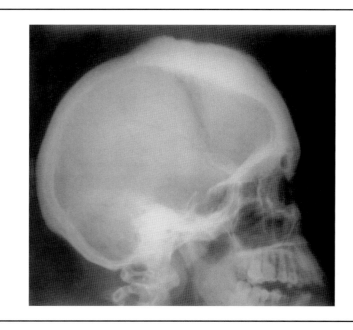

▲ **Fig. 5** Lateral skull plain radiograph showing skull vault hyperostosis due to meningioma.

- syringomyelic disturbance due to central destruction by intramedullary tumours;

- sensorimotor dysfunction due to cord compression.

Investigations/staging

- A MRI with gadolinium enhancement is the imaging technique of choice (Fig. 6).

- PET scan with ^{18}F-fluorodeoxyglucose, which accumulates in metabolically active tissues, may help to differentiate tumour recurrence from radiation necrosis (Fig. 7).

- Stereotactic biopsy is required to confirm the diagnosis, although occasionally tumours are

diagnosed on clinical evidence because a biopsy might be hazardous (eg in patients with brainstem gliomas).

Treatment

Some gliomas are curable by surgery alone and some by surgery and radiotherapy; the remainder require surgery, radiotherapy and chemotherapy, and these tumours are rarely curable.

- Surgical removal should be as complete as possible within the constraints of preserving neurological function.

- Radiation can increase the cure rate or prolong disease-free survival in high-grade gliomas, and may also be useful symptomatic therapy in patients with low-grade glioma who relapse after initial therapy with surgery alone.

- Chemotherapy (nitrosourea based or temozolomide) may prolong disease-free survival in patients with oligodendrogliomas and high-grade gliomas. However, its toxicity may not always merit this approach.

Therapy for meningiomas is surgical resection, which may be repeated at relapse. Radiotherapy reduces relapse rates and should be considered for high-grade meningiomas or incompletely resected tumours. Relapse rates at 5 years are 7% if completely resected and 35–60% if incompletely resected.

Complications

Early complications of radiotherapy (within the first 3–4 months) are due to reversible damage to myelin-producing oligodendrocytes that recover spontaneously after 3–6 months. This causes somnolence or

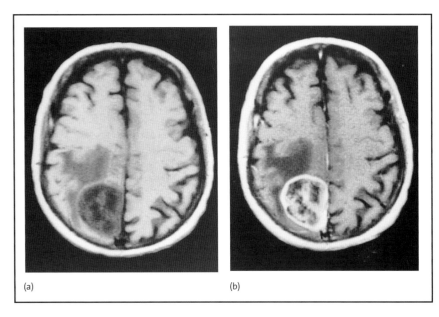

▲ **Fig. 6** (**a**) Before and (**b**) after intravenous gadolinium contrast MRI scans of the brain showing partially enhancing high-grade glioblastoma multiforme. There is adjacent low-density white matter due to extensive oedema.

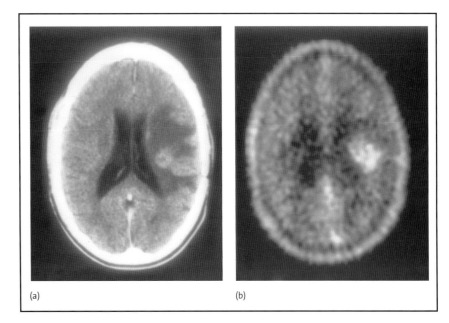

▲ **Fig. 7** Matched CT scan (**a**) and ^{18}F-fluorodeoxyglucose PET scan (**b**) from patient with paraventricular high-grade glioma demonstrating high glucose utilisation in tumour.

TABLE 5 THE 5-YEAR SURVIVAL RATES OF ADULT BRAIN TUMOURS

Tumour	5-year survival (%)
Grade I glioma (cerebellar)	90–100
Grade I glioma (all sites)	50–60
Grade II (astrocytoma)	16–46
Grade III (anaplastic astrocytoma)	10–30
Grade IV (glioblastoma multiforme)	1–10
Oligodendroglioma	50–80
Meningioma	70–80

exacerbation of existing symptoms in the brain and Lhermitte's sign in the cord (shooting numbness or paraesthesiae precipitated by neck flexion).

Late complications include irreversible radiation necrosis due to vessel damage. This may mimic disease recurrence, is radiation dose related and occurs in up to 15% of those treated, with the highest frequency in children who are also receiving chemotherapy. Single-photon emission computed tomography and PET scans may differentiate between radionecrosis and relapse.

Prognosis

Prognostic factors include histology, grade and size of tumour, age and performance status of the patient and the duration of their symptoms. Median survival of patients with anaplastic astrocytoma is 18 months; for those with glioblastoma multiforme it is 10–12 months. Meningiomas if completely resected are usually cured, the median survival being over 10 years (Table 5).

FURTHER READING

DeAngelis LM. Medical progress: brain tumors. *N. Engl. J. Med.* 2001; 344: 114–23.

2.3 Digestive tract cancers

Aetiology/pathophysiology/ pathology

Oesophagus

One-third are adenocarcinomas of the distal oesophagus and two-thirds squamous cell cancers, which are distributed as follows: 15% in the upper, 45% in the mid and 40% in the lower portions of the oesophagus.

- Risk factors for oesophageal cancer include smoking and alcohol, which are also implicated as carcinogens in oral and oropharyngeal cancers.

- Barrett's oesophagus, where gastric columnar epithelium extends over the distal oesophagus, is associated with an increased risk of adenocarcinoma of the distal oesophagus.

- Hereditary tylosis (an autosomal dominant trait that causes palmar and plantar hyperkeratosis) and Plummer–Vinson syndrome (sideroblastic anaemia, glossitis and oesophagitis) are associated with oesophageal cancer.

Gastric

- A very high incidence of gastric cancer is found in Japan, Chile and Costa Rica. Dietary carcinogens are thought to be responsible, especially nitrosamines and nitrosamides.

- *Helicobacter pylori* causes chronic active gastritis, which progresses to chronic atrophic gastritis. This is thought to be one of the early steps in the pathogenesis of gastric cancer. Several epidemiological studies have linked *Helicobacter pylori* to stomach cancer.

- Familial mutations of the E-cadherin gene (*CDH1*) are associated with an increased risk of gastric cancer.

Pancreas

- Smoking is the only well-established aetiological factor in pancreatic cancer; studies of alcohol and coffee consumption have been contradictory.

- Some studies have identified diabetes mellitus and chronic pancreatitis as risk factors; however, as both may develop as a consequence of pancreatic cancer the results have been questioned.

Over 90% of pancreatic cancers are adenocarcinoma of ductal origin, 5% are endocrine tumours arising in islet cells and 2% are acinar cell tumours.

Colorectal

In the UK in 2003 there were 16,107 deaths from colorectal cancer, comprising 10,416 from colon cancer and 5,691 from rectal cancer. Their incidence rises with age.

Two genetic predisposing syndromes are recognised that lead to colon cancer at a young age:

- familial polyposis coli (familial adenomatous polyposis, FAP);

- hereditary non-polyposis colon cancer (HNPCC).

	Percentage of all cancer registrations		**Rank of registration (all cancers)**		**Lifetime chance of cancer**		**Change in ASR 1993–2002 (%)**		**5-year survival (%)**
Tumour	**Male**	**Female**	**Male**	**Female**	**Male**	**Female**	**Male**	**Female**	
Oesophagus	3	1	7th	13th	1 in 75	1 in 95	+8	−2	7
Gastric	4	2	5th	9th	1 in 44	1 in 86	−20	−22	13
Pancreas	3	3	10th	8th	1 in 96	1 in 95	−4	−2	2
Colorectal	14	12	3rd	2nd	1 in 18	1 in 20	−2	−4	47

TABLE 6 GASTROINTESTINAL CANCER REGISTRATION DATA FOR THE UK IN 2001

ASR, age-standardised rate.

FAP affects less than 1% of people who develop colorectal cancer and presents before they are 40 years old. Gardner's syndrome is a variant of FAP also associated with desmoid tumours, osteomas and fibromas. HNPCC affects 2–5% people who develop colon cancer and is associated with an 80% lifetime risk of colon cancer (see Sections 1.1.3 and 3.12).

There is a 40% reduction in mortality from colorectal cancer in persons who use aspirin or other NSAIDs on a regular basis, and the level of cyclooxygenase 2, a target of NSAIDs, is elevated in colonic tumours.

Epidemiology
The new digestive system cancer registration data for the UK in 2001 is shown in Table 6.

Clinical presentation

Oesophagus
Patients present with dysphagia, weight loss and less often haematemesis (Fig. 8).

Gastric
Most patients will present with vague epigastric discomfort, weight loss, early satiety, anorexia, dysphagia or vomiting. Cancer spread to the left supraclavicular lymph glands (Virchov's node) is common. One-quarter of patients have metastases, usually to the liver, at presentation. Although rare, transcoelomic spread to the ovaries (Krukenberg tumours) is a well-recognised complication.

Pancreas
Two-thirds of pancreatic cancers are in the head of the pancreas. The sufferers present with epigastric pain, weight loss and jaundice (Fig. 9). The remaining one-third are in the tail and body of the pancreas and are frequently larger at the time of diagnosis than those in the head of the gland. They thus carry a worse prognosis. Occasionally, tumours are periampullary and cause obstructive jaundice at an early stage. These tumours have a better prognosis, with 5-year survival of up to 50%.

Tumours may extend directly into the duodenum, stomach, retroperitoneum and portal vein. Metastatic spread most frequently occurs to portal and para-aortic lymph nodes and the liver.

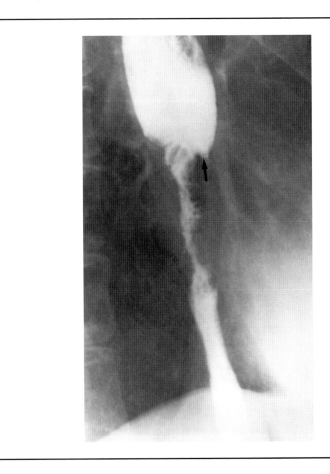

▲ **Fig. 8** Barium swallow showing oesophageal cancer causing an irregular stricture with shouldering at the upper end. Features of malignant oesophageal strictures include an irregular filling defect, extraluminal soft tissue, shouldering at margins (arrow), ulceration and proximal dilatation.

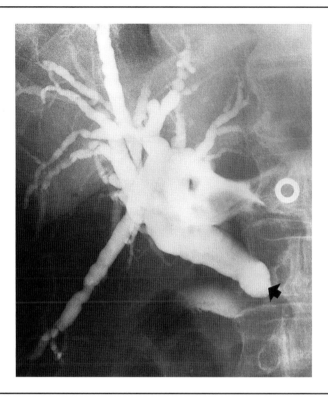

▲**Fig. 9** Percutaneous cholangiogram showing complete obstruction of the common bile duct (arrow) and dilated intrahepatic ducts due to pancreatic cancer.

For secretory endocrine tumour syndromes see Section 2.14.

Colorectal

The commonest symptoms are a change in bowel habit, rectal bleeding, abdominal pain and anaemia. Right-sided lesions classically present with microscopic anaemia and positive faecal occult blood, whereas left-sided lesions cause obstruction and blood to be smeared on the surface of stools. Colorectal cancer screening is covered in Section 3.4.

Treatment

Oesophagus

Only 40% of sufferers will have localised disease at presentation and thus be candidates for oesophagectomy, with or without preoperative neoadjuvant chemotherapy or chemoradiation. The surgery has a 5–20% mortality

rate, and may be complicated early by anastomotic leaks and later by strictures, reflux and motility disorders.

Locally advanced disease is present in 25% of sufferers. Small-volume inoperable disease may be considered for chemoradiation with curative intent, although this may cause oesophageal perforation or stricture, pneumonitis and pulmonary fibrosis. The majority of these patients are treated with stent insertion for dysphagia or palliative radiotherapy for pain or bleeding.

Around 35% of sufferers have metastases at presentation and these may be treated symptomatically, or with palliative chemotherapy if fit.

Gastric

The optimal surgery for patients with localised disease is radical subtotal gastrectomy and gastrojejunostomy. High cure rates

are only achieved with early lesions (those that are lymph node negative and where the tumour is confined to mucosa or submucosa); sadly these cases are uncommon in Europe. Despite the high relapse rate following surgery, adjuvant chemotherapy is rarely of benefit and adjuvant radiotherapy, although reducing locoregional relapse, does not alter chances of survival.

Patients with locally advanced disease may occasionally be rendered surgical candidates by neoadjuvant chemotherapy. Alternatively, they can be treated with chemoradiotherapy.

Metastatic disease may be treated with 5-fluorouracil-based combination chemotherapy schedules. These have response rates of around 35%, but do not improve survival rates.

Pancreas

Surgical resection is feasible for only 15% of tumours in the head of the pancreas (pancreaticoduodenostomy or 'Whipple procedure') and 10% of body and tail tumours (partial pancreatectomy). The operative mortality is high (up to 20%) and tumours are often found to be unresectable. Postoperative adjuvant chemoradiotherapy may be of benefit.

Most patients are treated symptomatically with endoscopic stenting for jaundice, and occasionally with surgical gastric bypass for duodenal obstruction and coeliac plexus nerve block for pain. Chemotherapy for advanced or metastatic pancreatic cancer can improve symptoms but is usually only administered in the context of a clinical trial.

Colorectal

Colorectal cancer staging is usually performed using the modified Dukes' classification.

- Dukes' A: cancer localised to bowel wall.

- Dukes' B: cancer penetrates wall.

- Dukes' C: cancer spread to local lymph nodes.

- Dukes' D: distant metastases.

Over 80% of patients undergo surgery with the aim of cure, although less than half of these will be alive 5 years later. Preoperative radiotherapy should be offered to patients with rectal cancer.

If locally advanced disease (Dukes' C) is found at surgery, adjuvant chemotherapy improves survival. Randomised studies in instances of advanced or recurrent disease reveal a prolonged median survival and symptom-free survival for early chemotherapy. The mainstay of colorectal chemotherapy is the combination of 5-fluorouracil and folinic acid.

Occasionally, patients with isolated hepatic metastases are candidates for curative hepatic resection, but only a minority (20%) will be cured.

Prognosis
See Table 7 for 5-year survival rates of digestive system cancers.

TABLE 7 THE 5-YEAR SURVIVAL RATES OF GASTROINTESTINAL CANCERS	
Tumour	**5-year survival (%)**
Oesophagus	7
Gastric	13
Pancreas	2
Colon (overall)	47
Dukes' A	83
Dukes' B	64
Dukes' C	38
Dukes' D	3

FURTHER READING

Bailey C. Stomach cancer. *Clinical Effectiveness*, 2005. Available at www.clinicalevidence.com/ceweb/conditions/onc/onc.jsp

Bazian Ltd. Pancreatic cancer. *Clinical Effectiveness*, 2004. Available at www.clinicalevidence.com/ceweb/conditions/onc/onc.jsp

Enzinger PC and Mayer RJ. Medical progress: esophageal cancer. *N. Engl. J. Med.* 2003; 349: 366–81.

Meyerhardt JA and Mayer RJ. Drug therapy: systemic therapy for colorectal cancer. *N. Engl. J. Med.* 2004; 351: 2519–29.

NHS Centre for Reviews and Dissemination. The management of colorectal cancer. *Effective Health Care* 1997; 3: 1–12.

NHS Centre for Reviews and Dissemination. The management of colorectal cancers. *Effective Health Care* 2004; 8: 1–12.

National Institute for Health and Clinical Excellence. *Colorectal Cancer Clinical Service Guidelines*, 2004. Available at www.nice.org.uk

Roy P and Last R. Colorectal cancer. *Clinical Effectiveness*, 2006. Available at www.clinicalevidence.com/ceweb/conditions/onc/onc.jsp

Ryan DP, Compton CC and Mayer RJ. Medical progress: carcinoma of the anal canal. *N. Engl. J. Med.* 2000; 342: 792–800.

Various. ABC of colorectal cancer. *BMJ* 2000; 321. Available at http://resources.bmj.com/bmj/topics/abc.

Various. ABC of diseases of liver, pancreas and biliary system. *BMJ* 2001; 322. Available at http://resources.bmj.com/bmj/topics/abc.

Various. ABC of diseases of the upper gastrointestinal tract. *BMJ* 2001; 323. Available at http://resources.bmj.com/bmj/topics/abc.

2.4 Genitourinary cancer

Aetiology/pathophysiology/pathology

Kidney cancer
Over 90% of renal tumours arise in the cortex, probably from cells of the proximal convoluted tubule, and are named renal cell carcinoma, renal adenocarcinoma, clear-cell carcinoma, hypernephroma or Grawitz tumours (these terms are synonymous). The remaining 10% are renal pelvis transitional-cell carcinomas and resemble tumours of the ureter, bladder and urethra (Fig. 10).

Rare familial cases of renal cell cancer are seen in von Hippel–Lindau syndrome and familial papillary renal carcinoma syndrome (mutation of *MET* oncogene on chromosome 7q31) (see Section 3.12).

Bladder cancer
The majority of bladder tumours are transitional-cell carcinomas (85%), with squamous cell cancers accounting for 10% and adenocarcinomas for 5%. Cigarette smoking is the most significant causative factor in the pathogenesis of bladder cancer, although recognised carcinogens including aryl amines, benzene and naphthylamines also play a part. *Schistosoma haematobium* causes squamous cell cancer of the bladder, the commonest bladder tumour in Egyptian men.

Testis cancer
Seminomas account for 40% of testicular germ-cell tumours (GCTs) and are the histological equivalent of ovarian dysgerminomas and pineal germinomas. The remaining 60% are non-seminomatous GCTs

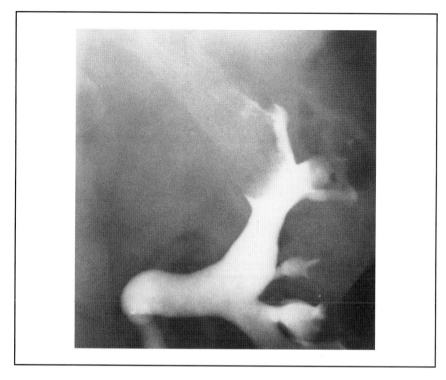

▲ **Fig. 10** Intravenous urogram showing irregular filling defect in an upper calyx due to renal pelvis transitional-cell carcinoma. These tumours constitute 10% of renal neoplasms in adults and may produce seedling tumours further down the urinary tract (ureter, bladder and urethra).

been implicated in hereditary prostate cancer (see Section 3.12). Overall, only 10% of cases have a familial pattern, although these men develop prostate cancer at a younger age than most sufferers.

There are racial differences in the incidence of prostate cancer: the order of incidence is black > white > Oriental. High levels of the androgen synthesis pathway enzyme 5α-reductase in African-Americans is associated with prostate cancer. The role of diet remains controversial. Although a high-fat, low-fibre intake may increase the risk of prostate cancer, soya beans and retinoids appear to protect against it.

Epidemiology

The new genitourinary cancer registration data for the UK in 2002 is shown in Table 8.

Prostate cancer

Prostate cancer is the commonest cancer in men in the UK. In 2002 there were 31,923 new cases diagnosed and around 10,000 deaths from prostate cancer in the UK. More than 60% of cases occur in men over 70 years old. Nearly half have metastatic disease at presentation, and a further quarter

(NSGCTs), comprising embryonal carcinoma, malignant teratoma, choriocarcinoma and yolk sac tumours. Many NSGCTs contain a mixture of these elements.

- Cryptorchidism is the only established risk factor for testis cancer, and the risk is reduced to normal if orchidopexy is performed before the age of 6.

- Extragonadal GCTs occur in the retroperitoneum, mediastinum and occasionally the pineal region. These tumours are thought to originate from residual midline germinal elements.

- Isochromosome 12p is a somatic abnormality found in up to 90% of GCTs and may be helpful in the differential diagnosis of extragonadal GCTs (Fig. 11).

Prostate cancer

Prostate cancers are adenocarcinomas that are graded

on a 5-point Gleason grading score. Family history is a major risk factor for the development of prostate cancer. Inherited *BRCA1* and *BRCA2* mutations (breast and ovarian cancer families) and hereditary prostate cancers due to mutations of *HPC1* (chromosome 1q24–q25) and *HPC2* (chromosome Xq27–q28) have

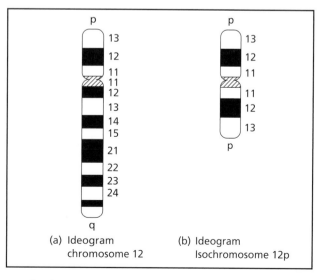

(a) Ideogram chromosome 12

(b) Ideogram Isochromosome 12p

▲ **Fig. 11** Ideogram of isochromosome 12p.

	Percentage of all cancer registrations		Rank of registration (all cancers)		Lifetime chance of cancer		Change in ASR 1993–2002 (%)	5-year survival (%)
Tumour	Male	Female	Male	Female	Male	Female		
Prostate	23	–	1st	–	1 in 14	–	+48	65
Testis	<1	–	15th	–	1 in 286	–	+5	96
Kidney	3	1	8th	14th	1 in 89	1 in 162	+18	45
Bladder	5	2	4th	11th	1 in 30	1 in 79	–27	58–67

TABLE 8 GENITOURINARY CANCER REGISTRATION DATA FOR THE UK IN 2002

ASR, age-standardised rate.

display localised extracapsular spread. In the USA it has been estimated that for a 50-year-old man, the projected lifetime risk of histological evidence of prostate cancer is 42%, of clinical disease is 9.5% and of death from prostate cancer is 3%.

Substantial increases in incidence have been reported in recent years for many countries around the world (including the UK) after correction for an ageing population. Some of this increase may be due to a real increase in risk but two other factors, the increasing use of transurethral resection (TUR) of the prostate during the 1980s and prostate-specific antigen (PSA) testing in the 1990s, have certainly increased the detection rate of the disease. In contrast, in the USA where the incidence is up to 10 times higher than in the UK, most of the two- to three-fold rise in incidence between 1973 and 1993 is due to widespread prostate cancer screening. For more details on prostate cancer screening see Section 3.4.

Clinical presentation

Kidney cancer
Although infrequent, the classical triad at presentation is loin pain, a mass and haematuria. Additional features include weight loss, fever and varicocele as well as signs of metastatic disease. Paraneoplastic manifestations are frequent with renal cell cancer, including anaemia, erythrocytosis, thrombocytosis, hypertension, hypercalcaemia, gynaecomastia, Cushing's syndrome, dermatomyositis, polymyositis and hepatic dysfunction without metastases (Stauffer's syndrome). Increasing numbers of renal cell tumours are diagnosed as incidental findings on abdominal imaging performed for other reasons.

Bladder cancer
Painless microscopic or macroscopic haematuria is the most frequent presenting sign of bladder cancer, although other lower urinary tract symptoms may be present. Metastatic disease at presentation occurs in fewer than 5% of cases. At diagnosis 70% of patients will have superficial papillary disease and 30% an invasive tumour.

Testis cancer
Testis cancer usually presents as a painless swelling, and minor trauma may bring this to the attention of the patient. Metastatic disease may present with abdominal fullness, backache, leg lymphoedema or a supraclavicular mass. Gynaecomastia may be present and occasionally patients present with superior vena cava obstruction (see Section 1.4.3 and Section 3.9). Extragonadal GCTs may occur in the midline anywhere from the sacrum to the pineal.

Serum tumour markers may be helpful in diagnosis (as well as prognosis and monitoring treatment). Of patients with seminoma, 10% have mildly raised human chorionic gonadotropin (HCG) levels (under 100 IU/L) but alpha-fetoprotein (AFP) is always normal. Of patients with NSGCTs, 85% have elevated HCG and/or AFP (see Section 3.3).

Prostate cancer
The incidence of prostate cancer increases with age; only 12% of clinically apparent cases arise before the age of 65 and only 20% of deaths occur in men under 70 years old. The most frequent presentation of symptomatic disease is with lower urinary tract symptoms or with bone pain from metastatic disease.

Treatment

Kidney cancer
Where possible radical nephrectomy should be undertaken as this may:

- be curative for early-stage disease;

- palliate symptoms of haematuria and pain in patients with locally advanced disease;

- improve the duration of survival in patients with metastatic disease who are subsequently treated with immunotherapy.

Spontaneous regression of metastases following nephrectomy, although well recognised, is extremely rare (occurring in less than 1% of cases) and is itself no longer considered to justify surgery.

Immunotherapy with interferon or interleukin-2 may be used in the management of metastatic disease (see Section 3.7). Antiangiogenic agents and tumour vaccines are showing promising results.

Bladder cancer

Superficial bladder cancer is treated by TUR. Those found to have high-risk disease likely to recur (high-grade histology, incomplete resection, multifocal disease or carcinoma in situ) should be treated with adjuvant intravesical bacille Calmette–Guérin (BCG).

Options for muscle-invasive bladder cancer range from TUR to radical cystectomy or radical radiotherapy depending on the performance status and age of the patient. Metastatic disease may be treated with combination chemotherapy in patients with good functional status, although complete remissions are rare.

Testis cancer

Testicular GCT is the most curable malignancy, even in the presence of metastases. Radical inguinal orchidectomy establishes the diagnosis.

For stage I disease where the tumour is confined to the testis, patients may be followed by close surveillance or be treated with adjuvant chemotherapy (seminoma or NSGCT) or radiotherapy (seminoma only).

Advanced disease should be treated with combination cisplatin-based chemotherapy. The standard regimen is bleomycin, etoposide and cisplatin. Following chemotherapy, residual masses should be removed surgically. If patients relapse after chemotherapy for advanced disease, they are candidates for high-dose chemotherapy and autologous peripheral blood stem-cell transplantation.

Prostate cancer

Localised disease The main options for treating clinically localised prostate cancer are 'watchful waiting', radiotherapy and radical prostatectomy. There is no evidence to support the superiority of any of these approaches.

- Watchful waiting varies from waiting until the patient presents with symptoms to a more active follow-up as an outpatient with regular PSA testing and physical examination. Although this strategy does not produce the physical or sexual complications associated with other treatments, it may increase anxiety. It is the best option for men with low-grade incidentally detected tumours and those who have a life expectancy of less than 10 years. For patients with a longer life expectancy, radical treatment will improve the local control rate but may adversely affect their quality of life.

- Radical radiotherapy is the most commonly used treatment in the UK. Complications include damage to adjacent organs, causing acute diarrhoea (in 50% of patients) and chronic proctitis (in 5–10%), incontinence (in 1–6%) and impotence (in 40%).

- Radical (total) prostatectomy complications include operative mortality (0.5% in skilled hands), complete incontinence (in 1–27% of patients) and impotence (in 20–85%). The published survival data for radiotherapy are worse than for surgery, but less fit patients will be referred for radiotherapy rather than surgery.

Advanced disease Metastatic prostate cancer is treated by endocrine therapy with orchidectomy, luteinising hormone-releasing hormone (LHRH) agonists with or without antiandrogens (such as flutamide, bicalutamide and cyproterone acetate), or oestrogens. Orchidectomy is associated with major psychological side effects as well as impotence and hot flushes. LHRH agonists produce an initial increase in testosterone levels that can cause the tumour to flare for the first 2 weeks of treatment. This may result in disease progression causing spinal cord compression, ureteric obstruction or increasing bone pain. For this reason an antiandrogen should be started 3–7 days before the LHRH analogue injection and be continued for 3 weeks after it. The advantage of using a combination of LHRH analogues and antiandrogens to maximally suppress androgen levels has been demonstrated in some studies, and a meta-analysis of all the trials showed a modest survival benefit over using an LHRH agonist alone. Diethylstilbestrol is now rarely used because of its toxic effects, including venous and arterial thrombosis, fluid retention and nausea.

Metastatic bone pain may be relieved by irradiation to localised sites or hemibody single-fraction radiotherapy if the disease is extensive. An alternative route of administration is an intravenous strontium (^{89}Sr) isotope, which is bone-seeking.

Prognosis

See Table 9 for 5-year survival rates of genitourinary cancers.

TABLE 9 THE 5-YEAR SURVIVAL RATES OF GENITOURINARY CANCERS

Tumour	5-year survival (%)
Kidney cancer	45
Bladder cancer	58–67
Bladder cancer (superficial)	80–90
Bladder cancer (invasive)	30–40
Testis cancer	96
Prostate cancer (incidental)	85
Prostate cancer (early localised)	78
Prostate cancer (locally advanced)	60
Prostate cancer (metastatic)	10–30
Prostate cancer	65

FURTHER READING

Bosl GJ and Motzer RJ. Testicular germ cell cancer. *N. Engl. J. Med.* 1997; 337: 242–53.

Cohen HT and McGovern FJ. Renal cell carcinoma. *N. Engl. J. Med.* 2005; 353: 2477–90.

Conn PM and Crowley WF. Gonadotropin-releasing hormone and its analogues. *N. Engl. J. Med.* 1991; 324: 93–103.

Dror Michaelson M, Smith MR and Talcott JA. Prostate cancer (metastatic). *Clinical Effectiveness*, 2003. Available at www.clinicalevidence.com/ceweb/conditions/onc/onc.jsp

Frydenberg M, Stricker PD and Kaye KW. Prostate cancer diagnosis and management. *Lancet* 1997; 349: 1681–7.

Gittes RF. Carcinoma of the prostate. *N. Engl. J. Med.* 1991; 324: 236–45.

International Germ Cell Cancer Collaborative Group. International Germ Cell Consensus Classification: a prognostic factor-based staging system for metastatic germ cell cancers. *J. Clin. Oncol.* 1997; 15: 594–603.

National Institute for Health and Clinical Excellence. *Urological Cancers Clinical Service Guidelines*, 2002. Available at www.nice.org.uk

Neal R, Stuart N and Wilkinson C. Testicular seminoma. *Clinical Effectiveness*, 2005. Available at www.clinicalevidence.com/ceweb/conditions/msh/msh.jsp

Nelson WG, De Marzo AM and Isaacs WB. Prostate cancer. *N. Engl. J. Med.* 2003; 349: 366–81.

Prostate Cancer Trialists' Collaborative Group. Maximal androgen blockade in advanced prostate cancer: an overview of the randomised trials. *Lancet* 2000; 355: 1491–8.

Raghavan D, Shipley WU, Garnick MB, Russell PJ and Richie JP. Biology and management of bladder cancer. *N. Engl. J. Med.* 1990; 322: 1129–38.

Wit L. Prostate cancer (non metastatic). *Clinical Effectiveness*, 2003. Available at www.clinicalevidence.com/ceweb/conditions/onc/onc.jsp

2.5 Gynaecological cancer

Aetiology/pathophysiology/pathology

Ovarian tumours

Suppressed ovulation appears to protect against the development of ovarian cancer, so pregnancy, prolonged breast-feeding and the high-oestrogen contraceptive pill have all been shown to reduce the risk of ovarian cancer.

Up to 7% of women with ovarian cancer have a positive family history. Two well-recognised familial patterns occur:

- hereditary breast/ovarian cancer families have mutations of *BRCA1* or *BRCA2*;

- Lynch-type II families have ovarian, endometrial, colorectal and gastric tumours and mutations of mismatch repair enzymes (see Section 3.12).

Endometrial tumours

Endometrial cancer is 10 times commoner in obese women. It is associated with elevated levels of free oestrogens due to decreased sex hormone-binding globulin, increased aromatisation of androgens (androstenedione to oestrone), or unopposed oestrogens, especially during hormone-replacement therapy and tamoxifen treatment.

Cervical tumours

The main risk factor for cervical cancer is infection with human papillomavirus (HPV) genotypes 16, 18, 31, 35 and 39. These are transmitted sexually: multiple sex partners, early onset of sexual activity and smoking are associated with cervical cancer. A vaccine for high-risk HPV genotypes is now available and under investigation in the prevention and treatment of cervical cancer.

Choriocarcinoma

Most cases of choriocarcinoma follow a hydatidiform molar pregnancy, although it may occur after both spontaneous abortion and

TABLE 10 GYNAECOLOGICAL CANCER REGISTRATION DATA FOR THE UK IN 2002					
	Percentage of all female cancer registrations	Rank of all female cancer registrations	Lifetime chance of cancer	Change in ASR 1993–2002 (%)	5-year survival (%)
Cervix	1	12th	1 in 116	−31	61
Endometrium	4	5th	1 in 73	+18	73
Ovary	5	4th	1 in 48	+5	36
ASR, age-standardised rate.					

normal-term pregnancy. If choriocarcinoma follows a molar pregnancy, molecular analysis will reveal that the tumour DNA is entirely androgenetic, being derived from the father, with loss of all maternal alleles. In contrast, post-term choriocarcinoma has a biparental genotype. Thus, all cases of choriocarcinoma include paternal DNA sequences that are absent from the patient's genome and can be used, if necessary, to confirm the diagnosis genetically.

Epidemiology

Ovarian, endometrial and cervical cancer are the fourth, fifth and twelfth most common cancers, respectively, in women in the UK (Table 10). In 2002, there were 6,900 new cases of and 4,600 deaths from ovarian cancer in the UK. Although breast cancer is five times commoner than ovarian cancer, deaths from breast cancer are only three times commoner than deaths from ovarian cancer. Ovarian cancer accounts for 5% of all deaths in women aged 40–60 years. Deaths from cervical cancer have fallen gradually over the last 20 years to around 1,100 per year in the UK.

Choriocarcinoma is a rare condition with approximately 100 cases per year in England and Wales, but higher rates in the Far East.

Clinical presentation

Ovarian tumours

Most women present with advanced disease and vague abdominal symptoms such as bloating, discomfort, altered bowel habit, backache or weight loss. The combination of ultrasound findings, serum CA125 and age can be used to differentiate between benign ovarian cysts and malignancy with 80–90% sensitivity and specificity, and have been studied for population screening (see Section 3.4).

Occasionally, umbilical peritoneal deposits are seen as Sister Joseph nodules (Fig. 12).

Rare ovarian tumours include the following.

- Germ-cell tumours (GCTs) resemble testicular GCTs in their histology and clinical management.

- Sex cord tumours include granulosa cell tumours, thecomas, Sertoli–Leydig cell tumours and gonadoblastomas. The sex cord tumours occasionally produce oestrogens, causing precocious puberty and postmenopausal bleeding, as well as androgens that cause virilisation.

Endometrial tumours

These tumours present in postmenopausal women as uterine bleeding. Postmenopausal bleeding is always abnormal and requires prompt investigation with

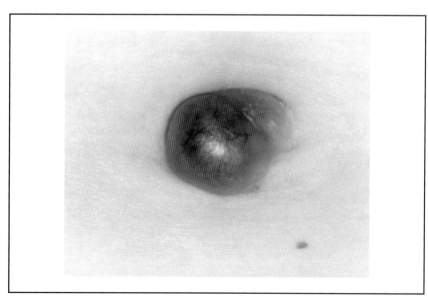

▲ **Fig. 12** Sister Joseph umbilical nodule due to advanced ovarian cancer.

dilatation and curettage or suction curettage.

Cervical cancer

In addition to asymptomatic patients identified from the screening programme, women with cervical cancer present with abnormal vaginal bleeding including postcoital bleeding, postmenopausal bleeding and irregular menses.

Choriocarcinoma

The clinical features of choriocarcinoma include:

- hyperemesis gravidarum;

- antepartum haemorrhage, especially the passing of grape-like particles;

- breast tenderness and gynaecomastia;

- thyrotoxicosis [human chorionic gonadotropin (HCG) shares β subunit with thyroid-stimulating hormone (TSH)];

- haemorrhagic metastases (especially lung, brain and vagina).

The most important investigations are pelvic ultrasonography, quantitative serum HCG assay and CXR. The serum HCG is elevated in all cases of choriocarcinoma but also during pregnancy and in 50% of non-seminomatous GCTs, and is found at low levels in 10% of seminomas. Serum thyroxine is often elevated because HCG acts as a weak TSH receptor agonist due to homology between the β subunits of HCG and TSH (molecular mimicry).

Differential diagnosis

Choriocarcinoma

- If presenting with lung metastases, choriocarcinoma may mimic pulmonary thromboembolic disease.

- If presenting with cerebral metastases, choriocarcinoma may mimic subarachnoid haemorrhage from an aneurysm or arteriovenous malformation.

It is always worthwhile performing a pregnancy test in a young woman with either presentation: a normal serum or urine HCG level excludes metastatic choriocarcinoma.

Treatment

Ovarian tumours

Surgery is the first intervention used to treat ovarian cancer, although complete clearance of a tumour will not be possible in most women. Nevertheless, debulking of as much tumour as possible has been shown to improve survival in women with advanced ovarian cancer. Following surgery the majority of women will be candidates for chemotherapy and at present the optimal treatment is a combination of paclitaxel and either cisplatin or carboplatin.

In the event of relapse, second-line chemotherapy is associated with a response rate of 20–40%, which is most likely if the treatment-free interval exceeds 12 months. Serum CA125 may be useful in predicting response to treatment, as falling values are associated with tumour regression. CA125 measurements are also used to monitor remission as rising values may precede clinical relapse by up to 3 months (see Section 3.3).

Endometrial tumours

Surgery is the initial therapy for endometrial cancer, and adjuvant pelvic radiotherapy is widely used in women with tumours that extend beyond the inner half of the myometrium. The combination of surgery and radiotherapy may produce long-term lymphoedema.

Neither chemotherapy nor endocrine therapy has been shown to reduce the chance of death in cases of advanced endometrial cancer.

Cervical cancer

Very early cervical cancer may be treated with cone biopsy or radiotherapy alone. More extensive disease requires radical hysterectomy followed by adjuvant chemoradiotherapy for women with adverse prognostic features (such as bulky or locally advanced disease, and lymph node or parametrium invasion).

Choriocarcinoma

Choriocarcinoma is exquisitely sensitive to chemotherapy. In the UK, all patients should be referred to the National Trophoblastic Tumour Service based at Charing Cross Hospital.

Prognosis

See Table 11 for 5-year survival rates of gynaecological cancers. Over 95% of women with choriocarcinoma can be cured.

TABLE 11 THE 5-YEAR SURVIVAL RATES FOR GYNAECOLOGICAL CANCERS

Tumour	5-year survival (%)
Ovary	36
Endometrium	73
Cervix	61

FURTHER READING

Advanced Ovarian Cancer Trialists' Group. Chemotherapy in advanced ovarian cancer: four systematic meta-analyses of individual patient data from 37 randomised trials. *Br. J. Cancer* 1998; 78: 1479–87.

Cancer Guidance Sub-group of the Clinical Outcomes Group. *Improving Outcomes in Gynaecological Cancers*, 1999. Available at www.nice.org.uk

Cannistra SA. Cancer of the ovary. *N. Engl. J. Med.* 2004; 351: 2519–29.

McGuire WP, Hoskins WJ, Brady MF, *et al.* Cyclophosphamide and cisplatin compared with paclitaxel and cisplatin in patients with stage III and IV ovarian cancer. *N. Engl. J. Med.* 1996; 334: 1–6.

NHS Centre for Reviews and Dissemination. Management of gynaecological cancers. *Effective Health Care* 1999; 5: 1–12.

Sundar S, Horne A and Kehoe A. Cervical cancer. *Clinical Effectiveness*, 2005. Available at www.clinicalevidence.com/ceweb/conditions/onc/onc.jsp

2.6 Head and neck cancer

Aetiology/pathophysiology/pathology

- Smoking, high alcohol intake and poor oral hygiene are well-established risk factors for the development of head and neck tumours.

- Epstein–Barr virus is implicated in the aetiology of nasopharyngeal carcinoma in southern China.

- Betel nut chewing is implicated in oral cancer in Asia.

- Wood-dust inhalation by furniture makers is implicated in nasal cavity adenocarcinomas.

Epidemiology

Head and neck tumours make up 5% of all tumours and account for 2.5% of cancer deaths. They are twice as common in men and generally occur in those over 50 years old. The sites in order of frequency are larynx, oral cavity, pharynx and salivary glands (Fig. 13).

Clinical presentation

- Most head and neck tumours present as malignant ulcers with raised indurated edges on a surface mucosa.

- Oral tumours present as non-healing ulcers with ipsilateral otalgia.

- Oropharyngeal tumours present with dysphagia, pain and otalgia.

- Hypopharyngeal tumours present with dysphagia, odynophagia, referred otalgia and neck nodes.

- Laryngeal cancers present with persistent hoarseness, pain, otalgia, dyspnoea and stridor.

- Nasopharyngeal cancers present with a bloody nasal discharge, nasal obstruction, conductive deafness, atypical facial pain, diplopia, hoarseness and Horner's syndrome.

- Nasal and sinus tumours present with a bloody discharge or obstruction.

- Salivary gland tumours present as painless swellings or facial nerve palsies.

Treatment

- Stage I and II tumours where there are no regional lymph node metastases should be treated with surgery or radiotherapy. This has a 60–69% cure rate.

- Patients with nodal metastases and more advanced local disease are treated with a combination of surgery and radiotherapy (often with concomitant chemotherapy as a sensitiser), with cure rates of less than 30%.

- Recurrent or metastatic tumour may be palliated with further surgery or radiotherapy to aid local control. In such circumstances, systemic chemotherapy has a response rate of around 30%.

- Second malignancies are frequent in patients who have been successfully treated for head and neck tumours (annual rate up to 3%) and all patients should be encouraged to give up smoking and drinking to lower this risk. In addition, a number of studies have addressed the role of

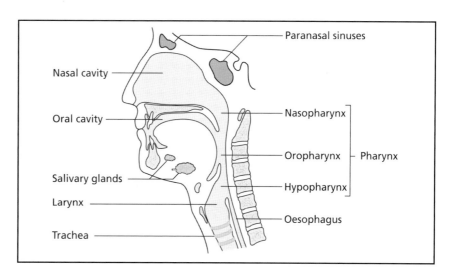

▲ **Fig. 13** Anatomy of head and neck.

retinoids and β-carotene as secondary prophylaxis but none has proved useful.

Prognosis

See Table 12 for 5-year survival rates of head and neck cancers.

TABLE 12 THE 5-YEAR SURVIVAL RATES FOR HEAD AND NECK TUMOURS	
Tumour	**5-year survival (%)**
Larynx	68
Larynx (glottic)	85
Larynx (supraglottic)	55
Oral cavity	54
Oropharynx	45
Nasopharynx	45
Hypopharynx	25
Salivary glands	60

FURTHER READING

Forastiere A, Koch W, Trotti A and Sidransky D. Head and neck cancer. *N. Engl. J. Med.* 2001; 345: 1890–1900.

2.7 Skin tumours

Aetiology/pathophysiology/pathology

Basal cell carcinoma and squamous cell carcinoma

Skin cancer is the commonest cancer overall, accounting for one-third of all cases of cancer; however, it accounts for only 2% of cancer deaths. Basal cell carcinoma (BCC) and squamous cell carcinoma (SCC) are the most common types of skin cancer, BCC being four times commoner than SCC.

Sun damage is the major cause of skin cancer, especially at UVB wavelengths (290–320 nm). The incidence of skin cancer is higher in latitudes closer to the equator. Light-exposed areas of the body are the most frequent sites for tumours, and occupations with high sun exposure (eg farmers) have an increased incidence of BCC and SCC. Ozone absorbs UVB so progressive destruction of the ozone layer by fluorinated hydrocarbons may lead to increased rates of skin cancer.

Genetic predispositions to skin cancer include xeroderma pigmentosum, Gorlin's basal cell naevus syndrome and familial melanoma syndromes (see Section 3.12). Familial melanoma is caused by inherited mutations of the *CDKN2* (*p16*) gene (chromosome 9p21), *CDK4* (chromosome 12q13) and *CMM* (chromosome 1p36).

Chemical carcinogens including arsenic are associated with SCC: in 1775 Percival Pott described scrotal cancers in chimney sweeps that are now thought to have been due to industrial exposure to coal tar. Furthermore, radiation is associated with an increased incidence of SCC, BCC and Bowen's disease (SCC *in situ*). Genotypes 5 and 8 of human papillomavirus have been found in some skin SCC.

Melanoma

Melanomas develop from melanocytes derived from neural crest tissue that migrate to the skin, eye, central nervous system and occasionally elsewhere. The incidence of melanoma is rising fast and has been shown to be related to sun exposure. The vast majority arise from pre-existing benign naevi and this emphasises the importance of watching for changes in moles.

- Fair-skinned and red-headed people are particularly prone, as are people who burn rapidly in the sun without ever tanning.

- Patients with a prior history of melanoma and with a large number of moles are at 8–10 times more risk.

- Patients with a strong family history or a giant pigmented hairy naevus (either >20 cm in diameter or >5% of body surface area) are at greater (100-fold) risk.

- Two precursor lesions are known: dysplastic naevi and congenital naevi.

There has been a three-fold increase in the incidence of melanoma mortality between 1950 and 1990. In the USA it is estimated that 1 in 100 white Americans will develop melanoma during their lifetime.

Epidemiology

The new melanoma registration data for the UK in 2002 are shown in Table 13.

Clinical presentation

Basal cell carcinoma

BCCs start as painless translucent pearly nodules with telangiectasia on sun-exposed skin (Fig. 14). As they enlarge they ulcerate and develop a rolled shiny edge, progressing slowly over many months and years. Fewer than 0.1% metastasise to regional lymph nodes. They occur mostly on the face (especially nose, nasolabial fold and inner canthus), usually in elderly people. They are commoner in men than women.

Squamous cell carcinoma

SCCs are red, irregular, hyperkeratotic tumours that ulcerate and crust (Fig. 15). They occur in sun-exposed areas and common sites are the face, neck, back, forearm and dorsum of the hand. Only 1–2% metastasise to regional lymph nodes. Unlike BCC, SCCs grow more rapidly over

TABLE **13** MELANOMA CANCER REGISTRATION DATA FOR THE **UK** IN **2002**

Tumour	Percentage of all cancer registrations		Rank of registration (all cancers)		Lifetime chance of cancer		Change in ASR 1993–2002 (%)		5-year survival (%)
	Male	Female	Male	Female	Male	Female	Male	Female	
Melanoma	1	3	11th	6th	1 in 147	1 in 117	+22	+38	77

ASR, age-standardised rate.

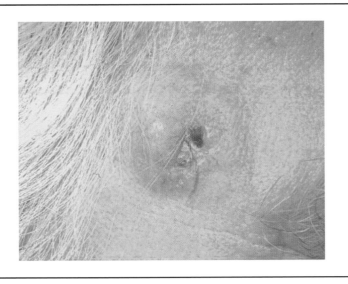

▲**Fig. 14** BCC. (Courtesy of King's College Hospital, London.)

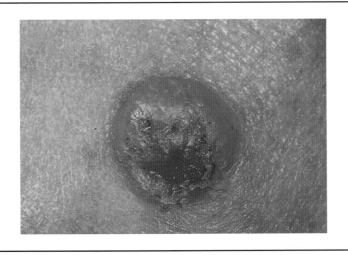

▲**Fig. 15** SCC. (Courtesy of King's College Hospital, London.)

months rather than years and occasionally bleed. Marjolin ulcers are SCCs arising in long-standing benign ulcers (eg venous ulcers) or scars (eg old burns).

Merkel cell carcinoma

These are highly malignant tumours in the basal layer of the epidermis, most commonly found in elderly white patients. They are rapidly growing, painless, shiny, purple nodules that may occur anywhere on the body. These tumours are thought to arise from neuroendocrine cells and are positive for neuron-specific enolase staining. They resemble small-cell lung cancer in their clinical course. Distant metastases are common and treatment is with combination chemotherapy, although relapses are frequent and the prognosis is poor.

Melanoma

Five clinical variants of moles are easily recognised:

- hairy naevi are intradermal;

- smooth naevi may be intradermal or compound (both intradermal and junctional);

- blue naevi are deep intradermal;

- Hutchinson lentigo are large junctional or compound lesions occurring in the elderly;

- juvenile naevi are junctional naevi that regress at puberty.

Only junctional and compound naevi, where melanocytes are present in the epidermis as well as the dermis, progress to melanoma. Changes in size, colour or edge of a naevus, or bleeding should alert to the possibility of melanoma.

The three major signs are:

- change in size;

- change in shape;

- change in colour.

The four minor signs are:

- inflammation;

- crusting or bleeding;

- sensory change (eg itch);

- diameter >7 mm.

Four types of melanoma are recognised (Table 14).

TABLE 14 CLINICOPATHOLOGICAL FEATURES OF FOUR COMMON FORMS OF MELANOMA

Type	Location	Age (median) (years)	Gender and race	Edge	Colour	Proportion (%)
Superficial spreading	All body surfaces, especially legs	56	White females	Palpable, irregular	Brown, black, grey or pink; central or halo depigmentation (Fig. 16)	50
Nodular	All body surfaces	49	White males	Palpable	Uniform bluish black (Fig. 17)	30
Lentigo maligna	Sun-exposed areas, especially head and neck	70	White females	Flat, irregular	Shades of brown or black, hypopigmentation (Fig. 18)	15
Acral lentiginous	Palms, soles and mucous membranes	61	Black males	Palpable irregular nodule	Black, irregularly coloured	5

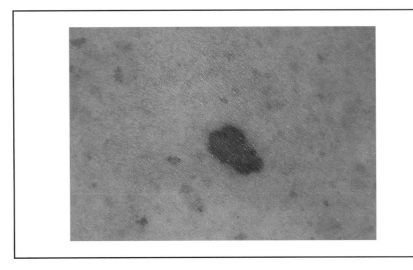

▲ **Fig. 16** Superficial spreading malignant melanoma. (Courtesy of King's College Hospital, London.)

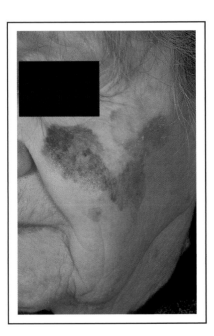

▲ **Fig. 18** Lentigo malignant melanoma. (Courtesy of King's College Hospital, London.)

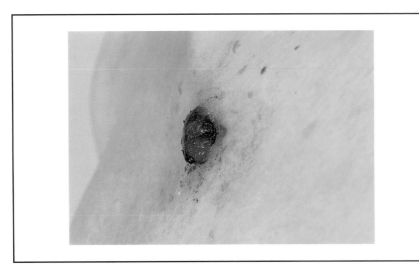

▲ **Fig. 17** Nodular melanoma. (Courtesy of Dr N. Stone.)

Ocular melanomas are the commonest intraocular malignancy and arise from uveal melanocytes. They progressively displace the retina inwards and may affect the lens and iris leading to secondary glaucoma. Occasionally patients present with occult primary melanoma, and they should be considered in the diagnostic work-up for unknown primary tumours. Immunocytochemical staining for S-100 is usually positive.

Treatment

Basal and squamous cell carcinoma

The goal of treatment for BCC and SCC is to eradicate local disease and achieve the best cosmetic appearance. The main options include the following.

- Surgery: offers a single brief procedure and histological confirmation of completeness of excision.

- Curettage: suitable for small nodular lesions (<1 cm) and yields good cosmesis.

- Cryotherapy: can be used for lesions <2 cm but may leave an area of depigmentation.

- Radiotherapy.

Radiotherapy has the following advantages: no pain, no hospitalisation, no keloids or contractures, preservation of uninvolved tissue and creation of smaller defects. However, it requires multiple visits and results in loss of hair follicles and sweat glands at the treated site. The decision between surgery and radiotherapy is based on the size and site of the disease, histology, age of the patient, recurrence rates and anticipated cosmetic results.

Melanoma

Early disease Melanoma is essentially a surgically treated disease. Surgical resection should be used for both primary lesions and localised metastases. Even distant metastases if unifocal should be considered for resection. Tumour thickness, as measured by the Clark level, correlates with the risk of lymph node metastases and of death.

- Clark level I: the melanoma is confined to the epidermis, never metastasises and has a 100% cure rate.

- Clark level V: the melanoma has penetrated to the subdermal fat; 65% of these cases have lymph node spread and only 10% are cured.

More recently most pathologists have adopted Breslow staging, which just measures tumour depth in millimetres.

Advanced disease Frequent sites of metastatic spread after regional lymph nodes include lungs, other sites in the skin, liver, bone and the brain. Solitary metastatic lesions may be resected.

- Radiotherapy and chemotherapy have a limited role in symptom palliation.

- Immunotherapy with interferons or interleukin (IL)-2 is associated with response rates of around 10–15% in metastatic melanoma, and interferon alfa has a role as adjuvant therapy in high-risk primary lesions (>1.5 mm thick or positive resected regional nodes).

- Lymphokine-activated killer (LAK) cells are the patient's own lymphocytes that are removed by leucapheresis and stimulated *ex vivo* by incubation with IL-2. These cells are then reinfused into the patient and have achieved durable remission in up to 20% of patients with metastatic melanoma. This therapy is toxic, causing a capillary leak syndrome that leads to cerebral, pulmonary and peripheral oedema. The targets of these LAK cells and tumour-infiltrating lymphocytes have been identified as melanoma-associated antigen proteins expressed by melanoma cells and other tumours, and melanoma differentiation antigens such as tyrosinase.

Prognosis

See Table 15 for 5-year survival rates of skin cancers.

TABLE 15 THE 5-YEAR SURVIVAL RATES FOR SKIN CANCERS

Tumour	5-year survival (%)
BCC	95–100
SCC	92–99
Melanoma	77

BCC, basal cell carcinoma; SCC, squamous cell carcinoma.

Prevention

Children should not be allowed to become sunburnt and white-skinned people should limit their total cumulative sun exposure. Lesions that are not obviously benign should be seen and removed in their entirety for pathological examination within 4 weeks of being examined.

FURTHER READING

Euvrard S, Kanitakis J and Claudy A. Skin cancers after organ transplantation. *N. Engl. J. Med.* 2003; 348: 1681–91.

Gilchrest BA, Eller MS, Geller AC, *et al.* The pathogenesis of melanoma induced by ultraviolet radiation. *N. Engl. J. Med.* 1999; 340: 1341–8.

Green A and Marks R. Squamous cell carcinoma of the skin (non metastatic). *Clinical Effectiveness*, 2006. Available at www.clinicalevidence.com/ceweb/conditions/onc/onc.jsp

Preston DS and Stern RS. Nonmelanoma cancers of the skin. *N. Engl. J. Med.* 1992; 327: 1649–62.

Rees J. Skin cancer. *J. R. Coll. Physicians Lond.* 1997; 31: 246–9.

Savage P, Crosby T and Mason M. Malignant melanoma (non metastatic). *Clinical Effectiveness*, 2005. Available at www.clinicalevidence.com/ceweb/conditions/onc/onc.jsp

2.8 Paediatric solid tumours

Aetiology/pathophysiology/ pathology

Many paediatric tumours are associated with recognised familial predispositions. These are due to inherited mutations of tumour-suppressor genes and are therefore inherited as autosomal dominant traits. Examples include:

- hereditary retinoblastoma (RB) (mutations of *RB* gene on chromosome 13q14);

- familial Wilms' tumour (mutations of *WT1* gene on chromosome 11p13) (see Section 3.12).

Epidemiology

After leukaemia (which accounts for 22% of childhood malignancies), central nervous system (CNS) tumours are the commonest (20%), occurring in 2.5 per 100,000 persons under 18 years old, followed by lymphoma (non-Hodgkin's 8% and Hodgkin's 6%), neuroblastoma (8%), Wilms' tumour (6%) and bone tumours (6%).

Clinical presentation

CNS tumours

In contrast to adult brain tumours, most paediatric CNS tumours (60%) are infratentorial and 75% are midline, involving the cerebellum, midbrain, pons and medulla:

- 45% are astrocytomas of varying grades, including optic nerve gliomas that are usually well-differentiated tumours;

- 20% are medulloblastomas, which may seed along the subarachnoid space;

- 5–10% are craniopharyngiomas that cause raised intracranial

pressure, visual defects and pituitary dysfunction (suprasellar calcification is a characteristic radiographic finding);

- 1–2% are pineal tumours, which present with Parinaud's syndrome (failure of conjugate upward gaze) – histologically, most pineal tumours are extragonadal germ-cell tumours (teratomas and germinomas).

The age distribution of paediatric CNS tumours is 15% between birth and 2 years, 30% from 2 to 5 years, 30% from 5 to 10 years and 25% from 11 to 18 years.

Neuroblastoma

These tumours are the commonest malignancy in infants and many are clinically apparent at birth. Tumours often have amplification of the N-*myc* oncogene on chromosome 1, either as small 'double minute' chromosomes or homogenously staining regions. They may arise from any site along the craniospinal axis derived from neural crest. These sites include non-pelvic abdominal sites (55%) such as the adrenal medulla (33%), pelvis (25%), thorax

(13%) and head and neck (7%), usually around the sympathetic ganglion or olfactory bulbs (the latter are more common in adults). The most common finding is a large, firm and irregular abdominal mass that crosses the midline.

Tumours may present with non-specific symptoms such as weight loss, failure to thrive, fever and pallor of anaemia, especially if widespread metastases are present.

At diagnosis, 70% are disseminated via lymphatic and haematogenous spread. Metastasis to bones of the skull is common and orbital swelling is a frequent presentation. Paraneoplastic opsoclonus/ myoclonus is a rare feature. These tumours have the highest spontaneous regression rate of any tumour, usually as a result of maturation to ganglioneuroma.

Other diagnostic investigations include:

- plain abdominal radiograph, which may show calcification (occurs in 70% of neuroblastomas and 15% of Wilms' tumours) (Fig. 19);

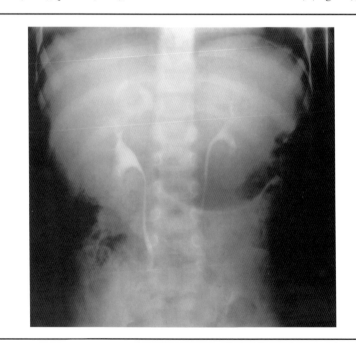

▲ **Fig. 19** Intravenous urogram showing right adrenal neuroblastoma with calcification.

- ^{131}I-metaiodobenzylguanidine scan;

- urinary catecholamines;

- serum neuron-specific enolase and ferritin.

Localised disease has a high cure rate with surgery and radiotherapy.

Wilms' tumour

This highly malignant embryonal tumour of the kidney is the most common malignant lesion of the genitourinary tract in children. Most occur in children under 5 years old and some are hereditary. Wilms' tumour is associated with congenital abnormalities including:

- aniridia as part of the syndrome of Wilms' tumour, aniridia, gonadoblastoma and mental retardation (WAGR);

- Denys–Drash syndrome (Wilms' tumour, male pseudohermaphroditism and diffuse glomerular disease);

- Beckwith–Wiedemann syndrome (organomegaly, hemihypertrophy and increased incidence of Wilms' tumour, hepatoblastoma and adrenocortical tumours).

Wilms' tumour presents in usually healthy children as abdominal swellings with a smooth, firm, non-tender mass (Fig. 20). One-quarter have gross haematuria, and occasionally children present with hypertension, malaise or fever. Up to 20% have metastases at diagnosis; lungs are the most common site of metastases.

Liver tumours

Liver cancers are rare tumours in children and may be divided into:

- hepatoblastoma (66%), which usually occurs before the age of 3 years;

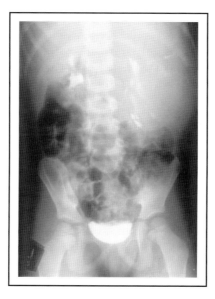

▲ **Fig. 20** Intravenous urogram showing Wilms' tumour (left) with distortion of renal pelvis.

- hepatocellular cancer (HCC) (33%), which occurs at any age.

Hepatoblastoma occurs as part of Beckwith–Widemann syndrome and is also associated with familial adenomatous polyposis. HCC is associated with hepatitis B virus and hepatitis C virus infection, tyrosinaemia, biliary cirrhosis and α_1-antitrypsin deficiency.

Retinoblastoma

RB most often occurs in children under 5 years old, and 30% of cases are bilateral. Up to 40% are hereditary due to germline mutations of the *RB* gene: these children frequently have bilateral RB and present at a younger age. Hereditary RB was the basis of Knudsen's two-hit model of tumour-suppressor genes. These tumours present with whitening of the pupil, squint or secondary glaucoma. RB is usually confined to the orbit and hence the cure rate with enucleation is high. However, hereditary RB is also associated with other malignancies, especially

osteosarcoma, soft-tissue sarcoma and melanoma. Genetic counselling is an integral part of therapy for RB. The siblings of all sufferers should be examined periodically, and DNA polymorphism analysis may identify relatives at high risk.

Complications

Late effects of multimodality therapy on a developing child are substantial, and the late sequelae cause considerable morbidity in this group of patients where long-term survival rates are high.

- Radiotherapy retards bone and cartilage growth, and causes intellectual impairment, gonadal toxicity, hypothalamic and thyroid dysfunction, pneumonitis, nephrotoxicity and hepatotoxicity.

- Late consequences of chemotherapy include infertility, anthracycline-related cardiotoxicity, bleomycin-related pulmonary fibrosis, platinum-related nephrotoxicity and neurotoxicity.

Second malignancies may be induced by chemotherapy and these occur most frequetly following combined chemotherapy and radiotherapy (see Section 3).

Prognosis

See Table 16 for 5-year survival of common paediatric cancers.

FURTHER READING

Crist WM and Kun LE. Common solid tumours of childhood. *N. Engl. J. Med.* 1991; 324: 461–71.

- - - - - - - - - - - - - - -

National Institute for Health and Clinical Excellence. *Improving Outcomes With Children and Young People With Cancer*, 2005. Available at www.nice.org.uk

TABLE 16 THE 5-YEAR SURVIVAL RATES OF PAEDIATRIC TUMOURS

Tumour	5-year survival (%)
Any paediatric CNS tumour	56
Low-grade glioma	80
High-grade glioma	25
Optic glioma	80
Brainstem glioma	5–50
Medulloblastoma	60
Ependymoma	60
Pineal germinoma	90
Pineal teratoma	65
Craniopharyngioma	90
Neuroblastoma	55
Wilms' tumour	80
HCC	25
Hepatoblastoma	70
RB	90

CNS, central nervous system; HCC, hepatocellular cancer; RB, retinoblastoma.

2.9 Lung cancer

Aetiology/pathophysiology/pathology

Lung cancer

Lung cancer can usefully be divided into two categories, which require different clinical management:

- 80% are non-small-cell lung cancer (NSCLC);

- 20% are small-cell lung cancer (SCLC).

Smoking The role of smoking in the pathogenesis of lung cancer has been established since Doll and Hill's classic epidemiological study of smoking in doctors was published in the 1950s. The relative risk of lung cancer in smokers is 17. The risk depends on the number of cigarettes smoked per day, duration of smoking history, age when smoking started, type of inhalation, tar and nicotine content of the tobacco smoked, and the presence of a filter. There is sufficient evidence demonstrating that passive smoking is responsible for the development of lung cancer in non-smokers living with smokers.

In the UK, smoking caused more than 120,000 deaths in 1995, including 46,000 deaths from cancer. A majority (82%) of smokers take up the habit during their teenage years; in 2002, 26% of 15-year-old girls were regular smokers compared with 20% of boys of the same age. Preventing the uptake of smoking in young people is a major focus of health promotion in the UK, although success has been limited. The prevalence of smoking had been declining since about 1970 but has increased since 1994, particularly amongst the young and women under 35 years old.

Occupational exposure to carcinogens Occupational exposure to carcinogens such as asbestos, acetaldehyde, formaldehyde, polycyclic aromatic hydrocarbons (from diesel exhausts), beryllium, cadmium, chromium, nickel and inorganic arsenic compounds is associated with higher incidences of lung cancer (independent of cigarette smoking). None of these carcinogens appears to be as toxic as tobacco (see Section 3.12).

Radon Radon is a naturally occurring, odourless, radioactive gas that emanates from rock. People living in areas with high radon levels (eg Devon and Derbyshire) are at increased risk of lung cancer.

Dietary factors Studies on the role of dietary antioxidant micronutrients such as carotenoids, vitamins C and E, and selenium, which were thought to protect against lung cancer, have been conflicting and no clear evidence of their role in preventing lung cancer is available.

Mesothelioma

Mesothelioma is a rare tumour (<1% of cancers) that is closely associated with asbestos exposure, although up to half the patients have no history of this. The risk of mesothelioma is greatest with blue asbestos (crocidolite) then brown asbestos (amosite) and least with white asbestos (chrysolite). The latency between exposure and diagnosis is up to 40 years. Mesothelioma occurs more frequently in men, reflecting the occupational exposure. Despite increasing awareness of the role of asbestos in these tumours and measures to reduce asbestos exposure, it is estimated that the incidence of mesothelioma will continue to rise until 2020 on account of the prolonged latency.

Epidemiology

In the past two decades the mortality rate for lung cancer has been stable and no improvement in survival can be reasonably anticipated. However, in the next century a decline in incidence is expected, due to reduced tar content in cigarettes and to educational programmes altering smoking habits. The new lung cancer registration data for the UK in 2003 is shown in Table 17.

Clinical presentation

Lung cancer

Lung cancer may present with the following symptoms:

- local disease (cough, dyspnoea, chest pain, haemoptysis and superior vena cava obstruction) (Figs 21 and 22) (see *Respiratory Medicine*, Sections 2.9.1);

	Percentage of all cancer registrations		Rank of registration (all cancers)		Lifetime chance of cancer		Change in ASR 1987–96 (%)		
Tumour	**Male**	**Female**	**Male**	**Female**	**Male**	**Female**	**Male**	**Female**	**5-year survival (%)**
Lung cancer	16	11	2nd	3rd	1 in 13	1 in 23	−22	+1	

TABLE 17 LUNG CANCER REGISTRATION DATA FOR THE UK IN 2003

ASR, age-standardised rate.

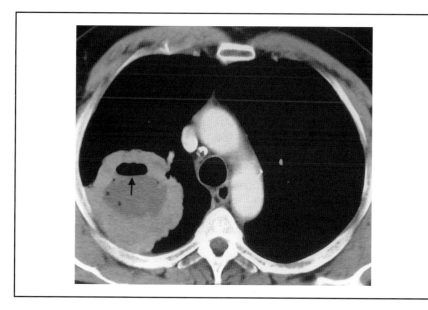

▲ **Fig. 21** Thoracic CT scan showing a cavitating primary carcinoma of the bronchus containing an air–fluid level (arrow). The thick wall with an irregular edge and an eccentric cavity are features suggestive of primary malignancy, particularly squamous cell lung cancer.

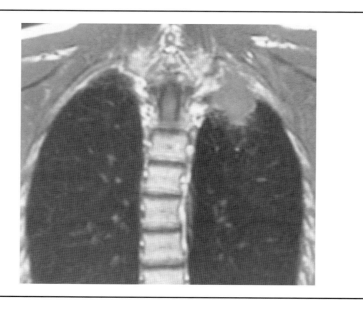

▲ **Fig. 22** T1-weighted coronal MRI scan revealing a Pancoast's tumour of the lung. These apical lung tumours spread locally to invade the brachial plexus, upper thoracic ribs and the thoracocervical sympathetic chain.

- metastases (bone pain, jaundice and cerebral symptoms);

- paraneoplastic syndromes (see Section 2.14).

The paraneoplastic syndromes, particularly endocrine and neurological, occur most frequently with SCLC. However, clubbing, hypertrophic osteoarthropathy (Fig. 23) and humoral hypercalcaemia due to secretion of parathyroid hormone-related peptide are more common with NSCLC.

Mesothelioma

Patients present with dyspnoea or non-pleuritic chest wall pain associated with a pleural effusion or pleural thickening. Pyrexia of unknown origin, sweats and weight loss are frequent; thrombocytosis, disseminated intravascular coagulation, thrombophlebitis and haemolytic anaemia also occur. Spread is predominantly by local invasion of the lung, adjacent organs in the mediastinum and the chest wall, and may track along chest drainage sites.

Treatment

Recent guidelines for the management and treatment of lung cancer are available.

Small-cell lung cancer

The first-line therapy for SCLC is chemotherapy, and the addition of surgery does not improve the outcome. Combination chemotherapy gives better results than single-agent therapy. Chemotherapy yields responses in around 80% of cases and the more effective regimens are generally more toxic, although dose intensification with stem-cell rescue does not offer an advantage. Patients with limited-stage SCLC (confined to one side of the chest) who achieve complete remission following

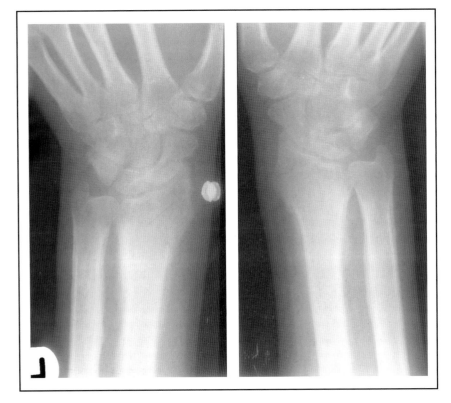

▲ **Fig. 23** Wrist and forearm radiograph demonstrating periosteal reaction in metaphysis and diaphysis of radius and ulna, and periarticular osteoporosis due to hypertrophic osteoarthropathy secondary to NSCLC (squamous cell).

chemotherapy may also benefit from radiotherapy to the thorax in order to prevent local relapse and to the brain to reduce the risk of brain metastases (prophylactic cranial irradiation).

Non-small-cell lung cancer

Early-stage non-small-cell lung cancer Only a minority of patients with NSCLC present with early-stage disease (Table 18) and are candidates for curative therapy.

Surgery remains the main hope of cure in early-stage NSCLC and patients need to be carefully selected to ensure that all who might benefit from this approach are offered it. Adjuvant chemotherapy following curative surgical resection has been developed.

To be considered for surgery:

• the tumour must be stage I or II, although on occasion patients with stage IIIa are considered;

• patients must have adequate respiratory reserves (forced expiratory volume in 1 second >1.0 L, $P\text{CO}_2$ <40 mmHg).

Prior to surgery, staging should include mediastinoscopy if mediastinal lymph nodes are present, although 18F-fluorodoxy glucose (FDG) PET is replacing this procedure. Adjuvant radiotherapy following surgery confers no benefit, whilst postoperative adjuvant chemotherapy is beneficial in good performance status patients. Neoadjuvant chemotherapy for stage IIIa tumours to downsize the disease prior to surgery is currently under investigation.

Patients with localised NSCLC who are not candidates for surgery should receive radical radiotherapy; this usually involves 4–6 weeks of treatment, and may be combined with chemotherapy. Continuous hyperfractionated accelerated radiation therapy, in which a lower total dose is given in small fractions three times daily for 12 consecutive days, yields better results than conventional radiotherapy alone, but with greater acute toxicity.

Advanced and metastatic non-small-cell lung cancer For patients with advanced or metastatic NSCLC, platinum-based chemotherapy leads to small improvements in survival and quality of life compared with no chemotherapy (increases median survival by 6 weeks and increases 1-year survival from 5 to 15%). Alternatively, advanced disease may be treated with palliative radiotherapy to alleviate symptoms.

Mesothelioma

Occasionally patients have operable stage I disease with a tumour confined to the ipsilateral pleural space, when either decortication (pleurectomy) or extrapleural

TABLE 18 STAGING FOR NSCLC		
Stage	**TNM**	**5-year survival (%)**
I	T1/2N0M0	60–80
II	T1/2N1M0	25–40
IIIa	T1/2/N2M0 or T3N0–2M0	10–30
IIIb	T1–3N3M0 or T4N0–3M0	<5
IV	Any T, any N and M1	<5

NSCLC, non-small-cell long cancer; TNM, tomour-node-metastasis.

pneumonectomy may be performed, followed by adjuvant radiotherapy. Radiotherapy may also be used for more advanced disease to control symptoms: the role of chemotherapy is not established but is under investigation.

In the UK, patients with asbestos-related mesothelioma are eligible for a lump sum payment in addition to their other benefit entitlements. Applications should be made to: Department of the Environment, Transport and the Regions, HSSD, Zone 1/B4, Eland House, Bressenden Place, London SW1E 5DU. Tel. 020 7890 4972.

Prognosis

See Table 19 for 5-year survival of lung cancers.

TABLE 19 THE 5-YEAR SURVIVAL RATES FOR LUNG CANCER AND MESOTHELIOMA

Tumour	5-year survival (%)
NSCLC	8
SCLC	5
Mesothelioma	5

NSCLC, non-small-cell lung cancer; SCLC, small-cell lung cancer.

FURTHER READING

Brown JS and Spiro SG. Update on lung cancer and mesothelioma. *J. R. Coll. Physicians Lond.* 1999; 33: 506–12.

Cancer Guidance Sub-Group of the Clinical Outcomes Group. *Improving Outcomes in Lung Cancer*, 2005. Available at www.nice.org.uk

Doll R, Peto R, Wheatley K, *et al.* Mortality in relation to smoking:

40 years' observations on male British doctors. *BMJ* 1994; 309: 901–11.

Eisen T, Hickish T, Smith IE, Sloane J and Eccles S. Small cell lung cancer. *Lancet* 1995; 345: 1285–9.

National Cancer Guidance Steering Group. *Improving Outcomes in Lung Cancer: The Research Evidence.* London: Department of Health, 1998 (available free from NHS response line 0541 555 455).

NHS Centre for Reviews and Dissemination. Preventing the uptake of smoking in young people. *Effective Health Care* 1999; 5: 1–12.

NHS Centre for Reviews and Dissemination. Management of lung cancer. *Effective Health Care* 1998; 4: 1–12.

Neville A. Lung cancer. *Clinical Effectiveness*, 2004. Available at www.clinicalevidence.com/ceweb/conditions/onc/onc.jsp

Robinson BWS and Lake RA. Advances in malignant mesothelioma. *N. Engl. J. Med.* 2005; 353: 1591–603.

Spira A and Ettinger DS. Multidisciplinary management of lung cancer. *N. Engl. J. Med.* 2004; 350: 379–92.

2.10 Liver and biliary tree cancer

Aetiology/pathophysiology/pathology

Hepatocellular carcinoma

The majority (80%) of cases of hepatocellular carcinoma are associated with chronic hepatitis B virus (HBV) infection. Although an effective vaccine for HBV has been available since 1982, more than 300 million people have chronic HBV. Most cases of hepatocellular carcinoma not associated with HBV are associated with hepatitis C virus (HCV) infection. The World Health Organisation estimates that 3% of the world population has been infected with HCV and that 170 million people are chronically infected. Approximately 20% of chronic HCV carriers will develop cirrhosis, of whom 7–14% will develop hepatocellular carcinoma over the ensuing 10 years.

- Aflatoxins are mycotoxins produced by the fungi *Aspergillus flavus* and *Aspergillus parasiticus* that contaminate food (eg peanuts and corn). Aflatoxins bind covalently to guanine (G) residues in DNA and can induce G→T (thymidine) mutations, and are associated with hepatocellular carcinoma.

- Alcoholic liver disease is associated with a high rate of HCV infection and patients with alcoholic cirrhosis have an increased risk of hepatocellular carcinoma. However, the contribution of each to the association is unclear.

- Other causes of cirrhosis are also associated with an increased risk of hepatocellular carcinoma including haemochromatosis, primary biliary cirrhosis, α_1-antitrypsin deficiency, glycogen storage diseases, Wilson's disease, hereditary tyrosinaemia and porphyrias.

- Iatrogenic liver tumours include hepatic angiomas induced by the oral contraceptive pill, which may possibly transform to hepatocellular carcinoma.

149

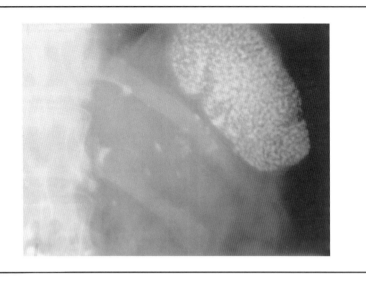

▲**Fig. 24** Abdominal radiograph showing lacy granular opacification of the spleen due to previous injection of Thorotrast. Thorotrast has been shown to increase the incidence of cholangiocarcinoma.

- Other identified human hepatic carcinogens include nitrosamines, carbon tetrachloride and polyvinyl chloride.

Liver cancers of childhood are covered in Section 2.8.

Biliary tract cancers

Biliary tract cancers have been divided into cancers of the gallbladder, extrahepatic bile ducts, ampulla of Vater and intrahepatic bile ducts.

- The term 'cholangiocarcinoma' may be applied to intrahepatic, perihilar and distal extrahepatic tumours.

- Perihilar tumours involving the bifurcation of the hepatic ducts are called Klatskin tumours and are often small and localised at presentation.

- Gallbladder tumours are associated with large often asymptomatic gallstones; however, the rate is still too low to justify prophylactic resection of the gallbladder.

- Cholangiocarcinoma is a complication of primary sclerosing cholangitis with a lifetime risk of 10%.

- In South-east Asia, infection with the liver flukes *Clonorchis sinensis* (Japan, Korea and Vietnam) or *Opisthorchis viverrini* (Thailand, Laos and Malaysia) are associated with a 25–500-fold risk of cholangiocarcinoma.

- The radiocontrast agent Thorotrast was associated with an increased risk of cholangiocarcinoma, hepatic angiosarcoma and hepatocellular carcinoma (Fig. 24).

Epidemiology

Hepatocellular carcinoma
Hepatocellular carcinoma is the third most common cause of death from cancer in men worldwide, most cases occurring in South-east Asia and sub-Saharan Africa. In contrast, primary liver cancers account for less than 0.5% of cancer deaths in the UK.

Biliary tract cancers
Biliary tract cancers account for less than 1% of cancer deaths in the UK.

Clinical presentation

Hepatocellular carcinoma
At diagnosis the majority of patients have advanced disease with abdominal pain, distension, weight loss and anorexia (Fig. 25). Patients with cirrhosis may present with unexplained worsening of ascites, fever, pain and a sudden rise in liver enzymes. Physical examination reveals hepatomegaly, right upper quadrant tenderness, occasionally an audible bruit, ascites and portal

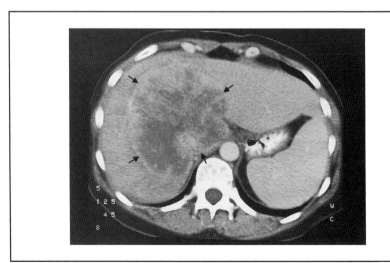

▲**Fig. 25** Abdominal CT scan showing large, well-defined, variable-density hepatoma (arrows).

hypertension with varices, splenomegaly and caput medusae.

Biliary tract cancers

Patients present with obstructive jaundice causing nausea, anorexia, epigastric pain, weight loss and pruritis. In one-third of cases the gallbladder is palpable (Courvoisier's sign).

Investigations/staging

Alpha-fetoprotein (AFP) may be a useful tumour marker for monitoring progress in hepatocellular carcinoma (see Section 3.3). At diagnosis 95% of patients will have raised AFP levels, as will 7% of patients with liver metastases from other primaries. In general, the latter will also have raised carcinoembryonic antigen (CEA) levels; therefore when AFP and CEA are used in conjunction, they may differentiate between primary hepatocellular carcinoma and liver metastases.

Benign liver diseases such as hepatitis may be accompanied by raised serum AFP, and levels are not raised in a significant proportion of patients with early resectable hepatocellular carcinoma. Thus, AFP has a limited role in screening for hepatocellular carcinoma. Nevertheless, in high-risk populations, specifically those positive for hepatitis B surface antigen (HbsAg) or HCV or those with chronic active hepatitis, cirrhosis or HCV/HBV acquired as a child, frequent serum AFP and liver ultrasound are recommended.

Treatment

Hepatocellular carcinoma

Surgical resection is the preferred option but is only feasible in a minority (around 15%) of patients who have limited-stage cancer and adequate hepatic reserves. Many

treatment approaches have been used for the majority of patients, but the variable course of the disease has made it difficult to evaluate their benefit, if any. Treatments used include intra-arterial chemotherapy, chemoembolisation, lipiodol chemoembolisation, external beam and internal radiotherapy, cryoablation, percutaneous ethanol injection and orthotopic liver transplantation.

The fibrolamellar variant of hepatocellular carcinoma has a better prognosis. As with all cancers, prevention remains the best approach, and in 1984 Taiwan introduced a mass HBV vaccination programme for neonates born to HBsAg carrier mothers and for children. After 10 years there was a significant decrease in the incidence of hepatocellular carcinoma in children in Taiwan.

Biliary tract tumours

Surgery is the only known curative treatment; however, only 20% of cholangiocarcinomas and 10% of gallbladder tumours are candidates for surgery. Periampullary tumours that present early are more frequently resectable and have a correspondingly better prognosis, as do papillary cholangiocarcinomas.

External beam radiotherapy with or without chemotherapy may be helpful in palliating symptoms but has not been found to improve survival.

Endoscopically or percutaneously placed stents are used to palliate cholestasis. Plastic stents need to be replaced every 3 months and occlude, whilst metal stents are less likely to occlude or migrate and tend to stay open longer on account of their larger diameter.

Prognosis

See Table 20 for 5-year survival of liver and biliary tract cancers.

TABLE 20 THE 5-YEAR SURVIVAL RATES OF HEPATIC AND BILIARY TRACT CANCERS	
Tumour	**5-year survival (%)**
Hepatocellular cancer	5
Gallbladder cancer	5
Cholangiocarcinoma	5
Periampullary cholangiocarcinoma	50

FURTHER READING

Chang M-H, Chen C-J, Lai MS, *et al.* Universal hepatitis B vaccination in Taiwan and the incidence of hepatocellular carcinoma in children. *N. Engl. J. Med.* 1997; 336: 1855–9.

- - - - - - - - - - - - - - - -

De Groen PC, Gores GJ, La Russo NF, *et al.* Biliary tract cancers. *N. Engl. J. Med.* 1999; 341: 1368–78.

- - - - - - - - - - - - - - - -

Various. ABC of diseases of liver, pancreas, and biliary system. *BMJ* 2001: 322.

2.11 Bone cancer and sarcoma

Aetiology/pathophysiology/ pathology

Soft-tissue sarcoma

Lymphoedema of the arm following breast surgery is associated with lymphangiosarcoma (Stewart–Treves syndrome). Radiation-induced sarcomas are rare, osteosarcoma being the most common and occurring in up to 1% after mantle radiotherapy for Hodgkin's disease.

Consistent chromosomal translocations have been found in

a number of soft-tissue tumours, both benign and malignant. These chromosomal rearrangements may be of help diagnostically, eg t(X;18)(p11;q11) translocation may be used to confirm the diagnosis of synovial sarcoma. The consequence of many of these translocations is the transcription of chimeric mRNA containing 5′ sequences of one gene and 3′ sequences from another gene, with translation to hybrid proteins. Many of the genes involved in these translocations are themselves transcription factors and it is postulated that the consequence of translocation is the aberrant expression of a number of downstream genes.

Genetic predispositions to sarcoma include (see Section 3.12):

- Li–Fraumeni syndrome (soft-tissue sarcoma and osteosarcoma);

- neurofibromatosis (15% develop neurofibrosarcoma, also known as neurogenic sarcoma, malignant schwannoma and malignant neurilemoma);

- basal cell naevus syndrome (soft-tissue sarcoma);

- hereditary retinoblastoma (osteosarcoma);

- Wilms' tumour (rhabdomyosarcoma).

Bone tumours

The incidence of bone tumours is highest during adolescence, although they only represent 3% of childhood cancers. Most tumours occur in areas of rapid growth in the metaphysis near the growth plate where cellular proliferation and remodelling are greatest during long-bone growth. The most active growth plates are in the distal femur and proximal tibia, and these are also the commonest sites for primary bone cancers.

- Prolonged growth and remodelling may account for the increased incidence of bone tumours associated with Paget's disease (osteosarcoma and giant-cell tumours) and chronic osteomyelitis (osteosarcoma).

- Chondrosarcoma may arise in pre-existing benign lesions such as enchondroma or osteochondroma.

- The transformation rate in Ollier's disease (multiple enchondromatosis) and hereditary multiple exostosis exceeds 10%.

- Other familial cancer syndromes with increased osteosarcoma incidence are retinoblastoma and Li–Fraumeni syndrome.

- Radiation has been identified as playing a role in the pathogenesis of osteosarcoma, chondrosarcoma and fibrosarcoma, both in the form of therapeutic radiotherapy and occupational exposure (eg radium dial painters).

Ewing's sarcoma This is a childhood bone malignancy of uncertain cellular origin that is associated with the t(11;22) chromosomal translocation that juxtaposes *EWS* and *Fli-1* genes, resulting in a hybrid transcript from these two transcription factor genes. This same chromosomal translocation occurs in peripheral neuroectodermal tumours and Askin lung tumours, suggesting a possible common origin. Peripheral neuroectodermal tumours are thought to arise from peripheral autonomic nervous system tissue and stain for neuron-specific enolase as well as S-100. Morphologically all three tumours are small, round, blue cell tumours, a group that also includes embryonal rhabdomyosarcoma, non-Hodgkin's lymphoma, neuroblastoma and small-cell lung cancer.

Epidemiology

Soft-tissue sarcoma

Sarcomas are rare tumours, comprising less than 1% of all cancers. They are commoner in children and rank as the fifth commonest tumour in those under 15 years old. Fibrosarcoma (22%), liposarcoma (20%), rhabdomyosarcoma (12%) and synovial sarcoma (7%) are the predominant types. Less common sarcomas include neurofibrosarcoma, angiosarcoma (haemangiosarcoma or lymphangiosarcoma), leiomyosarcoma and Kaposi's sarcoma (KS). Four forms of KS are recognised:

- AIDS-associated KS;

- post-transplant KS, which occurs in 1% of renal allograft recipients and may resolve with the reduction of immunosuppression;

- endemic African KS;

- classical/Mediterranean KS, which affects the lower extremities of elderly men.

All forms are associated with human herpesvirus 8 infection, an oncogenic virus with homology to Epstein–Barr virus.

Bone tumours

After bone metastases the commonest tumours in bones are haematopoietic tumours including leukaemia, myeloma and lymphoma. The origins of the remaining primary bone tumours are shown in Table 21.

TABLE 21 ORIGINS OF PRIMARY BONE TUMOURS

Origin	Benign	Malignant
Cartilage (21%)	Enchondroma Osteochondroma Chondroblastoma	Chondrosarcoma
Bone (19%)	Osteoid osteoma Osteoblastoma	Osteosarcoma
Unknown origin (10%)	Giant-cell tumour	Ewing's sarcoma Malignant fibrous histiocytoma

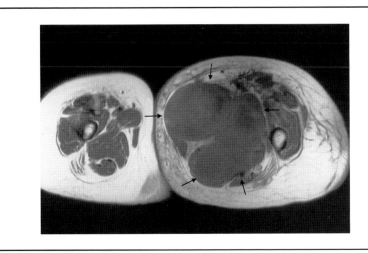

▲ **Fig. 26** T1-weighted MRI scan showing large soft-tissue mass in medial compartment of left thigh due to soft-tissue sarcoma (arrows).

Clinical presentation

Soft-tissue sarcoma

Most soft-tissue sarcomas present as masses that grow, becoming hard and painful (Fig. 26). Systemic effects include weight loss, pyrexia of unknown origin (PUO) and episodic hypoglycaemia, particularly with large retroperitoneal sarcomas. Sarcomas may appear anywhere on the body: 60% occur in the extremities, 30% on the trunk (including retroperitoneum) and 10% on the head and neck. Approximately 10–25% have metastases at presentation, most frequently in the lungs (Table 22).

Bone tumours

Most primary bone tumours present as painful swellings that may cause stiffness and effusions in nearby joints. Occasionally tumours present as pathological fractures. Systemic symptoms are uncommon except in Ewing's sarcoma when PUO, weight loss and night sweats occur.

TABLE 22 CLINICAL FEATURES OF SOFT-TISSUE SARCOMAS

Tumour	Age (years)	Commonest sites	Primary therapy	5-year survival (%)
Fibrosarcoma	20–50	Thigh, arm, head and neck	Wide excision and adjuvant radiation	90 (well differentiated), 50 (poorly differentiated)
Liposarcoma	40–60	Thigh, head and neck (rarely arise from lipoma)	Wide excision and adjuvant radiation	66 (myxoid), 10 (pleomorphic)
Embryonal rhabdomyosarcoma	0–10	Head and neck, genitourinary (botryoid)	Neoadjuvant chemoradiation and surgery	40
Alveolar rhabdomyosarcoma	10–20	Thigh	Neoadjuvant chemoradiation and surgery	60
Pleomorphic rhabdomyosarcoma	40–70	Thigh and upper arm	Wide excision and adjuvant radiation	10
Synovial sarcoma	20–40	Leg	Wide excision and adjuvant radiation	40
Angiosarcoma	50–70	Skin and superficial soft tissues	Wide excision and adjuvant radiation	15
Leiomyosarcoma	45–65	Retroperitoneal and uterine	Wide excision and adjuvant radiation	40

TABLE 23 FEATURES OF CARTILAGE-DERIVED BONE TUMOURS

	Enchondroma	Osteochondroma (exostosis)	Chondroblastoma	Chondrosarcoma
Age (years)	10–50	10–20	5–20	30–60
Site	Hands, wrists	Knee, shoulder, pelvis	Knee, shoulder, ribs	Knee, shoulder, pelvis
Location	Diaphysis	Metaphysis	Epiphysis prior to fusion	Metaphysis or diaphysis
Radiograph	Well-defined lucency, thin sclerotic rim and calcification (Fig. 27)	Eccentric protrusion from bone and calcification (Fig. 28)	Well-defined lucency, thin sclerotic rim and calcification	Expansile lucency, sclerotic margin, cortical destruction and soft-tissue mass (Fig. 29)
Notes	Ollier's disease = multiple enchondromas	1% transform to chondrosarcoma		

TABLE 24 FEATURES OF OSTEOID-DERIVED BONE TUMOURS

	Osteoid osteoma	Osteoblastoma	Osteosarcoma
Age (years)	10–30	10–20	10–25 and over 60
Site	Knee	Vertebra	Knee, shoulder, pelvis
Location	Diaphysis	Metaphysis	Metaphysis
Radiograph	Central lucency of <1 cm, surrounding bone sclerosis and periosteal reaction (Fig. 30)	Well-defined lucency, sclerotic rim, cortex preserved and calcification	Lytic/sclerotic expansile lesion, wide transition zone, cortical destruction, soft-tissue mass, periosteal reaction and calcification (Fig. 31)

TABLE 25 FEATURES OF BONE TUMOURS OF UNCERTAIN ORIGINS

	Giant-cell tumour	Ewing's sarcoma	Malignant fibrous histiocytoma
Age (years)	20–40	5–15	10–20 and over 60
Site	Long bones, knee	Knee, shoulder, pelvis	Knee, pelvis, shoulder
Location	Epiphysis and metaphysis post closure	Diaphysis and, less often, metaphysis	Metaphysis
Radiograph	Lucency with ill-defined endosteal margin, cortical destruction, soft-tissue mass and eccentric expansion (Fig. 32)	Ill-defined medullary destruction, small areas of new bone formation, periosteal reaction, soft-tissue expansion and bone/lung metastases (Fig. 33)	Cortical destruction, periosteal reaction and soft-tissue mass

Osteosarcoma developing in pagetic bones may present with pain, swelling and warmth that progresses rapidly over weeks. The features of cartilage-derived bone tumours are shown in Table 23, of osteoid-derived bone tumours in Table 24 and of bone tumours of uncertain origin in Table 25.

Treatment

Soft-tissue sarcoma

- The optimal therapy for most soft-tissue sarcomas is surgical resection with an adequate margin of normal tissue.

- For extremity lesions, limb-sparing approaches are possible in most cases, and offer survival rates equivalent to amputation without the associated morbidity.

- For high-risk patients, local control is improved with

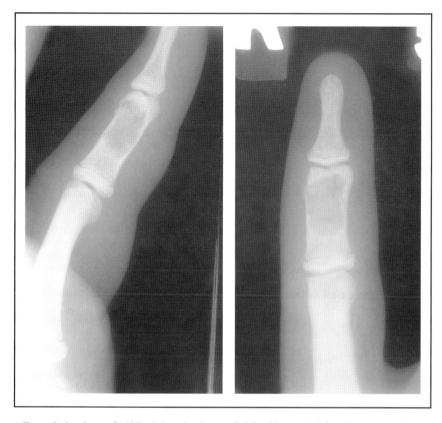

▲**Fig. 27** Enchondroma of middle phalanx showing a well-defined lucency and thin sclerotic rim with preserved cortex.

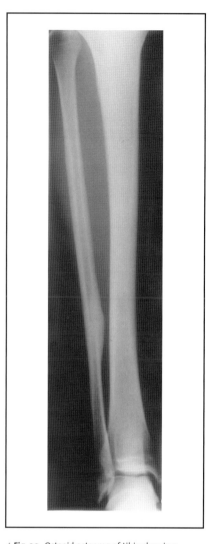

▲**Fig. 30** Osteoid osteoma of tibia showing eccentric dense bone expansion and central lucent nidus.

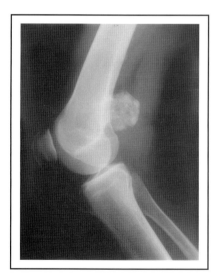

▲**Fig. 28** Osteochondroma of distal femur showing a well-defined eccentric protrusion in continuity with bone cortex.

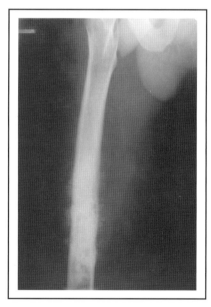

▲**Fig. 29** Chondrosarcoma of distal femur showing expansile lesion with sclerotic margin, cortical destruction and punctate internal calcification.

preoperative or postoperative radiotherapy. Local recurrence rates vary with the site; with extremity sarcomas only one-third recur. Recurrences nearly always occur within 3 years of initial presentation.

- Adjuvant chemotherapy improves disease-free survival but not overall survival.

- Isolated pulmonary metastases may be resected, with 20% survival at 3 years; however, metastatic disease is generally relatively resistant to chemotherapy.

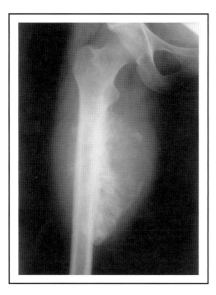

▲ **Fig. 31** Osteosarcoma of proximal femur showing sclerotic area with wide zone of transition, cortical destruction, soft-tissue mass, internal calcification and periosteal reaction with marked 'sunray' spiculation.

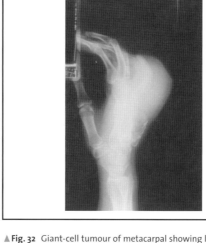

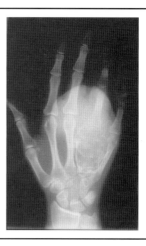

▲ **Fig. 32** Giant-cell tumour of metacarpal showing lucency with marked expansion, cortical destruction and soft-tissue mass. Internal cortical ridges produce a typical multilocular appearance.

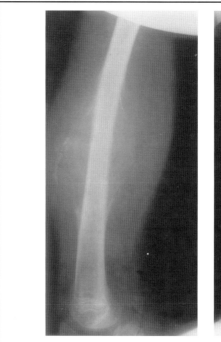

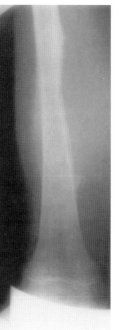

▲ **Fig. 33** Ewing's sarcoma of femur showing medullary destruction, lamellated periosteal reaction and soft-tissue extension.

Bone tumours

- The clinical management of bone tumours requires a specialist multidisciplinary unit including orthopaedic surgeons, plastic surgeons and oncologists, and should be in the context of an adolescent oncology unit because the majority of patients are in this age group, with all their special needs.

- Neoadjuvant chemotherapy plays an important role in shrinking the tumour in localised osteosarcoma and Ewing's sarcoma, hopefully enabling limb-sparing surgery without increasing relapse rates.

- Postoperative adjuvant chemotherapy and radiotherapy are useful in some tumours.

Prognosis

See Table 26 for 5-year survival of sarcomas and bone tumours.

TABLE 26 THE 5-YEAR SURVIVAL RATES FOR PRIMARY BONE CANCERS	
Tumour	**5-year survival (%)**
Osteosarcoma	15
Chondrosarcoma	40
Ewing's sarcoma	1–10

FURTHER READING

Arndt C and Crist W. Medical progress: common musculoskeletal tumors of childhood and adolescence. *N. Engl. J. Med.* 1999; 341: 342–52.

Clark MA, Fisher C, Judson I and Thomas JM. Soft tissue sarcomas in adults. *N. Engl. J. Med.* 2005; 353: 701–11.

2.12 Endocrine tumours

Aetiology/pathophysiology/ pathology

Thyroid tumours

Thyroid cancers account for less than 1% of all cancers. The four histological variants of thyroid cancer are:

- papillary (50–80%);

- follicular (8–25%);

- anaplastic (2–10%);

- medullary (7%), which arises from parafollicular C cells.

Radiation exposure is an established cause of papillary and follicular thyroid tumours. Children treated with thymic radiation or people exposed to radiation following the Chernobyl nuclear accident or atomic bomb testing in the Marshall Islands have an increased incidence of these thyroid cancers, which peaks 20 years after exposure. Thyroglobulin, normally produced by follicular cells of the thyroid, should not be detectable in patients following thyroidectomy, and may be helpful for following the course of papillary and follicular thyroid cancer.

Medullary thyroid cancer

Medullary thyroid cancer (MTC) occurs sporadically or in a familial form, either as part of multiple endocrine neoplasia (MEN) type 2a or 2b or as familial MTC without MEN. MTC produces calcitonin, and even where serum calcitonin levels are normal there may be an exaggerated calcitonin response to calcium and pentagastrin. Calcitonin may be used to screen patients with MEN-2 for MTC and may be used to monitor treatments for this condition.

Adrenal tumours

Adrenal cancer is rare and no aetiological factors have been identified except for a higher incidence in Li–Fraumeni syndrome (see Section 3.12). Phaeochromocytomas may be benign (90%) or malignant adrenal medulla tumours that secrete catecholamines. About 10% of phaeochromocytomas are familial. The incidence of phaeochromocytoma is increased in neurofibromatosis type 1, von Hippel–Lindau syndrome, MEN-2a and MEN-2b, and familial phaeochromocytoma.

Pituitary tumours

Pituitary tumours comprise 10% of intracranial neoplasms. There are no clues to the pathogenesis of these tumours.

Multiple endocrine neoplasia

Familial MEN syndromes are autosomal dominant traits with high penetrance: the associated tumours may be benign or malignant.

Multiple endocrine neoplasia type 1

MEN-1 is associated with pituitary adenoma, parathyroid hyperplasia or adenoma and a wide spectrum of pancreatic islet-cell tumours (pancreatic polypeptide-secreting tumour, gastrinoma, insulinoma, glucagonoma and vasoactive intestinal polypeptide-secreting tumour or growth hormone releasing factor-secreting tumour). MEN-1 is due to mutation of the *MEN1* gene on chromosome 11q13.

Multiple endocrine neoplasia type 2

Patients with MEN-2 have MTC and phaeochromocytoma. Parathyroid hyperplasia or adenoma are a feature of MEN-2a, whereas mucosal neuroma and marfanoid habitus are features of MEN-2b. Both forms of MEN-2 are due to mutations of the *RET* oncogene on chromosome 10q11, albeit at different sites within the gene.

Clinical presentation

Thyroid tumours

Thyroid cancers are two to four times commoner in women and the median age at diagnosis is 45–50 years. Patients present with an asymptomatic thyroid nodule, with cervical lymphadenopathy or with bone or lung metastases (Fig. 34).

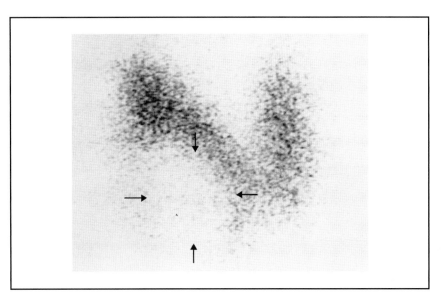

▲ **Fig. 34** ^{123}I radionuclide scan showing a large 'cold' area in the lower pole of the right lobe of the thyroid (arrows) due to follicular thyroid cancer.

TABLE 27 COMPARISON OF CLINICAL FEATURES OF PITUITARY TUMOURS

Tumour	Percentage	Morphology	Endocrine features	Neurological features
Prolactin-secreting adenoma	40	Macroadenoma	Amenorrhoea, galactorrhoea and hypopituitarism in men	Headache and visual field defects
Non-secretory adenoma	20	Macroadenoma	Hypopituitarism	Headache and visual field defects
Growth hormone-secreting adenoma	20	Macroadenoma	Gigantism in children and acromegaly in adults	Headache and visual field defects
Corticotropin-secreting adenoma	15	Microadenoma	Cushing's disease	Usually none
Gonadotropin-secreting adenoma	5	Macroadenoma	Panhypopituirarism	Headache and visual field defects
Thyrotropin-secreting adenoma	<1	Microadenoma	Hyperthyroidism	Usually none

Almost all patients are euthyroid. Although MTC secretes calcitonin, this has no metabolic effects.

Adrenal tumours

Non-functioning adrenal tumours present as large abdominal masses and are commoner in men. Functional tumours secrete steroids and may cause virilisation in females, Cushing's syndrome, feminisation in males or hyperaldosteronism, although the last two are very rare.

- Virilisation is caused by peripheral conversion of adrenal androstenedione and dehydroepiandosterone to testosterone.

- Cushing's syndrome with low plasma adrenocorticotropic hormone and virilisation are characteristic of adrenal cancers.

- Feminisation occurs rarely due to peripheral aromatisation of excess adrenal androstenedione to oestrone that results in gynaecomastia.

- Rarely, adrenal cancers present with features of primary hyperaldosteronism, although most patients with Conn's syndrome have idiopathic hyperaldosteronism or aldosterone-producing adenomas rather than adrenal cancers.

Phaeochromocytomas of the adrenal medulla are rare tumours that present with symptoms due to catecholamine secretion, including intermittent, episodic or sustained hypertension, anxiety, tremor, palpitations, sweating, flushing, headaches, gastrointestinal disturbances and polyuria.

Pituitary tumours

Pituitary tumours arise from the anterior lobe of the pituitary gland and produce their effects by uncontrolled production of specific hormones, destruction of the normal gland (hypopituitarism) or compression of adjacent structures (optic chiasm, hypothalamus and bony structures) (Table 27 and Fig. 35).

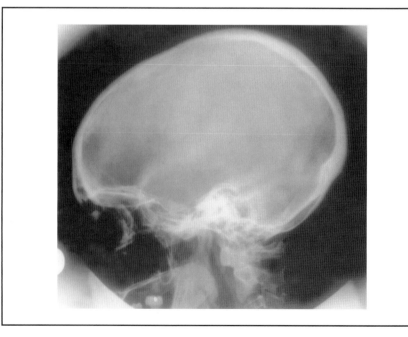

▲ **Fig. 35** Plain skull radiograph showing pituitary macroadenoma expanding sella turcica.

Treatment

Thyroid tumours

Localised thyroid tumours should be treated with total or near-total thyroidectomy followed by postoperative ^{131}I if iodine avid. The ^{131}I is given to:

- destroy occult metastases;

- destroy any remaining thyroid tissue and hence increase the sensitivity of thyroglobulin measurements;

- enable ^{123}I scanning to detect recurrence.

^{131}I therapy can cause acute nausea and sialadenitis, and occasionally mild pancytopenia if there are bone metastases. ^{131}I causes transient reduction in spermatogenesis and transient ovarian failure. It is recommended that pregnancy be postponed for 1 year after ^{131}I treatment, which should not be given to pregnant women.

External beam radiotherapy should be added if surgical excision is incomplete or the tumour is not iodine avid. Advanced thyroid cancer is usually treated with palliative radiotherapy.

Adrenal tumours

Localised adrenal cancers should be treated surgically, remembering that phaeochromocytomas will require preoperative and perioperative α- and β-adrenergic blockade.

Metastatic adrenal cancers are treated with endocrine therapy:

- metyrapone, which inhibits 11β-hydroxylation;

- aminoglutethimide, which blocks steroid aromatisation;

- mitotane, which blocks several enzymes in the steroid synthesis pathway;

- cytotoxic chemotherapy has a role in the management of metastatic adrenal cancer.

Metastatic phaeochromocytoma may be treated with ^{131}I-metaiodobenzylguanidine, a catecholamine precursor that is also used to image the tumours.

Pituitary tumours

The role of surgery in pituitary adenomas includes histological diagnosis; decompression of the optic chiasm, cranial nerves and obstructive hydrocephalus; and complete excision of adenomas. A transfrontal approach is needed for large tumours with extrasellar extension, whereas a trans-sphenoidal approach, which is safer and better tolerated, may be used for small tumours.

- Radiotherapy may be used as the primary treatment for intrasellar adenomas and as an adjunct to surgery for large tumours.

- Bromocriptine may be used to control prolactin secretion and can be used as the sole therapy for prolactin-secreting microadenomas, or in combination with surgery or radiotherapy for macroadenomas.

- Somatostatin analogues are used to control hormone secretion from growth hormone-secreting adenoma.

Prognosis

See Table 28 for 5-year survival of endocrine tumours.

TABLE 28 THE 5-YEAR SURVIVAL RATES OF ENDOCRINE TUMOURS

Tumour	5-year survival (%)
Papillary thyroid cancer	80
Follicular thyroid cancer	60
Anaplastic thyroid cancer	10
MTC	50
Adrenal cancer	<50
Pituitary adenoma	90

MTC, medullary thyroid cancer.

FURTHER READING

Cleland SJ and Connell JM. Endocrine hypertension. *J. R. Coll. Physicians Lond.* 1998; 32: 104–8.

Heath D. Multiple endocrine neoplasia. *J. R. Coll. Physicians Lond.* 1998; 32: 98–101.

Schlumberger M. Papillary and follicular thyroid carcinoma. *N. Engl. J. Med.* 1998; 338: 297–306.

Wass JAH and Sheppard MC. New treatments for acromegaly. *J. R. Coll. Physicians Lond.* 1998; 32: 113–17.

2.13 The causes of cancer

As with most diseases, the causes of cancer may be separated into environmental factors and genetic factors. Some examples of these are outlined below.

Environmental factors

Viruses

- Hepatitis viruses (B and C) in hepatocelluar cancer (HCC).

- Retroviruses (human T-cell leukaemia/lymphoma virus 1) in adult T-cell leukaemia.

- Papillomaviruses in cervical and anal cancers.

- Herpesviruses (Epstein–Barr virus and human herpesvirus 8) in nasopharyngeal cancer, Burkitt's lymphoma and Kaposi's sarcoma (KS).

Bacteria

- *Helicobacter pylori* in gastric mucosa-associated lymphoid tissue lymphomas.

Parasites

- Liver fluke (*Opisthorchis sinensis*) in cholangiocarcinoma.

- *Schistosoma haematobium* in squamous cell bladder cancer.

Radiation

- Ultraviolet radiation in cases of basal cell and squamous cell skin cancer, and melanoma.

- Nuclear explosions (Hiroshima and Pacific tests) in cases of leukaemia and solid tumours.

- Diagnostic, eg Thorotrast dye imaging (Fig. 24) in cholangiocarcinoma.

- Therapeutic, eg ankylosing spondylitis treatment in cases of acute myeloid leukaemia (AML).

- Occupational, eg uranium miners (lung cancer) and radium dial painters (osteosarcoma) (Table 29).

Chemical

- Dietary, eg aflatoxins in HCC.

- Cultural habits, eg alcohol (upper gastrointestinal cancer) and betel nut chewing (oral cavity cancers).

- Occupational, eg asbestos (mesothelioma) and benzene (leukaemia) (Table 29).

- Iatrogenic, eg cytotoxics (leukaemia) and oestrogens (endometrial cancer).

Carcinogenic drugs and their associated tumours.

- Cytotoxics: AML
- Cyclophosphamide: bladder cancer
- Immunosuppression: KS and post-transplantation lymphoma
- Oestrogens (unopposed): endometrial cancer
- Oestrogens (transplacental): vaginal adenocarcinoma
- Oral contraceptive pill: hepatic adenoma
- Androgenic anabolic steroids: HCC
- Phenacetin: renal pelvis transitional-cell carcinoma

Genetic factors

Inherited cancer predisposition syndromes are listed in Table 30. Germline mutations of key genes predispose to the development of cancer. These mutations may either be inherited and follow a familial pattern or may be sporadic new mutations. Examples of the classes of cancer predisposition genes are listed below.

TABLE 29 OCCUPATIONAL CARCINOGENESIS

Occupation	Carcinogen	Malignancy
Dye and rubber industries	Aromatic amines (benzidine, 2-naphthylamine 3,3'-dichlorobenzidine and 4-aminobiphenyl)	Bladder cancer
Leather and petroleum industries	Benzene	Acute leukaemia
Vinyl chloride manufacture	Vinyl chloride	Liver angiosarcoma
Nickel refining	Nickel and chromate	Nasal cavity and lung cancers
Hardwood furniture manufacture	Hardwood dust	Nasal cavity adenocarcinoma
Asbestos mining, shipbuilding and construction work	Asbestos	Mesothelioma
Steel and aluminium foundries, and coal gas manufacture	Polycyclic hydrocarbons	Lung cancer
Radium, uranium, haematite and fluorspar mining	Radon	Lung cancer
Pesticide manufacture and copper refining	Arsenic	Lung cancer and squamous cell skin cancer
Luminisers (clock and watch dials)	Radium	Osteosarcoma
Strong acid process in manufacturing	Isopropyl alcohol	Nasal sinus cancer

- Tumour-suppressor genes: *APC*, familial adenomatous polyposis; *VHL*, von Hippel–Lindau syndrome; *WT1*, Wilms' tumour syndromes; *RB1*, hereditary retinoblastoma; *NF1* and *NF2*, neurofibromatosis types 1 and 2; *p53*, Li–Fraumeni syndrome; *MEN1*, multiple endocrine neoplasia type 1; *BRCA1* (mutation on chromosome 17q21) and *BRCA2* (mutation on chromosome 13q12–13), breast/ovarian cancer syndromes.

TABLE 30 INHERITED CANCER PREDISPOSITION SYNDROMES

Syndrome	Malignancies	Inheritance	Gene
Breast/ovarian	Breast, ovary, colon and prostate	AD AD	*BRCA1* *BRCA2*
Cowden's syndrome	Breast, thyroid, gastrointestinal, pancreas	AD	*PTEN*
Li–Fraumeni syndrome	Sarcoma, osteosarcoma, leukaemia, glioma, breast, adrenal cortex	AD	*p53*
Prostate cancer	Prostate	AD XL	*HPC1* *HPC2*
Familial polyposis coli	Colon and upper gastrointestinal tract	AD	*APC*
HNPCC (Lynch type II)	Colon, endometrium, ovary, pancreas, gastric	AD AD AD AD	*MSH2* *MLH1* *PMS1* *PMS2*
Peutz–Jeghers syndrome	Colon, ileum, breast, ovary	AD	*STK11*
MEN-1	Pancreatic islet cell and pituitary adenoma	AD	*MEN1*
MEN-2	Medullary thyroid and phaeochromocytoma	AD	*RET*
Neurofibromatosis type 1	Neurofibrosarcoma, phaeochromocytoma, optic glioma	AD	*NF1*
Neurofibromatosis type 2	Vestibular schwannoma	AD	*NF2*
von Hippel–Lindau syndrome	Haemangioblastoma of retina and CNS; renal cell; phaeochromocytoma	AD	*VHL*
Retinoblastoma	Retinoblastoma and osteosarcoma	AD	*RB1*
Wilms' tumour	Nephroblastoma, neuroblastoma, hepatoblastoma, rhabdomyosarcoma	AD	*WT1*
Fanconi's anaemia	Leukaemia, hepatoma, oesophagus, skin	AR AR AR	*FACA* *FACC* *FACD*
Ataxia telangiectasia	Leukaemia, lymphoma, ovary, gastric, brain, colon	AR	*ATM*
Bloom's syndrome	Leukaemia, tongue, oesophagus, colon, Wilms' tumour	AR	*BLM*
Xeroderma pigmentosum	Skin, leukaemia, melanoma	AR AR AR AR	*XPA* *XPC* *XPD* (*ERCC2*) *XPF*
Melanoma	Melanoma	AD	*CDK2* (*p16*)
Gorlin's syndrome	Basal cell skin and brain	AD	*PTCH*
Papillary renal cell cancer syndrome	Renal cell cancer	AD	*MET*

AD, autosomal dominant; AR, autosomal recessive; CNS, central nervous system; MEN-1, multiple endocrine neoplasia type 1; MEN-2, multiple endocrine neoplasia; XL, X-linked.

- DNA damage response genes: hereditary non-polyposis colon cancer (HNPCC); *XPA*, *XPC*, *XPD* and *XPF*, xeroderma pigmentosum; *FACC*, *FACA* and *FACD*, Fanconi's anaemia; *SMAD4*, juvenile polyposis.

- Oncogenes: *RET* in MEN-2 and familial medullary thyroid cancer; *MET* in familial papillary renal cell carcinoma.

- Protein kinase inactivator, eg STK11 in Peutz–Jeghers syndrome.

- Growth factor receptor, eg TβR11 in hereditary colon cancer.

- Cell adhesion protein, eg E cadherin gene (*CDH1*) in hereditary gastric cancer.

Common hereditary cancers

Hereditary breast cancer Only 5–10% of breast cancer patients have a high-risk genetic predisposition. Half of these are due to inherited mutations of *BRCA1* or *BRCA2*. As with other genetic predispositions to cancer, *BRCA1* and *BRCA2* confer increased susceptibility to other tumours as well (Table 31).

Hereditary colorectal cancer
Only 5% of all cases of colorectal cancer are inherited and 80% of these are HNPCC or Lynch syndrome, due to mutations of DNA mismatch repair enzymes. The lifetime risk of colon cancer exceeds 80% and there is also an

increased risk of endometrial, gastric, genitourinary and ovarian cancers.

Adenomatous polyposis coli accounts for 1% of cases of colon cancer, and multiple polyps (>100) occur in 90% of carriers by 20 years of age. Colonoscopic surveillance is recommended from teenage years.

World Health Organisation Global Cancer Strategy
The current world population is 6 billion and there are 10 million new cancer cases annually and 6 million cancer deaths annually.

- Half of the cases occur in the developing world.
- Tobacco plays a major part in 3 million cancer cases (lung, oropharynx, larynx, bladder and kidney), which are preventable by smoking cessation.
- Diet contributes to a further 3 million cases (gastric, colon, oesophagus, breast, liver, oropharynx and prostate) and diet modification could reduce these by avoiding animal fat and red meat, increasing fibre, fresh fruit and vegetable intake, and avoiding obesity.
- Infections account for a further 1.5 million cases of cancer (cervix, stomach, liver, lymphoma, nasopharynx and bladder) and some of these could be reduced by infection-control measures and vaccination.
- The World Heath Organisation has established a priority ladder with the aim of reducing the global cancer burden by 25% by 2020.

FURTHER READING
Sikora K. Developing a global strategy for cancer. *Eur. J. Cancer* 1999; 35: 1870–7.

2.14 Paraneoplastic conditions

Non-metastatic manifestations of malignancy:

- occur because of the development of autoreactive antibodies and/or tumour secretion of growth factors;
- are most commonly associated with small-cell lung cancer (SCLC);
- in some, but not all, cases respond to successful therapy of the primary malignancy;
- are most commonly manifested in dermatological, neurological and endocrine systems.

Neurological manifestations

Myasthenic syndromes

Up to 50% of patients with thymoma have myasthenia gravis, whereas only 10% of patients with myasthenia gravis have thymoma. A special form of myasthenia, Lambert–Eaton myasthenic syndrome, can occur with SCLC. The diagnosis of myasthenia gravis can be confirmed by:

- an edrophonium (Tensilon) test, which will demonstrate brief but dramatic improvement in muscle power;

- electromyogram (EMG), which will show fatiguability on repeated supramaximal stimulation of peripheral nerve.

Table 32 shows the features of myasthenia gravis and Lambert–

TABLE 31 LIFETIME CANCER RISKS (%) FOR *BRCA1/BRCA2* MUTATION CARRIERS					
Gene	Female breast	Ovarian	Male breast	Colon	Prostate
BRCA1	80	60	0	6	6
BRCA2	80	27	5	0	6–14

TABLE 32 COMPARISON OF MYASTHENIA GRAVIS AND LAMBERT–EATON MYASTHENIC SYNDROME

	Myasthenia gravis	Lambert–Eaton myasthenic syndrome
Ocular/bulbar muscles	Involved	Spared
Effect of repetition on power	Power decreases	Power increases
EMG	Decremental response to repetitive stimulation	Incremental response to repetitive stimulation (post-tetanic facilitation)
Edrophonium effect	Improves power briefly	No effect
Guanidine effect	No change	Improves power
Antibodies	Anti-acetylcholine receptor antibodies	Bivalent IgG vs voltage-gated calcium channels

EMG, electromyogram.

Eaton myasthenic syndrome (see *Neurology*, Section 2.2.5).

The other paraneoplastic complications of thymoma include aplastic anaemia (common variable), hypogammaglobulinaemia, cytopenias, polymyositis, thyroiditis, systemic lupus erythematosus and chronic mucocutaneous candidiasis.

Other neurological manifestations

Other paraneoplastic neurological manifestations are listed in Table 33. (See *Neurology*, Section 2.11.1.)

Paraneoplastic endocrine syndromes

The most frequent paraneoplastic endocrine conditions are ectopic adrenocorticotropic hormone (ACTH) secretion, syndrome of inappropriate antidiuresis and humoral hypercalcaemia. Paraneoplastic hypoglycaemia is seen much less commonly. In addition, secretory endocrine tumours usually arising in the gastrointestinal tract may give rise to clinical features.

Ectopic ACTH secretion

This causes 15–20% of cases of Cushing's syndrome. When tumours grow rapidly there may not be time for the patient to develop typical physical features of steroid excess, and instead may present with weight loss, proximal muscle weakness, diabetes, hypokalaemia and alkalosis. Other products of the pro-opiomelanocortin gene may be produced, including melanocyte-stimulating hormone, which causes pigmentation.

Syndrome of inappropriate antidiuresis

Essential criteria for establishing this diagnosis include the following.

TABLE 33 PARANEOPLASTIC NEUROLOGICAL MANIFESTATIONS

Condition	Antibodies	Percentage paraneoplastic	Underlying malignancy
Encephalomyelitis	anti-Hu and anti-CV2	10	SCLC and/or thymoma
Subacute cerebellar degeneration	anti-Yo, anti-Hu, anti-VGCC and anti-Tr	50	SCLC, ovary and/or Hodgkin's disease
Opsoclonus–myoclonus syndrome	anti-Hu and anti-Ri	20–50	Neuroblastoma and/or breast
Retinal degeneration	anti-recoverin	10–20	SCLC and/or melanoma
Sensory neuropathy	anti-Hu	60	SCLC
Lambert–Eaton syndrome	anti-VGCC	5	SCLC
Myasthenia gravis	anti-AChR	10	Thymoma
Polymyositis		20	NSCLC, SCLC and/or lymphoma
Dermatomyositis			NSCLC, SCLC and/or lymphoma

AChR, acetylcholine receptor; NSCLC, non-small-cell lung cancer; SCLC, small-cell lung cancer; VGCC, voltage-gated calcium channel.

TABLE 34 COMPARISON OF CARCINOID TUMOURS BY SITE OF ORIGIN

	Foregut	Midgut	Hindgut
Site	Respiratory tract, pancreas, stomach, proximal duodenum	Jejunum, ileum, appendix, Meckel's diverticulum, ascending colon	Transverse and descending colon, rectum
Tumour products	Low 5HTP and multihormones[1]	High 5HTP and multihormones[1]	Rarely 5HTP and multihormones[1]
Blood	5HTP, histamine, multihormones[1] and occasionally ACTH	5HT, multihormones[1] and rarely ACTH	Rarely 5HT or ACTH
Urine	5HTP, 5HT, 5HIAA and histamine	5HT and 5HIAA	Negative
Carcinoid syndrome	Occurs but is atypical	Occurs frequently with metastases	Rarely occurs
Metastasises to bone	Common	Rare	Common

1. Multihormones include tachykinins (substance P, substance K and neuropeptide K), neurotensin, peptide YY, enkephalin, insulin, glucagon, glicentin, vasoactive intestinal polypeptide, somatostatin, pancreatic polypeptide, ACTH and the β-subunit of human chorionic gonadotropin.
5HT, 5-hydroxytryptamine (serotonin); 5HTP, 5-hydroxytryptophan; 5HIAA, 5-hydroxyindoleacetic acid; ACTH, adrenocorticotropic hormone.

- Plasma hypo-osmolality: plasma osmolality <275 mosmol/kg H_2O and plasma sodium <135 mmol/L.

- Concentrated urine: urine osmolality >100 mosmol/kg H_2O.

- Normal plasma/extracellular fluid volume.

- High urinary sodium: urine sodium >20 mmol/L on normal salt and water intake.

- Ensure that hypothyroidism, hypoadrenalism and diuretics are excluded as factors.

Supportive criteria for this diagnosis include the following.

- Abnormal water load test: the patient is unable to excrete more than 90% of a 20 mL/kg water load in 4 hours and/or fails to dilute urine to osmolality <100 mosmol/kg H_2O.

- Elevated plasma arginine vasopressin.

(See *Endocrinology*, Sections 1.4.1 and 2.7.3.)

Humoral hypercalcaemia
Malignancy is a common cause of severe hypercalcaemia, which may be associated with malignant solid tumours or haematological cancer, especially myeloma. Most cases are due to production of parathyroid hormone-related peptide by the tumour.
(See *Endocrinology*, Section 1.4.2; *Acute Medicine*, Section 1.2.22.)

Hypoglycaemia
Insulinomas typically present with symptoms of hypoglycaemia, when both insulin and C-peptide levels in the blood will be increased. Sarcomas and mesotheliomas rarely present with hypoglycaemia. (See *Endocrinology*, Sections 1.1.3 and 2.7.3.)

Carcinoid syndrome
Of patients with carcinoid tumours (Table 34), 5% develop carcinoid syndrome after the development of hepatic metastases, when first-pass metabolism of 5-hydroxyindoleacetic acid and kinins in the liver is avoided so that the systemic symptoms occur. The acute symptoms include vasomotor flushing (typically of the upper body that lasts up to 30 minutes), fever, pruritic wheals, diarrhoea, asthma and/or wheezing, borborygmi and abdominal pain. Chronic complications include tricuspid regurgitation, arthropathy, pulmonary stenosis, mesenteric fibrosis, cirrhosis, pellagra and telangiectasia.

Other gastrointestinal secretory endocrine tumours
These are shown in Table 35.

Dermatological manifestations
Paraneoplastic dermatological manifestations are listed in Table 36.

TABLE 35 CLINICAL MANIFESTATIONS OF SECRETORY ENDOCRINE TUMOURS

Tumour	Major feature	Minor feature	Common sites	Percentage malignant	Percentage MEN associated
Insulinoma	Neuroglycopenia (confusion and fits)	Permanent neurological deficits	Pancreas (β cells)	10	10
Gastrinoma (Zollinger–Ellison syndrome)	Peptic ulceration	Diarrhoea, weight loss, malabsorption and dumping	Pancreas and duodenum	40–60	25
VIPoma (Werner–Morrison syndrome)	Watery diarrhoea, hypokalaemia and achlorhydria	Hypercalcaemia, hyperglycaemia and hypomagnesaemia	Pancreas, neuroblastoma, SCLC, phaeochromocytoma	40	<5
Glucagonoma	Necrolytic migratory erythema, mild diabetes mellitus, muscle wasting, anaemia	Diarrhoea, thromboembolism, stomatitis, hypoaminoacidaemia, encephalitis	Pancreas (α cells)	60	<5
Somatostatinoma	Diabetes mellitus, cholelithiasis, steatorrhoea, malabsorption	Anaemia, diarrhoea, weight loss, hypoglycaemia	Pancreas (β cells)	66	Case reports only

MEN, multiple endocrine neoplasia; SCLC, small-cell lung cancer; VIPoma, tumour secreting vasoactive intestinal polypeptide.

TABLE 36 PARANEOPLASTIC DERMATOLOGICAL CONDITIONS

Name	Description	Malignancy
Acanthosis nigricans	Grey–brown symmetrical velvety plaques on neck, axillae and flexor areas	Adenocarcinoma, predominantly gastric
Acquired ichthyosis	Generalised dry, cracking skin; hyperkeratotic palms and soles	Hodgkin's disease, lymphoma and/or myeloma
Acrokeratosis paraneoplastica (Bazex's disease)	Symmetrical psoriasiform hyperkeratosis with scales and pruritis on toes, ears and nose; nail dystrophy	Squamous carcinoma of oesophagus, head and neck, and lung
Bullous pemphigoid	Large tense blisters	Lymphoma
Cushing's syndrome	Broad purple striae, plethora, telangiectasia and mild hirsuitism	SCLC, thyroid, testis, ovary and adrenal tumours, pancreatic islet cell tumours and/or pituitary tumours
Dermatitis herpetiformis	Pleomorphic symmetrical subepidermal bullae	Lymphoma
Dermatomyositis	Erythema or telangiectasia of knuckles and periorbital regions	Miscellaneous tumours
Erythema annulare centrifugum	Slowly migrating annular red lesions	Prostate, myeloma and others
Erythema gyratum repens	Progressive scaling erythema with pruritis	Lung, breast, uterus and/or gastrointestinal
Exfoliative dermatitis	Progressive erythema followed by scaling	Cutaneous T-cell lymphoma, Hodgkin's disease and other lymphoma
Flushing	Episodic reddening of face and neck	Carcinoid syndrome and/or medullary cell carcinoma of thyroid

TABLE 36 (CONTINUED)

Name	Description	Malignancy
Generalised melanosis	Diffuse grey–brown skin pigmentation	Melanoma, ACTH-producing tumours
Hirsutism	Increased hair in male distribution	Adrenal tumours and/or ovarian tumours
Hypertrichosis lanuginosa	Rapid development of fine long silky hair	Lung, colon, bladder, uterus and gallbladder tumours
Muir–Torre syndrome	Sebaceous gland neoplasm	Colon cancer and/or lymphoma
Necrolytic migratory erythema	Circinate area of blistering and erythema on face, abdomen and limbs	Islet-cell tumour of pancreas (glucagonoma)
Pachydermoperiostosis	Thickening of skin folds, lips and ears, macroglossia, clubbing and excessive sweating	Lung cancer
Paget's disease of nipple	Red keratotic patch over areola, nipple or accessory breast tissue	Breast cancer
Pemphigus vulgaris	Bullae of skin and oral blisters	Lymphoma and/or breast cancer
Pruritis	Generalised itching	Lymphoma, leukaemia, myeloma, CNS tumours and/or abdominal tumours
Sign of Leser–Trélat	Sudden onset of large number of seborrhoeic keratoses	Adenocarcinoma of stomach, lymphoma and/or breast cancer
Sweet's syndrome	Painful raised red plaques, fever, and neutrophilia	Leukaemia
Systemic nodular panniculitis (Weber–Christian disease)	Recurrent crops of tender violaceous subcutaneous nodules, may be accompanied by abdominal pain and fat necrosis in bone marrow and lungs	Adenocarcinoma of pancreas
Tripe palms	Hyperpigmented velvety thickened palms with exaggerated ridges	Gastric and lung cancer

ACTH, adrenocorticotropic hormone; CNS, central nervous system; SCLC, small-cell lung cancer.

Paraneoplastic nephropathy

Membranous glomerulonephritis is the most common glomerulonephritis associated with solid tumours. Clinical manifestations are the same as those of the idiopathic disease. The association of membranous glomerulonephritis with cancer is sufficiently common for it to be appropriate to consider investigation: perform a CXR and renal ultrasound in all cases, with a low threshold for investigation of gastrointestinal symptoms. The proteinuria typically resolves with successful treatment of the cancer.

Minimal-change glomerulonephritis is the most common glomerulonephritis associated with lymphoproliferative diseases. In general, however, the rarity of the association does not merit a work-up for occult malignancy in patients presenting with minimal-change disease. (See *Nephrology*, Section 2.3.)

FURTHER READING

Darnell RB and Posner JB. Paraneoplastic syndromes involving the nervous system. *N. Engl. J. Med.* 2003; 349: 1543–54.

Kulke MH and Mayer RJ. Carcinoid tumours. *N. Engl. J. Med.* 1999; 340: 858–68.

Le Roith D. Tumor-induced hypoglycemia. *N. Engl. J. Med.* 1999; 341: 757–8.

Newsom-Davies J. Paraneoplastic neurological disorders. *J. R. Coll. Physicians Lond.* 1999; 33: 225–7.

3.1 Investigation of unknown primary cancers

Why establish the site of the primary tumour?

- To enable diagnosis of any treatable disease.
- To avoid overtreating an unresponsive disease, thereby causing iatrogenic morbidity in resistant disease.
- To prevent complications related to an occult primary, eg bowel obstruction and pathological fracture.
- Prognostic clarification.

Approach to investigations and management

Identifying treatable tumours

There are five clinical presentations of cancer where the primary is unknown (cannot be localised) but where treatment can be effective:

- breast cancer;
- ovarian cancer;
- testicular tumours;
- neuroendocrine cancers;
- squamous cell carcinoma (SCC) of the head and neck.

These need to be identified because they require distinct management.

Treatable unknown primary tumours

Squamous cell carcinoma of the head and neck Patients with high cervical lymphadenopathy containing SCC may have occult head and neck tumours of the nasopharynx, oropharynx or hypopharynx. Radical neck dissection followed by extended-field radiotherapy that includes these possible primary sites may yield 5-year survival rates of 30%. However, note that adenocarcinoma in high cervical nodes and lower cervical adenopathy containing either histology have a much worse prognosis, and should not be treated in this aggressive fashion.

Breast cancer Women with isolated axillary lymphadenopathy (adenocarcinoma or undifferentiated carcinoma) usually have an occult breast primary. They should be managed as for stage II breast cancer and have a similar prognosis (5-year survival rate, 65%).

Ovarian cancer Women with peritoneal carcinomatosis (often papillary carcinoma with elevated serum CA125) should be managed in the same way as for stage III ovarian cancer.

Testicular tumours Men with extragonadal germ-cell syndrome or atypical teratoma present with features reminiscent of gonadal germ-cell tumours (GCT). They occur predominantly in young men with pulmonary or lymph node metastases. The GCT markers alpha-fetoprotein (AFP) and human chorionic gonadotropin (HCG) may be detected in serum and tissue by immunocytochemistry. Cytogenetic analysis for isochromosome 12p (which arises from abnormal centromere division and results in the duplication of the short arm of chromosome 12 and deletion of the long arm) is positive in 90% of patient's with testicular tumours (see Fig. 11). Empirical chemotherapy with cisplatin-based combinations yields response rates of more than 50% and long-term survival of up to 30%.

Neuroendocrine cancers Patients with neuroendocrine carcinoma of an unknown primary site overlap with extrapulmonary small-cell carcinoma, anaplastic islet-cell carcinoma, Merkel-cell tumours and paragangliomas. Patients often present with bone metastases and diffuse liver involvement. Immunocytochemical staining for chromogranin, neuron-specific enolase (NSE), synaptophysin and epithelial antigens (cytokeratins and epithelial membrane antigen) are usually positive. These tumours are frequently responsive to platinum-based combination chemotherapy.

Unknown primary tumours that respond poorly to treatment

Unfortunately, there is no curative treatment for the majority of unknown primary tumours, and the response rate to chemotherapy is less than 20%. These responses are usually short, with no impact on overall survival. The median survival is less than 12 months.

Investigations

These are directed towards establishing the primary site in metastatic disease.

Clinical, laboratory and radiological

Squamous cell carcinoma in cervical nodes Conduct the following investigations.

- Meticulous inspection of scalp and skin for primary tumour.

- Ear, nose and throat examination, and indirect laryngoscopy with or without examination under anaesthesia with blind biopsies from nasopharynx and base of tongue.

- CXR (with or without barium swallow).

- Colposcopy and cervical smear.

Anaplastic carcinoma in cervical nodes Conduct the following investigations.

- CXR and sputum cytology (most reliable in small-cell lung cancer).

- Thyroid scan and needle biopsy.

- Nasopharyngeal assessment.

Also consider the diagnosis of undifferentiated lymphoma (this can be excluded with immunophenotyping).

Axillary node adenocarcinoma in a woman Conduct the following investigations.

- Tumour hormone receptor: oestrogen receptor (ER) and progesterone receptor immunocytochemistry.

- Bilateral mammography (irrespective of ER result).

Metastatic adenocarcinoma Conduct the following investigations.

- ER and progesterone receptor expression by tumour in females.

- Serum prostate-specific antigen (PSA) and acid phosphatase in males.

- Serum AFP and HCG (if positive, histology needs review).

Also consider the diagnosis of poorly differentiated lymphoma, which can be excluded with immunophenotyping.

Retroperitoneal/mediastinal mass or multiple pulmonary metastases in a young man Conduct the following investigations.

- Serum AFP and HCG, with or without testicular ultrasound.

- FBC, differential, film and bone-marrow examination (to exclude lymphoma and T-cell leukaemia).

Squamous cell carcinoma in inguinal nodes Conduct the following investigations.

- Careful examination of legs, vulva, penis and perineum for primary tumour.

- Pelvic examination (to exclude vaginal/cervical cancer).

- Proctoscopy/colposcopy (to exclude anal/cervical cancer).

Histopathological

> 🔑 Clues to the origin of a metastatic tumour can often be found from careful histopathological studies.

Light microscopy In general for unknown primaries, 60% are adenocarcinoma, 35% are poorly differentiated carcinoma and 5% are SCC. There may be some additional clues from light microscopy to the origin of the tumour:

- signet-ring cells favour gastric primary;

- presence of melanin favours melanoma;

- presence of mucin is common in gut, lung, breast and endometrial cancers, but is less common in ovarian cancer and rare in renal cell or thyroid cancers;

- presence of psammoma bodies (calcospherites) is a feature of ovarian cancer (mucin positive) and thyroid cancer (mucin negative).

Immunocytochemical staining This can reveal many signs that will indicate the origin of a tumour:

- ER and/or progesterone receptor favours breast cancer (see Fig. 4);

- AFP, HCG and placental alkaline phosphatase all favour GCT;

- PSA and prostatic acid phosphatase favour prostate cancer;

- carcinoembryonic antigen, cytokeratin and epithelial membrane antigen favours carcinoma;

- chromogranin, NSE and synaptophysin favour a neuroendocrine tumour;

- thyroglobulin favours follicular thyroid carcinoma;

- calcitonin favours medullary thyroid carcinoma;

- S-100, vimentin and NSE favour melanoma;

- vimentin, desmin and muscle-specific actin favour rhabdomyosarcoma;

- vimentin and factor VIII antigen favour angiosarcoma;

- glial fibrillary acidic protein favours glioma;

- leucocyte common antigen (CD45) favours lymphoma.

Surface immunophenotypes
The pattern of immunoglobulin, T-cell receptor and cluster of differentiation antigen (CD) expression on the surface of lymphomas is helpful in their diagnosis and classification. Immunophenotyping can be achieved by immunohistochemical staining, immunofluorescent staining or flow cytometry.

Electron microscopy Intracellular features visualised by electron microscopy may indicate cellular origins of tumours, eg the presence of melanosomes in melanoma and dense-core granules in neuroendodermal tumours. Thus, electron microscopy may:

- distinguish adenocarcinoma and mesothelioma;

- characterise spindle-cell tumours (sarcomas, melanoma and squamous cell cancers) and small round-cell tumours;

- identify amelanotic melanoma (melanosomes) and carcinoids (neurosecretory granules).

Molecular analysis: lymphoid malignancies Monoclonal immunoglobulin gene rearrangements are characteristic of B-cell tumours and rearrangements of T-cell receptors are characteristic of T-cell tumours. In addition, a number of chromosomal translocations involving the immunoglobulin genes (heavy chain on chromosome 14q32, light chains on chromosomes 2p12 and 22q11) and T-cell receptor genes (TCRα on 14q11, TCRβ on 7q35, TCRγ on 7p15 and TCRδ on 14q11) occur in malignancies arising from these cell types. For instance:

- low-grade follicular lymphomas rearrange the *Bcl-2* gene on 18q21, eg t(14;18)(q32;q21);

- most Burkitt's lymphomas rearrange the *Myc* gene on 8q24, eg t(8;14)(q24;q32);

- most mantle-cell lymphomas rearrange the *Bcl-1* gene on 11q13, eg t(11;14)(q13;q32).

Molecular analysis: solid tumours
Other recurring chromosomal abnormalities have been found in solid tumours and may be detectable by molecular analysis. Some are helpful in establishing the diagnosis or classifying tumours, such as:

- GCTs, indicated by isochromosome 12p;

- Ewing's sarcoma and peripheral neuroectodermal tumours, indicated by t(11;22)(q24;q12).

In addition to translocations, gene amplification may be detected and may have prognostic significance, eg amplification of the N-*myc* oncogene in neuroblastoma is an adverse prognostic variable.

> **FURTHER READING**
>
> Hainsworth JD and Greco FA. Treatment of patients with cancer of an unknown primary site. *N. Engl. J. Med.* 1993; 329: 257–63.

3.2 Investigation and management of metastatic disease

Metastatic spread is the hallmark of malignant disease and occurs by lymphatic spread to regional lymph nodes and haematogenous spread to distant sites.

Brain and meninges
Up to 30% of solid tumours develop parenchymal brain metastases. Parenchymal brain secondaries are usually treated with whole-brain radiotherapy, although surgery may be considered for patients with solitary brain metastases and limited systemic disease.

Carcinomatous meningitis is less common and occurs most frequently with leukaemias and lymphomas. Carcinomatous meningitis presents with multiple widely separated cranial and spinal root neuropathies, and may be confirmed by finding malignant cells in the cerebrospinal fluid.

Treatment usually involves a combination of intrathecal chemotherapy and craniospinal radiotherapy.

Bone
The differential diagnosis of bone metastases is shown in Table 37.

Bone metastases are a substantial cause of morbidity in patients with cancer and often have a prolonged course. They cause:

- pain;

- reduced mobility;

- pathological fractures;

- hypercalcaemia;

- myelosuppression;

- nerve compression syndromes.

Tumours that commonly metastasise to bone include lung, breast, prostate, renal, thyroid and sarcomas. Note the following.

- Metastases are usually in the axial skeleton, femur or humerus; if elsewhere, consider renal cancer and melanoma as possible primary tumour sites.

- Most bone metastases are lucent lytic lesions. Occasionally, dense sclerotic deposits are seen in prostate (see Fig. 2), breast, carcinoid tumours and Hodgkin's disease.

TABLE 37 DIFFERENTIAL DIAGNOSIS OF BONE METASTASES

Diagnosis	Pain	Site	Age	Radiograph	Bone scan and/or CT/MRI	Biochemistry
Metastases	Common	Axial skeleton	Any	Discrete lesions, pathological fracture, loss of vertebral pedicles	Soft-tissue extension on MRI/CT	Raised ALP and calcium
Degenerative disease	Common	Limbs	Old	Symmetrical	Symmetrical uptake on bone scan	Normal
Osteoporosis	Painless (unless pathological fracture)	Vertebrae	Old women	Osteopenia	Normal bone scan and MRI	Normal
Paget's disease	Painless	Skull often	Old	Expanded sclerotic bones	Diffusely hot bone scan	Raised ALP and urinary hydroxyproline
Traumatic fracture	Always	Ribs	Any	Fracture	Intense linear uptake on bone scan	Normal

ALP, alkaline phosphatase.

Lung

The lungs are the second most common site for metastases via haematogenous spread. Tumours that commonly metastasise to the lung include lung, breast, renal, thyroid, sarcoma and germ-cell tumours. Carcinomatous lymphangitis can be seen (Fig. 36).

Surgical resection of pulmonary metastases is occasionally undertaken where the primary site is controlled and the lungs are the sole site of metastasis.

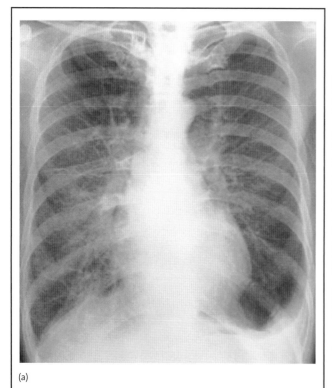

(a)

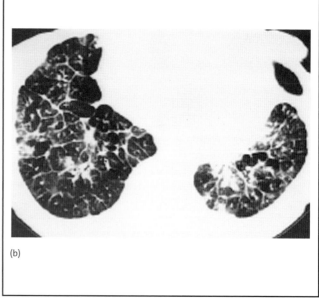

(b)

▲ **Fig. 36** (a) CXR and (b) thin-section high-resolution CT scan showing carcinomatous lymphangitis. The radiograph features widespread ill-defined linear and nodular shadowing with numerous septal lines (Kerley B lines) that may be associated with pleural effusions (as here at the left base) and mediastinal lymphadenopathy. The high-resolution CT shows irregular thickened interlobular septa.

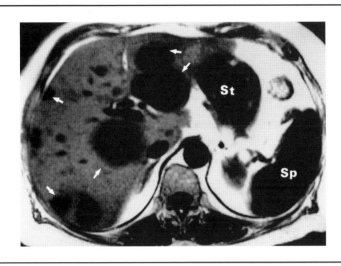

▲**Fig. 37** T1-weighted MRI showing multiple, rounded, low-signal areas (arrows) due to liver metastases. Multiple lesions with irregular edges and patchy enhancement with contrast favours metastases, whereas solitary well-defined lesions may be cysts or haemangiomas. St, stomach; Sp, spleen.

3.3 Tumour markers

Tumour markers are proteins produced by cancers that are detectable in the blood of patients. The minimal requirements for tumour markers are:

- reliable, quick and cheap assay;
- high sensitivity (>50%) and specificity (>95%);
- high positive predictive value and high negative predictive value.

Tumour markers may be used for:

- population screening;
- diagnosis;
- prognostication;
- monitoring treatment and the diagnosis of remission and relapse (Fig. 38);
- imaging of metastases.

A large number of serum tumour markers are available and each may be valuable for screening, diagnosis, prognostication or monitoring treatment (Table 38).

Liver

Liver metastases are most common in colorectal cancer (up to 60% of cases, including 20% at presentation), and also occur in melanoma (25%), lung cancer (15%) and breast cancer (5%) (Fig. 37).

Hepatic resection for patients with one to three metastases from colorectal cancer produces 5-year survival rates of 30% and is the best treatment available for selected patients.

Malignant effusions

Pleural effusion

The majority (80%) of malignant pleural effusions are due to lung and breast cancer, lymphoma and leukaemia. Treatment includes drainage followed by sclerosis with talc, bleomycin or tetracycline.

Pericardial effusion

Malignant pericardial effusions are less common than pleural effusions: breast and lung cancer account for 75% of cases. Metastases to the heart and pericardium are 40 times commoner than primary tumours at these sites. Only 15% will develop tamponade, which requires emergency percutaneous drainage (see *Cardiology*, Section 2.6.2). Subsequent treatment may involve surgical drainage by pericardial window.

Ascites

Malignant ascites is a common complication of ovarian, pancreatic, colorectal and gastric cancers and lymphoma. Treatment may involve the use of a peritoneovenous shunt.

FURTHER READING

Bower M and Rustin GJS. Serum tumour markers and their role in monitoring germ cell cancers of the testis. In: Vogelzang NJ, Scardino PT, Shipley WU and Coffey DS, eds. *Comprehensive Textbook of Genitourinary Oncology*. Baltimore: Williams and Wilkins, 1996: 968–80.

Fateh-Moghadam A and Stieber P. *Sensible Use of Tumour Markers*, 2nd edn. Basel: Editiones Roche, 1993.

TABLE 38 MOST COMMON SERUM TUMOUR MARKERS AND THEIR USES

	Natural occurrence	Tumours	Comments	Screening	Diagnosis	Prognosis	Follow-up
CEA	Glycoprotein found in intestinal mucosa during embryonic and fetal life	Colorectal cancer (especially liver metastases), gastric, breast and lung cancer	Elevated in smokers and instances of cirrhosis, chronic hepatitis, UC, Crohn's disease, pneumonia and TB (usually <10 ng/mL)	No	Yes	Yes	Yes
AFP	Glycoprotein found in yolk sac and fetal liver	GCT (80% non-seminomatous), hepatocellular cancer (50%), neural tube defects and Down's pregnancies	Role in screening in pregnancy not cancer. Only prognostic for GCT not HCC. Transient increase in liver diseases	No	Yes	Yes	Yes
PSA	Glycoprotein member of human kallikrein gene family. PSA is a serine protease that liquefies semen in excretory ducts of prostate	Prostate cancer (95%), also benign prostatic hypertrophy and prostatitis (usually <10 ng/mL)	Tissue-specific but not tumour specific, although level >10 ng/mL is 90% specific for cancer	(see Section 3.4)	Yes	No	Yes
CA125	Differentiation antigen of coelomic epithelium (Muller's duct)	Ovarian epithelial cancer (75%), also gastrointestinal, lung and breast cancers	Raised in cirrhosis, chronic pancreatitis, autoimmune diseases and any cause of ascites	(see Section 3.4)	Yes	No	Yes
HCG	Glycoprotein hormone, 14-kDa α subunit and 24-kDa β subunit from placental syncytiotrophoblasts	Choriocarcinoma (100%), hydatidiform moles (97%), non-seminomatous GCT (50–80%), seminoma (15%)	Screening post hydatidiform mole for trophoblastic tumours, also used to follow pregnancies and diagnose ectopic pregnancies	Yes	Yes	Yes	Yes
Calcitonin	32 amino acid peptide from C-cells of thyroid	Medullary cell carcinoma of thyroid	Screening test in MEN-2	Yes	Yes	Yes	Yes
β₂-microglobulin	Part of HLA common fragment present on surface of lymphocytes, macrophages and some epithelial cells	Non-Hodgkin's lymphoma and myeloma	Elevated in autoimmune disease and renal glomerular disease	No	No	Yes	Yes
Thyroglobulin	Matrix protein for thyroid hormone synthesis in normal thyroid follicles	Papillary and follicular thyroid cancer		No / No	Yes / Yes	No / No	Yes / Yes
PLAP	Isoenzyme of alkaline phosphatase	Seminoma and ovarian dysgerminoma (50%)					

AFP, alpha-fetoprotein; CEA, carcinoembryonic antigen; GCT, germ-cell tumours; HCC, hepatocellular cancers; HCG, human chorionic gondadotropin; HLA, human leucocyte antigen; MEN, multiple endocrine neoplasia; PLAP, placental alkaline phosphatase; PSA, prostate-specific antigen; TB, tuberculosis; UC, ulcerative colitis.

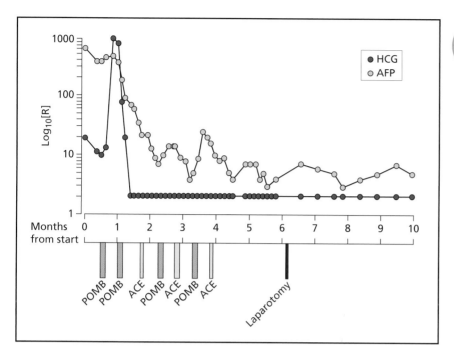

▲ **Fig. 38** Changes in serum levels of human chorionic gonadotropin (HCG) and alpha-fetoprotein (AFP) in a patient diagnosed with a metastatic non-seminomatous germ-cell tumour who was treated with combination chemotherapy followed by retroperitoneal lymphadenectomy for residual para-aortic lymph node mass, which revealed no residual viable tumour. The initial rise in serum HCG is due to tumour lysis.

Sources of bias in screening:

- Lead-time bias: by detecting tumours at an earlier (presymptomatic) stage, the subsequent survival is spuriously prolonged when compared with a symptomatic cohort.
- Length-time bias: at the start of a screening programme, more patients with indolent disease will be detected initially (since at any one time the prevalence of slowly growing tumours will be greater, even if the incidence of aggressive tumours is similar). This bias leads to an illusory survival improvement in the screened cohort.

3.4 Screening

As for all tests, it is essential to be aware of the following parameters.

- Specificity, the ability to detect negatives, calculated as: test negatives/(test negatives + false positives).
- Sensitivity, the ability to detect positives, calculated as: test positives/(test positives + false negatives).
- Positive predictive value, calculated as: test positives/(test positives + false positives).
- Negative predictive value, calculated as: test negatives/(test negatives + false negatives).

The following factors must be considered when assessing any screening programme.

- Is the disease curable if diagnosed early?
- What is the sensitivity of the test used?
- Is the disease common?
- How frequently should the test be done?
- What population should be tested?
- What are the disadvantages of screening?

Evaluation of a cancer screening programme should include:

- screening uptake rate in population;
- recall rate of screened population (true positives + false positives);
- biopsy rate;
- cancer detection rate;
- rate of interval cancers (cancers between screening tests);
- incidence rate in non-attenders;
- deaths from cancers.

Breast cancer screening

Mammographic screening represents an important advance in the management of breast cancer. A large percentage of screening-detected cancers are less than 2 cm without axillary nodal spread or are *in situ* tumours only. The suspicious mammographic features are microcalcification and soft-tissue density within the breast (Fig. 39).

Some randomised population-based trials have shown a reduction of 25% in breast cancer mortality. The age group found to benefit was 50–69 years; older women have not been adequately assessed and a benefit in younger women has not been proven. Most interval cancers occur in the third year after screening, suggesting that the optimal frequency may be every 2 years. In the UK, women aged 50–70 years are offered two-view mammographic screening every 3 years.

Colorectal cancer screening

Three randomised controlled studies have shown that population screening of people over 50 years old for faecal occult blood reduces

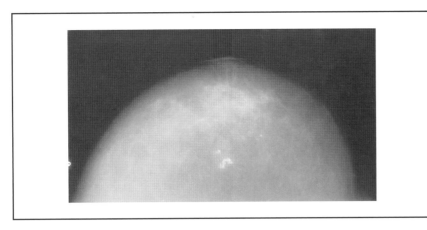

▲ **Fig. 39** Breast mammogram showing microcalcification due to small invasive ductal tumour.

colorectal cancer deaths. Case–control studies have also shown that sigmoidoscopy is effective for population screening. A routine screening programme is not in place in the UK. Members of families with familial adenomatous polyposis or hereditary non-polyposis colon cancer should have surveillance colonoscopy.

Gastric cancer screening

Early-stage gastric cancer is surgically curable and in Japan, where the incidence of gastric cancer is high, endoscopic screening has increased the number of cancers detected at an early stage and cured.

Prostate cancer screening

An early screening trial of serum prostate-specific antigen measurement and digital rectal examination in 18,000 men detected a cancer rate of 3.5%, of which over 90% were localised tumours amenable to radical curative therapy. This led to enthusiasm for prostate cancer screening, particularly in the USA. However, no randomised controlled trials have adequately addressed the impact of screening on survival. This is perhaps not surprising since no randomised controlled trials have evaluated the optimal therapy for localised early

prostate cancer either. Models of screening in the USA reveal part of the reason for this: 3% of men are expected to die of prostate cancer and the average reduction this produces in their natural lifespan is 9 years. Thus, for a group of 100 men an ideal screening programme coupled to a complete curative therapy could prevent three deaths and gain 27 years of life. This translates to an increased life expectancy for the whole screened cohort of 3 months.

Cervical cancer screening

Exfoliative cytology and Papanicolaou staining form the basis of cervical smear screening for the detection of premalignant cervical intraepithelial neoplasia (CIN). The detection of human papillomavirus in the cervix has recently been added to this screening algorithm. The cervical screening programme has reduced the incidence of squamous cell carcinoma of the cervix but is not able to detect adenocarcinomas that frequently develop deeper in the cervix and account for 15% of invasive cervical cancer.

Abnormal smears (CIN 2/3) should be followed by colposcopy (visualisation of cervix under

10–15× magnification with bright light and green filter to enhance vascular pattern) and biopsy. If colposcopic biopsy is incomplete, then patients should proceed to cone biopsy, removing the transition zone.

Ovarian cancer screening

Ovarian screening using measurement of serum CA125 tumour marker and/or transvaginal ultrasound is under investigation in randomised controlled trials. Although this approach is feasible and can detect tumours at an earlier and (in theory) more curable stage, there is as yet no evidence of improved survival in screened cohorts. Even in women with *BRCA1* or *BRCA2* there is no evidence to support screening.

Lung cancer screening

Screening for lung cancer by CXR and/or sputum cytology has not been found to be effective, even in high-risk populations. Four randomised trials have failed to show a reduction in lung cancer mortality. Low-dose CT screening has been shown to detect lung cancer at an earlier stage than would be detected in an unscreened population, but there is no evidence that survival is improved.

FURTHER READING

Anderson I, Aspergen K, Janzon L, *et al.* Mammographic screening and mortality from breast cancer: the Malmö mammographic screening trial. *BMJ* 1988; 297: 943–8.

Armstrong K, Eisen A and Weber B. Assessing the risk of breast cancer. *N. Engl. J. Med.* 2000; 342: 564–71.

Bell R, Petticrew M and Sheldon T. The performance of screening tests for ovarian cancer: results of a systematic review. *Br. J. Obstet. Gynaecol.* 1998; 105: 1136–47.

Catalona WJ, Smith DS, Ratliff TL, *et al.* Measurement of prostate-specific antigen in serum as a screening test for prostate cancer. *N. Engl. J. Med.* 1991; 324: 1156–61.

Eddy DM. Screening for breast cancer. *Ann. Intern. Med.* 1989; 111: 389–99.

Hardcastle JD, Chamberlain JO, Robinson MH, *et al.* Randomised controlled trial of faecal-occult blood screening for colorectal cancer. *Lancet* 1996; 348: 1472–7.

Jacobs IJ, Skates SJ, MacDonald N, *et al.* Screening for ovarian cancer: a pilot randomised controlled trial. *Lancet* 1999; 353: 1207–10.

Kronborg O, Fenger C, Olsen J, *et al.* Randomised study of screening for colorectal cancer with faecal-occult-blood test. *Lancet* 1996; 348: 1467–71.

Mandel JS, Bond JH, Church JR, *et al.* Reducing mortality from colorectal cancer by screening for faecal occult blood. *N. Engl. J. Med.* 1993; 328: 1365–71.

Roberts MM, Alexander FE, Anderson TJ, *et al.* Edinburgh trial of screening for breast cancer: mortality at 7 years. *Lancet* 1990; 335: 241–6.

Smith DS, Catalona WJ and Herschman JD. Longitudinal screening for prostate cancer with prostate specific antigen. *JAMA* 1996; 276: 1309–400.

Strauss GM, Gleason RE and Sugarbaker DJ. Chest X-ray screening improves outcome in lung cancer. A reappraisal of randomised trials on lung cancer screening. *Chest* 1995; 107: 270S–279S.

Tabar L, Gad A, Holmberg L, *et al.* Reduction in mortality from breast cancer after mass screening with mammography. *Lancet* 1985; ii: 829–32.

Woolf SH. Should we screen for prostate cancer? *BMJ* 1997; 314: 989–90.

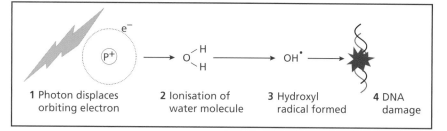

▲ **Fig. 40** Mechanism of radiation-induced DNA damage.

3.5 Radiotherapy

Principle

Radiotherapy is the use of ionising radiation for the treatment of disease. High-energy short-wavelength electromagnetic waves have sufficiently high energy to ionise atoms by displacing electrons and creating radicals (Fig. 40). DNA damage caused by radicals includes damage to bases and the sugar backbone, as well as cross-linkage between strands and single- and double-strand breaks. The effect of radiation is only expressed when cells attempt mitosis and fail. This accounts for the delay in tumour response and the timing of radiation reactions in normal tissue.

Practical details

Radiation can be delivered therapeutically by four possible routes:

- place a radioactive source into the tumour, either temporarily or permanently;
- place a radioactive source in a body cavity, eg endometrium;
- inject a radioactive isotope, eg strontium-89 for metastatic prostate cancer or phosphorus-32 for polycythaemia
- deliver an external beam of X-rays or electrons.

The latter requires careful planning and the shielding of normal tissues. This avoids toxicity while maximising the dose delivered to tumour. Radiotherapy planning thus involves simulation of the isodose distribution for each patient.

Complications

The normal tissue tolerance to radiotherapy is shown in Table 39. The normal organ tolerance to radiotherapy varies, and the timing of adverse reactions is shown in Table 40.

TABLE 39 NORMAL TISSUE TOLERANCE OF RADIOTHERAPY

Tissue	Radiation effect	Dosage (cGy)[1]
Testis	Sterility	200
Eye	Cataract	1000
Lung	Pneumonitis	2000
Kidney	Nephritis	2500
Liver	Hepatitis	3000
Central nervous system	Necrosis	5000
Gastrointestinal tract	Ulceration and haemorrhage	6000

1. Radiation dose is expressed in Gray (Gy): 1 Gy = 1 J/kg. 1 Gy = 100 rads (old units) and therefore units often expressed as centiGray (cGy) are equivalent to 1 rad.

TABLE 40 ADVERSE EARLY AND LATE REACTIONS TO RADIOTHERAPY

Timing	Tissue	Reaction
Early reactions	Skin	Dermatitis
	Oral mucosa	Stomatitis
	Bladder	Cystitis
	Oesophagus	Oesophagitis
	Bowel	Diarrhoea and ulceration
	Bone marrow	Myelosuppression
Late reactions	Central nervous system	Necrosis
	Kidney	Nephritis
	Liver	Hepatitis
	Lung	Pneumonitis and fibrosis
	Vascular endothelium	Fibrosis

Early reactions occur in tissues that divide rapidly, are expressed during the course of radiotherapy and may be reversible. Late tissue reactions occur when slowly dividing cells attempt division: these side effects can occur years after a course of radiotherapy and are less frequently reversible. An example of a late tissue reaction, postradiation fibrosis in the lung, is shown in Fig. 41.

FURTHER READING

Maisey M. Radionuclide imaging in cancer management. *J. R. Coll. Physicians Lond.* 1998; 32: 525–9.

O'Doherty M. Therapy and nuclear medicine. *J. R. Coll. Physicians Lond.* 1998; 32: 536–9.

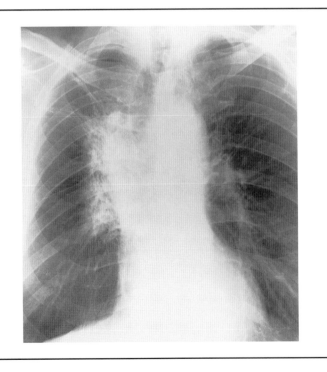

▲ **Fig. 41** CXR showing postradiation fibrosis of the right upper zone following radical radiotherapy for non-small-cell lung cancer. The features include geometrically delineated shadowing that corresponds to the radiation field and tracheal and mediastinal shift due to contraction of the irradiated lung.

3.6 Chemotherapy

Treatment with chemotherapy

The goal of treatment for cancer varies with tumour type, stage of disease and performance status of the patient. It ranges from cure to symptom palliation, with the aim of improving quality of life. Most curable cancers are early-stage diseases that are cured by complete surgical removal or, occasionally, radical radiotherapy. However, sometimes, cures may be achieved with chemotherapy in patients with very advanced metastatic disease if the histology shows:

- germ-cell tumours, particularly testicular cancer;
- choriocarcinoma;
- leukaemia;
- lymphoma, both Hodgkin's and non-Hodgkin's lymphoma;
- paediatric cancers, such as neuroblastomas and nephroblastomas.

The sensitivity and curability of various tumours with chemotherapy varies (Table 41).

In addition to the role of chemotherapy as a curative treatment and for symptom palliation, it has an increasing role as adjuvant therapy (Table 42).

- Adjuvant: treatment with chemotherapy, radiotherapy or hormone therapy in the absence of any detectable residual cancer after primary treatment (usually surgical).
- Neoadjuvant: treatment with chemotherapy, radiotherapy or hormone therapy before primary therapy, often with the aim of 'downsizing' the tumour to make surgery easier.

TABLE 41 SENSITIVITY AND CURABILITY OF SELECTED CANCERS TREATED WITH CHEMOTHERAPY

Sensitivity	Tumour
Sensitive and curable	Leukaemia, lymphoma, germ-cell tumours or childhood tumours
Sensitive and normally incurable (radical palliation)	Small-cell lung cancer or myeloma
Moderately sensitive (palliation or adjuvant treatments)	Breast, colorectal, ovary or bladder
Low sensitivity (chemotherapy of limited use)	Kidney, melanoma, adult brain tumours or prostate

TABLE 42 CANCERS EFFECTIVELY TREATED BY NEOADJUVANT AND ADJUVANT CHEMOTHERAPY

Therapy	Tumour
Neoadjuvant chemotherapy	Soft-tissue sarcoma Osteosarcoma Anal cancer Locally advanced breast cancer
Adjuvant chemotherapy	Wilms' tumour Osteosarcoma Breast cancer Colorectal cancer

Cytotoxic drugs act on cell division by interfering with normal cell replication. These agents are not tumour selective and are usually toxic. Cytotoxic drugs may be classified into groups based on their anticancer activity, sites of action and toxicity. Knowledge of the pharmacokinetics, including the metabolism and excretion, of cytotoxics is essential because impaired drug handling is frequent in cancer patients and may result in greatly enhanced toxicity if doses are not adjusted.

Functional classification of cytotoxics

Alkylating agents

- Nitrogen mustards: chlorambucil, cyclophosphamide, ifosfamide and melphalan.

- Nitrosoureas: 1,3-bis(2-chloroethyl)-1-nitrosourea (BCNU), lomustine and streptozotocin.

- Tetrazine compounds: dacarbazine and temozolomide.

- Aziridines: mitomycin and thiotepa.

- Busulfan.

Antimetabolites

- Purine analogues: 6-mercaptopurine and 6-thioguanine.

- Pyrimidine analogues: cytarabine and gemcitabine.

- Methotrexate: inhibits dihydrofolate reductase (DHFR).

- 5-Fluorouracil: inhibits thymidylate synthetase.

Hydroxycarbamide (hydroxyurea): inhibits ribonucleotide reductase.

Intercalating agents

- Platins: cisplatin and carboplatin.

- Antibiotics: anthracyclines (doxorubicin and daunorubicin), anthraquinones (mitozantrone), bleomycin, mitomycin, dactinomycin (actinomycin D).

Spindle-cell poisons

- Vinca alkaloids: vincristine, vinblastine, vindesine and vinorelbine.

- Taxanes: paclitaxel and docetaxel.

Topoisomerase inhibitors

- Topoisomerase I inhibitors: camptothecins (topotecan and irinotecan).

- Topoisomerase II inhibitors: epipodophyllotoxins (etoposide and teniposide).

Drug resistance

For most malignancies, combinations of drugs are used to overcome tumour resistance. These combinations rely on two principles:

- all drugs must have antitumour activity;

- different toxicity profiles allow maximum doses of each drug.

Ideally, the mechanisms of tumour resistance should also differ. A number of mechanisms of acquired tumour resistance to cytotoxics have been described.

- Reduced drug uptake: overexpression by a tumour cell of the *MDR1* (multidrug resistance 1) gene results in increased levels of P glycoprotein, a cell-membrane efflux pump that confers cross-class resistance to anthracyclines, vinca alkaloids, taxanes and topoisomerase inhibitors.

- Reduced drug activation: 5-fluorouracil requires phosphorylation to active moieties, and reduced levels of thymidine kinase and uridine kinase in tumour cells confer resistance.

- Increased detoxification: 6-mercaptopurine is inactivated to 6-thioxanthine by the enzyme xanthine oxidase, which is overexpressed in resistant tumour cells.

- Altered target levels: DHFR is the target of methotrexate, and resistant cells overexpress DHFR by amplifying the DHFR gene.

- Repair of drug-induced damage: O^6-alkylguanine DNA alkyltransferase repairs the DNA alkylation of nitrosoureas, and resistant tumour cells overexpress this repair enzyme.

Evaluation of chemotherapy

Evaluation of chemotherapy includes an assessment of:

- overall survival duration;

- response to treatment (chiefly radiological);

- remission rate;

- disease-free survival/response duration;

- quality of life;

- toxicity.

Uniform criteria have been established to measure these, including the UICC (Union International Contre le Cancer) criteria for response and the more recent response evaluation criteria in solid tumours and World Health Organisation toxicity grades. This allows clinicians to accurately

inform patients of the prognosis, effectiveness and toxicity of chemotherapy, and thus empowers patients to take an active role in treatment decisions.

In addition to conventional established treatments, oncologists actively enrol patients in studies to evaluate new agents. Three phases of clinical drug trials are widely recognised.

- Phase I studies determine the relationship between toxicity and dose schedules of treatment.

- Phase II studies identify tumour types for which the treatment appears promising.

- Phase III studies assess the efficacy of treatment compared with standard treatment including toxicity comparison.

Side effects

Many of the side effects of cytotoxic chemotherapy are predictable from their mode of action. The side effects may be divided into early and late complications.

Early complications

These generally occur with each cycle and within days, and include:

- extravasation injuries;

- nausea and vomiting;

- alopecia (this usually occurs after 4–8 weeks);

- myelosuppression, resulting in neutropenia, thrombocytopenia, anaemia and infections;

- gastrointestinal tract may be affected, leading to stomatitis, ulceration and diarrhoea.

Late complications

These may occur many years after treatment, and include:

- infertility;

- teratogenesis;

- second malignancies (especially acute leukaemia).

In addition, certain toxicities are associated with particular cytotoxic drugs.

Lung Pulmonary fibrosis: bleomycin, busulfan, methotrexate, mitomycin and BCNU (Fig. 42).

Liver

- Cholestasis: 6-mercaptopurine.

- Acute liver necrosis: high-dose methotrexate, L-asparaginase and mithramycin.

- Hepatic fibrosis: chronic low-dose methotrexate.

- Veno-occlusive disease: high-dose chemotherapy with autologous stem-cell rescue with or without radiotherapy.

Gastrointestinal tract

- Enteritis: 5-fluorouracil, dactinomycin (actinomycin D), cisplatin, methotrexate, hydroxycarbamide (hydroxyurea) and procarbazine.

- Oesophagitis: doxorubicin and cyclophosphamide.

Nervous system

- Peripheral neuropathy: cisplatin and vincristine.

- Cerebellar degeneration: 5-fluorouracil/high-dose arabinoside.

- Encephalopathy: ifosfamide and L-asparaginase.

- Myelopathy: intrathecal methotrexate and spinal cord radiotherapy.

- Reduced IQ: craniospinal radiotherapy for childhood leukaemia.

Opportunistic infections

Cryptococcal meningitis and progressive multifocal leucoencephalopathy.

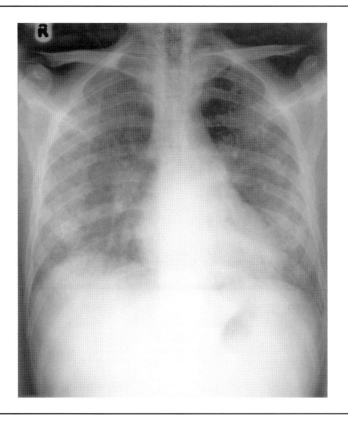

▲ **Fig. 42** CXR shows diffuse interstitial fibrosis, most prominent in the lower zones, typical of bleomycin fibrosis.

The late toxicities of treatment for cancer are increasingly recognised as successful treatment produces more long-term survivors.

Late complications of treatment for lymphoma including Hodgkin's disease:

- Hypothyroidism, especially following mantle irradiation.
- Infertility/hypogonadism, although this does not always occur.
- Peripheral neuropathy may persist, especially after vincristine.
- Secondary acute leukaemia: this is chiefly acute myeloid leukaemia 1–2 years after topoisomerase II inhibitors with abnormalities of chromosome 11q23, or 2–5 years after alkylating agents with abnormalities of chromosome 5q.

FURTHER READING

Hancock S, Cox R and McDougall I. Thyroid disease after treatment of Hodgkin's disease. *N. Engl. J. Med.* 1991; 325: 599–605.

Horning WJ, Hoppe RT, Kaplan HS, *et al.* Female reproductive potential after treatment for Hodgkin's disease. *N. Engl. J. Med.* 1981; 304: 1377–82.

Lowis S. Malignant disease and the adolescent. *J. R. Coll. Physicians Lond.* 2000; 34: 27–31.

Miller A, Hoogstraten B, Staquet M, *et al.* Reporting results of cancer treatment. *Cancer* 1981; 47: 207–14.

Morris Jones PH. The late effects of cancer therapy in childhood. *Br. J. Cancer* 1991; 64: 1–2.

Nooter K and Herweijer H. Multidrug resistance (mdr) genes in human cancer. *Br. J. Cancer* 1991; 63: 663–9.

Pedersen-Bjergaard J, Philip P, Larsen SO, Jensen G and Byrsting K. Chromosome aberrations and prognostic factors in therapy-related myelodysplasia and acute non-lymphocytic leukaemia. *Blood* 1990; 76: 1083–91.

Therasse P, Arbuck SG, Eisenhauer EA, *et al.* New guidelines to evaluate the response to treatment in solid tumours. *J. Natl Cancer Inst.* 2000; 92: 205–16.

Tucker MA, Coleman CN, Rosenberg SA, *et al.* Risk of second cancers after treatment for Hodgkin's disease. *N. Engl. J. Med.* 1988; 311: 876–81.

Urba WJ and Longo DL. Hodgkin's disease. *N. Engl. J. Med.* 1992; 326: 678–87.

Van Leeuwen FE, Klokman WJ, Hagenbeek, A, *et al.* Second cancer risk following Hodgkin's disease: a 20-years follow-up study. *J. Clin. Oncol.* 1994; 12: 312–25.

3.7 Immunotherapy

Both passive and active specific immunotherapy and non-specific immunotherapy have a limited role in the management of cancer.

Passive immunotherapy with monoclonal antibodies

- Rituximab (anti-CD20) for low-grade non-Hodgkin's lymphoma.

- Trastuzumab (anti-human epidermal growth factor receptor 2) for breast cancer.

Active immunotherapy

- Lymphokine-activated killer (*ex vivo*) cell therapy for renal cell cancer and melanoma.

Non-specific immunotherapy

- Interferon stimulates host immune responses in hairy cell leukaemia, chronic myeloid leukaemia, melanoma, renal cell cancer and Kaposi's sarcoma.

- Interleukin-2 stimulates host T-cell responses in melanoma and renal cell cancer.

- BCG administered into the bladder reduces recurrences in superficial bladder cancer.

3.8 Stem-cell transplantation

The dose-limiting toxicity of many cytotoxics is myelosuppression. This may occur in the linear phase of the dose–response curve for tumour cells, where further dose escalation would increase tumour-cell death. For some tumours this hurdle may be overcome by intravenous reinfusion of haematopoietic progenitor stem cells that are capable of re-establishing bone-marrow function after chemotherapy.

These progenitor cells may be harvested using multiple bone-marrow aspirations or peripheral blood leucapheresis, and may be obtained in one of two ways.

- Autologous cells (from the patient): these are used most commonly in the treatment of solid tumours.

- Allogeneic cells (from a donor): these have the disadvantages that (i) it is necessary to find a compatible sibling or donor closely matched for human leucocyte antigen (HLA) and (ii) the patient is likely to suffer the toxicity of graft-vs-host disease. Allogeneic cells may have the advantage of offering additional graft-vs-tumour effect, and are mostly used for younger patients with leukaemia.

Cancers treated effectively with high-dose chemotherapy and stem-cell transplantation are shown in Table 43.

FURTHER READING

Philip T, Guglielmi C, Hagenbeek A, *et al.* Autologous bone marrow transplantation as compared with salvage chemotherapy in relapses of chemotherapy-sensitive non-Hodgkin's lymphoma. *N. Engl. J. Med.* 1995; 333: 1540–5.

Shipp MA, Abeloff MD, Antman KH, *et al.* International consensus conference on high-dose therapy with haematopoietic stem cell transplantation in aggressive non-Hodgkin's lymphoma: report of the jury. *J. Clin. Oncol.* 1999; 17: 423–9.

3.9 Oncological emergencies

Superior vena cava obstruction

Superior vena cava obstruction (SVCO) by mediastinal tumour occurs most frequently with lung cancers, especially small-cell lung cancer, but also with lymphoma, germ-cell tumours (GCTs) and other metastatic tumours.

TABLE 43 CANCERS FOR WHICH HIGH-DOSE CHEMOTHERAPY AND STEM-CELL TRANSPLANTATION ARE USUAL

Disease	Stage	Transplant	Approximate 5-year disease-free survival rate (%)
CML	Stable phase	Allogeneic	30
ALL	Second remission	Allogeneic/autologous	40
AML	First remission	Allogeneic/autologous	50
High-grade NHL	Responsive relapse	Autologous	45
Hodgkin's disease	Responsive relapse	Autologous	45
Neuroblastoma	High-risk first line	Allogeneic/autologous	50
Neuroblastoma	Relapsed	Allogeneic/autologous	25
Non-seminomatous germ-cell tumour	Responsive relapse	Autologous	50
Myeloma	First line	Allogeneic/autologous	30

ALL, acute lymphoblastic leukaemia; AML, acute myeloid leukaemia; CML, chronic myelogenous leukaemia; NHL, non-Hodgkin's lymphoma.

Clinical features

Symptoms and signs include:

- headaches;

- dusky skin coloration over the chest, arms and face;

- oedema of the arms and face;

- distended neck and arm veins.

The severity relates to the rate of obstruction and the presence of compensatory venous collateral circulation. This may develop over a period of weeks, and the flow of blood in collaterals helps confirm the clinical diagnosis.

Investigations and management

SVCO is a medical emergency.

- Following suspicion of the diagnosis high-dose steroid therapy should be started (dexamethasone 10 mg iv stat and 4 mg po qds).

- Diagnosis can be confirmed by Doppler ultrasound or angiography (Fig. 43).

- A tissue diagnosis should be made urgently if possible: some tumours that cause SVCO are better treated with chemotherapy than radiotherapy, eg non-Hodgkin's lymphoma (NHL) and mediastinal GCTs.

- For most tumours the optimal treatment for SVCO is mediastinal radiotherapy: this relieves symptoms in 50–90% of patients within 2 weeks. If radiotherapy is ineffective or symptoms recur, then stenting of the superior vena cava may be possible.

See Section 1.4.3 for further discussion.

Spinal cord compression

Up to 5% of patients with cancer develop spinal cord compression.

- Around 30% will survive for 1 year.

- Residual neurological deficit usually reflects the extent of the deficit at the start of treatment.

- To prevent paraplegia the diagnosis of spinal cord compression must be made swiftly and treatment instituted quickly.

- Neoplastic cord compression is nearly always due to extramedullary, extradural metastases. This is most common from prostate cancer or myeloma, but also comes from breast, lung or renal cancers or lymphoma.

- Commonly, compression occurs by posterior expansion of vertebral metastases or extension of paraspinal metastases through the intervertebral foramina.

- Of cases of compression, 70% occur in the thoracic spine, 20% in the lumbar spine and 10% in the cervical spine.

Clinical features

The earliest symptom of cord compression is vertebral pain, especially on coughing and lying flat. Signs include sensory changes one or two dermatomes below the level of compression, progressing to motor weakness distal to the block and finally sphincter disturbance. Distal compression may cause conus medullaris or cauda equina compression (Table 44).

Investigations and management

Spinal cord compression should be treated as a medical emergency. The important aspects to note are listed below.

- Following suspicion of the diagnosis high-dose steroid therapy should be started (dexamethasone 10 mg iv stat and 4 mg po qds).

- Urgent MRI scan (Fig. 44) should be undertaken.

- Surgical decompression is appropriate in patients with one site of cord compression and very

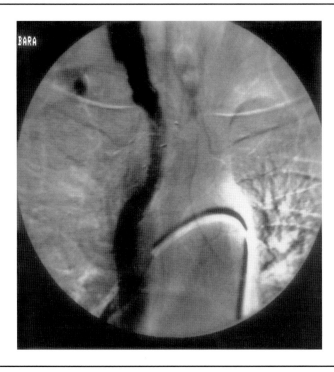

▲**Fig. 43** Angiogram showing superior vena cava compression at the level of the carina.

TABLE 44 COMPARISON OF FEATURES OF CORD, CONUS AND CAUDA COMPRESSION

Clinical feature	Spinal cord	Conus medullaris	Cauda equina
Weakness	Symmetrical and profound	Symmetrical and variable	Asymmetrical, may be mild
Reflexes	Increased or absent knee and ankle extensor plantar reflex	Increased knee and decreased ankle extensor plantar reflex	Decreased knee and ankle plantar reflex
Sensory loss	Symmetrical and sensory level	Symmetrical and saddle distribution	Asymmetrical and radicular pattern
Sphincters	Late loss	Early loss	Spared often
Progression	Rapid	Variable	Variable

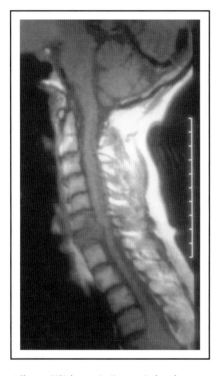

▲ **Fig. 44** MRI demonstrating cervical cord compression at C7 due to vertebral metastasis with soft-tissue extension.

limited disease elsewhere in the spine or systemically, especially if this is their first presentation of malignant disease (histology can then be obtained at the same time). Other indications for surgery are skeletal instability or recurrent compression following radiotherapy in patients without

extensive metastatic disease (see Fig. 3).

• In other patients urgent radiotherapy should be given.

See Section 1.4.2 for further discussion. See *Acute Medicine*, Section 1.2.28; *Neurology*, Section 1.4.1.

Hypercalcaemia

Hypercalcaemia is particularly common in some tumours, occurring in 50% of patients with myeloma and 20% of those with breast and non-small-cell lung cancer. In the majority of cases humoral hypercalcaemia is due to production of parathyroid hormone-related peptide by the tumour.

Clinical features

The symptoms of hypercalcaemia may mimic deterioration due to progressive malignancy. The common symptoms include drowsiness, confusion, nausea and vomiting, constipation, polyuria and polydipsia. As always, measured serum calcium should be corrected for albumin levels.

Management

All patients with symptomatic hypercalcaemia should receive 24-hour intravenous rehydration

with normal saline (2–4 L daily). The renal failure associated with hypercalcaemia is frequently due to dehydration, and hence administration of intravenous fluids may result in rapid symptomatic improvement.

Following rehydration, bisphosphonates (eg disodium pamidronate 30–90 mg by slow intravenous infusion) are optimal therapy. Disodium pamidronate will usually bring serum calcium levels to normal by day 5. Its duration of action is up to 4 weeks and doses can be repeated at 3–4 week intervals. Disodium pamidronate may also improve any bone pain caused by metastatic disease, as may oral bisphosphonates.

Hypercalcaemia is a sign of tumour progression and it should also prompt a review of the anticancer therapy. (See *Acute Medicine*, Section 1.2.22; *Endocrinology*, Section 1.4.2.)

Tumour lysis

Tumour lysis encompasses a number of metabolic derangements that complicate the treatment of bulky and highly proliferative tumours. The syndrome is rare: it occurs with Burkitt's lymphoma and other aggressive high-grade NHLs, acute lymphoblastic leukaemia with very high blast counts, and accelerated chronic myelogenous leukaemia.

Clinical features

Following chemotherapy, the lysis of tumour cells releases large amounts of intracellular urate, phosphate and potassium into the circulation. The metabolic consequences include hyperuricaemia, hyperphosphataemia, secondary hypocalcaemia and hyperkalaemia. Precipitation of urate or calcium phosphate in the renal tubules causes acute renal failure and further metabolic chaos. Cardiac dysrhythmias and encephalopathy occur subsequently.

Management

The most important aspect of tumour lysis is prevention. This can be achieved by:

- maintaining high fluid input prior to and during the first cycle of chemotherapy, and in the ensuing 3–5 days;

- administration of allopurinol.

These measures will prevent tumour lysis in most patients at risk. The management of tumour lysis includes these measures, alkalinisation of the urine with sodium bicarbonate to promote uric acid excretion, rasburicase and haemodialysis if necessary (see Section 1.4.1).

Neutropenic sepsis

Neutropenia (neutrophil count <1.0 × 10⁹/L) is:

- usually secondary to chemotherapy;
- can occur with radiotherapy if large amounts of marrow are irradiated;
- may be part of pancytopenia due to malignant infiltration of the marrow.

The risk of infection depends on:

- the degree of neutropenia and its duration;

- patient factors, such as the presence of a Hickman catheter.

Febrile neutropenia is defined as pyrexia of more than 38°C for over 2 hours in a patient with a neutrophil count $<1.0 \times 10^9$/L.

Investigations and management

Initial management should include an infection screen comprising:

- blood cultures (peripheral and from Hickman catheter if present);

- midstream urine;

- CXR;

- swabs for culture (throat and Hickman site).

No additional microbiological assessment is of benefit in the absence of localising signs of infection.

The standard approach is then to commence empirical antibiotics according to local hospital policies agreed with the microbiologists and based on the local antibiotic resistance patterns. In general, the following principles are observed.

- First-line empirical therapy is either monotherapy with an antipseudomonal β-lactam (in the UK this is usually ceftazidime, cefotaxime or meropenem) or a combination of an aminoglycoside and broad-spectrum penicillin with antipseudomonal activity (in the UK this is usually gentamicin and piperacillin).

- Metronidazole may be added if anaerobic infection is suspected, and flucloxacillin, vancomycin or teicoplanin can be added if Gram-positive infection is suspected.

- Antibiotics should be adjusted according to culture results, although these are often negative.

- If there is no response after 36–48 hours, review antibiotics with microbiological advice and consider antifungal cover with amphotericin.

Note the following.

- Remember drug levels for gentamicin and vancomycin.

- Starting doses of aminoglycosides and cephalosporins may need to be altered if impaired renal function is present, and particular caution is required in patients who have received cisplatin or other nephrotoxic drugs.

- Pay attention to fluid replacement if the patient is hypotensive or dehydrated.

- Pay attention to mouth care. Oral candidiasis may be treated with fluconazole 50 mg twice a day for 5 days or 100–400 mg single dose. Prophylaxis for oral *Candida* with triple therapy of nystatin suspension 1 mL, amphotericin lozenges and a mouthwash is only effective if given at least every 2 hours.

Colony-stimulating factors are not routinely used for all patients with neutropenia, and guidelines for their use have been established.

- Primary prophylaxis (ie with first cycle of chemotherapy): not routinely used except occasionally for pre-existing neutropenia, eg due to marrow infiltration.

- Secondary prophylaxis: only for curable tumours with proven importance of maintaining dose intensity (eg GCTs, choriocarcinoma and lymphoma).

- Febrile neutropenia: data do not support routine use of granulocyte colony-stimulating factor (G-CSF), but use in presence of pneumonia, hypotension, multiorgan failure or fungal infection.

- Peripheral stem-cell mobilisation prior to harvesting: G-CSF should not be started until 24 hours post chemotherapy.

Recently, some centres have adopted a risk-stratified approach to the management of neutropenic sepsis, with low-risk patients (ie absence of

hypotension, dehydration, altered mental state and respiratory failure, and adequate oral intake) receiving oral quinolones as outpatients. (See *Haematology*, Section 1.4.2.)

FURTHER READING

Lieschke GJ and Burgess AW. Granulocyte colony-stimulating factor and granulocyte–macrophage colony-stimulating factor. *N. Engl. J. Med.* 1992; 327: 28–35 and 99–106.

Pizzo P. Management of fever in patients with cancer and treatment-induced neutropenia. *N. Engl. J. Med.* 1993; 328: 1323–32.

Pizzo P. Current concepts: fever in immunocompromised patients. *N. Engl. J. Med.* 1999; 341: 893–900.

Strewler G. Mechanisms of disease: the physiology of parathyroid hormone-related peptide. *N. Engl. J. Med.* 2000; 342: 177–85.

ONCOLOGY: **SECTION 4**
SELF-ASSESSMENT

4.1 Self-assessment questions

Question 1

Clinical scenario
Figure 45 shows the pedigree of a family with hereditary polyposis.

Question
Which is the most likely polyposis syndrome illustrated in Fig. 45?

Answers
A Peutz–Jeghers syndrome
B Gardner's syndrome
C Familial adenomatous polyposis
D Turcot's syndrome
E Canada–Cronkhite syndrome

Question 2

Clinical scenario
A 62-year-old Vietnamese man presents with a 3-month history of abdominal pain and swelling. The pain is in the right upper quadrant of his abdomen and is constant without relief. He also reports generalised swelling of his abdomen with flatulence, nausea and constipation. Over the previous 6 weeks he had lost 10 kg in weight and developed anorexia. He emigrated to Britain in the 1980s and had previously been healthy apart from recurrent episodes of malaria when he lived in Asia.

On examination he is emaciated but not jaundiced. He is pyrexial (38°C). There is no peripheral lymphadenopathy. Abdominal examination reveals ascites and a tender enlarged liver with an irregular edge that extended 10 cm below the costal margin. The initial blood investigation results are as follows: haemoglobin 8.7 g/dL, white cell count 8.2×10^6/L, platelets 167×10^9/L, erythrocyte sedimentation rate 70 mm/hour, urea and electrolytes normal, glucose 3.2 mmol/L, bilirubin 15 umol/L, aspartate transaminase 57 u/L, γ-glutamyl transferase 469 u/L, alkaline phosphatase 1157 u/L, amylase 319 u/L, CXR normal.

Question
What are the two most likely diagnoses?

Answers
A Hepatocellular carcinoma
B Cancer of the head of pancreas
C Recurrent malaria
D *Opisthorchis viverrini* infection
E *Schistosoma mansoni* infection
F Metastatic colorectal cancer
G *Mycobacterium tuberculosis* infection
H Amoebic abscess
I Hepatitis A infection
J Crohn's disease

Question 3

Clinical scenario
A 28-year-old man presents with testicular swelling and undergoes an orchidectomy for a stage I testicular non-seminomatous germ-cell tumour.

Question
Which of the following is true regarding the use of tumour markers in testicular tumours?

Answers
A More than 90% of classical seminomas produce alpha-fetoprotein (AFP) or β-human chorionic gonadotropin (β-HCG)
B More than 20% of non-seminomatous germ-cell tumours produce no serum tumour markers

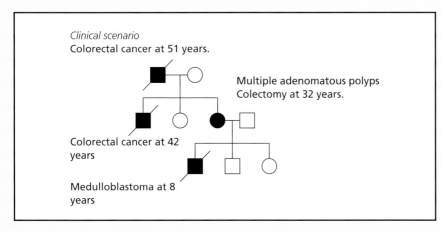

Clinical scenario
Colorectal cancer at 51 years.

Multiple adenomatous polyps
Colectomy at 32 years.

Colorectal cancer at 42 years

Medulloblastoma at 8 years

▲ **Fig. 45** Question 1.

C Both AFP and β-HCG should be measured to follow the progress of a tumour

D Serum tumour markers should be within the normal range 7 days following tumour resection if the resection has been complete

E β-HCG is identical to human luteinising hormone and has limited usefulness as a marker

Question 4

Clinical scenario

A 65-year-old man with known metastatic non-small-cell lung cancer develops lower back pain. Physical examination is normal, but plain radiographic films show sclerosis of T12 and L1.

Question

Which of the following would be appropriate in the management of this patient?

Answers

A Nerve conduction studies
B Lumbar puncture manometry
C Lumbar puncture and cerebrospinal fluid cytology
D MRI of the spinal column
E Corticosteroid therapy

Question 5

Clinical scenario

Figure 46 shows the bone scan of a 72-year-old man with newly diagnosed prostate cancer. His serum prostate-specific antigen level is 571 ng/ml.

Question

What is demonstrated?

Answers

A Paget's disease
B Osteoporosis
C Osteomalacia
D Metastatic deposits
E Hypertrophic osteoarthropathy

Question 6

Clinical scenario

A 41-year-old woman with metastatic breast cancer is treated with anthracycline-based combination chemotherapy and develops acute left ventricular failure. She was initially diagnosed with localised left-sided breast cancer 3 years previously and treated by wide local excision, followed by adjuvant radiotherapy and adjuvant chemotherapy.

Question

When considering doxorubicin cardiotoxicity, which of the following is *false*?

Answers

A Ventricular failure frequently develops 6 months or more after the last dose of doxorubicin

B Previous cyclophosphamide therapy increases the risk of doxorubicin cardiotoxicity

C Acute cardiotoxicity is usually brief and rarely serious

D Chronic cardiotoxicity occurs in less than 3% of patients whose lifetime dose is above 500 mg/m²

E Therapy with other anthracycline antibiotics increases the risk of doxorubicin cardiotoxicity

Question 7

Clinical scenario

A private GP refers a 47-year-old investment banker following a cancer screen. The patient, who is well, has had numerous serum tumour marker tests performed.

Question

Which of the following tumour markers have a role in screening?

Answers

A Carcinoembryonic antigen for gastric cancer

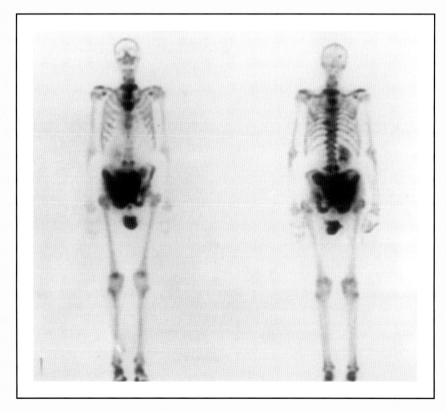

▲**Fig. 46** Question 5.

B Human chorionic gonadotropin for pure seminoma

C Calcitonin for medullary cell thyroid cancer

D β_2-microglobulin for myeloma

E Thyroglobulin for follicular thyroid cancer

Question 8

Clinical scenario

A 58-year-old farmer's wife is referred with a 6-month history of intermittent facial flushing. Episodes occur approximately once a week and last for 15 minutes. They are associated with bouts of watery diarrhoea lasting 1 day and cramping abdominal pains. Her periods stopped 6 years previously and she is not on hormone-replacement therapy. She has a long history of asthma, which had been well controlled, but recently noticed that she is wheezy more often and is using her salbutamol inhaler several times daily.

On clinical examination she is rather plethoric with multiple cutaneous telangiectasia and a rash of small blisters over her neck and hands. There are expiratory wheezes throughout both lung fields. There is a prominent venous wave in her neck, a third heart sound and a systolic murmur at her left sternal edge that is louder on inspiration. She has an enlarged liver measuring 6 cm below the costal margin in the mid-clavicular line which is pulsatile. There is no splenomegaly or peripheral adenopathy.

Question

Which of the following investigations is of *least* value in the clinical management of this patient?

Answers

A 24-hour urinary 5-hydroxyindoleacetic acid estimation

B Contrast-enhanced abdominal CT scan

C Somatostatin receptor scintigraphy

D Two-dimensional echocardiogram with Doppler flow studies

E Serum 5-hydroxytryptophan estimation

Question 9

Clinical scenario

Following curative bleomycin, etoposide and cisplatin combination chemotherapy for advanced testicular germ-cell tumour, a 36-year-old man develops progressive fatal pulmonary fibrosis.

Question

Pulmonary fibrosis is not a recognised complication of which of these anticancer therapies?

Answers

A Vincristine

B Busulfan

C Gefitinib (Iressa)

D Carmustine (BCNU)

E Radiotherapy

Question 10

Clinical scenario

A woman on chemotherapy for extensive small-cell lung cancer develops hyponatraemia with a serum sodium of 112 mmol/L.

Question

Which of the following cancer chemotherapy drugs does *not* cause or exacerbate the syndrome of inappropriate antidiuretic hormone secretion?

Answers

A Cyclophosphamide

B Dacarbazine

C Cisplatin

D Vinblastine

E Vincristine

Question 11

Clinical scenario

A 34-year-old Australian woman presents with a growing pigmented skin lesion suggestive of melanoma.

Question

Which of the following factors does *not* influence the likelihood of metastasis in malignant melanoma?

Answers

A Primary tumour site

B Level of invasion on histology

C Thickness of the primary lesion

D Geographical area of residence

E Presence or absence of tumour-infiltrating lymphocytes in the lesion

Question 12

Clinical scenario

During the course of a lung cancer multidisciplinary team meeting, the respiratory physician declares that 'there is no need to wait for the histology as all patients with paraneoplastic syndromes have small-cell lung cancer (SCLC)'.

Question

Which of the following paraneoplastic manifestations is least commonly associated with SCLC?

Answers

A Humoral hypercalcaemia

B Eaton–Lambert myasthenic syndrome

C Subacute cerebellar degeneration

D Cushing's syndrome

E Inappropriate antidiuretic hormone secretion

Question 13

Clinical scenario

A 36-year-old white woman presents with dull intermittent abdominal pain of 5 months' duration. The pain is located over her right upper quadrant and flank. It occurs five to six times per month. Over the past few months she has also noticed that diarrhoea often occurs at the same time and with the same frequency as the abdominal pain.

Question

Which of the following is *not* true of carcinoid syndrome?

Answers

A Elevated urinary excretion of 5-hydroxyindoleacetic acid (5-HIAA) may be associated with non-tropical sprue

B It is associated with primary non-metastatic tumours in the gastrointestinal tract

C Pharmacological blockade is clinically useful in most patients

D Flushing attacks may be associated with bronchoconstriction, periorbital oedema, salivation and excessive lacrimation

E Niacin supplementation can prevent pellagra in patients with marked elevation of urinary 5HIAA

Question 14

Clinical scenario

These skin lesions (Fig. 47) were present on a 40-year-old HIV-seropositive man from Zimbabwe.

Question

What initial treatment would you advocate for this patient?

Answers

A Antiretroviral therapy

B Single-agent anthracycline chemotherapy

C Combination chemotherapy

D Radiotherapy

E Interferon alfa treatment

Question 15

Clinical scenario

A homosexual barman was initially diagnosed HIV-positive in 1989 at the age of 38. He presented via the Accident and Emergency department with a 2-week history of frontal headaches and weakness of his right arm and leg, having recently returned from the USA. On examination there was marked muscle wasting, extensive orocutaneous Kaposi sarcoma

and oral candidiasis. He had expressive dysphasia and reduced power in his right arm and leg. His eyes and head deviated to the left. His right biceps, triceps, knee and ankle tendon reflexes were markedly brisk and his right plantar response was extensor. He had no neck stiffness. A CT scan confirmed a single ring-enhancing lesion in the left frontal cortex.

Question

Which of the following tests would you *not* perform to establish the diagnosis?

Answers

A *Toxoplasma* serology

B Cerebrospinal fluid examination for Epstein-Barr virus by polymerase chain reaction

C Bone marrow aspirate and trephine examination

D Two-week trial of anti-*Toxoplasma* therapy

E Fluorodeoxyglucose PET scan

Question 16

Clinical scenario

A 64-year-old retired secondary school teacher attended for the follow-up of metastatic breast cancer. She reported that she had been suffering for 2 weeks with a migraine, to which she was prone, but that this time the pain spread down into her neck. She had also noticed some numbness over her left upper lip and the left side of her nose. Neurological examination was normal except for sensory loss in the distribution of the left maxillary branch of the trigeminal nerve, and the loss of both ankle jerks and bilateral extensor plantar reflexes. Fundoscopy was normal.

Question

Which of the following are true of carcinomatous meningitis?

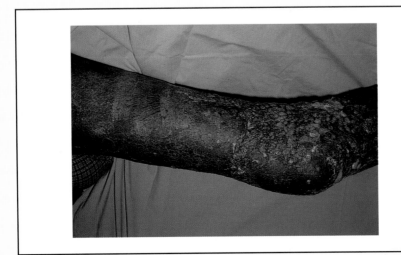

▲ **Fig. 47** Question 14.

Answers

A It is most common with gastrointestinal primary tumours

B Symptoms can be subtle and exist for several weeks prior to diagnosis

C Only 25% of patients have neurological signs of spinal cord involvement

D Approximately 30% of patients have positive cytology in the cerebrospinal fluid

E High-dose systemic chemotherapy is more effective than intrathecal chemotherapy

Question 17

Clinical scenario

A 67-year-old man with a 50 pack-year history of smoking presents with a cavitating lung tumour and has a CT-guided lung biopsy.

Question

What histological subtype is most likely?

Answers

A Small-cell lung cancer
B Bronchoalveolar lung cancer
C Adenocarcinoma of the lung
D Squamous cell lung cancer
E Bronchial carcinoid

Question 18

Clinical scenario

A 75-year-old retired miner presents with a 3-month history of a painful right upper arm with some swelling in the mid arm. His past medical history includes acute inferior myocardial infarction in 1993 and transurethral resection of the prostate in 1996 for bladder outflow obstruction. His current medication is aspirin, nifedepine and a salbutamol inhaler. He is a lifelong heavy smoker and his GP has diagnosed chronic obstructive airways disease.

On examination he is a well-built man with a prominent forehead and jaw. He has a hearing aid on his left ear and is apyrexial. His pulse rate is 80 beats/minute in sinus rhythm and his BP is 110/60 mmHg. JVP is raised at 4 cm above the angle of Louis and the apex beat is displaced to the mid-axillary line. Heart sounds are normal and there are no murmurs. There is mild bilateral ankle oedema and basal crepitations. Abdominal examination is unremarkable apart from an enlarged irregular prostate gland. His right mid-humerus is swollen and tender. Initial tests show the following: FBC, urea and electrolytes, calcium, albumin and phosphate are normal; alkaline phosphatase and acid phosphatase are increased; bone scan is diffusely hot but cold over right mid-humerus; and a radiograph of his right humerus shows lytic lesion with cortical bone destruction, but no periosteal reaction.

Question

Which of these investigations is most likely to establish the diagnosis?

Answers

A CT scan of his arm
B Whole-body PET scan
C Transurethral biopsy of his prostate gland
D Serum prostate-specific antigen
E Bone biopsy of arm lesion

Question 19

Clinical scenario

An 83-year-old retired sheet-metal worker presented as an emergency after coughing up fresh blood. He gave a 3-week history of breathlessness and swollen arms. He had a long history of ischaemic heart disease, with myocardial infarction 7 years previously, as well

as long-standing atrial fibrillation, hypertension and heart failure. His current medication included digoxin, co-amilofruse, salbutamol inhaler and warfarin. He was an ex-smoker, who had smoked heavily for many years. One week prior to admission his GP had prescribed a course of erythromycin for his chest symptoms.

Question

Which of the following characteristics would *not* be consistent with a diagnosis of superior vena cava obstruction (SVCO)?

Answers

A Clinical features of conjunctival suffusion, lower-extremity oedema and pulsus paradoxus

B High grade non-Hodgkin's lymphoma and small-cell lung cancer are the most common malignancies associated with SVCO

C SVCO is rarely a cause of death

D Definitive therapy should include local radiotherapy and if possible systemic chemotherapy

E Corticosteroids and diuretics may improve symptoms until a diagnosis is established

Question 20

Clinical scenario

A 28-year-old woman presents with respiratory symptoms and her CXR and subsequent CT scan reveal multiple metastases. The histological report from a CT-guided biopsy describes an undifferentiated anaplastic tumour. Serum tumour markers are sent. Serum β-human chorionic gonadotropin is raised, whilst CA19-9, carcinoembryonic antigen, CA15-3, CA125, inhibin and alpha-fetoprotein are all normal.

Question

What is the most likely primary diagnosis?

Answers

A Breast cancer

B Medullary cell thyroid cancer

C Melanoma

D Choriocarcinoma

E Granulosa cell carcinoma of ovary

Question 21

Clinical scenario

Following the breast cancer multidisciplinary team meeting, you are asked to prescribe tamoxifen to a 67-year-old woman with newly diagnosed metastatic breast cancer who was admitted with a pleural effusion.

Question

You should warn the patient about all the following possible side effects except one. Which one?

Answers

A Nausea

B Virilisation

C Acute hypercalcaemia

D Hot flushes

E Endometrial carcinoma in 1% of patients

Question 22

Clinical scenario

The 70-year-old mother of one of your friends has a colonoscopy for the investigation of diarrhoea and is told that she has colonic polyps. Your friend asks you about the diagnosis.

Question

Which of the following is *false* about adenomatous polyps of the colon?

Answers

A Most adenomatous polyps are clinically silent

B Tubular polyps are more likely to be malignant than villous adenomas

C The most common site for involvement is the rectosigmoid colon

D Risk of malignancy correlates with size of the polyp

E Endoscopic polypectomy is adequate therapy for an adenoma with evidence of carcinoma *in situ*

Question 23

Clinical scenario

A 64-year-old bank manager attends for outpatient review 7 months after hemicolectomy and adjuvant chemotherapy for Dukes' C colorectal adenocarcinoma. His serum carcinoembryonic antigen (CEA) level is elevated.

Question

Which of the following is *false* regarding CEA?

Answers

A Most patients with colon cancer have an elevated serum CEA

B Serum CEA can be elevated in smokers

C A decline in serum CEA suggests a favourable response to therapy

D Serum CEA can be elevated in inflammatory bowel disease

E Serum CEA can be elevated in benign biliary disease

Question 24

Clinical scenario

A 55-year-old ward sister presents with ascites and an elevated serum CA125. A CT scan demonstrates an adnexal mass and peritoneal seedlings.

Question

Which of the following is true about ovarian cancer?

Answers

A It has a peak incidence at 70 years of age

B It is more frequent in underdeveloped countries

C It can present with urinary frequency

D Associated pleural effusions are more common on the left

E Early disease often presents with abdominal distension

Question 25

Clinical scenario

A 73-year-old woman who presents with postmenopausal bleeding is found to have stage 1c endometrioid adenocarcinoma of the endometrium.

Question

Which of the following is true of endometrial cancer?

Answers

A Has a lower incidence in obese patients

B Is associated with an increase in sex hormone-binding globulin

C Should be treated with adjuvant progesterone

D Often presents with an enlarged uterus

E Is associated with polycystic ovaries

Question 26

Clinical scenario

A 78-year-old man who from the age of 30–50 years lived in the tropics presents with a suspicious skin lesion on his forearm.

Question

Which of the following is true about squamous cell carcinoma *in situ* of the skin (Bowen's disease)?

Answers

A Lesions require aggressive radiotherapy

B Lesions usually become invasive and metastasise early

C Is a risk factor for melanoma

D Is a risk factor for some carcinomas other than skin cancer

E The disease is associated with immunodeficiency

Question 27

Clinical scenario

A patient presents to her GP with a pigmented lesion on her foot. The patient states that the lesion was apparently present from birth and does not itch or bleed. However, it is not as homogeneous as it used to be.

Question

Which of the following is true?

Answers

A Early diagnosis would not affect prognosis

B It would be dangerous to perform an incisional biopsy of this lesion

C Bleeding and tenderness would be the first signs of malignant change

D Since the lesion has been present since birth, the risk of malignancy is low

E Change in colour is suspicious for malignant change

Question 28

Clinical scenario

Figure 48 shows a primary bone tumour of the upper humerus with an associated pathological fracture.

Question

Which of the following features favour a diagnosis of osteosarcoma rather than Ewing's sarcoma?

Answers

A Affects pelvic ischium

B Onion-skin periosteal reaction

C A previous history of Paget's disease

D Presence of t(11;22) chromosomal translocation in tumour cells

E Age under 10 years

4.2 Self-assessment answers

Answer to Question 1

D

Turcot's syndrome is an autosomal dominant familial polyposis syndrome with primary brain tumours, and is associated with mutations of the genes *APC*, *MLH1* or *PMS2* (mismatch repair genes mutated in hereditary non-polyposis colon cancer).

Peutz–Jeghers syndrome is an autosomal dominant disorder characterised by melanocytic macules of the lips, buccal mucosa and digits; multiple gastrointestinal hamartomatous polyps; and an increased risk of colon, small bowel, breast and ovarian cancers, as well as intussusception. It is caused by mutation of the STK11 gene on chromosome 19p13.

Gardner's syndrome is an autosomal dominant disorder characterised by colonic polyposis with extra-bowel tumours, especially osteomas and desmoid tumours of the mesentery and anterior abdominal wall. In addition sufferers have a characteristic retinal lesion

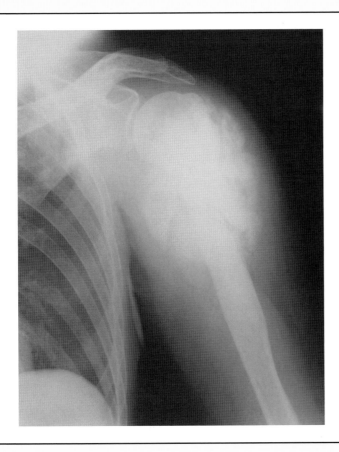

▲ **Fig. 48** Question 28.

(congenital hypertrophy of the retinal pigment epithelium) that can be a valuable clue to the presence of the gene in persons who have not yet developed other manifestations. Like familial adenomatous polyposis (FAP), Gardner's syndrome is caused by mutation in the APC gene.

FAP is an autosomal dominant disorder that typically presents with colorectal cancer in early adult life secondary to extensive adenomatous polyps of the colon. Polyps also develop in the upper gastrointestinal tract and malignancies may occur in other sites. It is caused by mutations of the APC gene on chromosome 5q21 that encodes a protein that interacts with L-catenin and E-cadherin.

Canada–Cronkhite syndrome is a non-hereditary, non-congenital disease. It is characterised by juvenile hamartomatous gastrointestinal polyps with a typically late onset, and is associated with alopecia, nail dystrophy and skin pigmentation.

Answer to Question 2

A and H

The next investigations should include a CT scan of the abdomen, fine-needle biopsy under imaging control and serum alpha-fetoprotein. Chronic liver disease due to any aetiology is associated with an increased incidence of hepatocellular cancer (HCC). Worldwide, hepatitis B virus infection is an important cause of chronic liver disease and subsequent HCC. Mycotoxins such as aflatoxin are found in foodstuffs in many parts of the world and are thought to be carcinogenic.

Answer to Question 3

C

Both alpha-fetoprotein (AFP) and beta-human chorionic gonadotropin (β-HCG) should be measured to follow the progress of a tumour. Pure seminomas usually produce no tumour markers, but over 90% of patients with non-seminomatous germ-cell tumours produce either AFP or β-HCG. The normal serum clearance half-life of HCG is 3 days and AFP 5 days, so these markers are present for some time after tumour resection and if the preoperative levels are very high it may take 30 days or more to return to normal values. Following treatment, unequal reductions of AFP and β-HCG may occur. This suggests that they are produced by heterogeneous clones within the tumour mass and therefore both markers should be monitored in the follow-up of the patient. HCG is similar to luteinising hormone, except for the distinctive β-subunit, but it is useful as a marker.

Answer to Question 4

D

This patient is most likely to have epidural spinal cord compression as a complication of metastatic lung cancer. Local or radicular pain is the most frequent and earliest clinical symptom. Clinical examination in the early stages can be unremarkable. However, subsequent weakness and bladder and bowel dysfunction can develop.

The diagnosis of spinal cord compression must always be considered even if the clinical examination is normal. The diagnosis can be confirmed by MRI, which is considered superior to CT imaging or myelography. Lumbar puncture should be avoided as herniation of the cord into

a decompressed region can result following the removal of cerebrospinal fluid. Manometry and cytological analysis are unlikely to give diagnostic information and may worsen the situation due to the lumbar puncture.

Patients with rapidly progressive neurological signs should be considered for neurosurgical decompression, and radiotherapy is useful in the treatment of slowly progressive lesions. Systemic chemotherapy and corticosteroids should not be used in place of surgery or radiotherapy, and may not influence the clinical situation.

Answer to Question 5

D

Technetium-99 pyrophosphate bone scan reveals multiple bone hotspots in the axial skeleton due to bone metastases, and a non-functioning left kidney due to long-standing obstruction. The diagnosis is metastatic and locally advanced prostate cancer.

Answer to Question 6

D

There are two types of doxorubicin cardiotoxicity. Acute cardiotoxicity produces ECG abnormalities such as dysrhythmias but is rarely serious. Chronic cardiotoxicity is unusual until the total lifetime dose exceeds 500 mg/m^2 and produces congestive cardiac failure that is unresponsive to digoxin therapy. Doxorubicin cardiotoxicity is more frequent in patients with previous cardiac irradiation, cyclophosphamide therapy or exposure to anthracycline compounds other than doxorubicin. Almost 50% of all cases of cardiotoxicity occur 6 months or more after the completion of therapy.

Answer to Question 7

C

Tumour markers have not proved useful in screening for the majority of tumour types. Human chorionic gonadotropin (HCG) is particularly useful in screening for gestational trophoblastic disease following a hydatidiform mole, but pure seminomas rarely produce markers. The only other established screening marker is calcitonin for medullary cell thyroid cancer, although there is some evidence for using CA125 for ovarian cancer and prostate-specific antigen for prostate cancer. However, their use is still confined to clinical trials designed to establish their efficacy and reliability (see Table 38).

Answer to Question 8

E

The most useful tests for confirming the diagnosis and extent of carcinoid syndrome include 24-hour urinary 5-hydroxyindoleacetic acid estimation and contrast-enhanced abdominal CT scan or somatostatin receptor scintigraphy to localise tumour and metastases. Two-dimensional echocardiogram with Doppler flow studies may confirm tricuspid regurgitation secondary to fibrosis of chordae tendineae, which is a complication of carcinoid tumours. Other associations include pellagra due to secondary niacin deficiency caused by metabolism of niacin by the tumour, arthropathy, pulmonary stenosis, mesenteric fibrosis and cirrhosis.

Answer to Question 9

A

Pulmonary complications are most commonly associated with bleomycin administration and are manifested by an interstitial pneumonitis leading to fibrosis, with substantial morbidity and mortality. In advanced cases widespread infiltrates are seen, occasionally with lobar consolidation, which can sometimes be confused with lung metastases and CT can be useful in the differentiation. Pulmonary function testing reveals a restrictive ventilatory defect with hypoxia, hypocapnia and chronic respiratory alkalosis due to impaired diffusion and hyperventilation. The incidence of bleomycin interstitial fibrosis has varied in published reports from 2 to 40%. Lung toxicity has also been reported with carmustine (BCNU), which produces features of pulmonary toxicity similar to bleomycin. The incidence is 20–30% and is dose related, but may be as high as 30–50% when a cumulative dose of 1500 mg/m^2 or greater is given. There is an increased risk with pre-existing lung disease and tobacco use. In children treated for brain tumours with BCNU and radiation, 35% of survivors died of lung fibrosis and delayed fibrosis has been seen up to 17 years after cessation of the drug. Although BCNU has been most commonly associated with pulmonary fibrosis, pulmonary toxicity has been reported with all other nitrosoureas. Pulmonary toxicity is infrequent with alkylating agents, but potentially lethal interstitial pneumonitis is the most common lesion. Atypical epithelial proliferation of the distal airways may result from busulfan. Gefitinib is an oral receptor tyrosine kinase inhibitor that inhibits epidermal growth factor receptors and is used mainly in the management of non-small-cell lung cancer. It is associated with interstitial lung disease in 1% of patients.

Lung toxicity is the dose-limiting toxicity of thoracic radiotherapy.

Answer to Question 10

B

Vincristine, vinblastine, cisplatin, ifosfamide and cyclophosphamide have all been reported to exacerbate the syndrome of inappropriate antidiuretic hormone secretion (SIADH). The mechanism is thought to be due to enhanced pituitary antidiuretic hormone release and as a consequence can lead to overt SIADH in cancer patients (see Section 2.14). Although rare, dacarbazine can cause hepatotoxicity and a flu-like syndrome that includes myalgia, fever and malaise that starts within 7 days of treatment.

Answer to Question 11

D

Primary malignant melanoma is the leading cause of death from all diseases arising in the skin. Geographic area of residence is an important factor in the development of melanoma, with a higher incidence in areas with greater sun exposure, but it does not influence risk of dissemination. The most common site for melanoma in males is the torso and lesions occurring here have a worse prognosis than those occurring on a lower extremity. Level of invasion and thickness of the primary lesion are predictive of dissemination and survival. The presence of lymphocytes infiltrating the melanoma has a favourable effect on prognosis.

Answer to Question 12

A

Small-cell lung cancer (SCLC) is associated with a number of paraneoplastic manifestations (see Section 2.14) that are due to the production of cross-reacting antibodies in the case of most neurological paraneoplastic phenomena, or the production of growth factors by the tumour in the case of most metabolic paraneoplastic manifestations.

Eaton–Lambert syndrome is characterised by proximal muscle weakness and electromyography showing increasing amplitude of contraction, and is almost exclusively associated with SCLC. Subacute cortical cerebellar degeneration is associated with cerebellar ataxia, dysarthria, deafness and with cerebellar atrophy on MRI of the brain. It has been linked with SCLC, cancer of the ovary and breast, and Hodgkin's disease. Cushing's syndrome (due to production of pro-opiomelanocortin-derived peptides by tumours) and the syndrome of antidiuretic hormone secretion (due to production of vasopressin by tumours) are associated with SCLC and many other tumours. Humoral hypercalcaemia is infrequently found with SCLC, although it is more frequently associated with squamous and large-cell cancers of the lung, due to parathyroid hormone-related peptide produced by the tumour.

Answer to Question 13

B

Carcinoid syndrome is caused by the production of serotonin and other vasoactive peptides by carcinoid tumours originating in the bronchus, gastrointestinal tract, pancreas and thyroid and in ovarian or testicular tumours. Quantification of urinary 5-hydroxyindoleacetic acid, the primary metabolite of serotonin, in a 24-hour urine

collection is the most useful diagnostic investigation. However, increases are associated with the excessive dietary intake of bananas and/or walnuts, acute intestinal obstruction and non-tropical sprue.

When released from a primary tumour into the gastrointestinal tract, the vasoactive peptides pass via the portal system to the liver, where they undergo complete first-pass metabolism. Therefore, there are no systemic effects. Carcinoid syndrome is only produced when there is metastasis, usually in the liver, or a primary outside the gastrointestinal tract, most commonly in the bronchus. Bronchial carcinoid can produce dramatic symptoms that include excessive lacrimation, salivation, periorbital oedema, bronchoconstriction, hypotension, tachycardia, anxiety, tremor, nausea, vomiting and explosive diarrhoea. Pharmacological blockade can reduce the symptoms in the majority of patients and is a useful adjunct to more definitive therapy.

Shunting large amounts of dietary tryptophan into the production of hydroxylated metabolites can result in niacin deficiency, producing a pellagra-like condition that may require supplemental niacin.

Answer to Question 14

A

Highly active antiretroviral therapy uses a combination of nucleoside reverse transcriptase inhibitors plus a protease inhibitor or non-nucleoside reverse transcriptase inhibitor. Subsequent systemic chemotherapy with liposomal anthracycline may well be necessary.

Answer to Question 15

C

A ring-enhancing focal cerebral lesion in an immunocompromised patient poses a difficult differential diagnosis. Conventional radiology (CT and MRI) is unable to reliably distinguish primary cerebral lymphoma (PCL) and cerebral toxoplasmosis, although a solitary large (2.5 cm) lesion located in the cerebral cortex favours PCL. Functional radiology, including PET, may be helpful as PCL is more likely to be hot. Cerebrospinal fluid examination for Epstein-Barr virus DNA by polymerase chain reaction amplification is positive in over 95% of patients with PCL associated with HIV infection, although not in immunocompetent patients with PCL. By definition PCL is confined to the central nervous system and will not involve the bone marrow.

Answer to Question 16

B

Carcinomatous meningitis is increasing in frequency because of the improved survival rates following systemic chemotherapy and increased awareness that it is a problem. Leptomeningeal involvement is seen most commonly with lymphoma, leukaemia, melanoma and cancers of the breast and lung. Most drugs fail to penetrate the blood–brain barrier and therefore carcinomatous meningitis can present without signs of disease progression outside the central nervous system. Symptoms depend on the extent of tumour involvement but can be subtle and exist for several weeks prior to diagnosis. Symptoms include headaches, nausea, vomiting, altered mental state, lethargy, impaired memory, diplopia, visual blurring, hearing loss and facial numbness.

More than 70% of patients have neurological signs due to spinal cord or nerve root involvement. The diagnosis can be confirmed by cytological analysis of cerebrospinal fluid (CSF). In a retrospective series, malignant cells were seen in the first, second and third CSF samples in 42–66%, 60–87% and 68–96% of cases, respectively. A normal lumbar puncture can occur with obstruction but more than 50% of patients will have one or more of:

- opening pressure >160 mmH$_2$O;

- increased white cell count;

- a reactive lymphocytosis;

- elevated CSF protein;

- decreased CSF glucose.

Brain metastasis can be seen in 20% of patients and CT or MRI should be undertaken in patients with suspected cord involvement. Treatment consists of intrathecal chemotherapy and radiation therapy to the area of neuraxis responsible for the neurological deficit. Therapeutic drug levels in the CSF are generally not achieved with systemic chemotherapy, although this can be achieved for high-dose methotrexate but at the expense of significant systemic effects.

Because of the high incidence of leptomeningeal involvement with acute lymphoblastic lymphoma and Burkitt's lymphoma, patients receive prophylactic intrathecal chemotherapy and whole-brain irradiation following complete remission with induction therapy.

Answer to Question 17

D

Squamous cell cancers may cavitate and are most frequently associated with ectopic parathyroid hormone production and hypercalcaemia.

Small-cell lung cancers often present with large mediastinal masses and distant metastases (40% bone, 30% liver and 15–25% bone marrow, including brain metastases). They are associated with paraneoplastic manifestations including ectopic adrenocorticotropic hormone production leading to Cushing's syndrome, the synrdrome of inappropriate antidiuresis and neurological paraneoplastic phenomena.

Adenocarcinomas of the lung generally arise in the periphery, unrelated to the bronchi. Bronchoalveolar carcinoma presents as a single nodular or multinodular pattern, and is associated with previous fibrotic lung disease, including repeated pneumonias, granulomas and idiopathic pulmonary fibrosis. It is not strongly associated with smoking. Bronchial carcinoid can produce dramatic symptoms that include excessive lacrimation, salivation, periorbital oedema, bronchoconstriction, hypotension, tachycardia, anxiety, tremor, nausea, vomiting and explosive diarrhoea. The vasoactive peptides released from a primary bronchial carcinoid, unlike a gastrointestinal tract carcinoid, are not delivered to the liver where they would be metabolised. Thus bronchial carcinoid can produce carcinoid symptoms in the absence of metastatic spread to the liver.

Answer to Question 18

E

The differential diagnosis is Paget's disease with osteosarcoma and metastatic prostate cancer. Although transrectal ultrasound-guided sextant biopsy and serum prostate-specific antigen may indicate prostate cancer, this is sufficiently common that it does not exclude

the presence of both diagnoses. Hence a biopsy is more likely to establish the diagnosis of the arm lesion definitively. Overall about 1% of patients with Paget's disease will develop a primary bone sarcoma: 85% are osteosarcoma and 15% fibrosarcoma. The most common sites are pelvis, femur and humerus. The radiological appearances are of osteolytic lesions with cortical destruction, but periosteal elevation is rare. Patients present with localised pain and most are dead within 2 years.

Answer to Question 19

A

There are a number of possible causes for the haemoptysis, including a prolonged INR because there is a well-known interaction between warfarin and erythromycin. However, the swollen arms is an unusual symptom that suggests superior vena cava obstruction (SVCO). SVCO is a complication of tumours that involve the mediastinum and upper lung fields, most commonly in lymphoblastic lymphoma (diffuse histiocytic lymphoma) and small-cell lung cancer. The syndrome is characterised by headaches, conjunctival injection and suffusion, plethoric facies, distension of the neck and arm veins, loss of venous pulsations and, in severe cases, convulsions. Pulsus paradoxus and lower-extremity oedema are more suggestive of pericardial tamponade, which can also be associated with mediastinal malignancy. Even though SVCO can be a serious medical condition, it is rarely the cause of death. Steroid and diuretic therapy may be useful, pending a diagnosis and the commencement of more specific therapy, which may include radiotherapy or systemic chemotherapy.

Answer to Question 20

D

Human chorionic gonadotropin (HCG) is a glycoprotein consisting of two non-covalently bound subunits. HCG-specific antisera are directed against various parts of the β chain. HCG is formed physiologically in the syncytiotrophoblast of the placenta. Its main uses are in diagnosing and monitoring pregnancy, gestational trophoblastic disease and germ-cell tumours (GCTs). The sensitivity is 100% for testicular and placental choriocarcinomas and for hydatidiform moles, 48–86% for non-seminomatous GCTs and 7–14% for seminomas. Pure choriocarcinomas are thus always HCG positive and alpha-fetoprotein (AFP) negative; endodermal sinus tumours (yolk sac tumours) are always AFP positive and HCG negative, whereas pure seminomas are always AFP negative but HCG positive in only 14% of cases.

Answer to Question 21

B

Tamoxifen is an antioestrogen used in the management of breast cancer. It is usually well tolerated but can be associated with nausea, hot flushes similar to menopausal symptoms, mild fluid retention producing slight weight gain, alteration in voice characteristics and acute hypercalcaemia. Virilisation is very rare. Endometrial carcinoma can develop in patients taking tamoxifen, although the incidence is less than 1% and patients with metastatic disease may not survive long enough to develop the condition.

Answer to Question 22

B

Adenomatous polyps of the colon are very common in the general population and their incidence increases with age. Detection is usually by barium enema or colonoscopy undertaken for occult blood loss. The majority of polyps occur in the rectosigmoid colon and a small percentage cause bleeding or intestinal obstruction. Polyps less than 1 cm have a 1% chance of malignant change, whereas 50% of polyps larger than 2 cm contain malignant cells. There are three histological types of polyps, tubular, tubulovillous and villous, with the latter tending to be the largest and having the greater risk of malignancy. Colonoscopic resection of carcinoma *in situ* is considered curative, as it does not tend to metastasise, although patients must subsequently be monitored carefully for synchronous lesions.

Answer to Question 23

A

Carcinoembryonic antigen (CEA) is a glycoprotein present in fetal serum and is found in association with certain malignant or inflammatory conditions. It is neither sensitive nor specific for gastrointestinal malignancy, although a very high serum level is strongly suggestive of malignancy. Once a diagnosis of cancer has been made, serum CEA can be used for monitoring the disease response and may herald disease progression. Mild elevations of serum CEA can be seen with smoking, sclerosing cholangitis and inflammatory bowel disease.

Answer to Question 24

C

Ovarian cancer predominantly affects postmenopausal women, with the majority of cases occurring between 50 and 75 years of age. The incidence of ovarian cancer increases with age and peaks in the mid-fifties. White women have a higher incidence than African-American women in the American population. The highest rates of ovarian cancer are seen in industrialised countries and the lowest in underdeveloped nations.

In the early stages this disease can be totally insidious and can enlarge considerably without causing any symptoms. A routine internal examination may reveal a mass. Once enlarged, symptoms of urinary frequency and rectal pressure may manifest. Patients with advanced disease can present with abdominal distension, ascites, a large pelvic mass, bladder or rectal symptoms, pleural effusions (more common on the right) and vaginal bleeding.

Answer to Question 25

E

Endometrial cancer is 10 times commoner in obese women and there is a higher incidence in individuals with diabetes or polycystic ovaries and in those who are nulliparous. It is associated with elevated levels of free oestrogens due to decreased sex hormone-binding globulin, increased aromatisation of androgens, or unopposed oestrogens, especially during hormone-replacement therapy and tamoxifen treatment. Patients may present with abnormal uterine bleeding, pelvic or abdominal pain and the uterus is frequently not enlarged on palpation. Treatment requires surgery and radiation for poorly differentiated tumours, cervical extension, deep myometrial penetration and regional lymph node involvement. Radiotherapy and progesterone should only be considered for patients with unresectable or recurrent disease.

Answer to Question 26

D

Squamous cell carcinoma of the skin *in situ* is best treated with surgical excision. Metastasis does occur, but in fewer than 2% of patients. Affected patients have an increased risk for developing carcinoma of the respiratory, genitourinary and gastrointestinal tracts. The risk is especially high in patients whose disease occurs on a region of skin not usually exposed to sunlight.

Answer to Question 27

E

The characteristics that distinguish a superficial spreading malignant melanoma from a normal mole include irregularity of its border, and variegation or colour. Loss of homogeneous coloration and disorderliness are suspicious. The first changes noted by patients developing a melanoma are a darkening in its colour or a change in the borders of the lesion. Irregularity of the border in an expanding darkening mole is melanoma until proved otherwise. Biopsy should be done promptly as early diagnosis and excision reduce the mortality rate.

Answer to Question 28

C

Ewing's sarcomas arise in diaphyses, including of flat bones. The radiological appearances are of onion-skin periosteal reaction rather than the sunburst reaction or Codman's triangle typically seen in osteosarcoma.

THE MEDICAL MASTERCLASS SERIES

Haematology and Oncology

HAEMATOLOGY

Cardiology and Respiratory Medicine

CARDIOLOGY

RESPIRATORY MEDICINE

Gastroenterology and Hepatology

GASTROENTEROLOGY AND HEPATOLOGY

Neurology, Ophthalmology and Psychiatry

NEUROLOGY

Endocrinology

ENDOCRINOLOGY

PACES Stations and Acute Scenarios 3

Investigations and Practical Procedures 165

Self-assessment 174

Nephrology

NEPHROLOGY

PACES Stations and Acute Scenarios 3

Rheumatology and Clinical Immunology

RHEUMATOLOGY AND CLINICAL IMMUNOLOGY

PACES Stations and Acute Scenarios 3

INDEX

Note: page numbers in *italics* refer to figures, those in **bold** refer to tables.